The Information Nexus

Capitalism is central to our understanding of contemporary economic and political life, and yet what does it really mean? If, as has now been shown to be the case, capital and property rights existed in pre-modern and pre-capitalist societies, what is left of our understanding of capitalism? Steven G. Marks's provocative new book calls into question everything we thought we knew about capitalism, from the word's very origins and development to the drivers of Western economic growth. Ranging from the Middle Ages to the present, *The Information Nexus* reveals that the truly distinctive feature of capitalism is business's drive to acquire and analyze information, supported by governments that allow unfettered access to public data. This new interpretation of capitalism helps to explain the rise of the West, puts our current Information Age in historical perspective, and provides a benchmark for the comparative assessment of economic systems in today's globalized environment.

Steven G. Marks is Professor of History at Clemson University. He has written books and articles on Russian economic and cultural history, including *How Russia Shaped the Modern World* and *Road to Power*.

The Information Nexus

Global Capitalism from the Renaissance to the Present

Steven G. Marks

Clemson University

CAMBRIDGE
UNIVERSITY PRESS

CAMBRIDGE
UNIVERSITY PRESS

University Printing House, Cambridge CB2 8BS, United Kingdom

Cambridge University Press is part of the University of Cambridge.

It furthers the University's mission by disseminating knowledge in the pursuit of education, learning and research at the highest international levels of excellence.

www.cambridge.org
Information on this title: www.cambridge.org/9781107108684

First published 2016

Printed in the United States of America by Sheridan Books, Inc.

A catalogue record for this publication is available from the British Library

Library of Congress Cataloging-in-Publication data
Marks, Steven G. (Steven Gary), 1958– author.
The information nexus : global capitalism from the Renaissance to the present / Steven G. Marks, Clemson University.
Cambridge, United Kingdom : Cambridge University Press, 2016.
LCCN 2016016321| ISBN 9781107108684 (hardback) | ISBN 9781107519633 (paperback)
LCSH: Capitalism – History. | Economic history. | Information networks.
LCC HB501 .M33165 2016 | DDC 330.12/209–dc23
LC record available at https://lccn.loc.gov/2016016321

ISBN 978-1-107-10868-4 Hardback
ISBN 978-1-107-51963-3 Paperback

To my mother and in memory of my father

Contents

Preface

Adam Smith never mentioned the word "capitalism."[1] Karl Marx used it arguably five times.[2] The first American president to invoke it was Harry Truman.[3] One of the most resonant terms of our modern vocabulary is thus a relative neologism. Awareness that the advent of the word occurred so recently compels us to alter our assumptions about the concept.

What Henry George wrote in 1879 about the word "capital" is also true of capitalism: "Most people understand well enough what capital is until they begin to define it."[4] The term is ubiquitous, but unlike similar grand historical concepts, such as feudalism or totalitarianism, whose validity historians have disputed, capitalism is assumed, by proponents and opponents alike, to be a given, like the air we breathe.[5]

The purpose of this book is to subject capitalism to a new critical inquiry. In doing so, I will question the myths pertaining to capitalism

---

[1] Adam Smith writes of "commercial society," in which "every man ... lives by exchanging" (*Wealth of Nations*, books I–III, ed. Andrew Skinner [London: Penguin, 1999], 126). According to Henry C. Clark, the eighteenth-century French political economists spoke of the "spirit of commerce," which he calls a "synechdoche for the 'public sphere.'" See his book *Compass of Society: Commerce and Absolutism in Old Regime France* (Lanham: Lexington Books, 2007), respective quotes on xvii and 6. In Germany in the nineteenth century, the terms that predated "capitalism" were the "Industry System" or the "Factory System": see Roman Köster, "Coerced Misunderstandings? The Transfer of the Concept of Capitalism from Germany to the United States," unpublished paper presented at conference on "Power and the History of Capitalism," The New School, New York City (April 16, 2011), with thanks to the author for sharing it with me.

[2] See the German texts of Marx's writings on the website "Stimmen der proletarischen Revolution," online at http://mlwerke.de/me/default.htm, keyword search "Kapitalismus" – bearing in mind that Marx's authorship of some of the relevant citations is in question.

[3] For the presidents, see John T. Woolley and Gerhard Peters, *American Presidency Project*, online at www.presidency.ucsb.edu/index.php, keyword search "capitalism." Herbert Hoover uttered the word "capitalism" once, in 1930, but only to dismiss it as a socialist term of abuse: see www.presidency.ucsb.edu/ws/?pid=22379.

[4] Henry George, *Progress and Poverty* (NY: D. Appleton and Co., 1886 [1879]), 32.

[5] Stephen Morillo, "A 'Feudal Mutation'? Conceptual Tools and Historical Patterns in World History," *Journal of World History* (Dec. 2003), 531–550; Susan Reynolds, *Fiefs and Vassals: The Medieval Evidence Reinterpreted* (Oxford: Oxford University Press, 1994); and Abbott Gleason, *Totalitarianism* (NY: Oxford University Press, 1995).

on all sides of the political spectrum and propose an alternative to traditional definitions of the concept. *The Information Nexus* demonstrates that the money-based economy is not unique to capitalism – and the same holds true for many of its other supposed attributes, from commodification to wage labor. Capital is essential for capitalism, but so was it for all pre-capitalist and non-capitalist societies. In short, I do not associate capitalism with the "cash nexus," as the Victorians first did.[6] Rather, I locate its distinctiveness in business' quest for information and usable knowledge.[7] What is unique about capitalism is not that it is capital-intensive, but that it is information-intensive.

The information nexus is synonymous with capitalism. A nexus is a series of connections linking things. What this book explores is the dense web of information seeking and generating that resulted from having ready access to a complex of ever-changing information, communications, and transportation technologies. The information nexus links people in capitalist economies and expedites all investment and spending decisions by firms and individuals. It has historically thrived under political systems that value freedom of expression – not because democratic political systems have refrained from economic intervention as the mythology of laissez-faire suggests, but because these governments have tolerated the free flow of information in their societies and permitted unfettered access to commercial and other forms of socially useful knowledge. This creates the optimal setting in which entrepreneurs, managers, employees, and consumers can flourish in a marketplace built and refereed by the state.[8]

---

[6] The conservative Scottish social critic Thomas Carlyle, in *Chartism* (London: James Fraser, 1840), 58, wrote that "*Cash Payment* had not then grown to be the universal sole nexus of man to man." But the first to use the exact phrase "cash nexus" was Elizabeth Gaskell in her 1855 novel *North and South* (Radford: Wilder, 2008), 348: "My only wish is to have the opportunity of cultivating some intercourse with the hands beyond the mere 'cash nexus.'" Most English translations of Karl Marx and Friedrich Engels's *Communist Manifesto* apply the phrase too, but there is nothing precisely like it in the original German: see sentence before page marker 465 in the online text at mlwerke.de /me/me04/me04_459.htm. For Victorian Britons' aversion to the cash nexus, see Raymond Williams, *Culture and Society, 1780–1950* (NY: Columbia University Press, 1983), 63, 76, 83, 92, 140, 240.

[7] For further explanation of my use of the term "information" and the theoretical framework of information economics, see Chapter 4.

[8] There is a rising consensus among scholars that the state has always played a strong role in the formation and functioning of capitalism. For examples from different disciplines, see Liah Greenfeld, *The Spirit of Capitalism: Nationalism and Economic Growth* (Cambridge, MA: Harvard University Press, 2001); Alice Teichova and Herbert Matis, eds., *Nation, State, and the Economy in History* (Cambridge: Cambridge University Press, 2003); Espen Moe, *Governance, Growth, and Global Leadership: The Role of the State in Technological Progress, 1750–2000* (Aldershot: Ashgate, 2007); and Pietra Rivoli, *The Travels of a T-Shirt in the Global Economy*, 2nd ed. (Hoboken: Wiley, 2009). See also Chapter 4, especially the references in footnote 78.

Commentators have identified a variety of types of capitalism, among them shareholder, stock-market, laissez-faire, or consumerist capitalism in the United States and Britain; stakeholder, welfare, or producerist capitalism in Western Europe; organized or managed capitalism in France, Germany, Japan, Singapore, South Korea, and Taiwan; "family capitalism," which is said to prevail in French, German, and Italian big business; and the recent concoction of "creative capitalism," according to which corporations aspire to do good deeds with their wealth and power.[9] Scholars have also labeled past eras according to purportedly dominant or vanguard modes of economic activity, from agrarian capitalism to war capitalism, finance capitalism, or industrial capitalism.[10] While some of these categories are more useful than others, they all seek to provide a comparative perspective that can yield insights into national cultures and explain more successful versus less successful economic strategies. But one feature that is neglected in these designations is the common denominator in all varieties of capitalism: a powerful drive for information acquisition.

The information nexus – and hence capitalism – sprouted in Europe during the Renaissance with the birth of double-entry bookkeeping and the appearance of printed books and newspapers, which allowed for the rapid circulation of political and commercial ideas and intelligence. But it first reached full flower in the early modern Dutch Republic and United Kingdom, where elite tolerance of free speech ushered in the financial press, the collapse of censorship, and the encouragement of open science. In later eras, the information nexus expanded via trains, automobiles, and airplanes; telegraph, radio, and television; computers and smartphones. No society had ever seen anything like the perpetual innovation in means

---

[9] David Coates, *Models of Capitalism: Growth and Stagnation in the Modern Era* (Cambridge: Polity, 2000); Ronald Dore, *Stock Market Capitalism: Welfare Capitalism: Japan and Germany versus the Anglo-Saxons* (Oxford: Oxford University Press, 2000); Peter A. Hall and David Soskice, eds., *Varieties of Capitalism: The Institutional Foundations of Comparative Advantage* (Oxford: Oxford University Press, 2001); Bob Hancké, ed., *Debating Varieties of Capitalism: A Reader* (Oxford: Oxford University Press, 2009); Harold James, *Family Capitalism: Wendels, Haniels, Falcks, and the Continental European Model* (Cambridge, MA: Belknap Press, 2006); Michael Kinsley, ed., *Creative Capitalism: A Conversation with Bill Gates, Warren Buffett, and Other Economic Leaders* (NY: Simon and Schuster, 2008); James Q. Whitman, "Consumerism versus Producerism: A Study in Comparative Law," *Yale Law Journal* (Dec. 2007), 340–406.

[10] Giovanni Arrighi, *The Long Twentieth Century: Money, Power, and the Origins of Our Times* (London: Verso, 1994), passim; T. H. Aston and C. H. E. Philpin, eds., *The Brenner Debate: Agrarian Class Structure and Economic Development in Pre-Industrial Europe* (Cambridge: Cambridge University Press, 1985), passim; Sven Beckert, *Empire of Cotton: A Global History* (NY: Knopf, 2014), chaps. 2–3, 6; and see Frederic Jameson, *Postmodernism, or, the Cultural Logic of Late Capitalism* (Durham, NC: Duke University Press, 1991).

of communication and information acquisition that took place in parts of Western Europe, the United States, and, in the last half-century, Japan and its emulators in East Asia.

The information nexus explains the rapid proliferation of factories in the Industrial Revolution, thanks to the dissemination of technical know-how and manufacturers' desire to achieve greater control over workers. In the late nineteenth and early twentieth century it accounts for the "managerial revolution," during which hierarchies of salaried managers emerged to develop new methods of collecting and processing information within large corporations. The information nexus gave rise to advertising through the mass media as a way of attracting and informing (or manipulating) consumers, as it did the distribution system that enabled businesses to produce and stock goods with greater responsiveness to consumer demand. Conversely, breakdowns in information flows were manifested in the mass mania of speculative investment in stocks or real estate, or, as in the Dutch Golden Age, tulips. In the Great Recession of 2008, as in the 1720 South Sea bubble, one of the major causes of financial crisis was the complexity of new types of derivatives and the dearth of information by which investors and governments could judge their worth.

No other authors approach capitalism from this vantage point. Comprising both historical synthesis and original research, the book brings to light what scholarly specialists now know about past eras of world economic life. I integrate the findings of the World History school, which has successfully challenged Eurocentric ways of viewing global societies. But I also offer a corrective to the argument that the rise of the West was primarily a matter of its willingness to project its power overseas. This book maintains instead that the "great divergence" occurred to a large extent because of the advantages that accrued to the West from the information nexus that is the quintessence of capitalism.[11] The culminating argument is twofold: our current Information Age, despite its new and transformative technologies, represents an amplification of a pattern of economic behavior originating in certain parts of early modern Europe. At the same time, restrictions on the information nexus, as can be seen in contemporary China, indicate the limits to the expansion of capitalism in the world today: a seeming paradox in light of the common perception that China epitomizes that expansion.

---

[11] The quotation is taken from Kenneth Pomeranz, *The Great Divergence: China, Europe, and the Making of the Modern World Economy* (Princeton: Princeton University Press, 2000). My argument in this respect parallels Jeremy Black's in *The Power of Knowledge: How Information and Technology Made the Modern World* (New Haven: Yale University Press, 2014), although his book, as a general reflection on information in history, does not place a reinterpretation of capitalism front and center.

I have structured the book first to critique the received wisdom on capitalism and second to offer an original interpretation of it. The chapters in Part I call into question what we think we know about the subject by recounting the history of the word "capitalism" and examining our deeply rooted misconceptions about it. Part II presents my view of capitalism, with chapters on the history of the information nexus that illuminate the qualities that separate capitalism from other economic systems past and present.

Acknowledgments

I would like to express my sincere appreciation to all the people who devoted their time to help me improve this book. Colleagues near and far referred me to readings and offered useful advice and assistance: Paul Anderson, Stephanie Barczewski, Amit Bein, Elizabeth Carney, Steven Grosby, Tom Kuehn, Pam Mack, Elisa Marks, Deirdre McCloskey, David Nicholas, Joe Peterson, Michael Silvestri, and Lee Wilson. I owe a large debt to those who read portions of the manuscript and offered invaluable criticism: Raquel Anido, James Burns, Pamela Kyle Crossley, Jonathan Daly, Bruce J. Dickson, Kent G. Deng, Steven J. Ericson, H. Roger Grant, Jacob D. Hamblin, Patricia Herlihy, Jonathan B. Imber, Michael Meng, David Moon, Carmi Neiger, Melissa Stockdale, and Christian Wolmar. I am deeply beholden to Henry C. Clark, Aviel Roshwald, and two anonymous referees for undertaking the laborious task of reading and commenting on the entire manuscript. My editor, Michael Watson, gave me extraordinary support and guidance, for which I am grateful. Copyeditor Matthew Bastock and production project manager Karthik Orukaimani expertly readied the text for publication. None of the above are responsible for the errors of fact and interpretation that are sure to remain.

Finally, I thank my wife and daughters for making such a wonderful life for me. But that has nothing to do with capitalism.

Part I

"Capitalism," word and concept

1   Cries of pain
The word "capitalism"

Throughout nineteenth-century Europe, industrialization and urbanization occurred rapidly and in tandem with wrenching socio-political transformation. Within several generations the continent experienced the
disappearance of cottage craft industries and explosive demographic
growth. Peasants fled their overcrowded farming villages for the shanty
towns and tenements of big cities that were bursting at the seams but
offered employment in factories, workshops, and retail stores. In the
nineteenth century, that could seem a mixed blessing because of the
lack of sanitation, the ubiquity of vermin, and the pollution: the inhabitants of Hamburg, Germany, saw "everything as if through a veil, for the
smoke from a thousand chimneys spread over everything like a drifting
mist."[1] To go from being a mainly farming society to a mainly industrial
and urban one was a jarring shift in the extreme. Polarities of wealth were
severe in the new metropolises, and, for many societies undergoing
industrialization for the first time, for at least a generation the wages
and living standard of workers were as likely to decline as improve.[2]
This is the general context in which the word "capitalism" emerged.

Unlike the word "capital," which dates to ancient Rome, and "capitalist,"
which was coined in mid-seventeenth-century Holland and Germany,
"capitalism" is of relatively recent vintage.[3] Before the mid-nineteenth

---

[1] Richard J. Evans, *Death in Hamburg: Society and Politics in the Cholera Years, 1830–1910*
(London: Penguin, 1987), chap. 2, with quote on 121.
[2] Theodore S. Hamerow, *The Birth of a New Europe: State and Society in the Nineteenth
Century* (Chapel Hill: University of North Carolina Press, 1983), 89–92, 104, and passim;
Daniel T. Rodgers, *Atlantic Crossings: Social Politics in a Progressive Age* (Cambridge, MA:
Belknap Press, 1998), 47, 49.
[3] On the word "capital," see Edwin Deschepper, "L'Histoire du mot capital (et
dérivés)," mémoire de licence, Université Libre de Bruxelles (1963–1964). For its earliest
antecedents, see Marc van de Mieroop, "The Invention of Interest: Sumerian Loans," in
The Origins of Value: The Financial Innovations that Created Modern Capital Markets, ed.
William N. Goetzmann and K. Geert Rouwenhorst (Oxford: Oxford University Press,
2005), 24. On the origins of "capitalist," see Deschepper, "L'Histoire du mot capital,"
123–125. The earliest English quotation cited in the *Oxford English Dictionary Online*
(2006), s.v. "capitalist," dates to 1792. But it had already appeared in America the

3

century it appeared scattershot in the European and American press.[4] Its consistent usage commenced in 1850, beginning with this passage by French socialist Louis Blanc in the ninth edition of his book *The Organization of Labor:* "What I would call *capitalism* ... [is] the appropriation of capital by the few, to the exclusion of the many." "Capitalism," he continues, is "the mortal enemy" of those who would make capital – "the hen that lays the golden egg" – accessible to the masses.[5] Later that same year, the anarchist-socialist Pierre-Joseph Proudhon mentioned the word in his personal correspondence, and in 1857 it made its appearance in one of his pamphlets. It makes sense that the word would have arisen in France in that time period: "socialism," "communism," and "liberalism" were coined there earlier in the century; adding "ism" to French words had become a natural linguistic reflex in the highly politicized atmosphere of class tensions and ideological conflict following the revolutions of 1789, 1830, and now 1848.[6]

For both Proudhon and Blanc, capitalism implied capitalists wielding power through capital; in other languages, the first instance of the word

previous year in staid sources that suggest it was not a neologism: see, e.g., *Pennsylvania Gazette* (Philadelphia) of August 17, 1791.

[4] The only instances I have found prior to Louis Blanc (see next note) are in *The Shamrock* of New York, NY (May 18, 1816) and *The Eagle* of Maysville, Kentucky (July 11, 1817), both reporting on events in Buenos Aires, and in *English Review, or, Quarterly Journal of Ecclesiastical and General Literature* (Dec. 1844). In all of these articles, the word "capitalism" hints at the power of great wealth, but the exact meaning is unclear. The term also appeared in early-nineteenth-century France, but it had a narrowly technical financial definition – "a system of capitalization" – that disappeared: see J. B. Richard de Radonvilliers, *Enrichissement de la langue française: dictionnaire de mots nouveaux*, 2nd ed. (Paris: Léautey, 1845), 52.

[5] Louis Blanc, *Organisation du travail: association universelle*, 9th ed. (Paris: Bureau du nouveau monde, 1850), 161, 162; the term does not appear in earlier editions. Emphasis in the original. For the etymology, in addition to online database searches, I have relied on J.-J. Hémardinquer, "'Capitalisme': mot et idée quarante-huitards? (Précision nouvelles)," *Annales* (March-April 1967), 442–446; Marie-Elisabeth Hilger et al., "Kapital, Kapitalist, Kapitalismus," in *Geschichtliche Grundbegriffe: Historisches Lexikon zur politisch-sozialen Sprache in Deutschland*, ed. Otto Brunner et al., vol. III (Stuttgart: Klett-Cotta, 1982), 399–454; and Richard Passow, *"Kapitalismus": Eine begrifflich-terminologische Studie* (Jena: G. Fischer, 1927), 2–3. Albert Dauzet et al., *Nouveau dictionnaire étymologique et historique*, 3d ed. (Paris: Larousse, 1974), 132, incorrectly claims that it first appeared in Diderot's *Encyclopédie*, where in fact the word is not found. Alain Rey et al., comps., *Dictionnaire historique de la langue française* (Paris: Dictionnaires le Robert, 1992), 343, dates the term to 1753, but without any evidence. David McLellan, *Karl Marx: His Life and Thought* (NY: Harper and Row, 1973), 217, is also incorrect when he states that the German radical Andreas Gottschalk used the word in 1848. The German source for this statement shows Gottschalk speaking of "*Kapitalherrschaft*" – the domination of capital – rather than "capitalism": see Hans Stein, *Der kölner Arbeiterverein (1848–1849)* (Cologne: Gilsbach, 1921), 96.

[6] Arthur E. Bestor, Jr., "The Evolution of the Socialist Vocabulary," *Journal of the History of Ideas* (June 1948), 259–302; Bestor does not discuss the origins of the word "capitalism."

was somewhat more restricted in its meaning. In English, the honor goes to the Victorian writer William M. Thackeray – the rival of Dickens who was much agitated by the condition of the urban poor – in his novel *The Newcomes* (1854). Here, capitalism refers specifically to having money invested in the stock market: because the character Paul de Florac had investments, it gave him a "sense of capitalism," which made him feel more "dignified."[7] In Germany, the first person to use the word in print was the Prussian conservative social reformer Karl von Rodbertus in a book on rural credit published in 1869. Although Rodbertus was the first person to call "capitalism ... an entire social system," all he was signifying was that money-lenders and speculators had gained too much influence over the disposition of landed property, the effect of which was to get landowners stuck in a "whirlpool of capitalism" – i.e., debt and bad investments.[8]

The word caught on only slowly. Karl Marx only mentioned it a few times late in life: the closest he came prior to that was "capitalist means [or mode] of production."[9] Books with "capitalism" in their titles were few and far between. In German, the first was political economist and social reformer Albert Schäffle's *Kapitalismus und Sozialismus* (1870), with the next one coming eleven years later.[10] In English, French, Italian, and Spanish, only a handful of books with "capitalism" in the title were published before the 1890s.[11] Keyword searches using database collections of the major English and American newspapers and French books indicate that the word did not regularly appear until after World War I (for reasons we will see), and often required an explanation for

---

[7] William Makepeace Thackeray, *The Newcomes* (London: Everyman, 1994 [1853–1855]), 467.

[8] Karl von Rodbertus-Jagetzow, *Zur Erklärung und Abhülfe der heutigen Creditnoth des Grundbesitzes* (Jena: Mauke, 1869), pt. 2, xiv–xvi, 377–379.

[9] For Marx, see German texts of his writings on the website "Stimmen der proletarischen Revolution" (mlwerke.de/me/default.htm), keyword search "Kapitalismus." As this chapter treats those who used the term "capitalism," it does not devote a specific section to Marx. But his legacy is inescapable and will be apparent throughout the first part of this book.

[10] Online catalogue searches of Deutsche Nationalbibliothek, Leipzig and Frankfurt am Main; and worldcat.org, s.v. "Kapitalismus." Worldcat.org gives the date of a pamphlet by the German socialist Heinrich Lux, *Die technische Revolution und der Kapitalismus* as 1870, but Lux was born only in 1863 and the real date of publication was 1895. See Hilde Schramm, *Meine Lehrerin, Dr. Dora Lux*, 2d ed. (Reinbek: Rohwolt, 2012), dritte Exkurs, 22–23, online at rowohlt.de/buch/Hilde_Schramm_Meine_Lehrerin_Dr_Dor a_Lux.2954762.html.

[11] Online catalogue searches of Biblioteca Nacional de España; British Library; Library of Congress; worldcat.org, and theeuropeanlibrary.org, s.v. "capitalism"; "capitalisme"; "capitalismo."

readers.[12] In 1908, for instance, Thorstein Veblen explained to other economists that it was a socialist term meaning a "large-scale industrial regime" – not the first thing that comes to mind when we think of capitalism today.[13]

An exception to that pattern was in Russia. The Russian intelligentsia was particularly sensitive to the rapid incursion of foreign models of economic development, and vigorously debated the ways Russia might cope with them. In doing so, its members made precocious use of the term "capitalism." There, the first occurrence of the word was in the title of the 1871–1872 translation of Schäffle's above-mentioned book.[14] The earliest appearance in an original Russian-language text that I have found comes from an anonymous Narodnik (Russian populist-socialist) article published in 1877 in a London-based exile journal.[15] The first Russian-authored book with "capitalism" in its title was also by a Narodnik economist, who was much troubled by the fate of native Russian handicrafts following the introduction of European-style factory production.[16] Regardless of their political position, most Russian thinkers of the late tsarist era would have agreed with the economist Nikolai-on (Nikolai F. Daniel'son) that capitalism had penetrated all realms of Russian life with the resulting disruption of traditional ties: "capitalism ... has destroyed all the age-old 'foundations' of the folk: economic, legal, moral."[17] The question was whether to oppose or embrace it: Marxists like Peter Struve argued that Russians needed to "recognize our backwardness and enter onto the path of capitalism," while Narodniks wanted to resist it for fear of what would happen to the once-flourishing but now fragile craft industries.[18]

---

[12] Keyword search in "ProQuest Historical Newspapers," "*Times* Digital Archive," and "Frantext" databases, s.v. "capitalism" or "capitalisme." Earliest appearance in the London *Times*: May 10, 1882, p. 7; in the *New York Times*: July 20, 1878, p. 3. Other first appearances of the word: *Washington Post* (Sept. 27, 1885), 1; *Los Angeles Times* (Oct. 13, 1890), 7; *Wall Street Journal* (Feb. 16, 1904), 1.

[13] Thorstein Veblen, "On the Nature of Capital," *Quarterly Journal of Economics* (Aug. 1908), 534.

[14] Al'bert E. Sheffle, *Kapitalizm i sotsializm* (St Petersburg: Tipografiia M. Khana, 1871–1872).

[15] "Ocherki uspekhov ekonomicheskoi ekspluatatsii v Rossii za polednie gody," *Vpered*, no. 5 (1877) (London), excerpted in *Narodnicheskaia ekonomicheskaia literatura: Izbrannye proizvedeniia*, comp. N. K. Karataev (Moscow: Izdatel'stvo sotsial'no-ekonomicheskoi literatury, 1958), 273, 656.

[16] V. V. [Vasilii Pavlovich Vorontsov], *Sud'by kapitalizma v Rossii* (St Petersburg: Tipografiia M. M. Stasiulevicha, 1882).

[17] Nikolai-on [Nikolai F. Daniel'son], *Ocherki nashego poreformennogo obshchestvennogo khoziaistva* (St Petersburg: A. Benke, 1893), 74–75, n1.

[18] James H. Billington, *Mikhailovsky and Russian Populism* (London: Oxford University Press, 1958), 165 (Struve quote); see also Nikolai-on, *Ocherki nashego poreformennogo obshchestvennogo khoziaistva*, 322, 335, 339, and, in general, Wayne Dowler,

By the early twentieth century, the term had entered such general usage among the Russian intelligentsia that medical doctors diagnosed the phenomenon as the cause of what they perceived to be a far-reaching "degeneration": they equated "capitalism" with a harmful Darwinian "struggle for existence" that was responsible for a deterioration of mental and physical health in the newly industrialized cities. In a 1907 book on the social diseases of tuberculosis, alcoholism, and syphilis, physician Lev B. Granovskii concluded that "struggle with [these manifestations of] degeneration ... should be directed at the removal of the capitalist order."[19] This type of medical analysis appeared in the West, too, where the critics of capitalism, whether they were socialist or not, believed that "evil capitalism makes people wicked and turns them into criminals and social parasites."[20]

With some exceptions, for the first couple of decades the word "capitalism" was predominantly part of the leftist vocabulary, adopted by other Marxists, anarchists, syndicalists, and an array of garden-variety socialists. This was true in China and Japan as well as in Europe and the United States. It started out as a term of abuse, adopted in order to describe what it was socialism was fighting against – or, better, to demonize what socialists hated about the modern world. If socialism was the dream of a perfect human future, free from all struggles and inequalities, then capitalism was the dreadful reality of suffering and oppression that had to be surmounted to achieve the wondrous promise of that freedom.[21]

"The Intelligentsia and Capitalism," in *A History of Russian Thought*, ed. William Leatherbarrow and Derek Offord (Cambridge: Cambridge University Press, 2010), 263–285, and Andrzej Walicki, *The Controversy over Capitalism* (Notre Dame: Notre Dame University Press, 1989 (1969)). One of the earliest academic articles explaining these Russian-intelligentsia debates to Western scholars was N. I. Stone, "Capitalism on Trial in Russia," *Political Science Quarterly* (March, 1898), 91–118.

[19] Daniel Beer, *Renovating Russia: The Human Sciences and the Fate of Liberal Modernity, 1880–1930* (Ithaca, NY: Cornell University Press, 2008), 80–88.

[20] Austrian (later American) legal philosopher Hans Kelsen, early 1920s, cited in Norbert Leser, "Otto Weininger und die Gegenwart," in *Otto Weininger: Werk und Wirkung*, ed. Jacques Le Rider and Norbert Leser (Vienna: Österreichischer Bundesverlag, 1984), 21.

[21] Deschepper, "L'Histoire du mot capital," 153; Martin Malia, *The Soviet Tragedy: A History of Socialism in Russia, 1917–1991* (NY: Free Press, 1994), 48–49; R. M. Hartwell and Stanley L. Engerman, "Capitalism," in *The Oxford Encyclopedia of Economic History*, ed. Joel Mokyr, vol. I (Oxford: Oxford, University Press, 2003), 321. In America, one of the earliest instances of the word was in an anti-private property tract published in 1877 by the Workingmen's Party of the United States, Adolf Douai's *Better Times!* (Chicago: Executive Committee, Workingmen's Party of the United States, 1877), 19, 23. On China and Japan see Wolfgang Lippert, *Entstehung und Funktion einiger chinesischer marxistischer Termini* (Wiesbaden: Franz Steiner Verlag, 1979), 145–153; and Andrew E. Barshay, *The Social Sciences in Modern Japan: The Marxian and Modernist Traditions* (Berkeley: University of California Press, 2004), passim.

The language associated with the word was, therefore, mostly negative, but with the promise of redemption. It drew from the deep well of ancient moralizing against money and merchants. Apostle Paul's counsel to Timothy in the New Testament epitomizes this enduring heritage of the classical Mediterranean: "They that will be rich fall into temptation and a snare, and into many foolish and hurtful lusts, which drown men in destruction and perdition. For the love of money is the root of all evil."[22] The echoes of admonitions such as Paul's resounded in the anti-capitalism of the modern era, but with a supplementary call to revolutionary action. In France, socialists of the 1860s and 1870s thundered against "parasitical capitalism," and on the eve of the violent insurrection of the Paris Commune, the latter-day Jacobin, Auguste Blanqui, seethingly remarked that "capitalism takes itself to the window and with utter tranquility views the people wallowing in the gutter."[23] The German socialist leader Wilhelm Liebknecht in 1872 castigated those who would sacrifice the working class to the "Moloch of capitalism" on the "battle-fields of industry."[24] Others blamed "all the evils of society" on capitalism, "this severe social disease" which involves the "excessive and illegitimate accumulation of capital" and turns workers into "raw materials, work tools, and beasts of burden."[25] The American Wobblie leader Big Bill Haywood decried the "slave bondage of capitalism" in a speech he gave in Chicago on June 27, 1905, before the "Continental Congress of the Working Class."[26]

Writing about this socialist movement and its bitter fury toward capitalism, French sociologist Émile Durkheim observed that it was "not a science" but "a cry of pain" in the face of the Industrial Revolution.[27] This was the most thorough-going and disruptive transformation of human affairs since the Neolithic birth of agriculture. Looked at in that context, we can understand why other ideological movements emitted cries of pain as they, too, latched onto the threat of "capitalism."

From socialists the term passed to Catholics, who were everywhere under assault by anti-clerical liberals and in Germany associated capitalist business with the harsh discrimination they faced in Bismarck's Lutheran- and Prussian-dominated, fast-industrializing nation.[28] Some

[22] 1 Timothy 6:7–10.   [23] Hémardinquer, "Capitalisme," 443.
[24] Hilger, "Kapital," 444.   [25] Passow, *Kapitalismus*, 10, 12, 23.
[26] Melvyn Dubofsky, *We Shall Be All: A History of the Industrial Workers of the World* (Chicago: Quadrangle Books, 1969), 81.
[27] Émile Durkheim, *Le socialisme* (1928), ebook version: http://classiques.uqac.ca/classiques/Durkheim_emile/le_socialisme/le_socialisme.html, 12.
[28] Wolfgang Hock, *Deutscher Antikapitalismus* (Frankfurt am Main: Fritz Knapp, 1960), 26; Paul Jostock, *Der deutsche Katholizismus und die Überwindung des Kapitalismus*

Catholic thinkers and politicians warmed to socialism, others moved to the far right, but either way they borrowed from socialist terminology as they sought to make sense of the bewildering challenges facing them in the nineteenth century. One statement encapsulates the mix of ideas in Catholic social thought of the period: "The enemy of the worker and of mankind in general was the vile spirit of egoism, which today rules the earth as capitalism and destroys Christian moral principles."[29]

From both socialists and Catholics, the word "capitalism" circulated to anti-Semites. According to the renowned economist Ludwig von Mises, writing in 1922, the term was a red cape waved by the "matadors of ultra-nationalist hate literature" to whip up the fury of the masses against free-market economics.[30] It was long standard fare for Jews to be associated with money lending and stock trading, but this ethnic minority became a more visible presence in certain arenas of economic life after gaining equal rights in Western Europe, and they were often scapegoats for the market crashes of the later nineteenth century. For anti-Semites, the "capitalist era" was synonymous with "control by the Jews."[31] "The Hebrew is the bearer of capitalism," a form of slavery imposed by these "subhumans" waging a "war of extermination . . . against the rest of humanity."[32] The Imperial German government had encouraged this link in the mind of the masses: Bismarck told an interviewer that he supported the anti-Semites of his day as "a safety-valve for reducing the pressure of the popular movement against capitalism in general. It deflected it from Socialist channels."[33] In France, too, many left-wing socialists and anarchists, as well as conservatives, were prone to anti-Semitism, which the historian Anatole Leroy-Beaulieu in the 1890s called

(Regensburg: Friedrich Pustet, 1933), 13; Joseph N. Moody, ed., *Church and Society: Catholic Social and Political Thought and Movements, 1789–1950* (NY: Arts, Inc., 1953), 519–520, 546–547; Passow, *Kapitalismus*, 12, 16–18, 25, 68–70. Cardinal Bourne of the English Catholic Federation tarred capitalism by association with the Protestant Reformation: "capitalism really began with the robbery of Church property in the sixteenth century" (London *Times* [Feb. 15, 1918], 4).

[29] Joseph Schwalber, *Vogelsang und die moderne christlich-soziale Politik* (Munich: Leohaus, Hauptstelle katholisch-sozialer Vereine, 1927), 12.

[30] Passow, *Kapitalismus*, 77n2.

[31] Heinrich Schnee, *Bürgermeister Karl Lueger* (Paderborn: Schöningh, 1936), 16 (quote), 30, 41. See also Kurt Wawrzinek, *Die Entstehung der deutschen Antisemitenparteien (1873–1890)* (Berlin: E. Ebering, 1927), 16–17; Bruce F. Pauley, *From Prejudice to Persecution: A History of Austrian Anti-Semitism* (Chapel Hill: University of North Carolina Press, 1992), 42, 158–159; and Schwalber, *Vogelsang*, 15–16.

[32] Ferdinand Roderich-Stoltheim [pseud. of Theodor Fritsch], *Die Juden im Handel und das Geheimnis ihres Erfolges* (Steglitz: Peter Hobbing, 1913), chap. 12 title, 144, 264.

[33] London *Times* (April 29, 1893), 7.

a manifestation of "anti-capitalism."[34] And in England, the Social Democratic Federation newspaper *Justice* stated that "the Jew financier" was the "personification of international capitalism" – an opinion repeated in the anti-Semitic diatribes of John A. Hobson, the socialist writer who wrote one of the earliest English books with "capitalism" in the title and helped to familiarize Britons with the concept.[35]

The German scholar Werner Sombart played a special role in furthering an anti-Semitic understanding of the relationship between Jews and capitalism.[36] His writings influenced right-wing extremists across Europe in the interwar years. As Sombart elucidated in numerous best-selling books, among them *The Jews and Economic Life* (1911), modern capitalism was devoid of any admirable Nordic qualities as it evinced a detestable Jewish spirit. By that he meant capitalism had taken on the allegedly nomadic, unrooted, and ultra-rational attributes of Judaism – all stereotypes rather than empirically derived characteristics. For Sombart, the "Jewish species" that created and dominated modern capitalism was epitomized by the unheroic trader "whose intellectual and emotional world is directed to the money value of conditions and dealings, who therefore calculates everything in terms of money" to the detriment of human considerations and the interests of the community.[37]

In the 1920s, in the wake of Germany's defeat in World War I and devastating hyperinflation, Sombart's musings became even more extremist. For Sombart, the modern era had entered the "chamber of horrors that was capitalism." He now believed that only German productive efficiency and technological greatness could serve as a bulwark against the greedy and conniving Jewish capitalist spirit that had pervaded the rest

---

[34] Stephen Wilson, *Ideology and Experience: Antisemitism in France at the Time of the Dreyfus Affair* (Rutherford: Farleigh Dickinson University Press, 1982), 248; see also chap. 10 and passim.

[35] John A. Hobson, *The Evolution of Modern Capitalism: A Study of Machine Production* (London: Walter Scott Press, 1894); Colin Holmes, "Anti-Semitism in British Society, 1876–1939," in *Hostages of Modernization: Studies on Modern Antisemitism, 1870–1933/39*, vol. I, ed. Herbert A. Strauss (Berlin: Walter de Gruyter, 1993), 326–329, 333 (quotes).

[36] See Friedrich Lenger, *Werner Sombart, 1863–1941: Eine Biographie*, 3rd ed. (Munich: C. H. Beck, 2012), chap. 9; Arthur Mitzman, *Sociology and Estrangement: Three Sociologists of Imperial Germany* (NY: Knopf, 1973), 22, 25–26, 251–259; Reiner Grundmann and Nico Stehr, "Why Is Werner Sombart Not Part of the Core of Classical Sociology?" *Journal of Classical Sociology*, vol. I, no. 2 (2001), 262–263; Jeffrey Herf, *Reactionary Modernism: Technology, Culture, and Politics in Weimar and the Third Reich* (Cambridge: Cambridge University Press, 1984), chap. 6; Jerry Z. Muller, *The Mind and the Market: Capitalism in Modern European Thought* (NY: Knopf, 2002), 253–257; Werner Sombart, "Capitalism," in *Encyclopedia of the Social Sciences*, ed. Edwin R. A. Seligman (NY: Macmillan, 1930), vol. III, 205.

[37] Cited in Grundmann and Stehr, "Why Is Werner Sombart Not Part of the Core of Classical Sociology?" 262–263.

of Europe. Only Germany could stand in the way of the "huge factory juggernauts," a Jewish creation that was destroying the traditional civilization he idealized – a point of view that patently overlooked the corrosive impact (primarily non-Jewish) German industries might have had.[38]

In his day, Sombart was a global celebrity, "the most influential, most widely known social scientist" in Germany and maybe the world.[39] Audiences mobbed his early 1914 lecture tour in Russia, and in 1928 the City University of Osaka, Japan, paid for the prestige of acquiring his personal library.[40] In his publications and speeches, Sombart reiterated Marx's anti-Semitic anti-capitalism under a scholarly veneer, and he channeled this particular aspect of Marx's thought to the German radical right when he moved in that direction after World War I. His position on capitalism and the Jews was instrumental in shaping the worldview of fascist circles in France and Germany and, one assumes, elsewhere among the many thousands of people who read his books.[41] One of those who integrated Sombart's anti-Semitic leitmotif into his own life's work was Joseph Goebbels, the Nazi Party propaganda leader: as he proclaimed in 1926, "I hate capitalism like the plague," above all because he associated it with the "dealer instincts" of the Jews, whose capitalist activities would come to "devour all peoples" if not stopped.[42] As the effects of the Great Depression wore on, the number of Europeans who sympathized with Goebbels – and Sombart – swelled across the continent.

"Made in Germany"

In 1911, Friedrich Naumann, a pastor and politician of the Wilhelmine empire, observed that "just as the French have their theme, namely 'What was the great Revolution?' so our national destiny has given us our theme

---

[38] Lenger, *Werner Sombart*, 149–150 (quotes).

[39] Grundmann and Stehr, "Why Is Werner Sombart Not Part of the Core of Classical Sociology?" 258 (quote), 261; Mitzman, *Sociology and Estrangement*, 223–224.

[40] Joachim Zweynert and Daniel Riniker, *Werner Sombart in Russland* (Marburg: Metropolis Verlag, 2004); Bernhard vom Brocke, *Sombarts "Moderner Kapitalismus": Materialen zur Kritik und Rezeption* (Munich: Deutscher Taschenbuch Verlag, 1987), 33.

[41] Klaus Bergmann, *Agrarromantik und Großstadtfeindschaft* (Meisenheim am Glan: Verlag Anton Hein, 1970), 198; Zeev Sternhell, *Neither Right nor Left: Fascist Ideology in France* (Berkeley: University of California Press, 1986), 159.

[42] Uwe Klussmann, "'Ich haße den Kapitalismus wie die Pest': Joseph Goebbels als nationaler Sozialist," in *Das Goebbels-Experiment*, ed. Lutz Hachmeister and Michael Kloft (Munich: Deutsche Verlags-Anstalt, 2005), 64, 66. See also Max Weinreich, *Hitler's Professors*, 2nd ed. (New Haven: Yale University Press, 1999), 204, 209; and Ritchie Robertson, *The "Jewish Question" in German Literature, 1749–1939* (Oxford: Oxford University Press, 1999), 191.

for a long time to come, namely 'What is capitalism?'"[43] German intellectuals of Naumann's (and Sombart's) time were preoccupied with this question, and their answers continue to shape our own outlook toward economic life.

Well before the turmoil of the interwar years, they were reacting to the changes wrought by the convulsive economic forces of the nineteenth and twentieth centuries. Many contemporaries celebrated the industrial and political might of the Kaiser's Germany. But others were apprehensive about the social unrest, moral corruption, and loss of traditions that seemed to accompany the introduction of railroads, cities, and factories. Germans debated the virtues and defects of the new type of society that was in the making, and German philosophical traditions, drawing on Romantic culture and Lutheran Pietism, both of which were hostile to commerce, gave one side of these debates an anti-capitalist thrust.[44] These anxieties are palpable in the work of Sombart, Max Weber, and the Austrian, later American, economist Joseph Schumpeter.

Sombart has been consigned to the back bench of the social sciences because of his sympathies for Nazism, but separate from his anti-Semitism he has had an important legacy in academic conceptualizations of capitalism. His theories of the relationship between Jews and capitalism were his riposte in an intellectual fencing match he initiated with his colleague Max Weber over the historical origins of capitalism. These two German scholars were largely responsible for popularizing the term "capitalism" among academics, whose serious engagement with the concept began after Weber claimed it was related to the rise of Calvinism and Sombart rejoined that it emanated from the spirit of Judaism.[45] The publication of Weber's *Protestant Ethic and the Spirit*

[43] Muller, *The Mind and the Market*, 229. Naumann's answer to his question was inconsistent, explaining it in one place as large-scale factory production and in another as a money economy and the victory of merchants over feudalism: see Passow, *Kapitalismus*, 22–23.

[44] Fritz Stern, *The Failure of Illiberalism: Essays on the Political Culture of Modern Germany* (NY: Knopf, 1972), 30ff.

[45] On the history of the debate between Weber and Sombart, see Hartmut Lehmann, "The Rise of Capitalism: Weber versus Sombart," in *Weber's Protestant Ethic: Origins, Evidence, Contexts*, ed. Hartmut Lehmann and Guenther Roth (Cambridge: Cambridge University Press, 1993), 195–208. The term "capitalism" also figured in the controversy over the nature of the pre-modern economy initiated by the publication of economic historian Karl Bücher's *Die Entstehung der Volkswirtschaft* (Tübingen: Laupp, 1917 [1893]); see 145–150 and passim. On that debate in Germany, see Alain Bresson, "Capitalism and the Ancient Greek Economy," in *The Cambridge History of Capitalism*, ed. Larry Neal and Jeffrey G. Williamson (Cambridge: Cambridge University Press, 2014), vol. I, 44–45. Separate from Weber, Sombart's work set off its own debate over the historical origins of capitalism: see Jairus Banaji, "Islam, the Mediterranean, and the Rise of Capitalism," *Historical Materialism*, vol. XV, no. 1 (2007), 47ff.

of Capitalism, first issued as a series of articles in the *Archive for Social Science and Social Policy* (*Arkhiv für Sozialwissenschaft und Sozialpolitik*) in 1905, and Sombart's retort, *The Jews and Economic Life* (first German publication, 1911), sparked the "longest running debate in modern social science" – still ongoing after more than a hundred years in the fields of economics, history, sociology, and political science.[46]

Their publications prompted a series of replies among scholars, who have continued ever since to deliberate on the so-called Weber thesis on the relationship between Protestantism, the work ethic, and capitalism. Besides Sombart, others challenged the idea, claiming it was medieval Italian traders, or Renaissance thinkers, or indeed Jews, who were responsible.[47] More recently, various academic authorities have labored to show that the Japanese, the Chinese, and other Asian mercantile peoples exhibit the same traits Weber identified as stimulating capitalism or reflecting a capitalist spirit: a theologically inspired work ethic and curtailment of consumption for the purpose of raising and investing capital.[48] We might add to that list the Catalans of eighteenth-century Barcelona, who were Catholics, but in the identical mold, placing a high premium on industriousness, thrift, and financial acumen.[49] From the beginning, there was also the argument that the commercial economy of early modern Europe shaped Calvinism as much as the other way around. Dutch scholars Jan de Vries and Ad van der Woude have endorsed that point of view: in the Netherlands, "the Reformation removed from its hinges the door leading to a rationalized commercial society. But, in

[46] Charles Camic et al., introduction to *Max Weber's Economy and Society: A Critical Companion*, ed. Charles Camic et al. (Stanford: Stanford University Press, 2005), 1 (quote); Lenger, *Werner Sombart*, 9. See also Hilger, "Kapital," 442, and Passow, *Kapitalismus*, 4–5, 8n1.

[47] Lehmann and Roth, eds., *Weber's Protestant Ethic*; Henri Sée, *Modern Capitalism: Its Origin and Evolution*, trans. Homer B. Vanderblue and Georges F. Doriot (NY: Adelphi, 1928 [1926]); Natalie Zemon Davis, "Religion and Capitalism Once Again? Jewish Merchant Culture in the Seventeenth Century," in *The Fate of "Culture": Geertz and Beyond*, ed. Sherry B. Ortner (Berkeley: University of California Press, 1999), 56–85.

[48] Robert N. Bellah, *Tokugawa Religion* (NY: Free Press, 1985 [1957]); Lawrence E. Harrison, *Who Prospers? How Cultural Values Shape Economic and Political Success* (NY: Basic Books, 1992), chap. 3. Most scholars now reject Weber's treatment of Asia, but his stimulus to scholarship on the region's economic history has been foundational. See, e.g., Syed Hussein Alatas, "The Weber Thesis and South East Asia," *Archives de sociologie des religions*, XV, no. 1 (1963), 21–34; Andreas E. Buss, ed., *Max Weber in Asian Studies* (Leiden: Brill, 1985); Tominaga Ken'ichi, "Die Modernisierung Japans und die soziologische Theorie Max Webers," in *Max Weber und das moderne Japan*, ed. Wolfgang J. Mommsen and Wolfgang Schwentker (Göttingen: Vandenhoeck & Ruprecht, 1999), 41–66.

[49] Raymond Carr, *Spain, 1808–1975*, 2nd ed. (Oxford: Oxford University Press, 1982), 30–32.

truth, that door was already open."[50] All the while, scholars down to the present have continued to stand by Weber while refining his original argument. For them, Protestantism did indeed add the leavening essential to the rise of capitalism.[51]

No matter where the truth lies, Weber and Sombart delinked capitalism from the socialist vocabulary and upended Marx's historical materialism by stressing the primacy of religious belief and cultural attitude in the birth of capitalism. In the work of Weber and Sombart, according to the economist John R. Commons, writing in 1934, "the capitalist spirit 'creates' capitalism. This is the reverse of Karl Marx whose capitalism created the capitalist spirit."[52] For Commons, this was an oversimplification of a complex reality. For other critics, the problem was that the idea of a capitalist spirit smacked of the eighteenth- and nineteenth-century German Romantic conceptions of the spirit of history and the nation, conceptions that had inspired the Kaiser's militarism and plunged Europe into World War I. This endowed the economic sphere with a dubious metaphysical essence, and it rubbed French historians Lucien Febvre and Marc Bloch the wrong way. Embittered by that war, like many of their contemporaries they rejected every manifestation of German culture, including the concept of capitalism, because it was "made in Germany."[53] On the other hand, this same emphasis on a distinctive national spirit goes a long way to explain the enormous influence Weber has had on Japanese analyses of capitalism.[54]

The notion of the spirit of capitalism à la Weber and Sombart would seem to be antithetical to how economics are perceived in the United States and United Kingdom, where economists tend to depict market forces as universals rather than endowed with qualities determined by

---

[50] Jan de Vries and Ad van der Woude, *The First Modern Economy: Success, Failure, and Perseverance of the Dutch Economy, 1500–1815* (Cambridge: Cambridge University Press, 1997), 165–172, with quote on 172. And see the work that launched the counterargument: R. H. Tawney, *Religion and the Rise of Capitalism* (NY: Mentor Books, 1954 [1926]).

[51] Notable recent works in this vein are Margaret C. Jacob and Matthew Kadane, "Missing, Now Found in the Eighteenth Century: Weber's Protestant Capitalist," *American Historical Review* (February 2003), 20–49; and Margaret C. Jacob, "Commerce, Industry, and the Laws of Newtonian Science: Weber Revisited and Revised," *Canadian Journal of History* (August 2000), 275–292.

[52] John R. Commons, *Institutional Economics*, vol. II (New Brunswick: Transaction Publishers, 1990 [1934]), 731.

[53] Hémardinquer, "Capitalisme," 443n2.

[54] Wolfgang Schwentker, *Max Weber in Japan: Eine Untersuchung zur Wirkungsgeschichte, 1905–1995* (Tübingen: Mohr Siebeck, 1998); and Wolfgang Schwentker, "Der 'Geist' des japanischen Kapitalismus: Die Geschichte einer Debatte," in *Max Weber und das moderne Japan*, ed. Mommsen and Schwentker, 270–298.

unique historical and cultural settings.[55] But the theory of the capitalist spirit was planted in Anglo-American academia thanks to Sombart's own English-language publications, selective translations of Weber by the Harvard sociologist Talcott Parsons beginning in the 1920s, and in the next decade by German scholars fleeing Nazism.[56] Social scientists in the United States canonized Weber as a prophet of Western capitalism against Marxist materialism, as they twisted his theory of the relationship between the Protestant ethic and capitalism to fit a triumphalist American (and especially American Protestant) ideology.[57]

Yet in some ways, Weber was just as pessimistic about capitalism as Sombart. Like many German intellectuals of his day, he expressed disquiet over the money economy, rapid industrialization and urbanization, mass consumption, and the loss of individual autonomy and community bonds. His body of work struggled with all the concerns about capitalism articulated by its critics everywhere.[58] He was not a socialist (he defended the economic benefit of stock markets), but for him the aforementioned "cries of pain" were fully justified. Weber endorsed the view that capitalism offered nothing but a "masterless slavery."[59] As he wrote in *The Protestant Ethic and the Spirit of Capitalism*, there was no longer any escape for humankind from the "iron cage" of capitalism, for we are all "bound to the technical and economic conditions of machine production which today determine the lives of all the individuals who are born into this mechanism, not only those directly concerned with economic acquisition, with irresistible force."[60]

[55] Axel R. Schäfer, "German Historicism, Progressive Social Thought, and the Interventionist State in the United States since the 1880s," in *Markets in Historical Contexts*, ed. Mark Bevir and Frank Trentmann (Cambridge: Cambridge University Press, 2004), 147–154.

[56] Roman Köster, "Coerced Misunderstandings? The Transfer of the Concept of Capitalism from Germany to the United States," unpublished paper presented at conference on "Power and the History of Capitalism," The New School, New York City (April 16, 2011); Sombart, "Capitalism," in *Encyclopedia of the Social Sciences*, 195–208; Talcott Parsons, "'Capitalism' in Recent German Literature: Sombart and Weber," *Journal of Political Economy* (Dec. 1928), 641–661; Wolfgang J. Mommsen, *The Political and Social Theory of Max Weber* (Chicago: University of Chicago Press, 1989), 179–188.

[57] Paul Münch, "The Thesis before Weber: An Archaeology," in *Weber's Protestant Ethic*, ed. Lehmann and Roth, 52; David Zaret, "The Use and Abuse of Textual Data," in *Weber's Protestant Ethic*, ed. Lehmann and Roth, 245.

[58] William Hennis, *Max Weber: Essays in Reconstruction* (London: Allen and Unwin, 1988), 50, 156, 158–159; Klaus Lichtblau, "The Protestant Ethic versus the 'New Ethic,'" in *Weber's Protestant Ethic*, ed. Lehmann and Roth, 179–193.

[59] Max Weber, *Economy and Society*, ed. Guenther Roth and Claus Wittich (Berkeley: University of California Press, 1978), vol. I: 600, vol. II: 1186.

[60] Max Weber, *The Protestant Ethic and the Spirit of Capitalism*, ed. Richard Swedberg (NY: Norton, 2009), 95–96. There is some controversy over the translation of the original

This is one of the bleakest assessments of capitalism that has ever been made. Via the neo-Marxists of the Frankfurt School, and many other iterations, this theory of technological domination lives on in the contemporary concept of "McDonaldization," the author of which, in describing the expansion of McDonald's (and IKEA and Starbucks, and so on) into every possible uncommodified area of the world, establishes a link "from the Iron Cage to the fast food factory."[61] Thus, one person might follow Weber to condemn capitalism while another can choose a different line of inquiry from the very same book and (without reading too closely) find cheerleading for a pro-capitalist ethos.

A similar process of selective borrowing of ideas about capitalism has taken place with the work of Joseph Schumpeter, the Austrian-born Harvard economist who during World War I served alongside Sombart and Weber as co-editor of the *Arkhiv für Sozialwissenschaft und Sozialpolitik*. Schumpeter is revered by many American defenders of a cut-throat variety of capitalism for accentuating the vital role of the brash and innovative entrepreneur and his articulation of the unavoidable process of "creative destruction." As Schumpeter wrote in 1950, capitalism "not only never is but never can be stationary": the "essential fact about capitalism" is that it produces a "perennial gale of creative destruction."[62] In assessing Schumpeter's interpretation, it is important to understand not only that he borrowed heavily from Sombart's writings on entrepreneurs, but that with the notion of "creative destruction," Schumpeter was refashioning an observation about the capitalist economy first made by Marx and Engels.[63] As they declared in the *Communist Manifesto* (1848),

German phrase "stahlhartes Gehäuse," as "iron cage": see editors' introduction to *The Protestant Ethic and the "Spirit" of Capitalism and Other Writings*, trans. and ed. Peter Baehr and Gordon C. Wells (NY: Penguin, 2002), xxiii–xxxiv. But it seems to me that "iron cage" comes closer to the spirit of the original than "shell as hard as steel" as proposed by Baehr and Wells. Either way, it does not negate my point about Weber's pessimism.

[61] Morton Schoolman, "Marcuse, Herbert," *Blackwell Encyclopaedia of Political Thought*, ed. David Miller (Oxford: Blackwell, 1991), 316; George Ritzer, *The McDonaldization of Society*, 5th ed. (Los Angeles: Pine Forge Press, 2008), 17ff, 47–48, chap. 2 (quote), and chap. 10. One assumes the title of Nicholas Carr's *The Glass Cage: Automation and Us* (NY: Norton, 2014), which is highly critical of the social impact of digital technologies, takes off from Weber, too, although there is no reference to him in the text.

[62] Joseph A. Schumpeter, *Capitalism, Socialism, and Democracy* (NY: Harper Perennial, 1976 [1950]), 82–84.

[63] John E. Elliott, "Marx's 'Grundrisse': Vision of Capitalism's Creative Destruction," *Journal of Post Keynesian Economics* (Winter, 1978–1979), 148–169; Hugo Reinert and Erik S. Reinert, "Creative Destruction in Economics: Nietzsche, Sombart, Schumpeter," in *Friedrich Nietzsche, 1844–1900: Economy and Society*, ed. Jürgen Backhaus et al. (NY: Springer, 2006), 55–85; Lenger, *Werner Sombart*, 234, 333.

The bourgeoisie cannot exist without constantly revolutionising the instruments of production, and thereby the relations of production, and with them the whole relations of society ... Constant revolutionising of production, uninterrupted disturbance of all social conditions, everlasting uncertainty and agitation distinguish the bourgeois epoch from all earlier ones. All fixed, fast-frozen relations, with their train of ancient and venerable prejudices and opinions, are swept away, all new-formed ones become antiquated before they can ossify.[64]

For Marx and Engels, this process enabled the deeper exploitation of the worker. Although this was not Schumpeter's emphasis, his debt to them is undeniable.

Like Sombart, Schumpeter was responding to Weber. Schumpeter believed the capitalist entrepreneur was a lone innovator who goes against the grain. He was neither Jewish nor Protestant in character, but a vestige of the aggressive aristocratic knight: as the entrepreneur strives to create a "private kingdom" he is "still the nearest approach to medieval lordship possible to modern man," driven by "the will to conquer: the impulse to fight, to prove oneself superior to others."[65] (Although he deflates that form of conquest when he writes elsewhere that capitalism is "unheroic in the knight's sense – no flourishing of swords about it, not much physical prowess, no chance to gallop the armored horse into the enemy ... and the ideology that glorifies the idea of fighting for fighting's sake ... understandably withers in the office among all the columns of figures.")[66]

However his writings have been interpreted, Schumpeter retained a deep pessimism about the human predicament under capitalism, which he shared with Weber and Sombart and which bore the heavy imprint of Marx. According to Schumpeter, the entrepreneur was a Nietzschean superman who, in disregard of mundane, rational conventions, shapes the world around him. His business endeavors acted like a dynamo to stir up waves of "creative destruction," which generated great industries and great wealth, but inevitably created losers as well as winners. Broad anti-capitalist social resentments followed; according to Schumpeter, these were an almost necessary by-product of capitalism.[67] Because industrial society required educated people and critical thinkers to function, it nurtured intellectuals, who by their nature would stoke the flames of discontent: "unlike any other type of society, capitalism ...

[64] Karl Marx and Friedrich Engels, *Communist Manifesto* (1848), online at marxists.org/archive/marx/works/1848/communist-manifesto/ch01.htm.
[65] Joseph Schumpeter, *The Theory of Economic Development* (Cambridge, MA: Harvard University Press, 1936), 93.
[66] Schumpeter, *Capitalism, Socialism, and Democracy*, 128.
[67] Schumpeter, *Theory of Economic Development*, chaps. 2, 5, 6; Muller, *Mind and the Market*, 293–294 and chap. 11 passim.

creates, educates and subsidizes a vested interest in social unrest."[68] Capitalism would always, therefore, generate hostility toward it from within, and this would regularly upend the social order.[69] "Can capitalism survive?" he asked in his bestselling book *Capitalism, Socialism, and Democracy* (1950). Spectator to the destructive anti-capitalism of communist and fascist movements, his answer was: "No, I don't think it can."[70]

Sombart, Weber, and Schumpeter were not alone in their despair over the fate of man under capitalism. Witnessing the rise of big business and industrial cartels, they assumed the truth of Marxist predictions of the inexorable growth and omnipotence of corporate monopolies (predictions which have so far not been fulfilled: as it has turned out, small and medium-sized companies have remained robust). All three thinkers contributed to and tapped into a trend among intellectuals in the twentieth century, which was to foretell either the impending demise of capitalism or its overpowering success, but in both scenarios with the same result: the final loss of individual autonomy and ethno-national particularities in a drab world dominated by statist, bureaucratized, large-scale enterprises.[71]

The American sociologist Daniel Bell, writing in the 1970s, fused the final-days economic prophesies of Schumpeter and Weber. According to Bell, we were already tangled up in the "cultural contradictions of capitalism." Our rich and hedonistic consumer society had come to be governed by the principle of "enjoy now, pay later," but capitalism was (or so he thought) rooted in Protestant-like frugality and hard work. As he sermonized, "we are witnessing the end of the bourgeois idea ... which has molded the modern era for the last two hundred years." This was, he

---

[68] Schumpeter, *Capitalism, Socialism, and Democracy*, 146 and passim.
[69] Schumpeter, *Capitalism, Socialism, and Democracy*, chaps. 12–14.
[70] Schumpeter, *Capitalism, Socialism, and Democracy*, 61.
[71] On this theme in general, see Howard Brick, *Transcending Capitalism: Visions of a New Society in Modern American Thought* (Ithaca, NY: Cornell University Press, 2006). Thomas K. McCraw, "Schumpeter Ascending," *American Scholar* (Summer 1991), 391, criticizes Schumpeter for his overreliance on Marx in this respect; the same can be said of Sombart and Weber. For the persistence of localized or small and medium-sized business despite the predictions of Marxists and a host of other social critics, see Michael J. Enright, "Organization and Coordination in Geographically Concentrated Industries," in *Coordination and Information: Historical Perspectives on the Organization of Enterprise*, ed. Naomi R. Lamoreux and Daniel M. G. Raff (Chicago: University of Chicago Press, 1995), 103–146; Mansel G. Blackford, *History of Small Business in America* (Chapel Hill: University of North Carolina Press, 2003); A. Shadwell, "Capitalism," pt. II, *Edinburgh Review* (Jan. 1921), 82–84; Heinz-Gerhard Haupt, "Small Shops and Department Stores," in *The Oxford Handbook of the History of Consumption*, ed. Frank Trentmann (Oxford: Oxford University Press, 2012), 268–269.

argued, a deterioration "from the Protestant ethic to the psychedelic bazaar." "The culture was no longer concerned with how to work and achieve, but with how to spend and enjoy ... By the 1950s American culture had become primarily hedonistic, concerned with play, fun, display, and pleasure." Along with his sometime co-author, the neoconservative forefather Irving Kristol, he warned that an economic system that promised endless shopping cannot offer "any vitality or a moral impulse that is a motivational or binding force ... [able to] hold society together."[72]

Bell's was a theory suited to the times, but in his attachment to a Weberian understanding of capitalism, he overlooked another line of inquiry about the nature and history of capitalism which stems from Sombart. Whereas Weber interpreted the ascetic Protestant renunciation of worldly goods as an essential quality of early capitalism, Sombart noted the importance of overt consumerism in its development. In his book *Luxury and Capitalism* (1913), he argued that as far back as the Renaissance, royal courts and their aristocracies desired luxury goods, which then stimulated manufacturing in the cities to supply those goods, and ultimately set the stage for industrialization. According to Sombart, consumer demand spurred capitalist activity, a point of view that has come into its own among scholars in recent years.[73] As American historian Jackson Lears and others have shown, not only were there certain strains of Protestantism that praised abundance instead of attempting to curtail this-worldly wealth, but in the nineteenth-century United States an "eroticizing of consumption" expressed in advertising catered to decadence and helped businesses turn a profit. This either clashed with or coexisted with ascetic Protestantism, but it existed early on.[74]

Bell's criticism imparts a sense of the fragility of cultures, communities, and individualism in an age of capitalist consumerism. Many other commentators have also sought to expose the abundance of consumer goods as a golden handcuffs for the masses, a modern capitalist variant of the

---

[72] Daniel Bell and Irving Kristol, *Capitalism Today* (NY: Basic Books, 1971), vii–viii; Daniel Bell, *The Cultural Contradictions of Capitalism* (NY: Basic Books, 1976), 54, 70, 84.

[73] Werner Sombart, *Luxury and Capitalism*, trans. W. R. Dittmar (Ann Arbor: University of Michigan Press, 1967); Daniel L. Purdy, *The Tyranny of Elegance: Consumer Cosmopolitanism in the Era of Goethe* (Baltimore: Johns Hopkins University Press, 1998), xii–xiii. For an overview of consumerism in Western social thought, see Ulrich Wyrwa, "Consumption and Consumer Society: A Contribution to the History of Ideas," in *Getting and Spending: European and American Consumer Societies in the Twentieth Century*, ed. Susan Strasser et al. (Cambridge: Cambridge University Press, 1998), 431–447.

[74] Jackson Lears, *Fables of Abundance: A Cultural History of Advertising in America* (NY: Basic Books, 1994), with quote on 47; Jackson Lears, "The Mormon Ethic and the Spirit of Capitalism," *New Republic* (Nov. 8, 2012), 50.

ancient Roman elite's practice of diverting the populace from political power through bread and circuses.[75] One might think of dismissing these critics for replaying "a well-known, much older morality tale: how the republican virtues of sobriety, civic pride, and bravery – in ancient Rome – led to victory and conquest which brought opulence and luxury, which in turn undermined those earlier virtues and destroyed the republic and eventually the empire."[76] But the truth is these intellectuals, like all those uttering "cries of pain," were also contending with something new in human history: large urban societies supplied by industrialized mass production. This demanded an all-encompassing term to both describe it and express their forebodings, and "capitalism" answered the call.

[75] Patrick Brantlinger, *Bread and Circuses: Theories of Mass Culture as Social Decay* (Ithaca, NY: Cornell University Press, 1983). At the same time, most American economists, politicians, and people came to support a consumption-oriented policy: see Gary Cross, *An All-Consuming Century: Why Commercialism Won in Modern America* (NY: Columbia University Press, 2000).

[76] Albert O. Hirschman, *Rival Views of Market Society* (Cambridge, MA: Harvard University Press, 1992), 113–114.

2 "Capitalism" in the mirror of the twentieth century

Chapter 1, for the most part, conveyed the views of scholars and politically active opponents of capitalism. But the word "capitalism" has had a deeper resonance due to its popular usage worldwide. It emerged as a mainstream term because of the geopolitics of the twentieth century, in reaction both to the specter of Russian communism and the rise of America as a military, commercial, and cultural superpower.

"Into the Russian looking glass"

With the victory of Bolshevism in Russia, anti-capitalist rhetoric posed a shiver-inducing threat that compelled a reexamination of American economic life. Russia became America's "dark double," and Americans came to understand their nation as its diametrical opposite, as the positive to its negative force.[1] In 1949, the writer and Librarian of Congress Archibald MacLeish lamented this pattern of thought for allowing the mental "conquest of the United States by the Russians." American political debate, he wrote, "was sung to the Russian tune; left-wing movements attacked right-wing movements not on American issues but on Russian issues, and right-wing movements replied with the same arguments turned round about." With respect to policy, "whatever the Russians did, we did in reverse." As America "wandered into the Russian looking glass," its perceptions of capitalism also took shape in the reflection.[2]

Nearly every one of the thousands of articles in the American press that mentioned the word "capitalism" from the 1880s to the 2000s defined it with reference to Russia or the Soviet Union, which in American opinion came to represent the polar opposite of the US political and economic system. This evidence leads to the conclusion that American views of

---

[1] David S. Fogelsong, *The American Mission and the "Evil Empire"* (Cambridge: Cambridge University Press, 2007), 6, 62, 228.

[2] Archibald MacLeish, "Conquest of America," *Atlantic* (Aug. 1949), 17–18. Thanks to Joe Peterson for the reference.

capitalism, whether conservative or liberal, developed out of America's preoccupation with Russia in the twentieth century. In existential rivalry with the USSR, Americans were forced to adopt the socialist term "capitalism" precisely because it was the object of communist abuse.[3]

As the press conveyed the earth-shattering events occurring in Russia, they adopted the word "capitalism" en route. Nearly every *New York Times* article that mentioned it in the 1920s was connected with the Soviet Union and its rulers Lenin, Trotsky, or Stalin.[4] Simple reporting on the USSR required adoption of the term, and editorializing necessitated defining it.

The definitions varied according to the political orientation of publications and their writers. By 1919, the first Red Scare was in full fury, and conservatives in the United States were denouncing Bolshevism as a "menace to Americanism."[5] Conversely, they put forth a defense of capitalism that contrasted with communism: "Capitalism is an evil you say? Nevertheless it is an evil that has permitted us to attain a high degree of material prosperity ... [And] the process of attaining communism is very much like committing suicide by the nation."[6]

The liberals writing for the *New Republic* had no enthusiasm for the Soviet experiment, but roundly critiqued the conservative position as well. They were bothered by the blind defense of free markets, "a capitalist utopia" based on a "myth of capitalistic rationality" as "mythical as any socialist utopia." Moreover, free markets did not work, the liberals argued, because they could not relieve poverty without some measure of government "economic control." The *New Republic* rejected the conservatives' depiction of the "present order as a great democracy of consumers," while corporations were able to apply "every device known to the psychology of advertising" to beguile buyers and relieve them of their hard-earned money.[7]

The arguments voiced in 1919 and the decade that followed would be familiar today. Public discussion of the American economic system is still framed essentially by the same ideological battle lines that were formed long ago in reaction to the Russian Revolution. Although rooted in the

---

[3] Articles were selected by keyword using library databases of periodical literature. Parts of this section have appeared in my article "The Soviet Union's Gift to America: The Word 'Capitalism,'" *Society* (March/April 2012), 155–163. They are used here with the kind permission of the publisher, Springer Science+Business Media.

[4] Keyword search of *New York Times* online archives.

[5] Joel H. Spring, *Images of American Life: A History of Ideological Management in Schools, Movies, Radio, and Television* (Albany: SUNY Press, 1992), 31, 40, 42.

[6] Hans Vorst, "Germany and the Danger of Bolshevism," *Living Age* (July 19, 1919), 135.

[7] *New Republic* (June 14, 1919), 205–207; (July 23, 1919), 372–375; (July 6, 1927), 164–165.

Gilded Age's antagonism between defenders and detractors of laissez-faire economics, positions hardened in debate over the inchoate concept of capitalism. They solidified further during the Great Depression, a capitalist calamity that happened to coincide with the staggering "super-industrialization" of the USSR.

In 1928, in the midst of the economic expansion and stock market boom of the Roaring twenties, Republican presidential candidate Herbert Hoover declared that "we in America today are nearer to the final triumph over poverty than ever before in the history of any land."[8] An editorial writer for the US Chamber of Commerce magazine *Nation's Business* gushed, "there is no doubt that the American businessman is the foremost hero of the American public today."[9]

But the reverence vanished like rain in the Dust Bowl with the onset of the Great Depression. The crash of Wall Street, the foreclosed farms, the failure of banks, and the 25 percent unemployment impugned the leader-ship of business and the old verities of laissez-faire economics. A nationwide debate ensued over the direction and nature of the eco-nomic system. The meaning of capitalism was a central issue.

There were a few holdouts: President Franklin D. Roosevelt never once mentioned the word in his public addresses, preferring "our economic system" or, on five occasions, "the capitalistic system."[10] Richard Whitney, the president of the New York Stock Exchange, told an audi-ence of brokers that "I prefer to avoid the term 'capitalism' and the 'profit system' as terms which have been badly abused" by the opponents of "freedom of the individual."[11] But he did not offer an alternative, and for nearly all others it was unavoidable – the word, with its socialist pedigree, was here to stay, but it became more contentious than ever as left, right, and center tried at a time of crisis to defend their positions through their own definitions of capitalism.

As Americans argued over the best course for their country after the catastrophic collapse, Russia was in everyone's mind as embodying the alternative to the US economy. This was illustrated in a film sponsored by the Westinghouse Corporation, *The Middleton Family at the New York World's Fair* (1939). The movie features a family whose middle-America

---

[8] *New York Times* (Aug. 26, 1928), sec. 8, p. 3. Hoover's Democratic opponent, Alfred E. Smith, retorted: "the Republican Party builds its case upon a myth."

[9] Herman Krooss, *Executive Opinion: What Business Leaders Said* (Garden City: Doubleday, 1970), 5.

[10] Keyword search of Woolley and Peters, *American Presidency Project*, Documents Archive (henceforth APP), online at www.presidency.ucsb.edu/ws/index.php; for the respective quotes, see Franklin D. Roosevelt, APP (www.presidency.ucsb.edu/ws/?pid=88410), parag. 23; and (www.presidency.ucsb.edu/ws/?pid=15578), parag. 11.

[11] Richard Whitney, "Economic Freedom," *Vital Speeches of the Day* (Dec. 31, 1934), 214.

values and assumptions about the "free enterprise system" are challenged by their daughter's boyfriend, Nick Makaroff, an abstract artist and communist with a suspiciously Russian-sounding name. He impresses the girl and horrifies the family when he denounces the fair as a "temple of capitalism" filled with machines that are "Frankenstein monsters," "where people are drooling over things that are taking away their jobs."[12] Fortunately, he is exposed as a cad and the girl returns to her original boyfriend, a clean-cut businessman and staunch defender of capitalism.

The basic spirit of the film, with its depiction of two antagonistic economic types, one good and one bad, one American and one Russian, lasted for decades.[13] As Americans argued over their country's response to the catastrophe of the Depression, Russia was in everyone's mind as embodying the alternative to the US economy. From the 1930s to the 1990s this pattern was cemented in place by introductory economics textbooks for colleges and high schools. They normally presented only two of the world's economic systems: American capitalism versus Soviet communism – with the addition of Fascist Italy and Nazi Germany while they existed. All of the other economies around the world were given short shrift or ignored altogether while implying the universality of the American and Russian models. Generations of American students saw the world through these lenses as their textbooks highlighted the functioning and superiority of the American system by emphasizing the shortcomings of the Soviet Union's.[14]

Not all of the comparisons were false. Certainly the differences between the American and Soviet systems were stark by any standard. But the reduction of economics to two possibilities was a great failure of imagination that made consideration of practical, non-ideological approaches to the Great Depression and the problems of capitalism then and later more

---

[12] The film can be viewed at archive.org/details/middleton_family_worlds_fair_1939.

[13] For the 1930s corporate public-relations campaigns on behalf of free enterprise and the "American Way," see Wendy L. Wall, *Inventing the "American Way"* (Oxford: Oxford University Press, 2008), pt. I; and William L. Bird, *"Better Living": Advertising, Media, and the New Vocabulary of Business, 1935–1955* (Evanston: Northwestern University Press, 1999).

[14] E.g., Edison L. Bowers and R. Henry Rowntree, *Economics for Engineers* (NY: McGraw-Hill, 1931), chap. 23; Harley L. Lutz et al., *New Introduction to Economics* (Evanston: Row, Peterson, 1933), 490ff; Howard C. Hill and Rexford G. Tugwell, *Our Economic Society and Its Problems* (NY: Harcourt, Brace, 1934), chap. 28; Walter E. Spahr, ed., *Economic Principles and Problems*, II. (NY: Farrar and Rinehart, 1940), chaps. 45–46; Frederic Benham and Francis M. Boddy, *Principles of Economics* (NY: Pitman Publishing, 1947), chap. 2; Paul A. Samuelson, *Economics*, 1st ed. (NY: McGraw-Hill, 1948), chap. 26; Paul A. Samuelson and William D. Nordhaus, *Economics*, 13th ed. (NY: McGraw-Hill, 1989), 837–844.

difficult. Truth be told, many on both sides had a rigid, simplistic, all-or-nothing view of capitalism. As agronomist and FDR advisor Mordecai Ezekiel complained, "the term 'capitalism' has become a slippery-smooth symbol of something all conservatives worship and something all radicals question."[15]

New Deal brain trusters and their supporters in the press were especially aggravated by the conservatives' refusal to accept government intervention in the economy on the grounds that it smacked of Stalinism. Liberal critics noted that conservatives paid no attention to places like Sweden, where "capitalism was controlled," yet economic and political freedoms were preserved.[16] Why? For Thurman W. Arnold, soon to be assistant US Attorney General, it was because the right wing had postulated a "true faith of Capitalism," and believed that critics of the faith were serving the forces of evil. For the followers of laissez-faire, the "national Devil ... is governmental interference," which will "lead the people astray" and condemn their country to a hell that looked a lot like communist Russia or Nazi Germany. The crusaders for a pure capitalism repudiated welfare assistance to the poor precisely "because Russia was a country in which government had assumed that obligation," and it had led "to the destruction of individual initiative ... and the downfall of Capitalism."[17]

The doom conservatives feared is what communists and other radical opponents of capitalism eagerly awaited. Few were the optimists who believed capitalism would pull through. *Collier's* magazine editorialized that "capitalism as a system is not endangered for the plain reason that no alternative seems more desirable ... However well Communism may suit the former subjects of the Russian czar, it has not attracted Westerners."[18] Columbia University economist Edwin R. A. Seligman told an interviewer that "it is the sheerest balderdash to say, merely because times are bad and Russia has a five-year plan, that capitalism is in danger." Quite the opposite: "Capitalism is in its merest beginnings."[19]

As Seligman's comment suggests, Soviet planning was attracting enormous attention. Even advocates of the market economy had to acknowledge that "with giant strides [Russia] advances its economic

[15] Mordecai Ezekiel, *Jobs for All through Industrial Expansion* (NY: Knopf, 1939), 278.
[16] Marquis Childs, "Sweden—Where Capitalism Is Controlled," *Harper's Magazine* (Nov. 1933), 749–758.
[17] Thurman W. Arnold, *Folklore of Capitalism* (New Haven: Yale University Press, 1937), 4–5, 8–10, 37.
[18] "Don't Choke the Future," *Collier's* (April 30, 1932), 54.
[19] Edwin R. A. Seligman, "Capitalism Has Just Begun," *Review of Reviews* (June 1931), 61–62.

development, while Capitalism flounders and sinks back."[20] The Soviet-inspired "cult of planning" provoked the envy of technocrats, who envisioned a society where *the engineer, rather than the business man or the financier is supreme. This is a stupendous conception and presents a real challenge to capitalism.*"[21]

America in the 1930s heard a cacophony of proposed economic plans. On the far left they intended to *abolish* capitalism; on the center-left they sought to *control* capitalism through industry cartels or a National Economic Board; in the center they stood for *stabilizing* capitalism by means of a managed currency, deficit spending, and public works.[22]

Conservatives critiqued both socialist and New Deal proposals, on the grounds that they would interfere with the laws of nature. "Capitalism," explained Dorothy Thompson to readers of *Good Housekeeping* and *Ladies' Home Journal*, "is a natural order of things, based upon man's nature and upon biological inequalities." She and numerous fellow conservatives warned that if government tinkered with this system it would lead to dictatorship on the model of Germany, Italy, Japan, and, above all, communist Russia.[23]

Liberal publicists, on the other hand, went to great lengths to justify planning in a capitalist society. They made a special effort to rebut the conservative critics of the New Deal, who reviled it as an attempt to "Sovietize the country" and undermine the "American system" – statements frequently found in the press releases of the National Association of Manufacturers and the US Chamber of Commerce.[24] The defenders of planning argued that "there is nothing Russian about its origin." Historian Charles A. Beard insisted that when the Russians adopted planning they were "laying aside Marx [and taking] up Frederick Winslow Taylor," the factory-efficiency guru.[25] Along with Beard, Mordecai Ezekiel maintained that "private capitalism is a man-made system," in which the state issued the laws, financed infrastructure, and employed civil servants from judges to firemen. It followed that national planning would not therefore deviate greatly from preexisting patterns of American life.[26]

[20] Arthur Dahlberg, *Jobs, Machines, and Capitalism* (NY: Macmillan, 1932), 1.
[21] Respective quotes in Paul Blanshard, "Socialist and Capitalist Planning," *Annals of the American Academy of Political and Social Science* (July 1932), 6, and Bowers and Rowntree, *Economics for Engineers*, 448. Emphasis in the original.
[22] Hill and Tugwell, *Our Economic Society*, chap. 29.
[23] Dorothy Thompson, *Dorothy Thompson's Political Guide* (NY: Stackpole Sons, 1938), 27–29, 60–63.
[24] Arnold, *Folklore of Capitalism*, 10–12, 73; Krooss, *Executive Opinion*, 23.
[25] Charles A. Beard, "'Five-Year Plan' for America," *Forum* (July 1931), 1–4.
[26] Ezekiel, *Jobs for All*, 271–279.

Parrying the conservative attack, New Dealers for the most part denied that there was any similarity between Stalinist and capitalist forms of planning. For radically different reasons, countercultural thinkers of the 1930s saw fit to highlight the similarities between the Soviet and American economic systems. On this point, the Southern Agrarian writers and back-to-the-land, small-is-beautiful advocates like Ralph Borsodi were in full agreement. Both the United States and the USSR, in the words of the writer Henry Blue Kline, "negate personality and ... reduce critical individuality to the zero deadness of a mass-mind."[27] In their romanticization of rural self-sufficiency and dislike of modern industry, they concluded that communism and capitalism had both built, according to Borsodi, "an ugly civilization. It is a civilization of noise, smoke, smells, and crowds – of people content to live amidst the throbbing of its machines; the smoke and smells of its factories; the crowds and discomforts of the cities of which it proudly boasts."[28] Both societies make "genuflections before the altar of mere bigness," and power and wealth seem "always to gravitate to the few." People should "cease permitting themselves to be fooled by collectivists of various kinds – industrialists, finance-capitalists, New Dealers, socialists, technocrats, communists, fascists," and favor instead "small, local enterprises."[29] Whether in the USSR or the United States, economic "insecurity and industrialism are Siamese twins. You can't have one without having to accept the other. Insecurity is the price we pay for our dependence upon industrialism for the essentials of life."[30]

Borsodi and Kline were not just intellectual outliers: it was hard to escape the assumption that the American and Russian economic systems were variations on a theme when widely read and well-respected studies of big business in the United States also pointed in that direction. Proto-convergence theories among conservatives and liberals drew especially on two influential books. *The Modern Corporation and Private Property* (1932), co-written by New Deal brain truster Adolf A. Berle and liberal economist Gardiner C. Means, contended that 200 large corporations dominated the US economy, and managers in bureaucracies rather than stock-holding owners ran those corporations.[31] In his best-seller *The Managerial Revolution* (1941), the Trotskyite-turned-conservative

[27] Henry Blue Kline, *I'll Take My Stand* (Baton Rouge: Louisiana State University Press, 1977 [1930]).
[28] Ralph Borsodi, *This Ugly Civilization* (NY: Harper and Bros., 1933), 1–46.
[29] Ralph Borsodi, *Prosperity and Security* (NY: Harper and Bros., 1938), 91–92, 300, 313.
[30] Ralph Borsodi, *Flight from the City* (NY: Harper and Bros., 1933), 144–146.
[31] Adolf A. Berle and Gardiner C. Means, *Modern Corporation and Private Property* (NY: Macmillan, 1932). And see Brick, *Transcending Capitalism*, 19–20, 56, 73–82, 217.

James Burnham reiterated the point more alarmingly by arguing that if all industrial societies were run by managerial elites, capitalism would disappear because of its inability to exploit technological and human resources as effectively as communism.[32] Both of these books strongly implied that if the United States had "capitalism without capitalists," then it was not so dissimilar from the USSR.[33]

This clouding of the conceptual dichotomies became more pronounced after the 1941 Nazi invasion of the USSR, which produced a US–Soviet alliance.[34] Wartime propaganda and the wishful thinking of the American public explain how Stalin quickly metamorphosed from being a bloodthirsty "big-nosed, mammoth-moustached" tyrant (as *Time* magazine portrayed him) into kindly ally Uncle Joe. His country no longer appeared in the press as a dreary slave labor camp, but as a "land of surprises" with a pioneer spirit just like ours.[35] Opinion polls in the United States registered high levels of sympathy for the Soviets and a new empathetic reading of their economy as a form of "modified" capitalism.[36] Even pro-business and anti-New Deal editorialists managed to convince themselves that the Soviet Union was a lot freer and more decentralized than Nazi Germany or Fascist Italy.[37] As *Fortune* magazine explained approvingly in January 1945, "Russia is in many ways not so very different from the US under the New Deal."[38]

In the years following World War II, the warm feelings Americans may have held toward their Russian allies gave way to panic. During the Cold War, fear of "totalitarianism" was the guiding conceptual framework of US foreign policy.[39] As Americans viewed the world through that prism, the United States represented itself as the opposite of everything the Soviet Union stood for. Typifying the era, American propagandists developed the socialist-sounding concept of "People's Capitalism."

---

[32] James Burnham, *Managerial Revolution* (NY: John Day, 1941), chap. 3 and passim.

[33] Max Nomad, "Capitalism without Capitalists," *Scribner's Magazine* (June 1934), 407–411.

[34] Abbott Gleason, *Totalitarianism* (NY: Oxford University Press, 1995), 36–37, 40–43, 54.

[35] Kimberly Eller, "Allies or Adversaries: The Evolving Popular American Image of the Russians, 1939–1950," MA thesis, Clemson University (1994), 23–85, with quotes on 33 and 53.

[36] John P. Diggins, *Up from Communism: Conservative Odysseys in American Intellectual History* (NY: Harper and Row, 1975), 202.

[37] E.g., Maxwell S. Stuart, *The American Way: Business Freedom or Government Control?* (n. p., 1944), 3–4.

[38] Peter H. Irons, "American Business and the Origins of McCarthyism," in *The Specter: Original Essays on the Cold War and the Origins of McCarthyism*, ed. Robert Griffith and Athan Theoharis (NY: Franklin Watts, 1974), 76.

[39] Gleason, *Totalitarianism*.

"People's Capitalism" was the brainchild of Eric Johnston, a moderate Republican who parlayed his earnings as a vacuum-cleaner salesman in Spokane, Washington, into an appliance-distribution empire across the western US and became president of the US Chamber of Commerce.[40] To counter the Soviet threat, Johnston's instinct kicked in: salesmanship on behalf of capitalism would win over the world.[41] Theodore Repplier, executive director of the Advertising Council, agreed with Johnston that "the American enterprise system needs 'reselling.'"[42] A PR organization whose mission was to improve the public image of business, the Ad Council had multiple links with the government. As a consultant to the US Information Agency, Repplier encouraged it to adopt "People's Capitalism" as its propaganda slogan.[43] "The purpose of US persuasion," he wrote, was "to whack Communism where it hurts": to combat the appeal of Communism in Asia and elsewhere in the world, it is important that we "make clear the fact that a new kind of capitalism has been born – a People's Capitalism which comes closer than any previous society to achieving man's age old goal of the good life for all."[44]

Behind the scenes many power brokers found the term hard to swallow. Bruce Barton, the advertising executive and author who had portrayed Jesus as a salesman in *The Man Nobody Knows* (1925), worried that the word "seems to bring up in too many minds the old cartoon of the pompous fat bellied old gentleman with a high silk hat elbowing his way down the street, and muttering to hell with the common people."[45] President Eisenhower, too, had doubts: "I would have liked to have seen some kind of adjective put between 'people's' and 'capitalism,' something of the order of, if not 'democratic' – something of the order of 'competitive' or something of that kind."[46]

But its defenders insisted. Claude Robinson, the head of the conservative, pro-business Opinion Research Corporation, had conducted preliminary polling on the People's Capitalism concept. He took Barton's point, writing in their correspondence that "there is no doubt but what

[40] See his obituary in *New York Times* (August 23, 1963), 1, 25.

[41] Eric Johnston, "Three Kinds of Capitalism," *Reader's Digest* (Sept. 1943), 124–126; Eric Johnston, *America Unlimited* (Garden City: Doubleday, Doran, 1944), chap. 8.

[42] Robert Griffith, "Selling of America: The Advertising Council and American Politics," *Business History Review* (Autumn, 1983), 388–412, with quote on 392.

[43] Walter L. Hixson, *Parting the Curtain: Propaganda, Culture, and the Cold War, 1945–1961* (NY: Palgrave Macmillan, 1998), 133.

[44] Theodore S. Repplier, "Persuasion under the Cherry Blossoms," *Saturday Review* (Oct. 1, 1955), 45–46.

[45] Bruce Barton, letter to Claude Robinson (Oct. 15, 1956), folder Roa-Rof (Claude Robinson), box 60, 1924–1961, Bruce Barton Collection, Wisconsin Historical Society. On Barton, see Bird, *"Better Living,"* passim.

[46] Dwight D. Eisenhower, APP (www.presidency.ucsb.edu/ws/?pid=10773).

[sic] the word 'capitalism' has its limitations." However, he added, "we have searched the dictionaries for a better word and do not seem to be able to find one." Most importantly, "the great advantage of the word 'capitalism' is that it places the issue in the people's minds of a privately owned economy vs. a government directed one" – i.e., the United States versus the USSR.[47] The popular American understanding of the word remains virtually unchanged to this day.

The USIA promoted the concept at international exhibitions, which coincided with a massive effort to convince domestic audiences of the virtues of free enterprise. Overseen by the Ad Council, the US Chamber of Commerce, and the National Association of Manufacturers, the intent, according to a National Cash Register executive, was to "indoctrinate citizens with the capitalist story." Companies supplied hundreds of millions of dollars to enable broadcasting of the corporate-driven message to millions of Americans through factory-employee lectures and discussion seminars, ads in print media, commercials on TV and radio, and pre-prepared talking points mailed to the molders of American opinion: pastors, teachers, and barbers.[48]

Given today's political rhetoric, it might surprise us to find that the enthusiasts of People's Capitalism also took pride in the American "mixed economy," with its unemployment and retirement benefits and Keynesian "efforts to tame the adversities of the so-called 'business cycle.'" In our capitalist society, they bragged, "we live in a welfare state which seeks to put a floor below which no one sinks but builds no ceiling to prevent man from rising."[49] Nowadays, conservatives would denounce all this as socialism, and then, too, a few voices warned against the "smiling mask" of the "Handout State" as inflationary and anti-capitalist and potentially totalitarian.[50] But most contemporary publications, including conservative ones, kept in concert with the spirit of the USIA and the Eisenhower administration in stressing the virtues of the

---

[47] Claude Robinson, letter to Bruce Barton (Nov. 5, 1956), folder Roa-Rof (Claude Robinson), box 60, 1924–1961, Bruce Barton Collection, Wisconsin Historical Society.

[48] Elizabeth A. Fones-Wolf, *Selling Free Enterprise* (Urbana: University of Illinois Press, 1994), 177 and passim.

[49] Leo Bogart, *Premises for Propaganda* (NY: Free Press, 1976), 90 (first quote); Herbert Harris, "Real Radicals: U.S. Businessmen," *Nation's Business* (July 1953), 29, 58 (second quote); "Lodge Tells What Capitalism Really Means," *US News and World Report* (Sept. 28, 1959), 106, (third quote). Grant Madsen, "Lessons of Victory: Occupying Germany and Japan, Discovering the 'People's Capitalism,'" doctoral dissertation, University of Chicago (2011), relates this quality to the personality of President Eisenhower and the unique international role America took on in the world in the immediate postwar era.

[50] E.g., Ernest L. Klein, *How to Stay Rich: The Story of Democratic American Capitalism* (NY: Farrar, Strauss, 1950), 11–12, 16, 116.

state–business partnership: they were content to make known how much better the American mixed economy was than the Soviet Union's, which couldn't even match People's Capitalism in its own supposed fields of strength, social welfare and labor relations.

The materialistic consumerism and lack of subtlety associated with the People's Capitalism slogan aroused the ire of the American intelligentsia, among them Harvard economist John Kenneth Galbraith. Our society should not, he argued, set "as its highest goal the production of private consumer goods" over investment for "human development."[51] Galbraith's assessment of the "affluent society" and the "new industrial society" emerging under the auspices of People's Capitalism was also highly negative on political grounds. The conservative "economic theology" of the free market allowed large corporations to concentrate too much power in their hands – as in the Soviet Union. Because big companies dominate the economy and have eliminated competition in the marketplace, Galbraith felt that the only way to protect the rights of labor and the citizenry was for government to erect a "countervailing power" to serve as a "restraint on private power" and restore the "autonomous self-regulation" of American capitalism.[52]

Traditionalist conservative thinkers were also leery of growing corporate power and the corporate boosterism associated with the push for People's Capitalism. As their cardinal philosopher, Russell Kirk, warned, "it is quite conceivable that the gigantic corporation, the gigantic union, and the gigantic state bureaucracy might give us the dreariest form of socialism without using the word" – a "socialist capitalism" whose "unholy alliance" of big-city "finance companies, contractors, and chain store executives" would destroy small family businesses and the distinctiveness of small towns by forcing them to "yield to a standardized mass commercialism," an "impersonal" and "standardized prosperity."[53]

Aware of the criticism of the People's Capitalism campaign at home and abroad, an MIT economic historian with close ties to the CIA, Walt W. Rostow, developed a more sophisticated theoretical framework for American capitalism that would substantiate its global triumph.[54]

---

[51] John Kenneth Galbraith, *The Affluent Society* (Boston: Houghton Mifflin, 1958), 275–276, 352.

[52] John Kenneth Galbraith, *The New Industrial State*, 3rd ed. (Boston: Houghton Mifflin, 1978 [1967]), 96–101; John Kenneth Galbraith, *American Capitalism* (Boston: Houghton Mifflin, 1962 [1952, 1956]), 17, 111, 128, 137, 151.

[53] Russell Kirk, "Little Shops and Socialist Capitalism," *National Review* (Oct. 23, 1962), 317.

[54] Latham, Adas, Gilman, Haefele, and Belmonte articles in David C. Engerman et al., eds., *Staging Growth: Modernization, Development, and the Global Cold War* (Amherst: University of Massachusetts Press, 2003).

The outcome was his short book *The Stages of Economic Growth: A Non-Communist Manifesto* (1960) – "a vivid and meaningful set of ideas that would bite and resist Communist alternatives," in the author's words.[55] Rostow replaced the Marxist stages of history (feudal, capitalist, communist) with stages correlating to the American model of economic development. Marx had been wrong. Class conflict was not the engine driving mankind forward to a day when private enterprise and private property would no longer exist. The only valid path to economic growth was the one blazed by the capitalist United States through representative democracy, mass consumerism, and social-welfare programs. Societies that aspired to the highest stage of economic achievement, exemplified by the United States, were moving on the right track toward development. Those that came under the sway of Marxist Russia would remain impoverished. Here was the birth of "modernization" theory in American social science, developed in answer to Russian communism, and a "capitalist mirror image" of Soviet teleology.[56]

We can empathize with Rostow for believing he had discovered in the United States the alchemical formula for transforming global poverty into prosperity. By the early 1960s, economist George Stigler was certain that America had "one foot through the door" of the capitalist "Golden Age."[57] On the fiftieth anniversary of the Russian Revolution, *Time* magazine assured its readers that the capitalist economic system was still "the most productive in human history."[58]

The optimism was short-lived, however. In the 1970s the US economy seemed to be rusting out. The mixed economy, it appeared, could not keep the machine running at full horsepower. This was when the majority of textbooks, college curricula, and academic journals began to extol "efficient markets ... [and] disparage all forms of regulation as equally suspect distortions of market forces."[59] The mathematically proven perfect market developed hand in hand with rational-choice theory to become the dominant paradigm in American economics scholarship in the last third of the twentieth century.[60]

---

[55] Mark H. Haefele, "Walt Rostow's Stages," in *Staging Growth*, ed. Engerman et al., 85.
[56] Michael E. Latham, "Introduction," in *Staging Growth*, ed. Engerman et al., 9.
[57] "Can Capitalism Survive?" *Time* (July 14, 1975), 56.
[58] "And 50 Years of Capitalism," *Time* (Nov. 17, 1967), 51.
[59] Robert Kuttner, *The Squandering of America* (NY: Knopf, 2007), 100.
[60] My treatment of the subject is based on S. M. Amadae, *Rationalizing Capitalist Democracy: The Cold War Origins of Rational Choice Liberalism* (Chicago: University of Chicago Press, 2003); Michael A. Bernstein, *A Perilous Progress: Economists and Public Purpose in Twentieth-Century America* (Princeton: Princeton University Press, 2001), chaps. 4–5; David Ciepley, *Liberalism in the Shadow of Totalitarianism* (Cambridge, MA: Harvard University Press, 2006), 178–180, 318; John Kay, "Rationale of the Market Economy," *Capitalism and Society*, vol. IV, no. 3 (2009), 2–3; Philip Mirowski,

These concepts grew in part out of the US Defense Department's sponsorship of the RAND Corporation and other Cold War think tanks. Here mathematicians, computer scientists, and economists formulated game theory to anticipate Soviet decision-making behaviors and guide American strategists in the hair-trigger atmosphere of the nuclear arms race. Economists found game theory irresistible and readily applied its modeling of human behavior to their own field of study. Positing cybernetically generated "laws of the market," they sidelined non-quantifiable factors in economics like human psychology, political cultures, and the weight of historical traditions as factors that "are not helpful ... [because] they don't predict anything ... [We] don't know which way human psychology will go wrong."[61]

Conservative economists of this bent drew conclusions that their colleagues to the left rejected.[62] If, as the conservatives argued, all business profits resulted from the sum total of choices made by individuals acting rationally in pursuit of their egoistic interests, then logically it followed that the most successful companies were beneficial to a society made up of those individuals, and the unrestricted market offered the only solutions to social ills that did not limit the individual's prerogatives – whereas the government, intervening in the economy through bureaucratic regulations, public spending, and communitarian impulses, could never accurately ascertain the wishes of the citizenry.

With its closed-circuit mathematical models, this brand of economics purported to have achieved "ideological neutrality" – which is why the word "capitalism" largely disappeared from its vocabulary. But not too far below the surface was a preoccupation with Soviet totalitarianism. For rational-choice theorists, capitalist democracy meant the "condition of non-dictatorship."[63] Soviet-bloc communist societies, and, potentially, social-welfare states, embodied the opposite principle, where citizens were incapable of making informed decisions because of political repression and/or imbalances in the economy brought about by government intrusion.

Machine Dreams: Economics Becomes a Cyborg Science (Cambridge: Cambridge University Press, 2002); and Yuval P. Yonay, *The Struggle over the Soul of Economics* (Princeton: Princeton University Press, 1998), 185–195, 204–205.

[61] Respective quotes from Mirowski, *Machine Dreams*, 283; and Conor Clarke, "Interview with Kenneth Arrow," *Atlantic* (July 27, 2009), online at theatlantic.com/politics/archive/2009/07/an-interview-with-kenneth-arrow-part-one/22213/.

[62] Kenneth Arrow, for example, was a father of rational-choice theory, but supported a classical-Keynesian synthesis balancing individual and community interests: see his review of Milton and Rose Friedman, *Free to Choose* in *New Republic* (March 22, 1980), 25–28.

[63] Respective quotes from Yonay, *Struggle over the Soul of Economics*, 204; and Amadae, *Rationalizing Capitalist Democracy*, 112.

Therefore the inference of efficient markets based on rational decision-making did not just represent a postscript to an older version of neo-classical economics dating from the nineteenth century, when economists first applied mathematics to demonstrate conditions of marginal utility and equilibrium. It was also a rebuttal of the ideological underpinning of the Soviet Union. As Robert Kuttner observed, "the corollary of resolute anticommunism seemed to be an equally fierce unreconstructed capitalism ... The Cold War and the laissez-faire imperative were mutually reinforcing."[64] Sociologist Daniel Bell, too, critiqued the rational-equilibrium hypothesis for generating its own "utopia of individualism" similar to the Marxist utopia of collectivism: both, he wrote, turned mankind into an "analytical abstraction." Instead of the messiness and often non-rationality of human affairs, neo-liberal economics reduced them to elegant mathematical equations that presented the free-market economy as "a jeweled set of movements, a celestial clockwork." For Bell, it was all a "convenient fiction," but for its conservative adherents, it betokened a higher truth.[65]

In this atmosphere, though, the conservative, laissez-faire views of capitalism that had been marginal since the 1920s gained currency once again. The libertarian, neo-classical, and neo-liberal schools of economics rocketed to prestige. Despite their disagreements, these overlapping schools of thought all sought the resurrection of laissez-faire and the demise of the mixed economy.[66] After the onset of the Great Depression, for forty years the prophets of the free market had wandered in the intellectual wilderness, sustaining themselves off their critiques and an idealized vision of a better world to come. The patriarchs of the movement were Friedrich A. Hayek, Ludwig von Mises, and Frank Knight. Hayek and Mises were Austrian-born economists celebrated by conservatives for their defense of laissez-faire. Knight was an American with degrees in German literature and economics, and a faculty member at the University of Chicago, which had become a redoubt of neo-classical and neo-liberal economics in no small part owing to Hayek's energetic crusading and fundraising. All three devoted their careers to battling the tenets of socialism. Repudiating state planning, they deployed their logical resources to convey "the impossibility of economic calculation" by

---

[64] Robert Kuttner, *End of Laissez-Faire* (Philadelphia: University of Pennsylvania Press, 1992), 9.

[65] Daniel Bell, "Models and Reality in Economic Discourse," in *Crisis in Economic Theory*, ed. Daniel Bell and Irving Kristol (NY: Basic Books, 1981), 57–58, 69–70.

[66] In general, see Philip Mirowski and Dieter Plehwe, eds., *Road from Mont Pèlerin: The Making of the Neoliberal Thought Collective* (Cambridge, MA: Harvard University Press, 2009); and Brian Doherty, *Radicals for Capitalism: A Freewheeling History of the Modern American Libertarian Movement* (NY: Public Affairs, 2007).

government bureaucrats, and warned of the "chaos and poverty for all [that] will unavoidably result."[67] On grounds of political freedom, too, they opposed the redistributive and interventionist economic policies of fascism, communism, and Keynesianism, which Hayek averred were taking the West down the very same "road to serfdom" – the title of his global best-seller, published in 1944, condensed in *Reader's Digest*, translated into twenty foreign languages, and still wildly popular among American conservatives today.[68] Hayek co-founded the Mont Pèlerin Society in Switzerland in 1947 as a kind of Libertarian International – in order, he said, to regenerate "the ideas of classical liberalism, . . . refute socialism, . . . and to work out . . . a philosophy of freedom."[69] It ended up accomplishing its goal in a way that could not have been expected at its creation.[70]

But judging by the number of books sold, the most popular of all these "radicals for capitalism," and the only consistent libertarian of the lot, was Ayn Rand.[71] Rand was born Alissa Rosenbaum, a Russian Jew, in the tsarist capital of St. Petersburg in 1905. Fiercely opposed to Bolshevism and dreaming of a career in Hollywood, she left the Soviet Union for the United States in 1925. Her libertarianism grew out of her seven-year experience of communism. She glorified the most materialistic and brutally competitive version of American capitalism as the antithesis of Russian communism. In the first place, man is "a sovereign individual who owns his own person, his mind, his life, his work and its products." In the second, he is "the property of the tribe (the state, the society, the collective) that may dispose of him in any way it pleases." "Is man free?" she asks. "In mankind's history, capitalism is the only system that answers: Yes." All others, she believed, including democratically elected social-welfare states, would lead to totalitarianism.[72]

Rand's influence, like that of Hayek and the Chicago School of neoliberal economics, penetrated Washington, DC, at the highest level.

---

[67] Ludwig von Mises, *Planned Chaos* (Irvington-on-Hudson: Foundation for Economic Education, 1947), 83.

[68] Friedrich A. Hayek, *Road to Serfdom* (Chicago: University of Chicago Press, 1944). For Hayek's importance to the American Tea Party movement, see Kate Zernike, "Movement of the Moment Looks to Long Ago Texts," *New York Times* (Oct. 1, 2010), online at nytimes .com/2010/10/02/us/politics/02teaparty.html?pagewanted=1&_r=1&hp.

[69] R. M. Hartwell, *A History of the Mont Pelerin Society* (Indianapolis: Liberty Fund, 1995), xiv.

[70] For its international network of adherents and institutional affiliates, see Dieter Plehwe, Bernhard Walpen, and Gisela Neunhöffer, eds., *Neoliberal Hegemony* (London: Routledge, 2006), pt. I.

[71] Jennifer Burns, *Goddess of the Market: Ayn Rand and the American Right* (Oxford: Oxford University Press, 2009), 195 and passim.

[72] Ayn Rand, *Capitalism: The Unknown Ideal* (NY: New American Library, 1966), 10.

Federal Reserve chairman Alan Greenspan was a member of Rand's inner circle and, as he put it, a "convert" to the "philosophy of unfettered market competition."[73] President Ronald Reagan had also been a kindred spirit since his days as a red-baiting Californian conservative in the McCarthy era. He spent his entire political career accusing liberals of consciously adopting what he (incorrectly) understood as Lenin's strategy in the Russian Revolution: implement social-welfare programs to push up inflation and taxes. These would destroy the middle class, crush "individual freedom and liberty," and yield absolute power to a socialist government.[74] Grouping the mixed economy with Soviet communism, he declared that "we're engaged in a struggle between the proponents of big government" and "our free system of democratic capitalism."[75]

Like Reagan, other conservatives – and, I would argue, most Americans – continued to glimpse capitalism through the shadows cast by the Soviet Union. This generation continued to idealize the American economy as the only alternative to communism, and American capitalism as the only system to guarantee democracy, freedom, and prosperity. "The force of the argument," explained economist Kenneth Arrow, "comes from one overwhelming and very ugly fact: the totalitarianism of the Soviet Union."[76] In the 1970s and 1980s, conceptions of capitalism in the United States derived from the same simplistic juxtapositioning of America versus Russia, the same fixation with communism that had been present since the early twentieth century.

These perspectives were not limited to conservatives. The pristine market economy imagined by Reagan Republicans was not far removed from what most Democrats had in mind. Although Republicans continued to assail Democrats during elections as "central planners" and socialists,[77] by the 1990s it had become routine for Democrats to advocate for tax reductions for the rich, financial deregulation, welfare reform, and free trade. During the Clinton administration – which was responsible for NAFTA (North American Free Trade Agreement), after all – the mantra in foreign and domestic policy was promoting "the market,"

---

[73] Alan Greenspan, *Age of Turbulence* (NY: Penguin, 2007), 52.

[74] Amos Kiewe and Davis W. Houck, *Shining City on a Hill: Ronald Reagan's Economic Rhetoric, 1951–1989* (NY: Praeger, 1991), 16–21, 26, 108. On Lenin's monetary policy, see Steven G. Marks, "The Russian Experience of Money, 1914–24," in *Russian Culture in War and Revolution, 1914–22*, book 2, ed. Murray Frame et al. (Bloomington: Slavica, 2014), 121–148.

[75] Ronald Reagan, APP (www.presidency.ucsb.edu/ws/?pid=41325).

[76] Kenneth Arrow contribution to "Capitalism, Socialism, Democracy: A Symposium," *Commentary* (April 1978), 30–31.

[77] E.g., Malcolm Forbes, "Three Cheers for Capitalism," *Forbes* (Oct. 25, 1993) 244, 246.

"market capitalism," or "democratic capitalism": phrases that appeared repeatedly in the speeches of the president and his cabinet.[78] This enthusiasm reflected, at least in part, Americans' response to the fate of the Soviet Union.

For Democrats and Republicans alike, the astonishing fall of communism sanctioned the new consensus on market economics with its distinctly neo-liberal flavor of capitalism. Social philosopher Francis Fukuyama proclaimed it the "end of history." His best-selling book of that title boiled down to one rousing thought: capitalism's "ultimate victory as the world's only viable economic system" went hand in hand with the "victory of liberal democracy in the political sphere."[79]

For many Americans, the collapse of Russian communism confirmed the near infallibility of capitalism. As President George H. W. Bush declared, "socialism's attempt to create the new Soviet man simply didn't work, because human nature cannot be destroyed and created anew." Capitalism, by contrast, "build[s] upon the strengths of human nature."[80]

The growing enthusiasm among conservatives for untrammeled capitalism suggests that when the threat of communism vanished, the "gentleman's agreement that was Keynesianism" became null and void.[81] Robert J. Eaton, chief executive of DaimlerChrysler, demonstrated this in the condescending lecture he gave to a German audience in 1999: "The idea that capitalism can be painless" is a delusion perpetrated by Western European social-welfare states – "the delusion that the costs of global capitalism can be avoided while the fruits of it are being enjoyed," the delusion that it is fair, or that it alleviates poverty. "Collectivism and redistribution won't work. They were tried. They failed. The [Berlin] Wall came down. End of story."[82]

The evidence for that assertion came not from Western Europe, but from Eastern Europe. Eaton could not recognize the difference between the social-welfare states of the West and the socialist dictatorships of the East, assuming as he did that if it was not laissez-faire capitalism it was not capitalism at all. He failed to recognize that Western European capitalism took a slightly different shape than it did in the United States. The confusion stemmed from a black-and-white understanding of

[78] William Clinton, APP (www.presidency.ucsb.edu/ws/?pid=46854; www.presidency.ucsb.edu/ws/?pid=52906; www.presidency.ucsb.edu/ws/?pid=48896; www.presidency.ucsb.edu/ws/?pid=48591).
[79] Francis Fukuyama, *The End of History and the Last Man* (NY: Free Press, 1992), 92–93.
[80] George H. W. Bush, APP (www.presidency.ucsb.edu/ws/?pid=19852).
[81] Naomi Klein, *Shock Doctrine: The Rise of Disaster Capitalism* (NY: Picador, 2007), 319.
[82] Robert J. Eaton, "Global Capitalism," *Vital Speeches of the Day* (Nov. 1, 1999), 39.

capitalism: like many Americans, Eaton was conditioned to believe that anything deviating from the American model or with government involvement beyond that "necessary for the efficient functioning of open markets" was some variant of socialism or communism. And with the end of the Cold War and disappearance of an ideological rival there was no longer a need for Americans to measure themselves against the practices of the Soviet Union.

This circumstance strengthened a dogmatic faith in the self-regulating market that was one of the causes of the financial crisis of 2008.[83] But even then, after the reputation of the American economic model suffered a global reversal of prestige, the comparisons with Russia remained in place, revealing how deeply intertwined they were to Americans' understanding of capitalism in their own society and how essential they were to justifying the particular forms it took.

The new era of "turbo-capitalism," it turned out, was dangerous at high speeds.[84] Without adequate traffic enforcement, the crash was inevitable. As the US government's Financial Crisis Inquiry Commission concluded, "what else could one expect on a highway where there were neither speed limits nor neatly painted lines?"[85] Francis Fukuyama attributed the Great Recession to the "unholy alliance of true believers and Wall Street firms" that had won the battle for financial deregulation. The economy was in a wreck, he contended, because "the Reagan revolution lost its way": it had "become an unimpeachable ideology," no longer "a pragmatic response to the excesses of the welfare state."[86]

For his part, recently retired Federal Reserve chairman Greenspan was in a "state of shocked disbelief" that deregulation had brought down the financial markets. As he testified before Congress, he was "very distressed" that there was a "flaw in the model" postulating that "the self-interest of lending institutions" would be sufficient for markets to correct themselves and prevent irrational or unethical behavior from bringing down the house. He was forced to admit that the "whole intellectual edifice . . . [had] collapsed."[87]

---

[83] The report of the US government's Financial Crisis Inquiry Commission makes this connection: see its *Financial Crisis Inquiry Report* (Washington, DC: Public Affairs, 2011), xviii, 53–54.

[84] The quote is from Edward N. Luttwak, *Turbo-Capitalism* (NY: HarperCollins, 1999).

[85] US Government, Financial Crisis Inquiry Commission, *Financial Crisis Inquiry Report*, xvii.

[86] Francis Fukuyama, "Fall of America, Inc.," *Newsweek* (Oct. 13, 2008), 30.

[87] "Testimony of Dr. Alan Greenspan" (Oct. 23, 2008), Committee of Government Oversight and Reform, House of Representatives, US Congress, online at gpo.gov/fdsys/pkg/CHRG-110hhrg55764/html/CHRG-110hhrg55764.htm.

Greenspan accepted that his theoretical foundation needed some repair. President Bush, on the other hand, was less inclined to question his assumptions and tried to put the financial crisis in perspective by contrasting capitalism and communism. His November 2008 speech to the Manhattan Institute repeated decades of American thinking on economics:

Ultimately, the best evidence for free market capitalism is its performance compared to other economic systems . . . Nations that have pursued other models have experienced devastating results. Soviet communism starved millions, bankrupted an empire, and collapsed as decisively as the Berlin Wall ... The record is unmistakable. If you seek economic growth, if you seek social justice and human dignity, the free market system is the way to go. And it would be a terrible mistake to allow a few months of crisis to undermine sixty years of success . . . [for] history has shown that the greater threat to economic prosperity is not too little government involvement in the market, it is too much government involvement in the market.[88]

Bush's account is a new version of the story we have heard since the Russian Revolution: there are two possible economic systems in the world, free market (American model) and collectivist (Russian model). America's won, the other lost. America's is free, the other is not. America's involves a minimal role for government, the other a large one. Obviously, something went wrong with the model prevailing in the United States. Bush blamed individual malefactors: "A relatively small group of people – many on Wall Street, some not – had gambled that the housing market would keep booming forever."[89] But the crisis could have had nothing to do with laissez-faire economic policies because the only alternative – "too much government involvement in the market" – was tantamount to communism.

Why is this comparison so persistent? Why are American discussions of capitalism still stuck in the same rut they were in as far back as the 1920s and 1930s? It is because the dominant American vision of capitalism was clouded by the country's apprehension over the rise of Russia. Americans sized up capitalism in relation to communism – to repeat Archibald MacLeish, they "wandered into the Russian looking glass." Over time the images of capitalism lodged in American minds to become, according to Indian writer Pankaj Mishra, a set of "passively internalized ideological beliefs."[90]

---

[88] George W. Bush, APP (www.presidency.ucsb.edu/ws/?pid=84854).
[89] George W. Bush, *Decision Points* (NY, 2010), 440.
[90] Pankaj Mishra, "It's a Round World after All," *Harper's Magazine* (Aug. 2007), 88.

My intent has not been to show that the dichotomizing of American capitalism and Russian communism was always a false position. Rather, it has been to call into question what we really know about capitalism by showing that at nearly every moment since the word came into use it was defined by way of comparison with the dreaded Soviet Frankenstein economy. As a result, American conceptions of capitalism have been, and still are, imbued with what economist Paul A. Samuelson once called the economic "science fiction of the right as well as of the left and center."[91]

Nor is the United States alone in this pattern of defining itself through comparison with a threatening foreign power: the rest of the world does something similar. In Europe and the non-Western world, perceptions of capitalism took shape as people there wandered into the *American* looking glass.

Into the American looking glass

Alongside Russian communism, "America was the dominant language through which modernity was debated in the twentieth century."[92] Global discussion of the phenomenon, whether positive or negative, circled around several keywords, including "Americanization," later "globalization," and always "capitalism."[93]

Paul Wengraf, a German art dealer of the Weimar era, wrote that Russia and the United States were "the two most modern states in the world."[94] Along with philosopher Martin Heidegger, many felt that their societies were caught "in the pincers between Russia and America, which are metaphysically the same."[95] But more typical was Sombart's belief that capitalism was synonymous with America while Russia represented its farthest remove.[96] Max Weber was in agreement with him about the Russians and the Americans: according to many of his writings, liberal modernity withered in the inhospitable Russian political climate, whereas

---

[91] Paul A. Samuelson, "Economic Scares," *Newsweek* (Sept. 11, 1978), 82.

[92] Mary Nolan, "Anti-Americanism and Americanization in Germany," *Politics and Society* (March 2005), 88–122, with quote on 102.

[93] This section relies in general on Richard Pells, *Not Like Us: How Europeans Have Loved, Hated, and Transformed American Culture since World War II* (NY: Basic Books, 1997), and Jessica C. E. Gienow-Hecht, "Always Blame the Americans: Anti-Americanism in Europe in the Twentieth Century," *American Historical Review* (Oct. 2006), 1067–1091.

[94] Mary Nolan, *Visions of Modernity: American Business and the Modernization of Germany* (NY: Oxford University Press, 1994), 25–26.

[95] Martin Heidegger, *Introduction to Metaphysics*, trans. Gregory Fried and Richard Polt (New Haven: Yale University Press, 2000 [1935, 1953]), 48.

[96] Sombart, "Capitalism," in *Encyclopedia of the Social Sciences*, 205.

in United States "the spirit of capitalism" reigned, as his examplar Ben Franklin illustrated.[97]

Whether in accord with Heidegger or Sombart and Weber, around the world a quest emerged to articulate "a third position between Soviet socialism and American capitalism," which future Argentine dictator Juan Domingo Perón in 1938 interpreted as the objective of Italian fascism (he later made it one of the guiding principles of his own governing doctrine).[98] And lest we think that this sentiment was restricted to political extremists, note that all the European Protestant denominations meeting in Amsterdam at the 1948 assembly of the World Council of Churches rejected capitalism along with communism – to the shock of the American delegation.[99]

These attitudes about America arose long before the Cold War and the emergence of the United States as superpower or, after the fall of communism, what Josef Joffe termed the global "Überpower."[100] The word "Americanization," like "capitalism," dates to the mid-nineteenth century and implied technical ingenuity, but by the *fin de siècle* was linked with the muscular American exports to Europe of bulk commodities and consumer goods – followed in the next decades by movies and music – all of which, in the minds of many intellectuals, threatened to obliterate distinctive European national identities.[101] From the 1880s onward, one prominent vision of the United States was as a barbarous place crowded with dehumanizing skyscrapers and slums, oscillating between excessive puritanism and sexual libertinism, but in either case a cultural wasteland because of its "worship of size, speed, mechanism, and money."[102] In contrast to Europe, so dominant and unquestioned was capitalism as a mode of life in the United States that Sombart was compelled to write a book to answer the question, *Why Is There No Socialism in the United States?* (1906). In it he portrayed the

[97] Max Weber, *The Russian Revolutions*, trans. and ed. Gordon C. Wells and Peter Baehr (Cambridge: Polity, 1995); Weber, *The Protestant Ethic and the Spirit of Capitalism*, ed. Swedberg, 23–25 and passim.

[98] David Rock, *Authoritarian Argentina: The Nationalist Movement, Its History, and Impact* (Berkeley: University of California Press, 1993), 3–4 21, 146 (quote), 160; Juan Domingo Perón, *Peron [sic] Expounds His Doctrine* (Buenos Aires: n.p., 1948), chaps. 7–14; Joseph A. Page, *Perón: A Biography* (NY: Random House, 1983), 89, 185, 221, 405. Cf. the quest for a "third way" in a German book from 1893 by Karl Jentsch titled *Neither Communism nor Capitalism*: see Rüdiger vom Bruch, "Bürgerliche Sozialreform im deutschen Kaisserreich," in *"Weder Kommunismus noch Kapitalismus,"* ed. Rüdiger vom Bruch (Munich: C. H. Beck, 1985), 62–179.

[99] "The Churches Speak to Business," *Fortune* (Dec. 1948), 122–123.

[100] Josef Joffe, *Überpower: The Imperial Temptation of America* (NY: Viking, 2006).

[101] Pells, *Not Like Us*, 7.

[102] British writer C. E. M. Joad cited in Martin J. Wiener, *English Culture and the Decline of the Industrial Spirit, 1850–1980* (Cambridge: Cambridge University Press, 1981), 89.

American working class as living in a land where "all Socialist utopias came to nothing on roast beef and apple pie." The workers were "well fed," the male dressed "like a gentleman and she like a lady," and had so much access to free land they were blithely unaware of their exploitation within the confines of the industrial system.[103] But then, as Sombart had once written during a visit to the United States, capitalism had filled American cities with an "artificial race of men."[104]

Negativism was the dominant mood in the discourse of the intelligentsia. As George Bernard Shaw wrote before the Great Depression, capitalism was a "runaway car" which "is taking its passengers over the brink of the precipice."[105] But together with the angst that produced anti-Americanism or anti-capitalism there was also enormous admiration of the United States, even among intellectuals. Not necessarily American democracy, which barely registered, but what the Germans called "Fordism," or mass production; as one author commented, Germany was beset by a "Ford psychosis." For many this presented a positive utopia of gleaming machinery, full production, low consumer prices, and corporate profits, just as for others it bespoke a dystopian nightmare in which humans became automatons.[106] Similarly in France in the 1920s, where anti-Americanism ran rampant, many supporters of business rationalization and high productivity via industrial efficiency and new technologies admired American advances in the factory and envied America's "practical spirit."[107] After World War II, young people in rebellion against the older generation embraced emblematic American consumer products such as t-shirts, blue jeans, chewing gum, and soft drinks. For pro- and anti-Americans, Coca-Cola symbolized the era as its executives bragged that it was "the essence of capitalism." Attitudes toward it were a barometer of opinion not only about the United States, but also capitalist economics.[108]

---

[103] Werner Sombart, *Why Is There No Socialism in the United States?*, trans. Patricia M. Hocking and C. T. Husbands (London: Macmillan, 1976 [1906]), with quotes on 105–106.

[104] Lenge, *Werner Sombart*, 143–148, 168, 342 with quote on 145.

[105] Bernard Shaw [sic], *The Intelligent Woman's Guide to Socialism, Capitalism, Sovietism, and Fascism* (Harmondsworth: Penguin Books, 1982 [1928]) 330–331.

[106] Nolan, "Anti-Americanism and Americanization," 94; Nolan, *Visions of Modernity*, chap. 3, with psychosis quote on 31.

[107] Richard Kuisel, *Capitalism and the State in Modern France* (Cambridge: Cambridge University Press, 1981), 86ff with quote on 90.

[108] Mark Pendergrast, *For God, Country, and Coca-Cola: The Definitive History of the Great American Soft Drink and the Company that Makes It* (NY: Basic, 2000), 240; H. B. Nicholason, "The Competitive Ideal," *Vital Speeches of the Day* (Dec. 15, 1952), 152; Richard F. Kuisel, "Coca-Cola and the Cold War," *French Historical Studies* (Spring 1991), 96–116.

One of the complaints about Coca-Cola was that it constituted a stealth American invasion: "cocacolonisation," according to the French Communist Party newspaper *L'Humanité*.[109] From World War I on, the suspicion that the United States sought to dominate Europe through the imposition of its form of capitalism was also a persistent theme in intellectual discourse, which the enthusiasm for the United States did not prevent, and in fact probably prompted. Thinkers of all political stripes railed against it. A recent analysis demonstrates that Hitler, from the very beginning of his rabble-rousing career, called on the German people to join his "struggle against capitalism." In connection with that he ranted against Jews, as we know, but even more so America as leader of Germany's "international world of enemies."[110] Likewise from the left, English philosopher Bertrand Russell warned against the "post-war domination [of Europe by] American capitalism": as he asserted in 1926, following the Dawes Plan and the Locarno treaties, "the government of France . . . has been shown . . . to be really in Wall Street."[111] Right-wing French nationalists Robert Aron and Arnaud Dandieu also alleged that France was becoming an "American colony." Their inflammatory writings of the 1930s agitated against "the American spirit," which, with its "two essential attributes, the religion of credit and the myth of production," was "the cancer of the modern world." In their eyes, the United States was leading Europe into "the capitalistic dance"; what many did not grasp, according to them, was that it was a "danse macabre" foretelling the death of Europe.[112]

These suspicions only became more pronounced after World War II, when the American military, economic, and cultural presence became overwhelming. This may have been filling the vacuum left by the devastation of the European continent, but the reflex of European thinkers on both the left and right was to attack American imperialism and capitalism for the steam-roller effect they would have on their societies. Antonio

---

[109] Kuisel, "Coca-Cola and the Cold War," 101.

[110] Brendan Simms, "Against a 'World of Enemies': The Impact of the First World War on the Development of Hitler's Ideology," *International Affairs* (March 2014), 317–336, with quotes on 322 and 330. The equation of the US, Jews, and capitalism has always been common in anti-American, anti-capitalist critiques, especially in Germany: see Andre S. Markovits, *Uncouth Nation: Why Europe Dislikes America* (Princeton: Princeton University Press, 2007), 62–64.

[111] Bertrand Russell, "Capitalism or What?" *Bankers' Magazine* (May 1926), 680, 725–726.

[112] Robert Aron and Arnaud Dandieu, "America: Europe's Cancer," *Living Age* (Oct. 1931), 117–123. Also see Denis Lacorne, "Anti-Americanism and Americanophobia: A French Perspective," in *With Us or Against Us: Studies in Global Anti-Americanism*, ed. Tony Judt and Denis Lacorne (NY: Palgrave Macmillan, 2005), 50–52; and Kuisel, *Capitalism and the State in Modern France*, 101.

Castro Villacañas, journalist of the Spanish Falange, put it plainly in 1948, the year the Marshall Plan was introduced: "We don't want progress, that romantic and liberal, capitalist and bourgeois, Jewish, Protestant, atheist, and Masonic Yankee progress. We prefer the backwardness of Spain, our backwardness."[113] At the same time, Simone de Beauvoir, the French feminist existentialist, bewailed the condition of love under capitalism, implying that while Europe was heading along this path, America was already at a dead end: because in modern industrial civilization "the mobility of capital allows its holder to own and dispose of his wealth without reciprocity," husband and wife are no longer "substantially attached," but "are only juxtaposed." This evolution was particularly noticeable in America, where modern capitalism had triumphed: divorce was going to flourish, and husbands and wives were no more than "provisional associates."[114] The entire cinematic oeuvre of Jacques Tati from the 1940s to 1970s spoofs the technological gadgetry, cars, corporate culture, and industrial uniformity which came to France from the United States or in imitation thereof. Humorously and gently, but insistently, Tati warns the French that their fascination with America will bring about the loss of their quaint, quirky, and beloved culture.[115] In 1981, a leader of the French New Right, Alain de Benoist, updated those tropes when he warned of Americanization and American-style capitalism as a subtle variant of totalitarianism that "leads to the creation of happy robots. It air-conditions hell and kills the soul."[116]

This was all very similar to the rhetoric coming out of the non-Western world. For African and Asian intellectuals, European imperialism had tainted capitalism by association. Liberation from the former seemed to necessitate rejection of the latter. Vietnamese guerilla leader Ho Chi Minh, who had turned to Marxism as an ideology of deliverance from imperialism, charged in a speech to the French Socialist Party at Tours in 1920 that "the hydra of western capitalism has for some time now been stretching its horrible tentacles toward all corners of the globe."[117] After World War II, under the influence of Soviet propaganda, anti-capitalism morphed into anti-Americanism when the civilizing mission of US-led

---

[113] Dorothy Noyes, "Waiting for Mr. Marshall: Spanish American Dreams," in *The Americanization of Europe*, ed. Alexander Stephan (NY: Berghahn Books, 2006), 313.

[114] Simone de Beauvoir, *The Second Sex*, trans. C. Borde et al. (NY: Knopf, 2010 [1949]), 140. Erich Fromm, *The Art of Loving* (NY: Harper and Row, 1956), 85, 105, makes similar points about capitalism, but without exclusive reference to America.

[115] Criterion Collection, *The Complete Jacques Tati*, Twelve-DVD Special Edition (2014).

[116] Lacorne, "Anti-Americanism and Americanophobia," 52.

[117] Odd Arne Westad, *The Global Cold War* (Cambridge: Cambridge University Press, 2007), 83.

modernization programs seemed to promise the "Third World" nothing but the continuation of the oppressive colonial relationship in a new guise.[118] In Latin America, "Yankee-phobia" transcended the left-right ideological divide to become a farrago of cross-fertilizing anti-Protestant Spanish Catholic spiritual aestheticism, Marxism, and fascism. But it mainly fed off of anger at the intervention of the United States and American multinational corporations in the region's affairs. "Where does Wall Street begin and where does it end?" pondered Juan José Arévalo, the former president of Guatemala, after the CIA orchestrated the overthrow of his successor, Jacobo Árbenz, in 1954.[119] By the 1970s in the Islamic world, radical, anti-capitalist, anti-American movements were proliferating in reaction to US policy and taking an ideologically syncretic form drawing from both the far left and the far right. Ibrahim Yazdi, first foreign minister of Khomeini's Iran, expressed the thrust of their implacable argument: "We know capitalism stops at nothing. It kills. It destroys." For him, like so many around the world, capitalism and the United States were synonymous.[120] In all non-Western societies one can find parallels with the European intellectuals' response to the rapid and unsettling introduction of industrialization in the nineteenth and early twentieth century, which is what spawned the word "capitalism" in the first place. Given America's weight in the world economy and given borrowings from the European intellectual tradition, it follows that non-Western thinkers and politicians would identify the United States with capitalism, and that it would have by and large negative connotations.

There were significant exceptions, like the Asian Tigers, whose governments crafted their own variant of capitalism under the dual influence of Japan and the United States.[121] And public-opinion polling shows that while many non-Western populations remain hostile to capitalism, others

---

[118] Peter T. Bauer, "Marxism and the Underdeveloped Countries," in *Marxist Ideology in the Contemporary World*, ed. Milorad M. Drachkovitch (NY: Praeger, 1966), 140, 146, 148, 151–153; Steven G. Marks, *How Russia Shaped the Modern World* (Princeton: Princeton University Press, 2003), 310–332.

[119] Greg Grandin, "Your Americanism and Mine," *American Historical Review* (Oct. 2006), 1042–1066, with Yankee quote at 1046, n20 and Arévalo quote at 1050; Juan Cole, "Anti-Americanism: It's the Policies," *American Historical Review* (October 2006), 1121; Rock, *Authoritarian Argentina*, 216.

[120] "Yazdi: 'Capitalism Kills,'" *Time* (Aug. 6, 1979), 54.

[121] Ezra F. Vogel, *The Four Little Dragons: The Spread of Industrialization in East Asia* (Cambridge, MA: Harvard University Press, 1991). For the complex multiplicity of interpretations of American capitalism in Japan, see Tessa Morris-Suzuki, *A History of Japanese Economic Thought* (London: Routledge, 1989), chaps. 4–6; and Barshay, *Social Sciences in Modern Japan*, 58–59. After World War II, Japanese economic policy also owed much to German economic thought and emulation of Germany: see Mark Metzler, *Capital as Will and Imagination: Schumpeter's Guide to the Postwar Japanese Miracle* (Ithaca, NY: Cornell University Press, 2013), chaps. 2, 8, 10.

46   "Capitalism," word and concept

(e.g., those in China, Egypt, Ghana, Nigeria) are today among the most supportive in the world. By contrast, European nations like France and Spain display the highest levels of disapproval, with more than 40 percent thinking "free market capitalism" is "fatally flawed."[122] This may be a temporary and understandable result of the Great Recession of 2008 combined with the ongoing euro crisis. But when we look at opinion sampling in Europe over the last half century we find a revealing situation: when polls used the term "capitalism" the responses were more negative – sometimes by twice as much – than if they asked people about the free market without mention of capitalism. This was not just left-wing prejudice: most respondents were unsympathetic to both communism and the American economic system, which they designated as the most extreme form of capitalism.[123] Interestingly, a similar pattern has prevailed in polling in the United States, too, where the word "capitalism" provokes apprehension over the unrestrained power of big corporations.[124]

Today, polling country to country indicates a mix of attitudes, but European discourse about capitalism remains consistently hostile regardless of political affiliation, with critics still singing the same anti-American lyrics from the interwar years even while the dance has changed in the post-Cold War globalized and digitized economy.[125] Despite (or maybe because of) the fact that the French economy has moved somewhat in the direction of the American one in recent decades, with the spread of chain stores, deregulation of equity markets, and privatization of many state industries, French Prime Minister Lionel Jospin could still in 1997 denounce American "ultra-capitalism." As sociologist Jean Baudrillard, no admirer of America himself, observed about the post–Cold War era, "a certain American triumphalism and our own relative decline has turned the idea [of a French exception] into an obsession."[126] In the early 2000s,

---

[122] globescan.com/84-press-releases-2012/179-economic-system-seen-as-unfair-global-po ll.html.
[123] Ralph K. White, "'Socialism' and 'Capitalism': An International Misunderstanding," *Foreign Affairs* (January 1966), 216–228; Pierangelo Isernia, "Anti-Americanism in Europe during the Cold War," in *Anti-Americanisms in World Politics*, ed. Peter J. Katzenstein and Robert O. Keohane (Ithaca, NY: Cornell University Press, 2006), 66–69.
[124] Herbert McCloskey and John Zaller, *The American Ethos: Public Attitudes toward Capitalism and Democracy* (Cambridge, MA: Harvard University Press, 1984), 102; *Economist* (Feb. 13, 2010), 63–64.
[125] An insight taken from Seth D. Armus, *French Anti-Americanism, 1930–1948* (Lanham: Lexington Books, 2007).
[126] Quotes from Roger Cohen, "Warring Versions of Capitalism," *New York Times* (Oct. 20, 1997), online at nytimes.com/1997/10/20/world/france-vs-us-warring-versions-of-capit alism.html; see also Richard F. Kuisel, *The French Way: How France Embraced and*

French opinion makers continued to accuse the United States of seeking to impose "its dictatorship of the market" on France and the world, this time through capitalist globalization, and the French government in 2005 urged a "yes" vote for the European Union constitution on the grounds that it would help to resist the onslaught of cold-hearted "Anglo-Saxon capitalism."[127] After the financial crisis of 2008, French President Nicolas Sarkozy hosted a symposium in Paris called "New World, New Capitalism," where he criticized financial capitalism for being a "perverted" and "immoral system" in which "the logic of the market excuses everything." Insisting that "either we re-found capitalism or we destroy it," he and other European leaders pressed for resistance against emulation of the American model and a new, gentler, form of capitalism with greater emphasis on the "social market" and consensus building: "I've always in my political life been a supporter of a close alliance with the United States but let's be clear: in the twenty-first century, a single nation can no longer say what we must do or what we must think."[128] And in 2014, Socialist French Economy Minister Arnaud Montebourg, a long-time advocate of cooperation as the quality lacking in capitalism, restated the complaint that French anti-capitalists and anti-Americans had been making for the entire preceding century when he urged legal action against Google because "what's at stake [for France] is our sovereignty itself."[129] With similar reverberations of the past, German Vice-Chancellor and Economics Minister Sigmar Gabriel sought heavier state regulation of Google in order to "tame Silicon Valley capitalism" and curb all the anarchic bustle that might be suitable to the United States but is an affront to Germans' instinctive desire for economic stasis.[130]

Rejected American Values and Power (Princeton: Princeton University Press, 2012), chap. 6.

[127] Respective quotes in Joffe, *Überpower*, 91 and 178.

[128] "French, German Leaders Call for 'Moralization' of Capitalism," *Deutsche Welle* (Jan. 8, 2009), online at dw.de/french-german-leaders-call-for-moralization-of-capitalism/a-39 30542; Amartya Sen, "Capitalism beyond the Crisis," *New York Review of Books* (March 26, 2009), 27. For former UK Prime Minister Tony Blair's milder critique, see his speech to the conference at "The Office of Tony Blair," online at tonyblairoffice .org/speeches/entry/speech-by-tony-blair-at-the-new-world-new-capitalism-confer ence/.

[129] Jean-Baptiste Duval, "Arnaud Montebourg encense le modèle coopératif," *LSA* (Aug. 28, 2012), online at lsa-conso.fr/arnaud-montebourg-encense-le-modele-coopera tif,132231#xtor=RSS-7; Sarah Drake, "Google's EU Antitrust Deal Challenged by European Companies," *Silicon Valley Business Journal* (May 26, 2014), online at bizjournals.com/sanjose/news/2014/05/16/googles-eu-antitrust-deal-challenged-by-eur opean.html (quote).

[130] Anna Sauerbrey, "Why Germans Are Afraid of Google," *New York Times* (Oct. 10, 2014), online at http://nyti.ms/1yfTl7v.

How do we explain the hostility evident in these statements and in the polls? Henry Kissinger offers a start: "The winners have few reservations about the system. But the losers – such as those stuck in structural misdesigns, as has been the case with the European Union's southern tier – seek their remedies by solutions that negate, or at least obstruct, the functioning of the global economic system."[131] Insofar as support for or opposition to capitalism waxes or wanes in parallel with economic conditions, he has a point. But not all of its opponents are "losers," and the history of the word "capitalism" suggests there is something more involved in the articulation of both positive and negative opinions about it.

Before, during, and after the Cold War, fears were persistent that the society in which Europeans lived and felt comfortable was changing under pressure from the forces of cultural homogenization. "Capitalism" and "Americanization" were the code words most commonly associated with these changes. Just as the United States had existential anxieties about the USSR, so Europeans have had existential anxieties about the power and influence of America – although conservative British Prime Minister Margaret Thatcher represented a strain of thought that is more comfortable with capitalism and America.[132] Just as Americans' apprehensions led them to express particular views of capitalism, so have Europeans used the term to articulate what has been good, bad, and unique about their own societies. The scholar Marie-France Toinet could be speaking for all Europeans when she writes, with echoes of Archibald MacLeish, "The French hold up the United States as a mirror to look, in fact, at themselves."[133]

---

[131] "Henry Kisinger on the Assembly of a New World Order," *Wall Street Journal* (Aug. 29, 2014), online at http://online.wsj.com/articles/henry-kissinger-on-the-assembly-of-a-n ew-world-order-1409328075?tesla=y.

[132] As indicated by keyword search for "capitalism" in her speeches: see "The Margaret Thatcher Foundation," online at margaretthatcher.org/speeches/results.asp? w=capitalism&pg=1.

[133] Gienow-Hecht, "Always Blame the Americans," 1079 (quote); and see Nolan, "Anti-Americanism," 103–105.

3   The myths of capitalism

Everything I have written so far establishes that capitalism is a socially and historically constructed concept, an emotionally loaded term whose proponents or antagonists invest it with assumptions based on their political or ideological orientations. Harsh or defensively self-righteous moral judgments have framed many of the assessments of this "contested truth," which is fundamental to discussion of modern history, politics, and the contemporary economy.[1] Of course, there have been plenty of reasonable moral objections to the particular ills of the existing economic order. That notwithstanding, polemicist critiques of capitalism have reflected and contributed to failures to understand what is truly distinctive about it.

The concept of capitalism appeared at a time when Europe had decisively pulled ahead of the rest of the world militarily and economically by making the sudden transition to an urbanized industrial existence. The concept was central to the critique (and later defense) of what historian William H. McNeill termed the "Victorian edifice," an architectural metaphor for the self-congratulatory nineteenth-century European worldview.[2] Capitalism's detractors wanted either to open the doors of the building wider or to pull it down altogether, but they, too, held the same presuppositions as everyone else about the bedrock foundations on which capitalism stood. Whether for it or against it, commentators "emphasized 'capitalism' as a new mode of production in Europe," ignoring the many identical patterns of economic life and behavior that existed elsewhere in the world.[3] The opponents of capitalism were just as "supremacist" as the supporters of capitalism because

---

[1] I borrow that phrasing from Daniel T. Rodgers, *Contested Truths: Keywords in American Politics since Independence* (NY: Basic Books, 1987).

[2] William H. McNeill, *The Shape of European History* (NY: Oxford University Press, 1974), 3–4.

[3] Jack Goody, *Metals, Culture, and Capitalism* (Cambridge: Cambridge University Press, 2012), xv.

49

they, too, automatically accepted the notion that while capitalist Europe was commercially dynamic, non-capitalist Asia had long been in a state of civilizational decay.[4]

This manner of thinking went back to the early Enlightenment. For many of the cosmopolitan philosophes of the eighteenth century, the high point in the evolution of civilization had been reached in Europe's "commercial society," specifically the Dutch Republic and England, both wealthy nations governed by law and reason where, in the words of Adam Smith, "every man ... lives by exchanging, or becomes in some measure a merchant."[5] For the next century or more the once-flourishing but now stagnant continent of Asia acted as a foil highlighting the exalted position Europeans saw themselves as occupying.[6]

Karl Marx and his associate Friedrich Engels, living in an age of European-led imperialism and economic globalization, had no reason to question their intellectual predecessors on this account. They hated what came to be known as capitalism, but believed it was a necessary stage on the road to socialism, which would originate in the advanced nations of Europe. China, in Engels' words, was the "rotting semi-civilization of the oldest state in the world." For Marx, "all the manifestations of the East ... [have] a common basis, namely the *absence of private landed property.*" Here he was referring to Turkey, Persia, and India, for in China he recognized that there were small privately owned peasant landholdings. In Marx's extensive commentary on India he noted that the English East India Company was no less despotic than its Mughal predecessors. He had much less to say about China. But even if he did not equate it with "Oriental despotism," the label he applied to other parts of Asia, China's small-scale agriculture and petty forms of industry and trade led him to identify it as an ossified society, "a giant empire ... vegetating in the teeth of time."[7]

[4] Quote from Gregory Blue, "China and Western Social Thought in the Modern Period," in *China and Historical Capitalism: Genealogies of Sinological Knowledge*, ed. Timothy Brook and Gregory Blue (Cambridge: Cambridge University Press, 1999), 77.

[5] Adam Smith, *The Wealth of Nations*, books I–III, ed. Andrew Skinner (London: Penguin, 1999), 126 (quotes), on Holland 194, 473, 505, and on England passim. For the intellectual context of Smith's statement, see Ronald L. Meek, *Social Science and the Ignoble Savage* (Cambridge: Cambridge University Press, 1976).

[6] Murray Milgate and Shannon C. Stimson, *After Adam Smith: A Century of Transformation in Politics and Political Economy* (Princeton: Princeton University Press, 2009), 191–194; Emma Rothschild and Amartya Sen, "Adam Smith's Economics," in *The Cambridge Companion to Adam Smith*, ed. Knud Haakonssen (Cambridge: Cambridge University Press, 2006), 320–325, 336; Maxine Berg, *The Machinery Question and the Making of Political Economy, 1815–1848* (NY: Cambridge University Press, 1980), 318–319, 333.

[7] Friedrich Engels, "Persia-China," *New York Daily Tribune* (May 22, 1857), online at marxists.org/archive/marx/works/1857/06/05.htm (first quote); Marx, letters to Engels (June 2, 1853, and June 14, 1853), in Karl Marx and Friedrich Engels, *Collected Works*,

Seeking to explain how the capitalist West had diverged from the rest of the world, Max Weber offered an argument that was indebted to Marx but more finely tuned. Weber laid out a typology of civilizations in which most pre-capitalist, non-Western societies of the world were "patrimonial" regimes where the ruler transmitted his personal authority through his enforcers. In patrimonial states, "the important openings for profit are in the hands of the chief and members of his administrative staff. In so far as productive enterprises are directly administered by the governing group itself, the development of capitalism is thereby directly obstructed." Even if there was some "opening to capitalistic development" in the form of individuals engaged in for-profit tax farming or provisioning for the military, "it is diverted in the direction of political orientation." What patrimonial states lacked were the "rationalization of economic activity" and freedom for "private acquisitive activity." The purest examples of this type of regime, besides imperial China, were the Persian empire, Ptolemaic Egypt, Byzantium, the Islamic caliphate, and, in Weber's own day, tsarist Russia. In the case of China, what Weber imagined to be extensive bureaucratic intervention in markets constituted effective state control of the empire's economy. Following Marx, he argued that slavery or other forms of unfree labor were standard features of these pre-capitalist societies, and that the state played an overarching role in their economic life – all of which stunted the market economy. For Weber, as for Marx, it was impossible for anything like the modern city or a capitalist middle class to develop in these circumstances.[8]

Weber's sociological paradigms were embellishments on views originating in the eighteenth century, which were so deeply entrenched that for a long time they were nearly unassailable in the scholarly literature. Writing in the 1970s, the French *Annaliste* Fernand Braudel rejected the old stereotypes in his expansive three-volume history *Civilization and*

vol. XXXIX (NY: International Publishers, 1983), 333–334 (second quote), 347 (third quote); Marx, "Trade or Opium?" *New York Daily Tribune* (Sept. 20, 2858), online at marxists.org/archive/marx/works/1858/09/20.htm (fourth quote). For analysis of Marx's position, see Marian Sawer, *Marxism and the Question of the Asiatic Mode of Production* (The Hague: Martinus Nijhoff, 1977), chap. 2; and Michael Curtis, "The Asiatic Mode of Production and Oriental Despotism," in *Marxism: The Inner Dialogues*, ed. Michael Curtis, 2nd ed. (New Brunswick: Transaction Publishers, 1997), 326–376.

[8] Max Weber, *Theory of Social and Economic Organization*, trans. A. M. Henderson and Talcott Parsons (NY: Free Press, 1947), 318, 346–358 (quotes); Weber, *Economy and Society*, vol. II: chap. 12 (on tsarist Russia, 1064–1068); Max Weber, *Essays in Economic Sociology*, ed. Richard Swedberg (Princeton: Princeton University Press, 1999), 148; Max Weber, *The Agrarian Sociology of Ancient Civilizations*, trans. R. I. Frank (London: Verso, 1988), 42 and passim. On Weber's debt to Marx in these respects, see Sawer, *Marxism and the Question of the Asiatic Mode of Production*, 59.

Capitalism by acknowledging that Asia had not been remotely stagnant over the centuries. Nevertheless, he, too, presented a sharp distinction between the West and the rest, between the modern (capitalist) and the pre-modern (non-capitalist): "there are two types of exchange: one is down-to-earth, is based on competition, and is almost transparent; the other, a higher form, is sophisticated and domineering ... The capitalist sphere is located in the higher form."[9] For Braudel, "capitalism and towns are basically the same thing in the West."[10] This, plus the long-distance trade directed by strong mercantilist states in alliance with European "finance capitalism," was what set Western economic life apart from the chiefly petty trade and money-changing of pre-modern economies.[11]

For all the breadth of his coverage, Braudel could not escape the legacy of another nineteenth-century conceptualization of society that nourished modern understandings of capitalism, namely the supposed division between *Gemeinschaft* (pre-modern, pre-capitalist community) and *Gesellschaft* (modern capitalist society), to use the terminology of German social theorist Ferdinand Tönnies in his influential 1887 book on the subject.[12] With roots in nineteenth-century German culture and European Romanticism, Tönnies' *Gesellschaft-Gemeinschaft* polarity posits the existence of a pre-capitalist, agrarian, or small-town past when things were "natural" and hand-made, rather than "artificial" and mass produced, when there was social cohesion, personal familiarity, and a concern with equality, family, and self-sufficiency in a localized world marked by cooperation, rather than the fixation on money and profit in the anonymous, depersonalized, urban economy.[13] As Sombart wrote in his own elaboration on the theme, the "asphalt culture" and "stone deserts" of the big city alongside the "bureaucratized capitalism" of big companies spelled "the end of traditional forms of life" and a "harmonious civilization." The elements making up the spirit of

---

[9] Fernand Braudel, *Afterthoughts on Material Civilization and Capitalism*, trans. Patricia M. Ranum (Baltimore: Johns Hopkins University Press, 1977), 62.

[10] Fernand Braudel, *Civilization and Capitalism*, vol. I, trans. Siân Reynolds (NY: Harper and Row, 1979), 514.

[11] Fernand Braudel, *Civilization and Capitalism*, vol. III, trans. Siân Reynolds (NY: Harper and Row, 1984), 601–609, 621, and passim. For a critique of Braudel's conception of capitalism based on his inadequate treatment of the non-Western world, see Jack Goody, *The Theft of History* (Cambridge: Cambridge University Press, 2006), chap. 7.

[12] Ferdinand Tönnies, *Community and Civil Society*, ed. Jose Harris, trans. Jose Harris and Margaret Hollis (Cambridge: Cambridge University Press, 2001 [1887]).

[13] Kenneth D. Barkin, *The Controversy over German Industrialization, 1890–1902* (Chicago: University of Chicago Press, 1970); Richard T. Gray, *Money Matters: Economics and the German Cultural Imagination, 1770–1850* (Seattle: University of Washington Press, 2008), 350–353.

capitalism were acquisitiveness, competition, and rationality; they had dissolved the more humane and communitarian values of the earlier era.[14]

The *Gemeinschaft-Gesellschaft* paradigm meshed with the example of the pre-revolutionary Russian peasant commune. Tönnies did not discuss it, but for many other intellectuals and scholars this served as the archetype of a pre-modern, pre-capitalist community, a vestige of the kinds of social arrangements that were once thought to have characterized all agrarian societies. Heavily touted by Russian Slavophiles and Narodniks as the antidote to Western capitalism, the rural Russian village, with its alleged lack of private property and cash-based relationships, functioned for social scientists as a lens allowing a backward glimpse of a vanished world. The major authority for that perspective was the widely read work of the revolutionary-era Russian economist and anti-industrial activist Alexander V. Chayanov (whose pro-peasant advocacy marked him for arrest and execution in the Stalinist Great Terror of the 1930s).[15]

These rigid sociological categorizations determined analyses by several generations of scholars working on the history of the peasantry, and have had implications for the historiography of capitalism.[16] To give one prominent example, Alan MacFarlane's depiction of the English medieval countryside was in part a projection of the Russian peasant commune onto his own subject.[17] Using that as a baseline for the pre-capitalist world, MacFarlane drew a sharp contrast between it and modern capitalism, which he endowed with qualities he admitted to have drawn from Marx and Weber.[18] Most interpretations of capitalism from recent years still unquestioningly accept these overly reductionist

[14] Lenger, *Werner Sombart*, 50, 101, 107, 118–123, 129–135, 137 (fourth quote), 140 (first quote), 149–150, 169 (second quote), 170 (fifth quote), 339 (third quote), 339; Sombart, "Capitalism," in *Encyclopedia of the Social Sciences*, 196–198.

[15] Tracy Dennison, *The Institutional Framework of Russian Serfdom* (Cambridge: Cambridge University Press, 2011), 6–17 and passim; Andrzej Walicki, *A History of Russian Thought: From the Enlightenment to Marxism*, trans. Hilda Andrews-Rusiecka (Stanford University Press, 1979), 108–109.

[16] A point also made by John Hatcher and Mark Bailey, *Modelling the Middle Ages: The History and Theory of England's Economic Development* (Oxford: Oxford University Press, 2001), 1–2 and passim.

[17] Alan MacFarlane, *Origins of English Individualism* (NY: Cambridge University Press, 1979), 14–17, 20–22, 32. For a critique of MacFarlane's overreliance on the model of the Russian peasant village, see Jane Whittle, *The Development of Agrarian Capitalism: Land and Labour in Norfolk, 1440–1580* (Oxford: Oxford University Press, 2000), 11–15 and passim.

[18] Alan MacFarlane, *The Culture of Capitalism* (Oxford: Basil Blackwell, 1987), 191–192, 223–227. A parallel can be found, although without reference to Chayanov, in Karl Polanyi's "primitivist" treatment of ancient and pre-modern economies. For refutations, see Morris Silver, "Karl Polanyi and Markets in the Ancient Near East: The Challenge of the Evidence," *Journal of Economic History* (Dec. 1983), 795–829; and Anthony

compartmentalizations of pre-capitalist and capitalist, pre-modern and modern, *Gemeinschaft* and *Gesellschaft*.[19] As the German historian Jürgen Kocka astutely observes, "'capitalism' was a concept of difference. It gained its vigor from contrasting the present with the past and an imagined future."[20]

We now know, though, that pre-emancipation nineteenth-century Russian village life was hardly static, self-sufficient, or governed by non-capitalist practices of "moral economy." Rather, it involved regular and complex interactions with the marketplace far beyond the village, full penetration of money and credit, and the extensive use of wage labor even among and between serfs.[21] Thus one of the strongest pieces of evidence for the old *Gemeinschaft–Gesellschaft* distinction can no longer be accepted as credible. As recent anthropological and historical scholarship shows, and overwhelmingly, *in all parts of the world*, from Russia to India to Africa to pre-Columbian America, pre-modern people engaged in rational calculation and profit-oriented market exchange just as much as inhabitants of modern, urban, capitalist societies participate in a range of economic interactions that are informed by close personal and social ties rather than purely monetary or narrowly self-interested choices.[22] Consider the Netherlands, which is one of the historical and contemporary market economies par excellence, but has long depended on public communal works to drain land and manage polders in a country half of

J. Barbieri-Low, *Artisans in Early Imperial China* (Seattle: University of Washington Press, 2007), 26–28.

[19] E.g., Robert L. Heilbroner, *The Nature and Logic of Capitalism* (NY: Norton, 1985), 34–35 and passim; Paul Bowles, *Capitalism* (Harlow: Pearson, 2007), xiv–xv and passim.

[20] Jürgen Kocka, "Writing the History of Capitalism," *Bulletin of the German Historical Institute* (Fall 2010), 9–10.

[21] Dennison, *Institutional Framework of Russian Serfdom*, passim. See also Alessandro Stanziani, *After Oriental Despotism: Eurasian Growth in a Global Perspective* (London: Bloomsbury, 2014), chap. 5 and passim; Catherine Evtuhov, *Portrait of a Russian Province: Economy, Society, and Civilization in Nineteenth-Century Nizhnii Novgorod* (Pittsburgh: University of Pittsburgh Press, 2011), chaps. 4–5 and passim; and Boris B. Gorshkov, trans. and ed., *A Life under Russian Serfdom: The Memoirs of Savva Dmitrievich Purlevskii, 1800–1868* (Budapest: Central European University Press, 2005).

[22] David Ludden, *Early Capitalism and Local History in South India* (New Delhi: Oxford University Press, 2005), 7, chap. 5, and passim; editor's introduction in Sanjay Subrahmanyam, ed., *Money and the Market in India, 1100–1700* (Delhi: Oxford University Press, 1994), 1–2, 4, 7–8, 12–19; Morten Jerven, "The Emergence of African Capitalism," in *The Cambridge History of Capitalism*, vol. I, ed. Larry Neal and Jeffrey G. Williamson (Cambridge: Cambridge University Press, 2014), 443–447; and Kenneth G. Hirth and Joanne Pillsbury, eds., *Merchants, Markets, and Exchange in the Pre-Columbian World* (Washington, DC: Dumbarton Oaks Research Library and Collection, 2013). Alain Bresson makes a similar argument about the ancient Greek economy contra Weber's stagnationism: see his article "Capitalism and the Ancient Greek Economy," in *Cambridge History of Capitalism*, ed Neal and Williamson, vol. I, 47–48.

which is below sea level.[23] And, as anyone who has ever been employed by a big company can attest, in our own capitalist age the *suppression* of individualism is essential for the millions of employees in modern corporate hierarchies.[24] In other words, there has always been plenty of *Gesellschaft* in the *Gemeinschaft*, and vice-versa.[25]

For such reasons, anthropologist David Graeber dismisses the "imaginary villages" of economics textbooks as a fantasy of a world without the discord caused by the existence of money.[26] As Jack Goody, also an anthropologist, maintains, this was not the "false capitalism" that many scholars, including Braudel, identified in pre-modern, non-Western commerce, but the real thing.[27] For Goody, all economic behavior in the history of the Eurasian continent has been on the same continuum going back to the ancient Bronze Age. Some places moved ahead and others behind, but interactions were constant, and the separation between the West and Asia was not as great as once imagined – except during the early stages of industrialization, but that gap, too, lasted only a historically short period of time. What Goody and a growing number of other scholars see is various shadings of capitalism all over the world, in the past and in the present, with constantly changing regional strengths and hegemons. At least in Eurasia, since the beginning of civilization in ancient Mesopotamia, markets have always existed, goods were always commodified, and the economy was always monetized. These elements may have disappeared during periods of political turmoil and collapse, but they always revived.[28]

[23] Peter Temin, *The Roman Market Economy* (Princeton: Princeton University Press, 2013), 8.
[24] Kenneth Lipartito, "The Utopian Corporation," in *Constructing Corporate America*, ed. Kenneth Lipartito and David B. Sicilia (Oxford: Oxford University Press, 2004), 94–119; Nicholas Abercrombie et al., *Sovereign Individuals of Capitalism* (London: Allen and Unwin, 1986); Anthony Sampson, *Company Man: The Rise and Fall of Corporate Life* (NY: Times Business, 1995).
[25] Don Slater and Fran Tonkiss, *Market Society* (Cambridge: Polity, 2001), 96–101ff.
[26] David Graeber, *Debt: The First 5,000 Years* (NY: Melville House, 2011), chaps. 2–3 and passim, with quote on 46.
[27] Goody, *Metals, Culture, and Capitalism*, 151. Frank Perlin makes a similar argument in his *Unbroken Landscape: Commodity, Category, Sign, and Identity* (Aldershot: Variorum, 1994), 58–59, 83. French sociologist Jean Baechler pointed toward some of these same problems with the historiography of capitalism in his book *The Origins of Capitalism*, trans. Barry Cooper (Oxford: Basil Blackwell, 1973 [1971]).
[28] Goody, *Metals, Culture, and Capitalism*; Goody, *Capitalism and Modernity* (Cambridge: Polity, 2004); Goody, *The East in the West* (Cambridge: Cambridge University Press, 1996). A kindred argument, which also dismisses Marxist periodization of defined historical stages, appears in Andre Gunder Frank and Barry K. Gills, eds., *The World System: Five Hundred Years or Five Thousand?* (London: Routledge, 1996).

I do not completely agree with Goody. As this book seeks to demonstrate, there is something different about the version of market economy associated with the Euro-Atlantic world beginning in the early modern era. The difference has to do with accelerating information acquisition. Before building a case for that characteristic as the quintessence of capitalism, it is necessary first to expose the myths and misconceptions that have accreted for almost two centuries to form the standard definition of capitalism. Based on an amalgamation from representative old and new scholarly works, the definition goes like this:

Emerging in modern Europe, capitalism is a new and unique economic system in which property is owned privately by the individual rather than communally or by the state, extended kin groups, or aristocratic landlords. There is a money-dominated, commercialized market economy, which is powered by the urge for profit, reliant on a predominantly wage-labor force, and entails the commodification of goods. Productive processes involve specialization and the division of labor for mass production, with coordination from rational forms of accounting and business organization. The keystone of the system is capital, the purpose of which is to generate new wealth through investment (whereas in olden times wealth chiefly served purposes of display to enhance the authority of monarchs and elites).[29]

Three other possible components of a standard definition are not included here because of the lack of consensus surrounding them: 1. the dating of the birth of capitalism – depending on the scholar, this is said to have occurred at different moments between the end of the Middle Ages and the mid-nineteenth century;[30] 2. the role of the state, which some would argue laid the foundations for capitalism and actively shepherds it, while others, mainly American libertarian conservatives, assume, in alignment with this Ayn-Randian formulation, that "capitalism is the social system that separates economy and state completely";[31] and 3. the dominance of the bourgeois social class in the capitalist system.

The rest of the book treats the first of these components, the chronology of capitalism, so I will leave it aside for now. On the role of

---

[29] Definition derived from Bowles, *Capitalism*, 8; *Encyclopedia Britannica: The New Volumes*, 11th ed., vol. XXX (London: Encyclopedia Britannica, 1922), s.v. "Capitalism," 565–571; James Fulcher, *Capitalism: A Very Short Introduction* (Oxford: Oxford University Press, 2004), 14–15; Sandra Halperin, *Re-Envisioning Global Development* (London: Routledge, 2013), 32–33; Heilbroner, *Nature and Logic of Capitalism*, 34–35; Jürgen Kocka, *Geschichte des Kapitalismus* (Munich: C. H. Beck, 2013); MacFarlane, *Culture of Capitalism*, 191–192, 223–227; Sombart, "Capitalism," in *Encyclopedia of the Social Sciences*, 196; Weber, *Economy and Society*, vol. I, 165.

[30] *Cambridge History of Capitalism*, vols. I–II, ed. Neal and Williamson, is unusual in tracing capitalism to ancient times.

[31] Clemson Institute for the Study of Capitalism website, online at clemson.edu/capitalism/resources.html.

the state, see Chapter 2 on American views of capitalism and references to the subject throughout the book. Regarding the bourgeoisie and social class, suffice it to say that, in opposition to the inflexible categories of the Marxists, scholars today approach the topic with an appreciation of its multidimensionality and complexity.[32] Historian Jerrold Siegel goes so far to aver that the bourgeoisie created a style of life in the cities of nineteenth-century Europe, but it was never a clear-cut or unified social or political class.[33] Moreover, as Karl Marx himself began to conclude toward the end of his life, landed aristocratic elites had a political and economic weight equal to that of the bourgeoisie in the age of industrialization; as other authorities have shown, that remained the case well into the twentieth century in the capitalist societies of both Germany and Great Britain.[34]

Besides those features, I will also not make further comment at this point on rational accounting or business organization, as they are major subjects within subsequent chapters. Otherwise, in what follows I will bring to bear recent research from both world and European history to review each piece of the (flawed) definition I have amalgamated: private property; profit-seeking, commercialization, and the commodification of goods; capital; the division of labor and mass production; and wage labor. I cannot pretend to offer a comprehensive survey in this limited space, but even a brief overview such as this will be enough to cast doubt on the existing definition of capitalism.

Private property

Perhaps the most prevalent misconception is the belief that private property receives unique protections under capitalism. But it is now

---

[32] See, e.g., Dennis Dworkin, *Class Struggles* (Harlow: Pearson Longman, 2007); and Peter Calvert, *The Concept of Class: An Historical Introduction* (NY: St. Martin's, 1982).

[33] Jerrold Siegel, *Modernity and Bourgeois Life: Society, Politics, and Culture in England, France, and Germany since 1750* (Cambridge: Cambridge University Press, 2012), chap. 1.

[34] In the last volume of *Capital*, Marx writes of the "wage laborers, capitalists, and landowners, [who] make up the three great classes of modern society based on the capitalist mode of production" – whereas in the *Communist Manifesto* he and Engels include only the bourgeoisie and proletariat: see Jonathan Sperber, *Karl Marx: A Nineteenth Century Life* (NY: Liveright, 2013), 448–452. On the undiminished importance of the aristocracy, see Sandra Halperin, *In the Mirror of the Third World: Capitalist Development in Modern Europe* (Ithaca, NY: Cornell University Press, 1997), chap. 4. According to Paul Kingsnorth, "High House Prices? Inequality? I Blame the Normans," *Guardian* (Dec. 17, 2012), two-thirds of the land in Britain today is owned by 0.3% of the population, mostly descendants of aristocrats who received the land from William the Conqueror in the aftermath of the Norman Conquest: see online at theguardian.com/c ommentisfree/2012/dec/17/high-house-prices-inequality-normans.

well attested that private property in goods and real estate, including landholding, existed extensively and received legal guarantees as far back as the Bronze Age in Egypt under the Old and Middle Kingdoms, Assyrian and Neo-Babylonian Mesopotamia, the Persian empire, and throughout Roman history – all places once thought to be lacking in either private property or private property rights, if not devoid of them altogether. These states and their religious hierarchies also had significant landholdings which would not come under the category of private property, but that does not detract from the fact that they issued laws to protect individuals' property and by and large respected them.[35]

The same was true of China. Contracts proving property ownership were already common by the Yuan dynasty (1271–1368), but existed as early as the first century AD, if not before – a realization that also upends Victorian legal historian Sir Henry Maine's assertion that the transition from "status to contract" was a modern and Western phenomenon. By the mid-1500s, during the Ming dynasty, the vast majority of land in the realm was held as private property. Even if families retained some customary rights over land and even if ownership of the subsoil was a complex matter, in the eighteenth century the Qing state was working to eliminate these traditional practices and simplify the law, clarifying individuals' abilities to alienate land and defend it in the courts, where even peasants routinely took their property disputes for litigation. The courts did not always decide these cases fairly, but that was no different than in Western countries. Additionally, as in medieval and early modern Europe, where merchant courts, guilds, and other voluntary associations adjudicated such matters, there were equivalent Chinese venues which enforced contracts over property and other business matters outside of the state legal system.[36]

[35] Silver, "Karl Polanyi and Markets in the Ancient Near East," 801, 805, 807; Marvin A. Powell, "Merchants and the Problem of Profit," *Iraq* (Spring 1977), 23–29; Philip D. Curtin, *Cross-Cultural Trade in World History* (Cambridge: Cambridge University Press, 1984), 63–64; Goody, *Metals, Culture, and Capitalism*, chaps. 1–5, 8 passim; Temin, *Roman Market Economy*, chap. 7 and passim; Mario Liverani, "The Near East: The Bronze Age," *in The Ancient Economy*, ed. J. G. Manning and Ian Morris (Stanford: Stanford University Press, 2005), 50–54; Peter R. Bedford, "The Economy of the Near East in the First Millennium BC," in *The Ancient Economy*, ed. Manning and Morris, 78ff; Michael Jursa, "Babylonia in the First Millennium BCE: Economic Growth in Times of Empire," in *Cambridge History of Capitalism*, vol. I, ed. Neal and Williamson, 36.
[36] Kenneth Pomeranz, *The Great Divergence: China, Europe, and the Making of the Modern World Economy* (Princeton: Princeton University Press, 2000), 71–77; Valerie Hansen, "How Business Was Conducted on the Chinese Silk Road during the Tang Dynasty, 618–907," in *The Origins of Value: The Financial Innovations that Created Modern Capital Markets*, ed. William N. Goetzmann and K. Geert Rouwenhorst (Oxford: Oxford University Press, 2005), 43–53; Valerie Hansen, *Negotiating Daily Life in Traditional*

If anything, private property in capitalist England was less secure than it was in many ancient and non-Western societies. After the Glorious Revolution of 1688, property rights actually weakened in the face of a strong central state that actively forced the compulsory sale of large swathes of land for infrastructural projects, including 911 new turnpikes in acts of eminent domain which Parliament authorized between 1695 and 1839, and tens of thousands of acres in large-scale expropriations deemed necessary for the construction of a wide network of canals and railroads.[37] The early modern English government was not in the habit of arbitrarily seizing people's property, but then neither was China, nor Rome, nor any of the others on the list above. And perhaps the confiscations in the United Kingdom served the greater good of society by encouraging economic growth and industrial development. But if the legal system of what was in the eighteenth and nineteenth centuries the most preeminent capitalist nation permitted the periodically large-scale contravention of the sanctity of private property, while reputedly despotic empires did not, then how can one claim that the sanctity of private property is an exclusive feature of capitalism? Sheilagh Ogilvie and A. W. Carus make a distinction between the English protection of generalized property rights as opposed to particularist property rights such as feudal land-ownership. The state encroached on the latter in order to make way for more productive use involving railroads and other new industrial technologies.[38] Even so, it is necessary to revise our

China: How Ordinary People Used Contracts, 600–1400 (New Haven: Yale University Press, 1995), 1–3, 5–8, 31, 43, 39ff; Melissa Macauley, "A World Made Simple: Law and Property in the Ottoman and Qing Empires," *Journal of Early Modern History*, vol. V, no. 4 (2001), 334–342; R. Bin Wong, "Formal and Informal Mechanisms of Rule and Economic Development: The Qing Empire in Comparative Perspective," *Journal of Early Modern History*, vol. V, no. 4 (2001), 391–400; Gang Deng [Kent G. Deng], *The Premodern Chinese Economy: Structural Equilibrium and Capitalist Sterility* (London: Routledge, 1999), chap. 2; Jean-Laurent Rosenthal and R. Bin Wong, *Before and Beyond Divergence: The Politics of Economic Change in China and Europe* (Cambridge, MA: Harvard University Press, 2011), chap. 3; Madeleine Zelin, Jonathan K. Ocko, and Robert Gardella, eds., *Contract and Property in Early Modern China* (Stanford: Stanford University Press, 2004). For the importance of contracts in medieval Islamic law, see Abraham L. Udovitch, *Partnership and Profit in Medieval Islam* (Princeton: Princeton University Press, 1970), 86ff. For extra-judicial means of contract enforcement among the Jewish traders of North Africa and the Mediterranean in the eleventh century, see Avner Greif, *Institutions and the Path to the Modern Economy: Lessons from Medieval Trade* (Cambridge: Cambridge University Press, 2006), chap. 3.

[37] Julian Hoppit, "Compulsion, Compensation, and Property Rights in Britain, 1688–1833," *Past and Present* (Feb. 2011), 93–128.

[38] Sheilagh Ogilvie and A. W. Carus, "Institutions and Economic Growth in Historical Perspective," *in Handbook of Economic Growth*, vol. 2A, ed. Philippe Aghion and Steven N. Durlauf (Amsterdam: Elsevier, 2014), 447–459, and 403–490 passim.

understanding of the relationship between private property and capitalism.

Profit-seeking, commercialization, and the commodification of goods

As with private property, market economies in which merchants, farmers, and craft producers sought profit were also the rule rather than the exception – further weakening the standard definition of capitalism. *All* of the texts relating to the cattle and fishing businesses in ancient Sumer in the third millennium BC make clear that the profit motive was the basic economic principle guiding merchant undertakings.[39] The vocabulary of every era and every regional ascendancy, whether Akkadian, Old and Neo-Babylonian, Hittite, Hurrian, or Ugaritic, includes a long list of words for profit and loss, investing for profit, and the like.[40] In Neo-Babylonian Mesopotamia (626 to 539 BC), the Egibi family, which rose from humble origins, had a wide-ranging family business empire that included producing and exporting textiles made from wool and renting out farmland to sharecroppers, who shifted from grain to date palms to enhance profits. This was what motivated the Egibis' contemporary Iddin-Marduk of the Nūr-Sîn family, who specialized in raising onions to capture profits in a niche market: in areas serving cities, such cash-crops were a well-established form of agriculture, with produce grown by farmers who contracted with middlemen to market it.[41]

Moving east to the example of China, how do we even begin to describe its incomparable commercialization? Spanning the millennium from the 600s to the 1600s, the T'ang, Song, and Ming dynasties saw the steady growth of profit-seeking in local, provincial, and national markets.[42] By the

[39] Powell, "Merchants and the Problem of Profit," 28; Benjamin R. Foster, "Commercial Activity in Sargonic Mesopotamia," *Iraq* (Spring 1977), 31–43.

[40] Gerd Steiner, "Kaufmanns- und handelsprachen im Alten Orient," *Iraq* (Spring 1977), 11–17; Foster, "Commercial Activity in Sargonic Mesopotamia," 40.

[41] Cornelia Wunsch, "Neo-Babylonian Entrepreneurs," in *The Invention of Enterprise: Entrepreneurship from Ancient Mesopotamia to Modern Times*, ed. David S. Landes, Joel Mokyr, and William J. Baumol (Princeton: Princeton University Press, 2010), 47–48, 50; Jursa, "Babylonia in the First Millennium BCE," 32–33.

[42] For this paragraph and the one that follows, in addition to references cited at quotes, see Denis Twitchett, "Merchant, Trade, and Government in Late T'ang," *Asia Major*, vol. XIV, no. 1 (1968), 63–95; Martin Heijdra, "The Socio-Economic Development of Rural China during the Ming," in *The Cambridge History of China*, ed. Denis Twitchett and Frederick W. Mote, vol. VIII (Cambridge: Cambridge University Press, 1998), 496–578; Timothy Brook, *The Confusions of Pleasure: Commerce and Culture in Ming China* (Berkeley: University of California Press, 1998), 218–222; Antonia Finnane, *Speaking of Yangzhou: A Chinese City, 1550–1850* (Cambridge, MA: Harvard University Press, 2004); R. Bin

ninth century, self-sufficient villages were already rare, with house after house shuttered because "the inhabitants ... had all gone off to trade," in the words of a contemporary.[43] In that era the great western market at Ch'ang-an filled "an area as big as the whole of medieval London."[44] But much earlier, according to a poem about Ch'ang-an from 78–139 AD, there were already "countless shop rows ... Precious wares arriving from all quarters, gathered like birds, amassed like fish scales. Sellers earned double profit, but buyers were never lacking ... The peddlers, shopkeepers, and common people, male and female vendors, selling cheap, sold good quality mixed with the shoddy."[45] As for the transport of merchandise to market, a traveler in the 1580s gives us a glimpse of the intense commercial traffic over the mountain passes in the area of Minbei: "Not one day passes but the silks of Fuzhou, the gauzes of Zhangzhou, the indigo of Quanzhou, the iron-ware of Fuzhou and Yanping, the oranges of Zhangzhou, the lichees of Fuzhou and Xinghua, the sugar of Quanzhou, and the paper [products] of Shunchang go through the Fenshui mountain pass and the pass at Pucheng and down to Zhejiang ... and Jiangsu ... like flowing water."[46]

In early modern China, farmers grew these and many other cash crops, including cotton. Large and small manufacturers produced silk, paper, ceramics, and lacquerware, all destined for domestic as well as foreign markets, whose range extended from the nomadic territories of the western grasslands to the coastal regions of East and Southeast Asia. A 1746 gazetteer from the Lake T'ai region reported that "in every village near a town, residents were devoting their energies entirely to earning a living from silk. The wealthy hired others to weave, and the poor wove themselves." Similarly from a gazetteer published in 1512: "the [cotton] textile industry is not limited to the rural villages, but is also seen in the city. Old rural women enter the market at dawn carrying yarn and, after trading it for raw cotton, return home. The next morning they again leave home carrying yarn. There is not a moment of rest. The weavers finish a bolt a day, and there are some who stay awake all

Wong, "The Political Economy of Agrarian Empire and Its Modern Legacy," in *China and Historical Capitalism*, ed. Brook and Blue, 217–220.

[43] Shiba Yoshinobu, *Commerce and Society in Sung China*, trans. Mark Elvin (Ann Arbor: University of Michigan Press, 1970), 209; and see passim.

[44] Denis Twitchett, "The T'ang Market System," *Asia Major*, vol. XII, no. 2 (1966), 211; and see 202–248.

[45] Barbieri-Low, *Artisans in Early Imperial China*, 116; and see 40–43.

[46] Lucille Chia, *Printing for Profit: The Commercial Publishers of Jianyang, Fujian (11th–17th Centuries)* (Cambridge, MA: Harvard University Press, 2002), 21.

night."[47] It is important to note that these Ming- and Qing-era merchants and craftspeople were working overtime to meet a steady demand for regularly changing fashions in clothing. Confucian moralizing may have formed the heart of Chinese state ideology, with its expressions of disdain for merchants and lauding of peasant self-sufficiency. But in the face of dynamic market forces, government officials could do little to fight effectively against the riptide current.

In England, too, medieval scholars have pushed back the timeline of profit-seeking commercialization and commodification, which further erodes the standard definition of capitalism as a modern phenomenon.[48] By the late thirteenth century, self-sufficiency did not exist anywhere in England as households of all social strata bought and sold goods, services, and labor, and to facilitate that activity habitually entered into credit arrangements as borrowers or lenders. English peasant farms were too small to produce enough to feed and clothe the family. At weekly markets in rural villages, one could find bread, ale, meat, candles, and charcoal for sale alongside the services of shoemakers, tailors, weavers, dyers, smiths, and carpenters – all in response to the penetration of money and strong consumer demand even on the lower half of the social scale. In towns there was even greater occupational diversity. By 1330, most English wool and more than a third of grain were sold for a profit at market.

Over the course of the fourteenth and fifteenth centuries, if not before, an active market in land and real estate had also developed in England, with the regular participation of peasants. Medievalist Christopher Dyer speaks of "property portfolio[s]" among the nobility, as by around 1400 most aristocratic lands were leased out for a profit, and over the next hundred years landlords began pushing hard to enclose their properties to ensure maximum efficiency and revenue growth.[49] There may have been some customary restraints on peasant properties inherited from village communities, extended families, or aristocratic overlordship, but none of that disaffirms the fungible quality land had taken on as a tradable commodity. Expressing the profit-seeking that was by then universal, probate records from 1464 include the will of a woman from the town of Fakenham in Norfolk County who instructed executors to sell her land

---

[47] Timothy Brook, "Communications and Commerce," in *Cambridge History of China*, ed. Twitchett and Mote, vol. VIII, respective quotes on 688 and 690; and see 670–707.

[48] For this paragraph and the next, see Bruce M. S. Campbell, "Factor Markets in England before the Black Death," *Continuity and Change*, vol. XXIV, special issue 01 (May 2009), 79–106 passim; Hatcher and Bailey, *Modelling the Middle Ages*, 135–137, 140ff, 144, 151–152; Whittle, *Development of Agrarian Capitalism*, chaps. 3–4; Christopher Dyer, *A Country Merchant, 1495–1520: Trading and Farming at the End of the Middle Ages* (Oxford: Oxford University Press, 2012), 9, 11–12, 14–18.

[49] Dyer, *Country Merchant*, 11–12 (quote).

for "the best price in cash."[50] A similar situation prevailed in other commercialized parts of Europe – besides eastern England, the Low Countries, the Paris basin, Italy, and Catalonia – where all strata of the populace participated in a "lively market economy" in land.[51]

In light of the foregoing it is worth revisiting the views of the Marxist philosopher Georg Lukacs. Following Marx, Lukacs wrote that "commodity fetishism is a *specific* problem of our age, the age of modern capitalism." While simple commodity exchange existed previously, "when society was still very primitive," only under capitalism did it become "dominant, permeating every expression of life." Contrary to what Lukacs and Marx supposed, however, commodification permeated life early on in human history, as the preceding paragraphs indicate. Yet I do believe there is something exceptional about capitalism and that neither Lukacs nor Marx were mistaken in fingering it. But to me what explains the permeating nature is not commodification so much as the pervasiveness of the information nexus that was beginning to be witnessed so acutely in the nineteenth and twentieth centuries, as the succeeding chapters of this book will make apparent.[52]

Capital

In a speech of 2003, the former Prime Minister of Thailand Thaksin Shinawatra said that "capitalism needs capital, without which there is no capitalism."[53] True enough, but every economic system in which profit-seeking commerce takes place has always needed and always used capital. This runs counter to the standard definition of capitalism, which

---

[50] Christopher Dyer, *An Age of Transition? Economy and Society in England in the Later Middle Ages* (Oxford: Oxford University Press, 2005), 121 (quote).

[51] Karl Gunnar Persson, "Markets and Coercion in Medieval Europe," in *Cambridge History of Capitalism*, vol. I, ed. Neal and Williamson, 238–242; and Bas van Bavel, "The Medieval Origins of Capitalism in the Netherlands," *BMGN-Low Countries Historical Review*, vol. CXXV, no. 2–3 (2010), 45–80. For continental Western Europe, as opposed to England, Martha C. Howell, *Commerce before Capitalism in Europe, 1300–1600* (Cambridge: Cambridge University Press, 2010), 5–16, 38–39, 40, stresses the persistence of traditional ties and non-capitalist economic relations in the Middle Ages, while also recognizing the presence of strong market- and profit-oriented elements. Her argument is that a worldview in which fungibility took central place had to emerge before we can label this society capitalist. Her timing meshes with my own, although as will become clear in Chapter 4, I emphasize crossing an informational threshold.

[52] Georg Lukacs, *History and Class Consciousness*, trans. Rodney Livingstone (Cambridge, MA: MIT Press, 1971), 84 and 83–222 passim; Karl Marx, *Capital*, vol. I, trans Ben Fowkes (London: Penguin, 1990), 974–975. Thanks to Raquel Anido and Michael Meng for prompting these insights.

[53] Richard Bernstein, "Thailand: Beautiful and Bitterly Divided," *New York Review of Books* (Nov. 20, 2014), 51.

implies by its very etymological root that it is somehow special in this regard. Examples from the pre-capitalist world show that it is not.

In medieval England, as elsewhere in Europe, money and credit relations penetrated the economy once it revived after the long post-Roman collapse. According to Chris Briggs, "it is now clear that in a typical year, peasants throughout [fourteenth-century] Europe might, for example, sell animals or grain for a deferred payment, borrow from a fellow [peasant] to pay taxes or fund a marriage, or lease out land to pay off an existing obligation, thereby becoming involved in extensive and complex networks of credit." Just because at that time there was not yet a securities market for the purchase and sale of transferrable shares does not mean the employment of capital was negligible. Local farmers and merchants accumulated earnings on their sales, which they then invested in other operations or which they lent to others at a profit (when coins were in short supply, as they sometimes were, the profit came in the form of goods). In many instances Jews provided the money as a business investment of their own. After their expulsion from England in 1290, local moneylenders or northern Italians filled the gap there and elsewhere in Northern Europe. These were not occasional or incidental practices, but widespread.[54]

And it was by no means a new phenomenon or one restricted to England or Europe. The oldest written loan contracts, some of them including calculations of interest, date to the 2200s BC in northern Mesopotamia, where by the next century agricultural credit, commercial loans, and consumer borrowing had become ordinary facets of everyday life. In the Assyrian empire, debts (in silver or grain) marked in cuneiform on clay tablets became negotiable themselves. Silver was the precious metal required for venture-capital investments in long-distance trade operations: according to the Hammurabi Code (c. 1750 BC), "if a man gives silver to another man for investment in a partnership venture, before the god they shall equally divide the profit or loss." After clearing losses from the books and assessing assets and expenditures, merchants in Sumer called the surplus "liquid capital" and applied the wealth as businessmen the world over would, by investing it. A letter from Assyrian times urged the reader to "inform me of all that you hear from the mouth of my investors!"[55] By the middle of the first millennium BC in

---

[54] Chris Briggs, *Credit and Village Society in Fourteenth-Century England* (Oxford: Oxford University Press, 2009), passim, with quote on 2; Laurence Fontaine, *L'Économie morale: Pauvreté, crédit et confiance dans l'Europe préindustrielle* (Paris: Gallimard, 2008); Campbell, "Factor Markets in England," 92–96; Dyer, Country Merchant, 96, 120–125.

[55] Roman Bogaert, "Banking in the Ancient World," *in A History of European Banking*, ed. Herman van der Wee and Ginette Kurgan-van Hentenryk (Antwerp: Fonds Mercator, 2000), 14–17; Marc van de Mieroop, "The Invention of Interest: Sumerian Loans," in

Babylonia, legally recognized joint-stock funds financed the international caravan trade. Debt notes were transferrable then, too, functioning like medieval bills of exchange.[56]

Except for the more limited range of financial securities, accounting methods, and communications technologies that restricted informational flows, these capital operations have a strikingly modern feel to them. Perhaps nothing illustrates this better than a quotation from Demosthenes (384–322 BC), the orator and statesman of ancient Athens who wrote that "the Athenian bank is a business operation that produces risk-laden revenues from other people's money." Demosthenes' statement only hints at the sophistication of classical Greek finance, from money-changing (about 265 cities issued coins by the late 500s BC), bank deposits for money and valuables, consumer and commercial bank lending with variable interest rates according to market conditions, giro transfers between banks, pawn broking, specialized maritime loans, and maritime insurance.[57] Demosthenes himself kept 4,600 drachma on deposit at two banks (plus with a relative) and earned money from a 7,000-drachma maritime loan and another large loan earning 12 percent. He also owned a sword factory and a furniture factory, both manned by slaves, another capital investment.[58]

In ancient Rome, too, moneylenders calculated the rate of return on loans for agricultural or commercial enterprises or maritime loans for overseas trade, with the standard interest rate being 12 percent per annum, although with much variation and fluctuation depending on the place and market conditions. These loans were also transferrable. Commercial banks were located throughout the empire. Temples and private citizens alike owned banks, all of them existing to turn a profit. They accepted deposits and made loans using those funds. They transferred money between their own branches and other banks. They earned income from mortgage loans whose recipients offered their houses as security; land, which was easily bought and sold, also served as collateral. Furthermore, the Roman society of publicans (*societas publicanorum*)

Origins of Value, ed. Goetzmann and Rouwenhorst, 17–30; Wunsch, "Neo-Babylonian Entrepreneurs," 52 (quote from Hammurabi code); Powell, "Merchants and the Problem of Profit," 25–27 (liquid capital quote); Mogens Trolle Larsen, "Partnerships in the Old Assyrian Trade," *Iraq* (Spring 1977), 119–145, with quote about Assyrian investors on 128; Silver, "Karl Polanyi and Markets in the Ancient Near East," 802–804.
[56] Jursa, "Babylonia in the First Millennium BCE," 28–29.
[57] Edward E. Cohen, *Athenian Economy and Society: A Banking Perspective* (Princeton: Princeton University Press, 1992), 111(Demosthenes quote) and passim; Bogaert, "Banking in the Ancient World," 23–43.
[58] M. I. Finley, *The Ancient Economy*, updated ed. (Berkeley: University of California Press, 1999), 116.

"anticipated the modern corporation and, in particular, the use of fungible shares with limited liability." The publicans contracted with the Roman state to supply the Roman republic's armies, collect taxes and tolls, or lease public property. Private citizens could hold their shares as a long-term investment, or trade them near the Temple of Castor on the Roman Forum. Shares differed in value according to the company, and their price rose and fell according to the success of the company and general economic conditions. Ownership was extensive among citizens by the second century BC.[59]

A quotation from Cicero in 66 BC, referring to events two decades earlier, points to the interconnectedness of financial markets, and again suggests a modern understanding of capital flows that the standard definition of capitalism would seem to preclude:

For, coinciding with the loss by many people of large fortunes in Asia, we know that there was a collapse of credit at Rome owing to suspension of payment. It is, indeed, impossible for many individuals in a single State to lose their property and fortunes without involving still greater numbers in their ruin . . . Believe me when I tell you . . . that this system of credit and finance which operates at Rome, in the Forum, is bound up in, and depends on capital invested in Asia; the loss of the one inevitably undermines the others and causes its collapse.[60]

Commercialized market exchange, profit-seeking, commodification, and complex methods of investing and wielding capital were all fundamental to pre-modern, non-capitalist economies. Neither the division of labor for the purposes of mass production nor wage work (by which labor becomes a commodity) were all-encompassing until the age of industrialization, but they existed to a far greater extent in earlier times and in non-Western societies than the standard definition of capitalism would allow. I look at each in turn.

The division of labor and mass production

The division of labor within single enterprises appeared in modern times after having been constrained in medieval societies by inadequate demand.[61] But it was actually a *reappearance* as, prior to that, in the

---

[59] Temin, *Roman Market Economy*, chaps. 7–8; Ulrike Malmendier, "Roman Shares," in *Origins of Value*, ed. Goetzmann and Rouwenhorst, 31–42, with publicans quote at 32.

[60] Temin, *Roman Market Economy*, 178–179.

[61] Karl Gunnar Persson, *An Economic History of Europe* (Cambridge: Cambridge University Press, 2010), 24–25. And see Jan de Vries, *The Industrious Revolution: Consumer Behavior and the Household Economy, 1650 to the Present* (Cambridge: Cambridge University Press, 2008), 72 and passim for the relationship between consumer demand, the division of labor, and industrialization from the eighteenth century.

flourishing economies of ancient Rome and pre-modern China, we find that vigorous consumer demand stimulated the extensive mass production of commodities. Mass production then necessitated the division of labor to achieve more efficiency on the work floor and higher levels of output.[62]

In the early imperial period, the Roman economy had one of the highest living standards prior to the industrial era, due in part to excellent maritime and land communications and specialized regional agriculture. The Roman government contracted with private companies to supply it with all manner of goods, including the *annona*, the grain distributed to the populace.[63] Strong demand across the social spectrum spurred manufacturers to adopt standardized mass fabrication of consumer durables such as African Red Slipware pottery, iron knives for cutting food, glassware, bricks, architectural marble, sarcophagi, ceramics, nails, and oil lamps. Large-scale preparation of food staples was also the rule, especially olive oil, wine, salted fish for the popular condiments *garum* or *liquamen*, and bread made in bakeries using large-batch processes. For the mass production of these goods, the owners of firms directed workers to perform specialized tasks in factory-like buildings, as floor plans uncovered by archeologists have revealed. Like Adam Smith, who observed the division of labor in the making of pins centuries later, many Roman writers were aware of and analyzed the phenomenon – St. Augustine in the fifth century AD, for example, who wrote about "the street of the silversmiths, where one vessel, so that it may go out perfect, passes through many craftsmen, when it might have been finished by one perfect craftsman. But the reason why a multitude of workmen was thought necessary was so that individual workers could learn individual parts of an art quickly and easily, rather than that they should all be compelled to be perfect in one entire art, which they could only attain slowly and with difficulty."[64]

Analogous to their Roman counterparts, Chinese writers also commented on the division of labor, anticipating Adam Smith by a good two thousand years.[65] A 1,200-year-old shipwreck of an Arab dhow recently

---

[62] Large-scale production outside of the household was itself not new to Rome or China. Archeologists have discovered textile workshops in late-third-millennium BC Babylonia which employed hundreds of female spinners and weavers in numerous cities as well as large enterprises from the seventh to fifth centuries BC producing oil jars at Ugarit: see Silver, "Karl Polanyi and Markets in the Ancient Near East," 810–812.

[63] Temin, *Roman Market Economy*, 2, 222–225, and chaps. 2 and 5 passim.

[64] Andrew I. Wilson, "Large-Scale Manufacturing, Standardization, and Trade," *in The Oxford Handbook of Engineering and Technology in the Classical World*, ed. John Peter Oleson (Oxford: Oxford University Press, 2008), 393–417, with Augustine quote on 395. For Adam Smith's famous description of pin production, see his *Wealth of Nations*, books I–III, ed. Skinner, 109–110.

[65] Barbieri-Low, *Artisans in Early Imperial China*, 43–44.

discovered in the Java Sea proves that commercialized mass production for export was a major attribute of the T'ang-dynasty economy. Archeologists retrieved tens of thousands of pieces of made-to-order pottery: identical inkpots, spice jars, and pitchers of various sizes, as well as Changsha tea bowls, which were in high demand as far away as Persia from the eighth to tenth centuries. Large Chinese ceramics firms fired them in their kilns after applying decorations for specific export markets: Buddhist lotus symbols on some, Koranic inscriptions on others. They were packed in rice straw to prevent breakage on board ship.[66]

This type of production was evident in China from the third century BC, during the Han dynasty, around the same time it first emerged in Rome. Both state-owned and private firms implemented a precise division of labor in their factories, where artisans performed distinct and highly specialized tasks to produce high-demand items like lacquer cups and other vessels, bronze mirror casings, arrows, and stone tombstones. Besides the division of labor, among the mass-production techniques they utilized were stenciling with uniform patterns, modular parts, standardized tools, and regularized quality controls. For those who could not afford the expensive models, firms offered knockoffs at a lower price. Eager to generate sales and profits, manufacturers often marketed them with advertising slogans like the text found on the back of a "Shangfang brilliant mirror" made in 145 AD: "I have harmoniously combined the three auspicious metals, and refined the white [tin] and the yellow [copper] by a secret formula. As brilliant as the sun or the moon, its reflection enables one to see to the ends of the earth. It will enable one to extend his life and have eternal happiness without end. For one who buys this mirror, may his family become rich and prosperous."[67]

As time went on, more and more items were being mass produced, including multiple varieties of paper. By the Ming dynasty, there were more than thirty paper mills in the manufacturing town of Jiangxi alone, each hiring up to two thousand workers. In part the paper went into making books, which were also commodities whose sale required intensive marketing. Publishers listed forthcoming titles on cover pages, distributed sample pages before publication, added illustrations to the text, decorated covers, and targeted distinct types of audiences with publicity on individual books.[68]

[66] Simon Worrall, "Made in China," *National Geographic* (June 2009), 112–123.
[67] Barbieri-Low, *Artisans in Early Imperial China*, 29, 43–44, 74–75, 78–81, 93–94, 114, 116–152, with mirror advertisement on 146–147.
[68] Kai-wing Chow, *Publishing, Culture, and Power in Early Modern China* (Stanford: Stanford University Press, 2004), 32, 73–75, 79–89, 250.

Wage labor

All the people working in those Chinese manufactories were employees who received set wages. That is because in early modern China, there was "a relatively mobile free labor force. At least by the late Ming, and probably earlier, the majority of Chinese were free of any legal or social encumbrances to their movement between places and between occupations."[69]

To be sure, the vast majority of the population worked their own small farms raising goods for market. But recognition that wage labor was present to a significant degree in this pre-modern, non-Western society erodes the ground around one of the pillars holding up the standard definition of capitalism, namely that the workforce in the communitarian, non-monetarized, pre-capitalist past was made up of serfs or slaves, self-sufficient peasants, and solo artisans banging out a few handicrafts in their small shops.

Many authorities have rehearsed Marxist or Weberian scripts about labor in the ancient world, like German philosopher Jürgen Habermas, who wrote that "the political order, as is well known, rested on a patrimonial slave economy."[70] But although slavery was ever-present, in reality it was not the main source of surplus labor for elites in Rome or Mesopotamia (the evidence is less decisive for ancient Greece, but it leads toward the same conclusion).[71] There were "considerable numbers" of free, wage-earning farm workers in Mesopotamia by the mid-2000s BC, with clearly specified wages paid by the day, month, or year in silver or in barley denominated in shekels. For the next several hundred years, craft mills, large estates, and public works paid their workhands wages.[72] By the mid-500s BC, the *majority* of Babylonian urban and rural workers – including those in the temple and palace sectors – were not unfree laborers, but hired in return for contractually established remuneration at market rates.[73] In Rome, slaves made up at most 10–20 percent of the labor force depending on the period. The rest consisted of free, hired workers whom employers paid wages guaranteed by contract at amounts also set by the interaction of labor-market supply and demand. In general,

[69] Madeleine Zelin, *The Merchants of Zigong: Industrial Entrepreneurship in Early Modern China* (NY: Columbia University Press, 2005), 116.

[70] Jürgen Habermas, *The Structural Transformation of the Public Sphere*, trans. Thomas Burger (Cambridge, MA: MIT Press, 1989), 3.

[71] Morris Silver, "Slaves versus Free Hired Workers in Ancient Greece," *Historia: Zeitschrift für Alte Geschichte*, no. 3 (2006), 257–263.

[72] Silver, "Karl Polanyi and Markets in the Ancient Near East," 808–809.

[73] Jursa, "Babylonia in the First Millennium BCE," 30–31, 35.

they had more of a right to quit and change jobs than did factory workers in nineteenth-century England.[74]

After the fall of Rome, while Europe was yet to recover, the economies of the Islamic world grew fast between the seventh and tenth centuries.[75] In North Africa and the Middle East there was a high degree of specialization in handicrafts and manufacturing, trade, and agriculture, as befit the large free-market trading zone that it was (the same percentage of the population was engaged in commercial pursuits as in Victorian England). The sources tell of a complex, ever-changing mix of free, slave, and other forms of coerced labor. But a mobile wage-labor force was very active in medieval Islamic cities: between the seventh and ninth centuries, 100,000 workers were hired to build Baghdad and 10,000 to refurbish and enlarge Córdoba. In reaction to political disturbances or in return for inducements, massive numbers of skilled workers migrated from one region to the next, and wherever it was they could always count on receiving monetary compensation according to the going rates for their expertise.[76]

When the Western European money economy revived, as in medieval England by the 1080s, lords quickly shifted to hiring laborers for cash (or goods when coins were in short supply) instead of retaining them by virtue of customary or servile relationships. Prior to 1300, a wage-earning labor force already existed in England. In the next century it rose to represent more than 30 percent of the total working population, and up to two-thirds in the more economically vibrant east (the remainder were self-employed or unpaid members of the family). Servants, construction workers, craftsmen, and, most numerously, farm workers on aristocratic estates were the categories of laborers that would have received wages, with the market setting pay

---

[74] Chris Wickham, "Marx, Sherlock Holmes, and Late Roman Commerce," *Journal of Roman Studies* (Nov. 1988), 188; Temin, *Roman Market* Economy, chap. 6.

[75] Maya Shatzmiller, "The Role of Money in the Economic Growth of the Early Islamic Period (650–1000)," in *Sources and Approaches across Disciplines in Near Eastern Studies: Proceedings of the 24th Congress of L'Union Européenne des Arabisants et Islamisants, Leipzig, 2008*, ed. Verena Klemm et al. (Leuven: Uitgeverij Peeters, 2013), 271–305; Jairus Banaji, "Islam, the Mediterranean, and the Rise of Capitalism," *Historical Materialism*, vol. XV, no. 1 (2007), 57–62.

[76] Maya Shatzmiller, *Labour in the Medieval Islamic World* (Leiden: Brill, 1994), 12, 27, 101–174, 215, 259–260, and passim; Maya Shatzmiller, "Human Capital Formation in Medieval Islam," *Workers of the World – International Journal on Strikes and Social Conflict. Special Issue: Global Labour History* (May 2013), 60, 65; Bas van Bavel, Michele Campopiano, and Jessica Dijkman, "Factor Markets in Early Islamic Iraq, c. 600–1100 AD," *Journal of the Economic and Social History of the Orient*, vol. LVII, no. 2 (2014), 271–278.

rates.[77] In Europe as a whole, around half of the populace performed wage labor by the late Middle Ages, although in agricultural areas it was seasonal, and the totals were higher in more urban economies such as those of the Low Countries.[78] As Christopher Dyer points out, wage earning in the Middle Ages was not always full time and did not always last for long periods of time.[79] But it is a larger phenomenon than once thought and signifies the commodification of labor in the pre-modern commercialized economy.

****

Under the weight of that evidence, accumulating in recent decades, yet unfamiliar to most people, the standard definition of capitalism collapses. *All* of the features we once thought comprised capitalism existed in combination with one another beforehand or outside the West, and to a substantial degree. Our understanding of the term is flawed because the paradigm rests on faulty premises, fiery rhetoric, and simplistic stereotypes. I am not rejecting everything that has been said about capitalism. But I am contending that it is not what we think it is. By showing that the traits we normally associate with capitalism were not unique to it, this chapter leaves us with a question: What is distinctive about capitalism? The answer is the information nexus.[80] That is the subject of the rest of the book.

---

[77] Nicholas Mayhew, "Wages and Currency: The Case in Britain up to c. 1600," *in Wages and Currency: Global Comparisons from Antiquity to the Twentieth Century*, ed. Jan Lucassen (Bern: Peter Lang, 2007), 212–214; Campbell, "Factor Markets in England before the Black Death," 84–88; Whittle, *Development of Agrarian Capitalism*, chap. 5; Dyer, *Age of Transition?*, chap. 6.

[78] Persson, "Markets and Coercion in Medieval Europe," 248–251; Oscar Gelderbloom and Joost Jonker, "The Low Countries," in *Cambridge History of Capitalism*, vol. I, ed. Neal and Williamson, 314–356 passim.

[79] Dyer, *Age of Transition?*, 213–214.

[80] Joyce Appleby gets close to the heart of the matter when she writes "at the cultural heart of capitalism is the individual's capacity to control resources and initiate projects." But she does not develop the theme. See her book *The Relentless Revolution: A History of Capitalism* (NY: Norton, 2010), with quote on 14.

Part II

The information nexus

4 Early modern Europe's expanding field of vision
The origins of capitalism

In 1870, workmen in a house in Prato, Italy, near Florence, knocked down a wall and came upon an old boarded-up stairwell filled with sacks of documents. It turned out they belonged to Francesco di Marco Datini, the head of a late-fourteenth-century import-export firm, and included more than 150,000 letters, 500 account books, 400 insurance policies, 300 deeds of partnership, and tens of thousands of commercial bills and instruments.[1] This was the discovery of a medieval "database" compiled by a businessman who spent so much time sending and receiving letters that one can imagine him adjusting very quickly to email had it been introduced in the 1300s.[2]

It is important to understand that Datini was not all that unusual for his time and place. Nor would he be out of place in today's world – although he might store his documents in a file cabinet or online rather than in sacks. If his obsession with collecting and communicating information seems familiar from the behavior of corporations in the twenty-first century, that is because Renaissance Italy's merchants had the same need to find out news that might affect their business and the same need to achieve coordination and control of their operations.[3]

Why the similarity? Because business, whether ancient, medieval, or modern, needs information to function. The most basic feature of a market economy is a price, which is a "mechanism for communicating information" about any product being bought or sold.[4] Besides supply and demand, what economists call "transaction costs" influence prices. The cost of doing business is obviously less, for instance, if property rights are protected, contracts are enforced, and transportation is more

[1] Iris Origo, *The Merchant of Prato: Francesco di Marco Datini* (NY: Knopf, 1957), vi.
[2] John Micklethwait and Adrian Wooldridge, *The Company: A Short History of a Revolutionary Idea* (NY: Modern Library, 2003), 10.
[3] Jonathan Barron Baskin and Paul J. Miranti, Jr., *A History of Corporate Finance* (Cambridge: Cambridge University Press, 1997), 29–30.
[4] Friedrich A. Hayek, "The Use of Knowledge in Society," *American Economic Review* (Sept. 1945), 526.

advanced, as these make it easier to buy, sell, and produce. Conversely, the costs are higher if these conditions do not exist. The lower such transaction costs, the more efficient the market.[5]

Acquiring information about something one might buy, sell, or invest in is another transaction cost with an impact on market efficiency. Following the lead of economists dating back to the eighteenth century, Friedrich A. Hayek emphasized that relationship in his writings of the 1930s and 1940s: "The economic problem of society," he wrote, "is a problem of the utilization of knowledge not given to anyone in its totality."[6] Several decades later, George Stigler won a Nobel Prize for coming to grips with the implications of Hayek's statement. Stigler argued that information costs had to be considered in economics, especially since businessmen or consumers make most decisions on the basis of incomplete information about almost everything: the future cost of raw materials, the exact price shoppers are willing to pay, or the quality of a product.[7] Similarly, in a study of used-car sales called "The Market for Lemons," George A. Akerlof laid bare the problem of "hidden information" in all economic transactions.[8] They and other economists who studied the impact of information – or the lack thereof – ended up qualifying standard neo-classical assumptions about the functioning of the free market: without fully accessible information, economic

[5] Douglass C. North, "Markets," in Oxford Encyclopedia of Economic History, ed. Joel Mokyr, vol. III (Oxford: Oxford University Press, 2003), 432–433; Douglass C. North, "Institutions, Transaction Costs, and the Rise of Merchant Empires," in The Political Economy of Merchant Empires, ed. James D. Tracy (Cambridge: Cambridge University Press, 1991), 22–40; Douglass C. North and Robert Paul Thomas, The Rise of the Western World (Cambridge: Cambridge University Press, 1973). Although North considers the acquisition of information as a transaction cost, his main emphasis is on law.

[6] Hayek, "Use of Knowledge," 519–520. Hayek was prompted to consider the issue in reaction to post–World War I socialist ambitions for economic planning, which presupposed the omniscience of government. But economists for over a hundred years before him were conscious of the problem of inadequate information. See Fritz Machlup, Knowledge: Its Creation, Distribution, and Economic Significance, vol. III: The Economics of Information and Human Capital (Princeton: Princeton University Press, 1984), 15–17 and passim; Philip Mirowski, Machine Dreams: Economics Becomes a Cyborg Science (Cambridge: Cambridge University Press, 2002), 370; Yuval P. Yonay, The Struggle over the Soul of Economics (Princeton: Princeton University Press, 1998), 131; Frank H. Knight, Risk, Uncertainty, and Profit (Boston: Houghton Mifflin, 1921), 197 and chaps. 7–8 passim; Robert E. Wright, The Wealth of Nations Rediscovered: Integration and Expansion in American Financial Markets, 1780–1850 (Cambridge: Cambridge University Press, 2002), 214.

[7] George J. Stigler, The Organization of Industry (Chicago: University of Chicago Press, 1968), chap. 16.

[8] George A. Akerlof, "The Market for Lemons: Quality Uncertainty and the Market Mechanism," Quarterly Journal of Economics (Aug. 1970), 488–500. I borrow the term "hidden information" from John Cassidy, How Markets Fail (NY: Farrar, Straus and Giroux, 2009), chap. 12.

decision-making can be flawed, which implies that the market economy is not perfectly constructed.[9]

But businessmen have always intuited this. It is precisely because the information available is imperfect that they strive to gather as much as they can: the more of it they have and the faster they get it, the better able they are to make decisions that help them earn a profit and best their competitors. For a company, information acquisition entails a reduction of transaction costs, uncertainties, and risks, and with that an enhancement of opportunities.[10]

That takes us to the heart of my argument: in parts of early modern Western Europe, businessmen overcame informational deficiencies to an unprecedented degree. They made the collection and transfer of information, to borrow the terminology of another economist, less "sticky" than they had ever been before.[11] For reasons we will explore, the societies they lived in and the political regimes they lived under made it easier for them to open information channels and reduce informational blockages, thereby diminishing transaction costs. The sheer volume of information seeking, accumulating, analyzing, and dispensing was unprecedented in human history.

To elaborate, by information I mean more than the narrow consideration of price or an enterprise's profitability; I include in this institutions that expand useful knowledge in the widest sense.[12] Therefore, transportation, communications, literacy, book production, and the press all play a large role in this chapter. Information encompasses everything from inventing new accounting methods to sniffing out shifts in the political winds that would affect market conditions. As we will see, all of these manifold efforts reflect societies that were driven to learn about the world

---

[9] Naomi R. Lamoreaux, Daniel M. G. Raff, and Peter Temin, "Introduction," in *Learning by Doing in Markets, Firms, and Countries*, ed. Naomi R. Lamoreaux, Daniel M. G. Raff, and Peter Temin (Chicago: University of Chicago Press, 1999), 5–6; Cassidy, *How Markets Fail*, chap. 12; Kenneth J. Arrow, "Limited Knowledge and Economic Analysis," *American Economic Review* (March 1974), 1–10.

[10] John J. McCusker, "Information and Transaction Costs in Early Modern Europe," in *Weltwirtschaft und Wirtschaftsordnung*, ed. Rainer Gömmel and Markus A. Denzel (Stuttgart: Franz Steiner Verlag, 2002), 69.

[11] Eric von Hippel, "'Sticky Information' and the Locus of Problem Solving," in *The Dynamic Firm*, ed. Alfred D. Chandler, Jr. et al. (Oxford: Oxford University Press, 1998), 60–77. Von Hippel identifies the nature of the problem in today's world, but does not delve into the history of information transfer.

[12] A distinction is often made between "information," which some economists define as unprocessed data, and "knowledge," which they define as applied or "socially useful" information: see Joel Mokyr, *The Gifts of Athena: Historical Origins of the Knowledge Economy* (Princeton: Princeton University Press, 2002), chap. 1, and David Warsh, *Knowledge and the Wealth of Nations* (NY: Norton, 2006), 295–297. Since my emphasis is on the *potential* for acquiring information and knowledge, the distinctions between them are less important and I will use the two terms interchangeably.

in all its dimensions and developed the tools to do so.[13] Europe's expanding field of vision helps to account for the economic successes of Western business and the relative deficiencies of the leading Asian economies. With that assessment, this chapter challenges the "California" school of economic history, which argues that the "great divergence" between East and West occurred only late in the day, around 1800, and resulted from Western Europe's access to "coal and colonies," the twin juggernauts of imperialism and industrialization.[14] In doing so, the chapter also disputes the implication in the works of anthropologist Jack Goody that all notions of Western uniqueness are Eurocentric myths, which he labels "the theft of history."[15] What I am arguing is that the initial divergence took place much earlier, and was a by-product of the information deficit within Asia and the superior information-gathering abilities of the West. This is what opened the door of economic development for the one and shut it (at least for a while) for the other.

The dense information nexus that was first built in Italy, Holland, and England is the essence of capitalism. Yes, the profit motive is an essential driving force of the system, which is lubricated by credit and cash. But as argued in Chapter 3, these also existed in many other places and time periods, so we cannot say capital or the "cash nexus" are defining aspects of capitalism, despite the name. As we saw in Chapter 3, most people still view capital, wage labor, the division of labor, and private property rights as the fundamental features of the capitalist system. Yet however crucial these features may be, they have existed in so many places that they cannot be taken to constitute the building blocks of capitalism as a unique economic system. The only characteristic that is *exclusive* to capitalism is the enhanced ability to marshal information.

The information nexus has its roots in the Middle Ages and first came to fruition in certain nations of early modern Western Europe. This is why

---

[13] Similar arguments for the early industrial era can be found in Joel Mokyr, "The Market for Ideas and the Origins of Economic Growth in Eighteenth Century Europe," online at http://faculty.wcas.northwestern.edu/~jmokyr/Marketforideas.PDF; Robert C. Allen, *The British Industrial Revolution in Global Perspective* (Cambridge: Cambridge University Press, 2009), chap. 10; and Margaret C. Jacob, *The First Knowledge Economy: Human Capital and the European Economy, 1750–1850* (Cambridge: Cambridge University Press, 2014).

[14] Kenneth Pomeranz, *The Great Divergence: China, Europe, and the Making of the Modern World Economy* (Princeton: Princeton University Press, 2000). Peer Vries, in both a review essay, "Are Coal and Colonies Really Crucial? Kenneth Pomeranz and the Great Divergence," *Journal of World History* (Fall 2001), 407–446, and a book, *Escaping Poverty: The Origins of Modern Economic Growth* (Goettingen: V&R unipress, 2013), offers a sustained rebuttal of Pomeranz et al., but does not consider information as a factor in the debate as I do here.

[15] Jack Goody, *The Theft of History* (Cambridge: Cambridge University Press, 2006).

bestselling authors Alvin Toffler and Peter Drucker, among others, are mistaken when they announce that in our own digital age, knowledge and information have "gone from being an adjunct of money power" to being "the most important ingredient of force and wealth."[16] In reality, we entered the "Information Age" centuries ago. Let us return to Datini's day and see how it came about.

The Middle Ages: Communications and commercial revolutions

Stepped-up information gathering and processing in Renaissance Italy of the kind we see evidenced in Datini's sacks of documents were both the cause and effect of a revolution in commerce and communications that took place in medieval Europe.

After the long hiatus following the collapse of the Roman empire, aristocrats and peasants alike were drawn into a money economy. From the twelfth century onward, trade boomed, both locally and across national boundaries. In the long run, even deadly outbreaks of warfare and plague could not keep it in check. Regularly scheduled fairs tied all the commercial activity together and improved information exchange about commodities, credit, and the reputations of fellow traders. The largest fairs were French, and served as meeting grounds for Northern and Southern European merchants: the Champagne fairs of Provins, Troyes, Lagny, and Bar-sur-Aube; to the south and east in Chalon, Geneva, and Lyons; and to the west at Saint-Denis near Paris. Soon they also appeared in the Low Countries, southwest Germany, Italy, and Castile. In England, over the course of the thirteenth and fourteenth centuries people congregated at well over a thousand local fairs and markets, plugging small towns into regional and international trade grids that were pulsating with commercial life.[17]

[16] Quote from Alvin Toffler, *Powershift* (NY: Bantam Books, 1990), xix, 18. For similar statements, see Peter F. Drucker, *Post-Capitalist Society* (NY: HarperBusiness, 1993), 5–6; Manuel Castells, *The Rise of the Network Society*, vol. I (Oxford: Blackwell, 1996), 469–478; and Thomas Stewart, *Intellectual Capital: The New Wealth of Organizations* (NY: Currency Doubleday, 1997), xx.

[17] Peter Spufford, *Power and Profit: The Merchant in Medieval Europe* (London: Thames and Hudson, 2002), 48–50, 144–150; John Hatcher and Mark Bailey, *Modelling the Middle Ages: The History and Theory of England's Economic Development* (Oxford: Oxford University Press, 2001), 142–144; S. R. Epstein, *Freedom and Growth: The Rise of States and Markets in Europe, 1300–1750* (London: Routledge, 2000), 74–88. For a glimpse at the thriving regional and international trade of Iberia in the high Middle Ages, see Bernard F. Reilly, *The Medieval Spains* (Cambridge: Cambridge University Press, 1993), 140–144.

Commerce grew as conditions for transportation eased on upgraded land, river, and sea routes across Western Europe in the Middle Ages. Local and regional authorities constructed thousands of small bridges, expanded ports, opened mountain passes, canalized riverways, and repaired Roman highways that had fallen into disuse centuries earlier. This was an interlinked, "integrated transport network for carrying goods," a "road revolution" that affected the entire continent. Medieval thoroughfares were now clogged with mercantile travelers taking advantage of wagons, whose newly invented front axles and iron-rimmed wheels offered a higher carrying capacity for freight. A dense network of inns cropped up, where innkeepers often provided money-changing and other banking services.[18]

People in the northern Italian city-states were the first to capitalize on these developments. Some of their businesses became large multi-branched firms financed in part through transferable shares. Investors who congregated in the financial quarters formed bourses – the earliest being the open-air *Loggia dei Mercanti* located on the Piazza di Rialto in Venice from 1322. Wealthy individuals ploughed their money into these shares or government bonds. Companies like the Datini, Acciaiuli, Peruzzi, and Bardi groups started as family firms, then grew into separate and multiple partnerships whose international operations spanned banking, mining, textile manufacturing, and the bulk trade in grain. They had more employees than contemporary government bureaucracies and opened satellite offices to capture new business. In 1335, the Peruzzi Company had five agents in England, four in France, four in Avignon, four in Flanders, six in Sicily, six in Naples, and five at the grain exporting port of Barletta. In the next century, the Medici Bank had branches in eleven cities.[19]

---

[18] Spufford, *Power and Profit*, 12ff, 48ff, chaps. 3–4, with quotes on 164 and 181; Christopher Dyer, *An Age of Transition? Economy and Society in England in the Later Middle Ages* (Oxford: Oxford University Press, 2005), 170–172; Hatcher and Bailey, *Modelling the Middle Ages*, 146–149, 154–156. This picture based on recent scholarship is a rebuttal of Fernand Braudel, who insisted on the sluggishness of late medieval communications, perhaps because he was comparing them to the modern era: see his *The Mediterranean and the Mediterranean World in the Age of Philip II*, trans. Siân Reynolds, vol. I (NY: Harper and Row, 1972), 283–284, 355–375 passim, and *Civilization and Capitalism*, vol. I: *The Structures of Everyday Life*, trans. Siân Reynolds (NY: Harper and Row, 1981), 424. Citing new documentary and archeological evidence, Michael McCormick, *Origins of the European Economy: Communications and Commerce, AD 300–900* (Cambridge: Cambridge University Press, 2001), finds extensive international maritime and overland travel by Europeans in an even earlier period. But it was nothing compared to what occurred later.

[19] Edwin S. Hunt and James M. Murray, *A History of Business in Medieval Europe, 1200–1550* (Cambridge: Cambridge University Press, 1999), chap. 5; Spufford, *Power*

The Italian companies were able to establish a permanent presence away from their home bases because of numerous innovations in communications and control that allowed for a flow of regular information from the field to headquarters. Among them were seemingly simple but new devices that helped track commercial activity like invoices, bills of lading, and shipping manifests.[20] Perhaps most momentous was the development of a regular mail service. Starting in the 1260s, courier services called *scarselle* (after the leather letter bags) began operating between Italy and the French fairs. By the 1340s, seventeen firms in Florence agreed to support a joint mail cooperative called the *Scarsella dei Mercanti Fiorentini* to avoid duplicating costs. The *scarselle genovesi* regularly ran correspondence between businesses in Genoa and their agents in Barcelona, Paris, Cologne, and Bruges. Routes crisscrossed Italy and reached as far as England, but companies could always hire their own private couriers if they needed to send something faster than the average 50 kilometers a day (which meant around a month and a half for a letter to go between Naples and London). Private entrepreneurs ran most of these services, which profited from the massive number of letters being mailed: the Datini company alone was responsible for at least 10,000 a year for three decades. But in the 1300s, the Venetian government founded its own postal system, the *Compagnia dei Corrieri*. Beginning in 1516, the Habsburg crown farmed out postal operations between Austria and their dominions in the Low Countries, Burgundy, Italy, and Spain to the Taxis family (Tassis in Italy and France), whose Italian forbears had been postmen in Lombardy. This was the "first public communications system in Europe," available for use by everyone.[21]

What was in these letters?[22] Information on market conditions, for one. In the 1380s, for example, darker furs came into style for men of

---

and *Profit*, 19–25, 43, 50–52; Baskin and Miranti, *History of Corporate Finance*, 40–41; David Abulafia, "The Impact of Banking in the Late Middle Ages and the Renaissance, 1300–1500," in *Banking, Trade, and Industry: Europe, America, and Asia from the Thirteenth to the Twentieth Century*, ed. Alice Teichova et al. (Cambridge: Cambridge University Press, 1997), 24; Micklethwait and Wooldridge, *The Company*, 7–10.

[20] Baskin and Miranti, *History of Corporate Finance*, 33.

[21] Wolfgang Behringer, "Communications Revolutions: A Historiographical Concept," *German History* (Aug. 2006), 340–346, with quote on 342. Spufford, *Power and Profit*, 25–29; Peter Burke, "Early Modern Venice as a Center of Information and Communication," in *Venice Reconsidered*, ed. John Martin and Dennis Romano (Baltimore: Johns Hopkins University Press, 2000), 391; Andrew Pettegree, *The Invention of News* (New Haven: Yale University Press, 2014), 43–46, 51–57, 168–181.

[22] For a sample of mainly Italian international commercial correspondence, see Robert S. Lopez and Irving W. Raymond, eds, *Medieval Trade in the Mediterranean World* (NY: Columbia University Press, 1990), chap. 23.

substance, which shifted demand from Russian squirrel to black sable; those merchants with the fastest communications link to the Russian suppliers of the fur profited (judging from a later traveler's account, it could have taken up to ten months to go from Hamburg to Moscow via Riga on the Baltic coast, and thence over land and river routes).[23] Letters often included political news relevant to investment conditions and sales opportunities – whatever could be gleaned from friends, contacts, diplomats, spies, and gossip-mongers about the financial needs of monarchs or their inclination toward war and peace.

But above all, it was commodities prices and exchange rates that were the sought-after information in these missives, prices being the basic indicator of supply and demand in every market, a signal of where to conduct business and what to buy and sell. A 1588/1589 price list from Venice included the values of currencies from other Italian states, Germany, France, and England; the prices of gold, silver, various kinds of cloth, metals, grain; and a panoply of spices and herbs: pepper, ginger, gum Arabic, asafoetida, sugar, mastic, camphor, and on and on. A similar document from Florence in 1631 includes these items plus almonds, apples, amber, cinnamon, nutmeg, saffron, and verdigris.[24] These lists were usually appended to letters and transcribed in standardized form. What the Italians called *listini dei prezzi* covered every commodity from every potential market of Europe and the Levant. At first, such firms as the Datini or, in the German lands, the giant financial and commercial concern of the Fugger family wrote them up internally. Soon price lists were more widely distributed for sale in manuscript form and by the late sixteenth century in print – due to the invention of the Gutenberg printing press. These so-called "commodity price currents" were the earliest precursors of our business press.[25]

---

[23] Jean Favier, *Gold and Spices: The Rise of Commerce in the Middle Ages*, trans. Caroline Higgitt (NY: Holmes and Meier, 1998), 65–67. On the Russian side of the business, see Janet Martin, *Treasure of the Land of Darkness: The Fur Trade and Its Significance for Medieval Russia* (Cambridge: Cambridge University Press, 1986), chaps. 3–4. For the slow and difficult travel conditions even centuries later, see Samuel H. Baron, trans. and ed., *The Travels of Olearius in Seventeenth-Century Russia* (Stanford: Stanford University Press, 1967), chap. 1.

[24] John J. McCusker and Cora Gravesteijn, *The Beginnings of Commercial and Financial Journalism: The Commodity Price Currents, Exchange Rate Currents, and Money Currents of Early Modern Europe* (Amsterdam: Nederlands Economisch-Historisch Archief, 1991), 192 on Florence, 397 on Venice.

[25] John J. McCusker, "The Demise of Distance: The Business Press and the Origins of the Information Revolution in the Early Modern Atlantic World," *American Historical Review* (April 2005), 299; John J. McCusker, "Information and Transaction Costs in Early Modern Europe," in *Weltwirtschaft und Wirtschaftsordnung*, ed. Gömmel and Denzel, 74–76; McCusker and Gravesteijn, *Beginnings of Commercial and Financial Journalism*, 22–23, 38n20; Spufford, *Power and Profit*, 28–29.

Add political information and you have the birth of newspapers. These were essential tools for merchants, who were the main suppliers and consumers of news in Europe in the late medieval and early modern periods. In Venice, known by European contemporaries as the "metropolis of news," *reportiste* (reporters) wrote *avvisi* (notices) by hand; after Gutenberg the *gazette*, or printed newsletter, appeared – a word derived from the Venetian halfpenny, which was the price of each copy.[26] With the publishing of commodity price currents, a greater number of people engaged in commerce could now exploit this kind of intelligence, which was formerly restricted to a tiny, well-connected merchant elite. That number was still relatively small, but it was an important step in making commercial expansion possible.

If the birth of newspapers was directly related to the European adoption of the world-changing invention of printing with moveable type, so was the expansion of book production. That too helped encourage the profit-seeking activities of businessmen by giving them ready access to new techniques and broadening their horizons with information about the world at large. Surpassing all others as a book-publishing center was Venice, which in the first fifty years after Gutenberg issued 4,500 titles, amounting to 2.5 million copies of books. In Europe as a whole by 1600, around 150,000 titles had come out, with estimates of the number of books in circulation before that date ranging from 150,000,000 to 230,000,000.[27]

Aside from religious and secular literature in every European and Middle Eastern language, publishers issued numerous aids to business-men with the sale of almanacs, atlases, descriptions of tradable goods, multilingual dictionaries, travel itineraries, etiquette guides for behavior in foreign emporia, tips on maneuvering around customs in every port, and an array of manuals designed to shortcut calculations and currency conversions. Books for the merchant were as popular as do-it-yourself, self-help, and inspirational books aimed at the businessman are today.[28]

---

[26] Burke, "Early Modern Venice as a Center of Information," 397; Pettegree, *Invention of News*, 5–6; Paul Arblaster, "Posts, Newsletters, Newspapers," *Media History*, XI, nos. 1–2 (2005), 22–23, 34n9.

[27] Burke, "Early Modern Venice as a Center of Information," 392, 398, 400–402; Erdmann Weyrauch, "Das Buch als Träger der frühneuzeitlichen Kommunikationsrevolution," in *Kommunikationsrevolutionen: Die neuen Medien des 16. und 19. Jahrhunderts*, ed. Michael North, 2nd ed. (Cologne: Böhlau Verlag, 2001), 2–3; Eltjo Buringh and Jan Luiten van Zanden, "Charting the 'Rise of the West': Manuscripts and Printed Books in Europe, A Long-Term Perspective from the Sixth through Eighteenth Centuries," *Journal of Economic History* (June 2009), 417.

[28] Spufford, *Power and Profit*, 52–56; Lopez and Raymond, *Medieval Trade in the Mediterranean World*, 342–343 and chap. XXI passim; Armando Sapori, *The Italian Merchant in the Middle Ages*, trans. Patricia Ann Kennen (NY: Norton, 1970), 36.

Among the books that had the greatest impact were those on accounting and financial analysis – both of which aided the continuing growth of business in the West. The bible of medieval finance was *Liber Abaci* (The Book of the Abacus), published in 1202, a practical guide on the mathematics of money, trade, arbitrage, and the calculation of profits written by Fibonacci, a.k.a. Leonardo of Pisa.

Fibonacci's father had been a customs official in the Pisan colony of Bugia (now Bejaia) in Algeria. There the son learned the Arabic language and Arabic numerals – he was in fact the first person to demonstrate to Europeans their convenience for business purposes. To quote Fibonacci, he traveled widely throughout the Mediterranean region and studied "with whoever was learned in [mathematics], from … Egypt, Syria, Greece, Sicily."[29] What he did was to bring together the advanced mathematical traditions of the East – the Arab world and India – and bestow them upon subsequent generations in the West. As *Liber Abaci* begins, "these are the nine figures of the Indians: 9 8 7 6 5 4 3 2 1. With these nine figures and with this sign 0 which in Arabic is called *zephirum*, any number can be written, as will be demonstrated."[30]

But he also surpassed his Asian predecessors – and allowed European commerce to surpass them – insofar as he was the first anywhere to analyze relative value and present value mathematically. How does one decide, for instance, which is worth more when dealing with Arab merchants: their saffron or their pepper? How does one decide whether to speculate in grain or invest in the government annuities offered by the Italian city-states in return for the purchase of their bonds? How does one divide profits among partners with different amounts of capital invested in a company? These problems, all presented in *Liber Abaci*, had never been addressed before, although they drew on Asian mathematical principles. The book was translated almost immediately from Latin into the vernacular Italian and imparted in the business schools that were appearing in the late thirteenth and early fourteenth centuries in every Italian commercial city. The hundreds of Renaissance-era business math textbooks that were first handwritten then printed in Italy, France, and beyond all drew directly or indirectly on Fibonacci.

Robust commercial exchange and international trade created a ready-made audience for Fibonacci, and it also gave rise to "Italian

---

[29] William M. Goetzmann, "Fibonacci and the Financial Revolution," in *The Origins of Value: The Financial Innovations that Created Modern Capital Markets*, ed. William M. Goetzmann and K. Geert Rouwenhorst (Oxford: Oxford University Press, 2005), 123–143, with quote on 127.

[30] Jane Gleeson-White, *Double Entry: How the Merchants of Venice Created Modern Finance* (NY: Norton, 2011), 19.

bookkeeping," as it was long known. Double-entry bookkeeping was invented in the thirteenth century in northern Italy, where the complexity of business operations made accounting necessary to monitor the large amounts of money changing hands between clients, suppliers, investors, and customers. Like Fibonacci's work, it was taught in the proliferating business schools of Renaissance Italy. It spread farther and wider with the publication of *Summa di Arithmetica* (Venice, 1494). The author was Luca Bartolomeo de Pacioli, a neo-Platonist philosopher and friend of Leonardo da Vinci, whose fame throughout Europe came with his aphoristic nuggets of practical wisdom: "If you cannot be a good accountant, you will grope your way forward like a blind man and may meet great losses."[31] Not only was double-entry bookkeeping, once invented, recommended for making sure one's business was not "a confusion of Babel," in the words of another fifteenth-century writer, it was also how the owners of the Italian super-companies mentioned above could keep control of their long-distance operations: that is, through regular accounting audits of their highly paid branch managers.[32]

What Pacioli was saying seems obvious: the more information you have and the more effectively it is analyzed the stronger your business; conversely, those who fail to adopt new methods of information-processing limit the scope and scale of their operations and risk being outrun by their competitors. But self-evident though Pacioli's words are to us, in his day they had the force of novelty. European businessmen also had access to new techniques and new ideas that made it possible for them to follow his advice. Why that was so has to do with a unique concatenation of circumstances to be explained more fully below. For now, suffice it to say that the seeds were planted in parts of Western Europe during the Middle Ages, to sprout in the early modern era and come to fruition in later centuries. In other parts of the world, by contrast, it was much harder to acquire the kinds of information Western European merchants increasingly had available to them thanks to steadily improving means of communications, above all the business and financial press.

---

[31] Alfred W. Crosby, *The Measure of Reality: Quantification and Western Society, 1250–1600* (Cambridge: Cambridge University Press, 1997), 212–216, with quote on 216; Gleeson-White, *Double Entry*, chaps. 2–4; Spufford, *Power and Profit*, 29–31; and Lopez and Raymond, *Medieval Trade in the Mediterranean World*, chap. XXII. On the first English translation of Pacioli in 1543, see Geoffrey Poitras, *The Early History of Financial Economics, 1478–1776* (Cheltenham: Edward Elgar, 2000), 117.

[32] Baskin and Miranti, *History of Corporate Finance*, 42, 44. The quote is from Benedetto Cotrugli, *Della mercatura et del mercante perfetto* (Naples, 1458), excerpted in Lopez and Raymond, *Medieval Trade in the Mediterranean World*, 377.

To support those claims we need to examine the status of information in medieval and early modern China, Japan, India, and the Middle East, then follow with the early modern Dutch Republic, England, and France.

The non-Western world: The gap opens

The fact is, Asian or North African merchants were also naturally interested in gathering business information, and they had more tools available for that purpose than many of us realize. But – and this is the crux of the matter – such tools only saturated parts of Western Europe beginning in the seventeenth and eighteenth centuries and thereafter manifesting themselves in higher economic growth. But the story is not a straightforward matter of European advance and Asian decline.

For Max Weber, a key difference between the West and the East lay in the development of European bookkeeping and accounting techniques, which he regarded as a signpost of the rationalist approach to the management of business and society as a whole. But scholarship since his time has disproven his assertions. The Chinese might not have had true double-entry bookkeeping of the Italian type, but as early as the T'ang dynasty (618–907), and certainly throughout the Ming (1368–1644), extensive records can be found of rents, taxes, merchant sales, pawnshop and other shopkeepers' transactions, temple finances, and gambling debts. By the late Song dynasty (960–1279), private accounts involved a four-column system with balance forward, new receipts, expenditures, and present balance. This system and similar ones – the so-called "three-legged" and "four-legged" account books – that developed in commercial regions of China during the Ming and Qing dynasties (the latter 1644–1912) were fairly close to the Italian system. Chinese partnerships from the mid-Ming onward were able to calculate profits according to the different percentages of capital invested by various partners. For elite families, a self-help book from around 1200 – Ni Ssu's *Assorted Notes from the Hall of Tilling with the Classics* – urged keeping of both monthly and annual plans following daily and yearly budgets for household expenditures.[33] On the other hand, at the shop level, Westerners in late-nineteenth-century China reported chaos in bookkeeping, with "entries . . . not set down in columns, so as to be consistently added, but strung along a page like stockings on a clothes-line" – giving at best an

[33] Goody, *The East in the West*, 77–79; Hsu Tzu-fen, "Traditional Chinese Bookkeeping Methodology," *Chinese Business History*, vol. II, no. 1 (Nov. 1991), 1–2; William T. Rowe, *Hankow: Commerce and Society in a Chinese City, 1796–1889* (Stanford: Stanford University Press, 1984), 73; Joseph P. McDermott, "Family Financial Plans of the Southern Song," *Asia Major*, 3d series, vol. IV (1991), 19–21, 23, 33–35, 45–47, 48n90.

"approximate estimate of [a merchant's] gains and losses in any particular transaction or in his trade for a given period."[34]

In South Asia and the Arab-speaking world, bookkeeping was similarly developed.[35] In medieval Cairo, the writer Ibn 'Abd Rabbihi advised "for kings the study of genealogy and histories, for warriors the study of battles and biography, and for merchants the study of writing and arithmetic."[36] Egyptian merchants used unwieldy Greek (or, if Jews, Hebrew) numerals until learning about Arabic numerals from their Western trading partners in the late Middle Ages. Before the introduction of Italian bookkeeping methods, for an overall picture of their financial position merchants often had to rely on their memories of numbers, prices, and goods bought and sold.[37] Yet, in northern India by the seventeenth century, in what seems to be a trend originating indigenously, merchants adopted Hindu arithmetic and adhered to the guidelines of Persian accounting manuals. It appears governments and businesses used a form of double-entry bookkeeping.[38]

Although there were some deficiencies, we should not discount the viability of the accounting systems that existed outside the West, and Weber's claim that Europeans were more advanced than Asians in this regard cannot be sustained. Even if we think of Fibonacci and Pacioli it is not clear, judging by accounting practices, that the Asians were beginning to lag behind. A few English merchants with international trade ties might have adopted double-entry bookkeeping in the sixteenth and seventeenth centuries, but most used a system that was no better than the ones prevalent in China: as an instruction manual of 1682 reported, "the best of them are confused, the others so blotted and blurr'd, so cross'd and raced, that neither Head nor Tail can be discovered."[39] Even in the early-twentieth-century United States, the nation that for Weber exemplified rational, capitalist society, there was a great imprecision in accounting. In his 1869 manual for retailers, Samuel Terry stated that

[34] Robert P. Gardella, "Commercial Bookkeeping in Ch'ing China and the West," *Ch'ing-shih wen-t'i*, vol. IV, no. 7 (1982), 59.

[35] Goody, *The East in the West*, 72–75; Subhi Y. Labib, "Capitalism in Medieval Islam," *Journal of Economic History* (March 1969), 92.

[36] Abraham L. Udovitch, *Partnership and Profit in Medieval Islam* (Princeton: Princeton University Press, 1970), 237–238.

[37] S. D. Goitein, *A Mediterranean Society*, vol. I (Berkeley: University of California Press, 1967), 204–209.

[38] Prasannan Parthasarathi, *Why Europe Grew Rich and Asia Did Not: Global Economic Divergence, 1600–1850* (Cambridge: Cambridge University Press, 2011), 82–84.

[39] Christopher Dyer, *A Country Merchant, 1495–1520: Trading and Farming at the End of the Middle Ages* (Oxford: Oxford University Press, 2012), 92–93, 95–97; Craig Muldrew, *The Economy of Obligation: The Culture of Credit and Social Relations in Early Modern England* (Houndmills: Macmillan, 1998), 61–63, with quote on 62.

"ignorance of the principle and practice of 'double-entry' bookkeeping, simple though they are, is astonishingly universal." As John D. Rockefeller observed about his competitors, "many of the brightest kept their books in such a way that they did not actually know when they were making money on a certain operation and when they were losing." Among American and also British experts at the time, lamentations about businessmen and their weak knowledge of accounting were common.[40]

We might even minimize the differences between Asia and the West in transportation and communications infrastructures. In many parts of Asia these were well developed. We have to recognize the vast trade and political/administrative networks that spread across all of central Eurasia and the Indian Ocean beginning in the ancient Bronze Age. The medieval Mongol empire functioned with an expansive iteration of that network: among its servitors there was an extraordinary geographical mobility, with Italians, Franks, Flemings, Greeks, Germans, Scandinavians, Russians, Hungarians, Armenians, Georgians, Arabs, Persians, Mongols, Uighurs, Tibetans, and Chinese all working for the Mongol state and many moving back and forth across the length of its vast territory. Couriers brought messages routinely between the Mongolian court of the Yuan dynasty in China and the Mongolian Il-khan rulers of Iran.[41] Across the medieval Islamic lands, too, from the Middle East to Spain, regular mail services run both by governments and private entrepreneurs also existed in what S. D. Goitein portrays as an intercontinental free-trade zone. These were reliable enough to be inexpensive. As for business travel throughout that zone, it was also robust on land and sea.[42]

---

[40] Rockefeller quote from Ron Chernow, *Titan: The Life of John D. Rockefeller, Sr.* (NY: Vintage, 1998), 46; Terry quote from David Sellers Smith, "The Elimination of the Unworthy: Credit Men and Small Retailers in Progressive Era Capitalism," *Journal of the Gilded Age and the Progressive Era* (April 2010), 201; and see 209. For other testimonies to that effect from the US and the UK, see Irving Fisher, *The Nature of Capital and Income* (NY: Macmillan, 1906), 63–64; and Sidney Pollard, *The Genesis of Modern Management: A Study of the Industrial Revolution in Great Britain* (Cambridge, MA: Harvard University Press, 1965), 233–245. It is noteworthy that the first books on depreciation accounting were not published in Britain until the late nineteenth century: see Paul Johnson, *Making the Market: Victorian Origins of Corporate Capitalism* (Cambridge: Cambridge University Press, 2010), 203.

[41] Thomas T. Allsen, *Culture and Conquest in Mongol Eurasia* (Cambridge: Cambridge University Press, 2004); Christopher I. Beckwith, *Empires of the Silk Road: A History of Central Asia from the Bronze Age to the Present* (Princeton: Princeton University Press, 2009), 63–64, 252ff.

[42] S. D. Goitein, "The Commercial Mail Service in Medieval Islam," *Journal of the American Oriental Society* (April–June 1964), 118–123; S. D. Goitein, *Mediterranean Society*, vol. I, pt. IV; Adam J. Silverstein, *Postal Systems in the Pre-Modern Islamic World* (Cambridge: Cambridge University Press, 2007).

It was no different in late medieval and early modern China, where in the 1540s a Portuguese sailor who had been transported as a prisoner in the coastal region between Quanzhou and Fuzhou commented on the quality and upkeep of the roads. The Chinese government encouraged local officials and wealthy merchants to build bridges and local byways. From the fourteenth century onward, the central authorities invested heavily in river transport, and early in the following century renovated the Grand Canal, which stretched a thousand miles on the eastern seaboard from Beijing to Hangzhou. For both military and administrative purposes, the Song dynasty had established a series of postal or courier stations for government officials traveling on important riverine and over-land routes. By the early to mid-Ming dynasty there were more than 1,900 such stations 35–40 kilometers apart.[43]

Chinese and Western sources comment on the vast number of people on the go – from southern China in 1733 came a report that "one sees a perpetual movement of boats, barks, and rafts everywhere . . . and they resemble so many moving towns."[44] Or we can quote a sixteenth-century stele that describes merchants in Shui-ch'üan as "coming and going like shooting stars."[45] Commercial boat transport was plentiful and cheap, and on land one could hire sedan chairs, carts, or horses. As business travel became common, a choice of guidebooks appeared for purchase, among them Huan Pien's *Water and Land Routes at a Glance for Traveling Merchants*, published from 1570 onward with many pirated editions and originally relying on information collected from businessmen who were queried about their experiences on the road.[46]

Obviously China at this time was by no means the stagnant society that Marx, Weber, and many others portrayed it to be. But Chinese transportation and communications systems did have significant short-comings compared to those in Western Europe. Travel in most places was difficult. Mainly it took place on rivers, which in China run parallel to each other on an east–west axis and were rarely connected. River travel was slow (especially upstream), although steady.[47] Regions without

[43] Timothy Brook, "Communications and Commerce," in *The Cambridge History of China*, ed. Denis Twitchett and Frederick W. Mote, vol. VIII (Cambridge: Cambridge University Press, 1998), 580–583, 585, 588, 609–611.
[44] Braudel, *Civilization and Capitalism*, vol. I, 421.
[45] Brook, "Communications and Commerce," 620.
[46] Brook, "Communications and Commerce," 612–615, 619–620, 631–633.
[47] Brook, "Communications and Commerce," 608, 621–623; Timothy Brook, *The Confusions of Pleasure: Commerce and Culture in Ming China* (Berkeley: University of California Press, 1998), 126; Lucille Chia, *Printing for Profit: The Commercial Publishers of Jianyang, Fujian (11th–17th Centuries)* (Cambridge, MA: Harvard University Press, 2002), 19–21.

substantial rivers were therefore substantially less developed than those areas with them, and trade flowed more readily into commercial towns like Hankou from the Yangtze River, rather than from the interior.[48]

The Chinese courier and postal services were also not as far-reaching as they might seem, for they were by law restricted to government use. Private individuals bribed the soldiers who served as postmen to carry letters or deliver goods, but mostly people had to rely on friends or trust their parcels to unfamiliar merchants who happened to be passing through. A private commercial mail service also emerged late in the Ming dynasty.[49] The Shanxi banks (so called because many of their owners came from Shanxi province) of the eighteenth and nineteenth centuries ran their own courier services, bearing similarities to those of their medieval Italian counterparts, designed to circumvent banditry and other difficulties of travel.[50] These various services fluctuated as government finances were shaken by warfare, but even at their highpoint they only existed on the main roads between provincial capitals and bypassed most other towns.[51] As the classic novel *Chin P'ing Mei*, which chronicles daily life of the sixteenth century, illustrates, travel from most communities to the center was sluggish: when evil protagonists in the book want sexual rivals out of the way they manage to send them on routine business trips that they know will take months or years.[52]

These comparisons with European transportation might not be considered unfavorable, but they are glaringly so in the realm of publishing. This is perhaps unexpected given the big head start in printing that China had. Xylographic or woodblock printing was invented there in the ninth century and was not introduced into Europe until the fifteenth. Hundreds of years before Gutenberg, in the mid-eleventh century the Chinese had also invented printing with moveable type. Book publishing was a large commercial industry, and in the Ming dynasty there was no censorship: although books could be banned for political reasons after publication, this was rare until the Qing dynasty in the late eighteenth century. As the Ming economic expansion went on and demand rose, large mills processed

[48] Martin Heijdra, "The Socio-Economic Development of Rural China during the Ming," in *Cambridge History of China*, ed. Twitchett and Mote, vol. VIII, 499–500.

[49] Brook, "Communications and Commerce," 639–642; Brook, *Confusions of Pleasure*, 185–190.

[50] Linsun Cheng, *Banking in Modern China* (Cambridge: Cambridge University Press, 2003), 10ff; email correspondence with Professor Kent Deng of the London School of Economics regarding his unpublished research in the Shanxi bank archives (July 25, 2014).

[51] Brook, "Communications and Commerce," 588–596; Brook, *Confusions of Pleasure*, 173–174.

[52] *The Plum in the Golden Vase, or, Chin P'ing Mei*, vol. I, trans. David Tod Roy (Princeton: Princeton University Press, 1993), passim.

bamboo and cotton fibers into paper, allowing the production of cheap editions – "vulgar and commercial" in the words of a contemporary – for a mass market in law books, examination primers, guides to etiquette, entertainment, and morality, household encyclopedias, almanacs, divination manuals, gazetteers, route books, popular fiction, plays, accounts of foreign customs, and erotica, including regularly updated lists of brothels.[53] But the publication record is far less impressive than in Western Europe, where the number of titles printed in the period 1500–1650 was at least forty times that of China.[54]

Japan's commercial life was more dynamic than China's. Like Northwestern Europe, in the early modern era urbanization was steadily increasing in Japan, whereas the urban population of China remained stagnant at about 4 percent.[55] The population of Japan living in cities was around 15 percent in 1700, with Edo (the future Tokyo) reaching a million inhabitants, probably the largest city in the world, while Osaka and Kyoto were the same size as London or Paris. Consumer shopping in Japan thrived, much as it did in the towns of the Netherlands, England, and France.[56] Among other things, the townsfolk wanted to buy books – or borrow them from the many existing rental libraries. In the seventeenth and eighteenth centuries, there were over a thousand commercial publishing houses in the cities of Japan (although they are hard to count as many folded after only a year in business). The Tokugawa equivalent of our "Yellow Pages" – comprehensive urban directories for the wide variety of products and services available, from artists and teachers to prostitutes and every type of retail and wholesale merchant – were issued in multiple, regularly updated editions. So were popular books like primers of commercial terminology, or manuals of household management, bookkeeping, and business practices.[57]

---

[53] Kai-wing Chow, *Publishing, Culture, and Power in Early Modern China* (Stanford: Stanford University Press, 2004), 20–33, 42–43, 54–59, 252, with quote on 43; Chia, *Printing for Profit*, 6–10, 66, 74–77, 126–146, 149–150, 153, 186, 190–191, 228, 236–238; Brook, "Communications and Commerce," 647–649, 659–664; Brook, *Confusions of Pleasure*, 129–133; Brook, "Censorship in Eighteenth-Century China: A View from the Book Trade," *Canadian Journal of History* (Aug. 1988), 177–196.

[54] Buringh and van Zanden, "Charting the 'Rise of the West,'" 437.

[55] Vries, *Escaping Poverty*, 187–188.

[56] Penelope Francks, *The Japanese Consumer: An Alternative Economic History of Modern Japan* (Cambridge: Cambridge University Press, 2009), chaps. 2–3.

[57] Mary Elizabeth Berry, *Japan in Print: Information and Nation in the Early Modern Period* (Berkeley: University of California Press, 2006); Katsuhisa Moriya, "Urban Networks and Information Networks," in *Tokugawa Japan: The Social and Economic Antecedents of Modern Japan*, ed. Chie Nakane and Shinzaburō Ōishi, trans. Conrad Totman (Tokyo: University of Tokyo Press, 1990), 115–118; Richard Rubinger, *Popular Literacy in Early Modern Japan* (Honolulu: University of Hawaii Press, 2007), 84.

Still, the publishing industries in Japan, like China's, paled beside Western Europe's, where printing and publishing were on an astronomical scale. In the second half of the eighteenth century, per-capita book production in Japan was seven per million, which was more than twice that of China's three per million, but in the Netherlands it was 538, Sweden 219, and Britain 198.[58] These statistics are vital to my argument, since econometric analysis indicates that there was a strong correlation between GDP growth and book production in the early modern era. China (as well as India and Indonesia) saw stagnant or negative economic performance in the nineteenth century, which relates closely to low measures of human capital formation, including publishing activity. The highest levels of growth in GDP per capita occurred in the same period in the United States, Switzerland, Germany, France, and Belgium; that is, only those places where the number of books being produced was also high.[59] Adding to this all the other factors related to information that I adduce below only strengthens the case for a gap between Europe and Asia emerging in this period rather than after the onset of imperialism and industrialization.

Like China and Japan, India in the medieval and early modern eras was also hardly stagnant, but in informational terms already disadvantaged in comparison to the West. Offering proof of the region's economic vitality were the commercial ports of the subcontinent and the robust trade of its merchants in the Indian Ocean; the flexible response of Indian cotton-textile manufacturers to local tastes and European demand; and the deep penetration of money, credit markets, and commerce across the land.[60] As historian Prasannan Parthasarathi argues, just as some European early-industrial technologies diffused among skilled craftsmen who learned and taught about them orally rather than in writing, the same

[58] Joerg Baten and Jan Luiten van Zanden, "Book Production and the Onset of Modern Economic Growth," *Journal of Economic Growth* (Sept. 2008), 230–231. See also Buringh and van Zanden, "Charting the 'Rise of the West,'" 439.
[59] Baten and van Zanden, "Book Production and the Onset of Modern Economic Growth," 217–235.
[60] Simon Digby, "The Maritime Trade of India," in *The Cambridge Economic History of India*, vol. I: *c. 1200–c. 1750*, ed. Tapan Raychaudhuri and Irfan Habib (Cambridge: Cambridge University Press, 1982), 125–159; Janet Abu-Lughod, *Before European Hegemony: The World System A.D. 1250–1350* (NY: Oxford University Press, 1989); Sanjay Subrahmanyam, *The Political Economy of Commerce: Southern India, 1500–1650* (Cambridge: Cambridge University Press, 1990); B. R. Grover, "An Integrated Pattern of Commercial Life in the Rural Society of North India during the Seventeenth and Eighteenth Centuries," *in Money and the Market in India*, ed. Sanjay Subrahmanyam (Delhi: Oxford University Press, 1994), 219–243; Prasannan Parthasarathi and Giorgio Riello, "From India to the World: Cotton and Fashionability," in *The Oxford Handbook of the History of Consumption*, ed. Frank Trentmann (Oxford: Oxford University Press, 2012), 145–170.

was true of India, where literacy was low.[61] Nor did South Asia exist in an information vacuum. In the eighteenth century, Indian states and the East India Company alike commissioned public and private handwritten newsletters, which were often read out loud in local communities.[62]

More to the point, there were no printing presses or newspapers at all in India until the 1820s.[63] And unlike the steady erosion of the monopoly position Latin held in Europe, in early modern India Sanskrit was not replaced by vernacular languages more readable and accessible down the social scale – but without that, popularization of scientific or technological knowledge could not occur. The persistence of Sanskrit in India as a language only accessible to a small elite implies that there was a limit to the ready availability of socially useful information.[64]

One of the greatest and most consequential differences between Western Europe and Asia was in the circulation of news. Beginning in the Song dynasty, the Chinese government from its capital at Kaifeng issued official "capital reports" for circulation. The *Beijing Gazette* announced edicts, memoranda, and news of the emperor, as well as disasters and foreign and military affairs. This circulated among government officials, who would often post information from it for local public consumption. After 1638, the *Beijing Gazette* appeared in printed form to circulate over a wider expanse of the country. From the late sixteenth century onward there were also a few private newspapers, but mostly they plagiarized from the *Beijing Gazette*, or just fabricated stories; as a high-ranking state official alleged in the 1590s, "news bureau entrepreneurs who are out for the miniscule profits" were spreading false information about the military situation on the northern border. An independent press did not come into being in China until the nineteenth century.[65]

---

[61] Parthasarathi, *Why Europe Grew Rich and Asia Did Not*, 203–222.

[62] C. A. Bayly, "Colonial Rule and the 'Informational Order' in South Asia," in *The Transmission of Knowledge in South Asia*, ed. Nigel Crook (Delhi: Oxford University Press, 1996), 298–299 and 280–315 passim.

[63] C. A. Bayly, *Empire and Information: Intelligence Gathering and Social Communication in India, 1780–1870* (Cambridge: Cambridge University Press, 1996), 1–2, 5, 10–55; Francis Robinson, "Islam and the Impact of Print in South Asia," in *The Transmission of Knowledge in South Asia*, ed. Crook, 63, 70.

[64] Sheldon Pollock, "The Languages of Science in Early Modern India," in *Forms of Knowledge in Early Modern Asia*, ed. Sheldon Pollock (Durham, NC: Duke University Press, 2011), 19–48. One can say much the same about Ottoman Turkish before the nineteenth century: see Miri Shefer-Mossensohn, *Science among the Ottomans: The Cultural Creation and Exchange of Knowledge* (Austin: University of Texas Press, 2015), 91ff.

[65] Brook, "Communications and Commerce," 638–639, 645–646; Brook, *Confusions of Pleasure*, 171–172 (quote); Anthony Smith, *The Newspaper: An International History* (London: Thames and Hudson, 1979), 14; email correspondence with Dr. Kent Deng (July 25, 2014).

Newspapers in Japan were of the same order. Palanquin operators distributed single-page gossip sheets involving information about the court, but their content was paper thin.[66] The Tokugawa government circulated one copy of its decrees to villages and required officials to notify villagers and pass it on to the next village.[67] Otherwise, here as in China, political news was simply unavailable, as publication of information about military families and foreign policy (as well as Christianity) was outright forbidden.[68] This prevented merchants from being able to assess opportunities and risks on the same scale as in Europe.

As we have seen, a business press, however rudimentary, had come into existence in early modern Europe and grew more widespread by the year. Its main function initially was to grease the wheels of commerce by providing ready access to prices. In Asia, the business press was nonexistent until the nineteenth century, and digging up price data was far more difficult. Asian merchants did have a sense of prices and took advantage of the possibilities that flowed therefrom: Chinese shipping brokers at every river port exploited their near-exclusive familiarity with the local market to buy, sell, and store goods as needed. They had enough information to practice "time arbitrage" – taking advantage of price fluctuations in silk, salt, cotton, lumber, metals, and foodstuffs to buy when the supply was high and the price low, or vice-versa.[69] Intimate familiarity with prices and market conditions was also evident in seventeenth-century Japan, which, as a commercialized urban society, was the economy that was more similar to that of Northwestern Europe than anywhere else. Japan had banking, wholesale and retail firms, brokerages, and the ability to make large payments by check rather than coin via the private trading and financial institutions called *ryogae-sho*. At the sophisticated Dojima rice market of eighteenth-century Osaka, a fully functional futures exchange existed.[70] There was no national Japanese post office before the Meiji era, but during the Tokugawa shogunate, mail services were similar to those in Renaissance Italy: tens of private courier companies – *hikyaku* – carried

[66] Smith, *The Newspaper*, 14–15.
[67] Tsuneo Satō, "Tokugawa Villages and Agriculture," in *Tokugawa Japan*, ed. Nakane and Ōishi, 61–62.
[68] Berry, *Japan in Print*, 51–53.
[69] Ramon H. Myers, "Some Issues of Economic Organization during the Ming and Ch'ing Periods," *Ch'ing-shih wen-t'i*, vol. III (Dec. 1974), 88–89; Mark Elvin, *The Pattern of the Chinese Past* (Stanford: Stanford University Press, 1973), 144.
[70] Ulrike Schaede, "Forwards and Futures in Tokugawa-Period Japan: A New Perspective on the Dojima Rice Market," *Journal of Banking and Finance*, vol. XIII (1989), 496, 498–499, 503; Yoshiaki Shikano, "Currency, Wage Payments, and Large Funds Settlement in Japan, 1600–1868," in *Wages and Currency: Global Comparisons from Antiquity to the Twentieth Century*, ed. Jan Lucassen (Bern: Peter Lang, 2007), 129–137; Rubinger, *Popular Literacy in Early Modern Japan*, 82ff.

freight, letters, bills of exchange, and cash between Kyoto, Osaka, and Edo along roads designated for the samurai military elite but increasingly used by merchants for trade and information exchange.[71]

Price information circulated in other parts of the non-Western world, too. In medieval Cairo, most private letters from merchants came with an attached list of commodity prices from around the Mediterranean and Middle East.[72] And in eighteenth-century India, grain dealers employed spies and special agents whose seismographic sensitivity to supply, demand, and the prices that resulted from their interplay was such that they knew exactly when to withhold or dump their stocks of grain. Contemporary British officials in charge of purchasing foodstuffs were frustrated at being so completely at the mercy of indigenous merchants, who kept information on the cost of grain close to their breast.[73] Other governments seem to have been more successful at keeping track of prices: it was the job of local Chinese officials during the Ming to record prices at daily and periodic markets to make sure the government was getting a fair deal on its own purchases.[74] In medieval Egypt, official "masters of the market" compiled similar price lists in consultation with local merchants.[75]

But all of this was fairly crude, and comparisons to Western Europe suggest the limits to the potential expansion of economic activity. A good picture of information collection in mid-nineteenth-century British India comes from Rudyard Kipling's novel *Kim* (1901), wherein the protagonist, Kim, and his mentor, the Afghan horse dealer Mahbub Ali, make political and business decisions based on back-breaking effort and serendipitous encounters in towns and market places while trekking across thousands of miles of northern India. It is not that the information was necessarily bad or even imperfect – it can be today too – but it was the arduousness and hence the high cost of acquiring the information that is at issue.[76] Conditions may not have been as daunting in Japan or China or the Middle East, but even there, each merchant had to gather his own price information and news,

---

[71] Charles Andrews, "Nittsū's Company History as a Guide to the Early Modern Origins of Japan's Modern Communications," *Shashi*, I, no. 1 (2012), online at shashi.pitt.edu/ojs/index.php/shashi/article/view/3; Moriya, "Urban Networks and Information Networks," 107–114.

[72] Goitein, *Mediterranean Society*, vol. I, 201.

[73] Kum Kum Banerjee, "Grain Traders and the East India Company: Patna and Its Hinterland in the Late Eighteenth and Early Nineteenth Centuries," in *Merchants, Markets, and the State in Early Modern India*, ed. Sanjay Subrahmanyam (Delhi: Oxford University Press, 1990), 175–176.

[74] Brook, *Confusions of Pleasure*, 67–68.

[75] Goitein, *Mediterranean Society*, vol. I, 218–219.

[76] On the real-life inspiration for the character of Mahbub, see Peter Hopkirk, *Quest for Kim: In Search of Kipling's Great Game* (Ann Arbor: University of Michigan Press, 1996), chap. 3.

essentially reinventing the wheel as he did so. In Europe too that was the case at one time, but no longer following the creation of the business and financial press. That allowed merchants to make decisions with less time, expense, and trouble than their counterparts in Asia could do until the Europeans introduced newspapers into their empires in the nineteenth century.

The most commercially active parts of Asia were, at best, like Western Europe in the Middle Ages, and both were akin to the modern Moroccan bazaar, in which

information is generally poor, scarce, maldistributed, inefficiently communicated and intensely valued ... The level of ignorance about everything from product quality and going prices to market possibilities and production costs is very high, and a great deal of the way in which the bazaar is organized and functions (and within it, the ways its various sorts of participants behave) can be interpreted as either an attempt to reduce such ignorance for someone, increase it for someone, or defend someone against it.[77]

To refer back to the concepts introduced at the beginning of the chapter, Asians were not gaining traction in reducing transaction costs related to communications, transportation, or information acquisition. Europeans were. Or, to be more precise, we should say it was certain Europeans, primarily the Dutch and the English, whose innovations ultimately transformed the entire continent.

Amsterdam and London: "Freshest advices" and the birth of capitalism

The gap between the West and the rest was beginning to open during the Italian Renaissance. It then grew into a gulf of oceanic proportions with the emergence of Holland and England as great economic powers in the succeeding centuries. Here in Northwestern Europe is where the information nexus of capitalism came into its own; and forever after, "the annual markets [and fairs] ... gave way to the ceaseless market places of the cities."[78]

One might think, based on standard conceptions of capitalism, that the reason the English and Dutch were unblocking informational channels and making more rapid strides economically than Asians was because

---

[77] Clifford Geertz, Hildred Geertz, and Lawrence Rosen, *Meaning and Order in Moroccan Society* (Cambridge: Cambridge University Press, 1979), 124–125, 228, 230–231.

[78] McCusker and Gravesteijn, *Beginnings of Commercial and Financial Journalism*, 24. For medieval Bruges as an antecedent to Amsterdam in this respect, see James M. Murray, *Bruges, Cradle of Capitalism, 1280–1390* (Cambridge: Cambridge University Press, 2005), chap. 6 and passim.

European states allowed more space for private enterprise than Asian governments did. But it is more complicated than that. Giving the lie to stereotypes of Asian despotism versus limited European government, taxation was in fact quite low in China, as also in Mughal India, and there was far less intervention in the economy by the central authorities in both of those societies than in Europe, where bureaucracies were relatively large. Compare, for instance, Britain, with 16,000 civil servants in the eighteenth century, the highest per capita in the world, with China's 20,000 in a country with thirty times the population of the United Kingdom (300 million versus 10 million). Perforce, the Asian empires had a far more laissez-faire approach to the economy than England did.[79]

As we noted in Chapter 3, Western thinkers also once saw nothing but stagnation in the Imperial Chinese economy. While it is true that China did not develop anything like the unique financial devices, political

[79] This and the three paragraphs that follow rely on insights gained from reading the following works: Daren Acemoglu, Simon Johnson, and James Robinson, "The Rise of Europe: Atlantic Trade, Institutional Change, and Economic Growth," *American Economic Review* (June 2005), 546–579; Pin-Tsun Chang, "Work Ethics without Capitalism: The Paradox of Chinese Merchant Behavior, c. 1500–1800," in *Maritime Asia*, ed. Karl Anton Sprengard and Roderich Ptak (Wiesbaden: Harrassowitz Verlag, 1994), 66–72; Epstein, *Freedom and Growth*; Gang Deng [Kent G. Deng], *The Premodern Chinese Economy: Structural Equilibrium and Capitalist Sterility* (London: Routledge, 1999), 84, 195–199; Jack A. Goldstone, "Efflorescences and Economic Growth in World History: Rethinking the 'Rise of the West' and the Industrial Revolution," *Journal of World History* (Fall 2002), 339–360; Regina Grafe, *Distant Tyranny: Markets, Power, and Backwardness in Spain, 1650–1800* (Princeton: Princeton University Press, 2012), chap. 1 and passim; F. W. Mote, *Imperial China, 900–1800* (Cambridge, MA: Harvard University Press, 1999), 613–617, 717–722; M. N. Pearson, "Merchants and States," in *Political Economy of Merchant Empires*, ed. Tracy, 52–61 and passim 41–116; Patrick Karl O'Brien, "Fiscal and Financial Preconditions for the Formation of Developmental States in the West and the East from the Conquest of Ceuta (1415) to the Opium War (1839)," *Journal of World History* (Sept. 2012), 526, 528–529, 532–537, 546; Patrick Karl O'Brien, "The Formation of States and Transitions to Modern Economies: England, Europe, and Asia Compared," in *The Cambridge History of Capitalism*, ed. Larry Neal and Jeffrey G. Williamson, vol. I (Cambridge: Cambridge University Press, 2014), 364–380; Sheilagh Ogilvie, *Institutions and European Trade: Merchant Guilds, 1000–1800* (Cambridge: Cambridge University Press, 2011), 175–180; Peter C. Perdue, "What Price Empire? The Industrial Revolution and the Case of China," in *Reconceptualizing the Industrial Revolution*, ed. Jeff Horn, Leonard N. Rosenband, and Merritt Roe Smith (Cambridge, MA: MIT Press, 2010), 312–319; P. H. H. Vries, "Governing Growth: A Comparative Analysis of the Role of the State in the Rise of the West," *Journal of World History* (Spring 2002), 67–138, with the statistics on civil servants on 105; Peer Vries, "Public Finance in China and Britain in the Long Eighteenth Century," Department of Economic History, London School of Economics, Working Paper no. 167/12 (Aug. 2012), online at lse.ac.uk/economicHistory/working Papers/economicHistory/2012.aspx; R. Bin Wong, *China Transformed* (Ithaca, NY: Cornell University Press, 1997), 107, 129–138, 146–148; R. Bin Wong, "The Political Economy of Agrarian Empire and Its Modern Legacy," in *China and Historical Capitalism: Genealogies of Sinological Knowledge*, ed. Timothy Brook and Gregory Blue (Cambridge: Cambridge University Press, 1999), 221–222.

arrangements, or industrial technologies that materialized in early modern England, Chinese living standards were improving in the eighteenth century with the adoption of New World crops, intensified rice cultivation, the spread of a cotton-textile industry, and improved techniques in the production of both silk and ceramics. The country was, therefore, capable of stimulating economic growth. Yet England and then Western Europe industrialized and China did not.

Why were these two regions of the world so different? From the sixteenth century onward, European states were involved in balance-of-power wars on the continent and intense competition for overseas territory in both the Atlantic littoral and the Indian Ocean. These conflicts required far more revenue than any of the Chinese government's undertakings at the same time. In China, the imperial state's deep-seated belief was that political stability depended in part on light taxation. In any case, it faced no extraordinary fiscal challenges on the magnitude of what the European powers did as they ventured overseas and fought war after war with one another. Although large Chinese flotillas had once sailed across Southeast Asia and for a while into the Indian Ocean, the Ming government stopped sponsoring these expeditions after the 1430s due to the cost and a focus on domestic affairs and its unstable northern border. This policy left the maritime trade in Asian waters either to individual Chinese traders and peddlers plying the coasts on junks and sampans, or to European charter companies backed by strong mercantilist states engaged in intense competition among themselves.

As befit the Chinese emperors' conception of their realm as an agrarian empire, there was much less interest in merchants and their activities than in Western Europe. Dating to the Middle Ages, European monarchs had formed alliances with towns and the wealthy merchants who dominated them in joint opposition to locally entrenched feudal aristocracies which embodied the "jurisdictional fragmentation" and "multiple sovereignty" that were the legacies of early-medieval political upheaval.[80] Unlike their Chinese counterparts, European merchants over centuries developed a cohesive corporate sense and an institutionalized voice. This prepared the way for the early modern financial revolution in the Dutch Republic and the United Kingdom. Convening in parliaments and other corporate bodies, merchants worked with the English and Dutch governments to engage in experimental financing of military operations and overseas business ventures that created new kinds of capital markets.

---

[80] Epstein, *Freedom and Growth*, 30–31, 36–37, 170, 173–174.

As the Italian states succumbed to constant foreign military intervention in the sixteenth century, the Dutch Republic and England consolidated their strengths. With growing empires, a substantial export and re-export trade, booming home manufacturing, and the resulting capital accumulation, the Dutch Republic became the dominant economic power of Europe in the seventeenth century and England in the eighteenth. Each one overcame internal conflict – the Dutch war of independence against Spain (1568–1648), and in England the civil war and Glorious Revolution (1642–1651; 1688) – and benefited furthermore from the financial institutions that were born primarily as a result of wars with the French in the seventeenth and eighteenth centuries.

The financial revolution was launched in Amsterdam and eagerly adapted in London, especially when the stadholder of Holland, William of Orange, became King William III of England in 1688. It involved the establishment of a de facto national bank and autonomous securities markets buttressed by a free business press. These were conceived with some inspiration from northern Italian, Flemish, French, and German antecedents, as most European treasuries had had greater or lesser degrees of reliance on private finance prior to this. In truth, William was reluctant to subordinate his powers to merchant investors. But he was desperate for military financing to counter the aggressions of Louis XIV and ultimately saw that he had no choice but to tap private capital markets to cover the costs of warfare.[81] This was a departure from the routine fiscal methods favored by European monarchies, which normally involved coercing contributions from the wealthy or imposing crippling taxation on the poor.[82] The financial revolution availed the Dutch and English governments of a level of cash flow which rival states could not match.

Besides giving advantages that led to victory on the battlefield, these advances helped the economy to grow and develop. The broad and

---

[81] Anne L. Murphy, *The Origins of English Financial Markets: Investment and Speculation before the South Sea Bubble* (Cambridge: Cambridge University Press, 2009), 4, 14–15ff, 43–48ff; Marjolein 't Hart, "'The Devil or the Dutch': Holland's Impact on the Financial Revolution in England, 1643–1694," *Parliaments, Estates, and Representation* (June 1991), 39–52.

[82] Larry Neal, "How It All Began: The Monetary and Financial Architecture of Europe during the First Global Capital Markets, 1648–1815," *Financial History Review* (October 2000), 118; Paul J. Miranti, "Stock Markets," in *Oxford Encyclopedia of Economic History*, ed. Mokyr, vol. V, 23. James Macdonald, *A Free Nation Deep in Debt: The Financial Roots of Democracy* (NY: Farrar, Straus, and Giroux, 2003), attributes the development of responsive and open democratic governments in the modern world to government debt financing through the capital markets, as opposed to the popular view that it was the other way around, where free political institutions allowed for the rise of capitalist institutions.

complex financial markets that then emerged sustained the English Industrial Revolution. Nearly all firms, from artisans on up, tapped into the capital markets for short-term liquidity and long-term investment capital. Large and small financing set off the "wave of inventions, innovations, and adaptations in all sectors of the economy (agriculture, transport, manufacture, trade, and finance) in hard technology as well as organization, which contributed substantially to total economic growth" and swept over Holland, England, and eventually much of the rest of Western Europe.[83]

Emphatically, the financial, consumer, and industrial revolutions could not have occurred in Northwestern Europe as they did without the information nexus: for the new financial infrastructure to function properly, it was vital that information about capital markets and business opportunities flow as freely as possible. The financial and industrial revolutions in Holland and Britain were manifestations of the birth of capitalism, which correlates to the information nexus connecting businessmen, inventors, craftsmen, consumers, financiers, and governments.[84] Scholars have established that higher productivity in the Dutch and English economies was the outcome of both the abundance of new sources and methods of finance and the stepped-up ability of merchants to distribute their goods to consumers. Economic growth depended as much on the information-digesting and information-generating services sector as it did on industrial production (and, as Chapter 5 will show, information was the *sine qua non* of all industrial

---

[83] See Peer Vries, "Challenges, (Non)-Responses, and Politics," *Journal of World History* (Sept. 2012), 648 (quote), 652; Wright, *The Wealth of Nations Rediscovered*, chap. 8; Larry Neal, "The Finance of Business during the Industrial Revolution," in *The Economic History of Britain since 1700*, vol. I: *1700–1860*, ed. Roderick Floud and Deirdre McCloskey, 2nd ed. (Cambridge: Cambridge University Press, 1994), 151–181; M. J. Daunton, *Progress and Poverty: An Economic and Social History of Britain, 1700–1850* (Oxford: Oxford University Press, 1995), chap. 9; Stephen Quinn, "Money, Finance, and Capital Markets," in *The Cambridge Economic History of Modern Britain*, vol. I: *Industrialisation, 1700–1860*, ed. Roderick Floud and Paul Johnson (Cambridge: Cambridge University Press, 2004), 147–174. My point should not be negated by the fact that the Netherlands itself was slow to industrialize. Into the nineteenth century "its financial institutions still dominated European capital," it "remained amongst the leading economic nations of the world," and its "prosperity was intimately related to the economic fortunes of its neighbors": respective quotes by A. T. van Deursen, "The Dutch Republic, 1588–1780," in *History of the Low Countries*, ed. J. C. H. Blom and E. Lamberts, trans. James C. Kennedy (NY: Berghahn Books, 1999), 211, and Michael Wintle, *An Economic and Social History of the Netherlands, 1800–1920* (Cambridge: Cambridge University Press, 2000), 72, 245; and see 238–247, where the author argues that Dutch economic choices resulted in part from considerations of comparative advantage.

[84] This is in alignment with the thesis of Jacob, *First Knowledge Economy*.

firms). This was a huge difference with India or China or Japan, where none of the above was occurring.[85]

What the Dutch and British authorities did was remarkable, if unintended and in their own self-interest: winning wars and competing for market share on the high seas, not concern for private property rights or individual freedom, led them to place their trust in the free market and allow for a financial press. This required them to give up a certain amount of control and subject themselves to the scrutiny of independent investors. But their governments became stronger in consequence. France might have been a major contender, too, but as we will see the Bourbon monarchy rejected the methods and policies associated with the financial revolution and instinctively dammed up the flow of information that powered the Dutch and English economies.

Before returning to the information nexus that made it all possible, I will survey the key institutions of the financial revolution. The Bank of Amsterdam (Wisselbank van Amsterdam) was founded by the city council in 1609 as a convenience to business. The bank combined for the first time in one institution the full range of banking transactions, many of them borrowed from Italian and Flemish antecedents: municipal deposit, transfer, and multilateral clearing. It licensed money changers and reduced the reliance of merchants on cash by honoring all bills of exchange and monitoring those Dutchmen and foreigners who were dependent on them. With its requirement of full reserves and assertion of a legal monopoly over large-value payments in the city, it eliminated the circulation of debased coins and produced a stable money of account, the bank guilder. It did not issue convertible banknotes – i.e., paper money – which only entered usage in England in the next century, although its receipts for cash deposits became a reliable medium of exchange. Nonetheless, the creation of this proto-central bank produced a single, integrated financial system in Holland that accelerated the free movement of capital, stabilized interest rates, and made Amsterdam the international money market for all Europe in the seventeenth and eighteenth centuries, until London, expanding on Dutch techniques, replaced

---

[85] Stephen Broadberry and Bishnupriya Gupta, "The Early Modern Great Divergence: Wages, Prices, and Economic Development in Europe and Asia, 1500–1800," *Economic History Review*, LIX, no. 1 (2006), 10 and passim; and see 16, 22, 25, for a critique of the view put forth by Prasannan Parthasarathi and others that Indian economic productivity was equal to Western Europe's before the Industrial Revolution. According to Indrajit Ray, *Bengal Industries and the British Industrial Revolution (1757–1857)* (London: Routledge, 2011), 253–254, in the early industrial era Indian manufacturers failed to take advantage of export opportunities precisely because they were not knowledgeable enough about foreign markets (although discriminatory measures taken against them by the English government and East India Company were also part of the problem).

it. In these ways the Bank of Amsterdam contributed enormously to the commercial expansion of early modern Europe.[86]

Dutch officials provided for their fellow merchants with other developments that also shaped the course of modern economic history. Following the example of nearby Antwerp, the city of Amsterdam planned its Bourse or Exchange in 1607–1608 to bring together in one building commodity, financial, and insurance transactions. It opened for business in 1611. Commodities dealing and speculation were by that time already well advanced in the Netherlands and only grew more intense with the coming of the bourse. Before it opened, the most common commodities were Baltic grain, herring, pepper, coffee, cacao, saltpeter, brandy, whale oil, whale bone, and tulip bulbs; by 1640, over 350 additional commodities were being traded, and within a few decades the number nearly doubled.[87]

Many of these products involved futures contracts, and in this respect Holland long remained more sophisticated than England, where Parliament tried throughout the eighteenth century to combat futures trading as immoral and unnatural speculation. British legislators failed to see that it was a convenient way for producers of commodities to hedge their risks and gain some kind of protection from the vagaries of nature and the market. The Dutch had qualms about it, too, since it sometimes smacked of heavy-duty gambling, but they understood its beneficial aspects, allowed it, and tried to regulate it.

The Amsterdam Bourse also saw trading in corporate shares, although mainly of the Dutch East India Company (VOC), or its Caribbean equivalent, the West India Company. Subscribers could not demand back their capital in these companies, but were able to retrieve their investment by selling shares to a third party; this liquidity attracted investors seeking to adjust their portfolios. Dutch capitalists at the bourse

[86] The entire section on the Netherlands relies on the following sources: Neal, "How It All Began," 121–123; Larry Neal, "The Monetary, Financial, and Political Architecture of Europe, 1648–1815," in *Exceptionalism and Industrialisation*, ed. Leandro Prados de la Escosura (Cambridge: Cambridge University Press, 2004), 176–178; Herman Van der Wee, "European Banking in the Middle Ages and Early Modern Times," in *A History of European Banking*, ed. H. Van der Wee and G. Kurgan-van Hentenryk, 2nd ed. (Antwerp: Mercatorfonds, 2000), 212, 226–227; Jan de Vries and Ad van der Woude, *The First Modern Economy: Success, Failure, and Perseverance of the Dutch Economy, 1500–1815* (Cambridge: Cambridge University Press, 1997), 113–117, 140; Stephen Quinn and William Roberds, "The Big Problem of Large Bills: The Bank of Amsterdam and the Origins of Central Banking," *Federal Reserve Bank of Atlanta: Working Paper Series*, Working Paper 2005–16 (August 2005).

[87] Jonathan I. Israel, *Dutch Primacy in World Trade, 1585–1740* (Oxford: Oxford University Press, 1989), 74ff; Oscar Gelderblom, *Cities of Commerce: The Institutional Foundations of International Trade in the Low Countries, 1250–1650* (Princeton: Princeton University Press, 2013), chap. 3.

developed all manner of risk-reducing and speculative activity involving those shares, among them hedging, options trading, and purchases on margin, which laid the foundations for the practices of all financial markets to come. Here were the first European derivatives market and the first secondary market for corporate stock (albeit largely in one company). To give an indication of the amount of trading being done, within a year of the bourse's opening, 360 officially registered brokerage houses were in business, and over 700 solo freelancers buzzed around the city's coffee houses hawking equities, commodities, and real estate, in addition to loans and insurance.[88]

Although emulation of Dutch methods seems to have been in the works earlier, many elements came to London from Amsterdam when William III brought Dutch financiers with him to England in 1688. Only when the London Stock Exchange was organized in 1693 could anonymous investors trade shares in English joint-stock companies. But the English monarchy soon surpassed Holland in its fiscal inventiveness.[89]

In London, no single bank served as a centralized clearinghouse for international bills of exchange the way the Bank of Amsterdam did. The English financial system involved many players and was decentralized and self-monitoring: bankers adhered to mercantile law and upheld the integrity of commerce by sharing news of defaulting merchants. The Bank of London (later called the Bank of England) was founded in 1694 not to replace this system, but to issue banknotes and loan its capital to the crown to finance the nation's wars with France under King Louis XIV. Shares of the bank – as well as shares in the East India Company and the more recently formed South Sea Company – could be bought and sold on the stock exchange. The three corporations owned the bulk of the sovereign debt, which they paid off by selling their stock to investors. This arrangement created a transferable public debt that allowed for the continuous refinancing of government operations through the free market. Since the Bank of London held only fractional reserves instead of 100 percent as in Amsterdam, the specie in the bank could be circulated as loan

---

[88] Marjolein 't Hart, Joost Jonker, and Jan Luiten van Zanden, *A Financial History of the Netherlands* (Cambridge: Cambridge University Press, 1997), 53–54; de Vries and van der Woude, *First Modern Economy*, 150–152; Larry Neal, *The Rise of Financial Capitalism: International Capital Markets in the Age of Reason* (Cambridge: Cambridge University Press, 1990), 45; Oscar Gelderblom and Joost Jonker, "Completing a Financial Revolution: The Finance of the Dutch East India Trade," *Journal of Economic History* (Sept. 2004), 641–672.

[89] Larry Neal, "Venture Shares of the Dutch East India Company," in *Origins of Value*, ed. Goetzmann and Rouwenhorst, 165–175; Oscar Gelderblom and Joost Jonker, "Amsterdam as the Cradle of Modern Futures and Options Trading, 1550–1650," in *Origins of Value*, ed. Goetzmann and Rouwenhorst, 189–205.

capital for an even greater revenue source. For the time being, no other nation had the financial reserves that were at the disposal of the English state and its military.[90]

Buying and selling of shares grew briskly – not only in government debt but also in the increasing number of English joint-stock companies: fifteen in 1685; 100 ten years later. It happened not because there was such faith in the government's "credible commitment" to pay on its debts. Rather, it was because there was already a lot of liquidity in the form of an active shares market, as well as plentiful information about and for customers of financial services. The shares market then called forth more such information.[91] The stock market licensed traders and issued regular price lists, but at first all activity continued to take place in the coffee houses of Exchange Alley near the Bank of England. It is no coincidence that the new financial markets located themselves in the publishing district, the "IT" center of early modern London, where vendors sold books, business news-papers, and business stationery, and where every pillar was pasted over with an untidy pastiche of advertisements and notices.[92]

These revolutionary innovations in Holland and England were obviously not conjured out of thin air, but could only be conceived in societies that were prepared for them. They were grounded in a whole series of extraordinary developments in information transmission without parallel in any other European society at the time, let alone Asia. In the words of Dutch scholar Clé Lesger, Amsterdam became the economic power it did because it was an unequaled "center of information exchange."[93] This gave its merchants and their companies a huge advan-tage over other nations – and we can say the same thing about London in

[90] E. Victor Morgan and W. A. Thomas, *The Stock Exchange: Its History and Functions* (London: Elek Books, 1962), 20–22; Ranald C. Michie, *The London Stock Exchange: A History* (Oxford: Oxford University Press, 1999), online version, 18; Neal, "How It All Began," 64–65; Larry Neal, "On the Historical Development of Stock Markets," in *The Emergence and Evolution of Markets*, ed. Horst Brezinski and Michael Fritsch (Cheltenham: Edward Elgar, 1997), 64–65, 71–73; Neal, *Rise of Financial Capitalism*, 47ff; Stephen Quinn, "Securitization of Sovereign Debt: Corporations as a Sovereign Debt Restructuring Mechanism in Britain, 1694 to 1750," *Social Science Research Network* (March 2008), online at http://ssrn.com/abstract=991941; Larry Neal and Stephen Quinn, "Markets and Institutions in the Rise of London as a Financial Center in the Seventeenth Century," in *Finance, Intermediaries, and Economic Development*, ed. Stanley L. Engerman et al. (Cambridge: Cambridge University Press, 2003), 13–18, 31–33. On the northern Italian origins of the market in government debt in the Middle Ages, see Luciano Pezzolo, "The Via Italiana to Capitalism," in *Cambridge History of Capitalism*, ed. Neal and Williamson, vol. I, 296–304.
[91] Murphy, *Origins of English Financial Markets*, chaps. 1 and 6 passim.
[92] Natasha Glaisyer, *The Culture of Commerce in England, 1660–1720* (Woodbridge: Boydell Press, 2006), 32–34.
[93] Clé Lesger, *The Rise of the Amsterdam Market and Information Exchange*, trans. J. C. Grayson (Aldershot: Ashgate, 2006), 10, 183.

the next century. There was simply nothing like it anywhere else in the world.

Until the invention of the telegraph, communications began – or ended – with transportation. In the late eighteenth century, Simon Vorontsov, Catherine the Great's ambassador to London, remarked on the relationship between the speed of travel in England and its rising prosperity.[94] Prior to 1715, pack horses carrying heavy loads of freight along wet English roads left them a rutted and muddy wreck. In the decades thereafter, high demand by distributors and newly founded stagecoach services for passengers required improvements to roads as well as canals. By mid-century, well-maintained turnpikes connected London to the major cities of the country and were lined with inns and coach services. Bridges replaced fords and ferries. Roadwork was common throughout Western Europe in the eighteenth century, but after passage of the General Turnpike Act of 1773, the English turnpike trusts, run by local elites, leased out the rights to toll collection, yielding economic benefits to the locales where they existed and making British roads perhaps the best on earth. On the surface this may have seemed to be a nod to private enterprise and the profit motive, but like the financial markets it reflects the power of the English government, which gave the trusts the right to charge tolls. This was the beginning of what Joanna Guldi calls the "infrastructure state," an invention of the British government which in the century 1750–1850 oversaw construction of a national network of highways and railroads that encouraged economic and political interactions across the land. Elsewhere in Europe, for instance in Spain, the crown could never run roughshod over entrenched local interests the way the British administration could, even when it would have been economically beneficial. Roads were not as good as a result. And merchants outside of England continued to travel with their own merchandise, rather than entrusting them to haulage firms, a type of service unknown even in France until the nineteenth century. All in all, between 1700 and 1800, travel time in England was cut in half and traffic multiplied, "suck[ing] the dark corners of the land into the hectic economy of exchange and consumption."[95]

[94] Fernand Braudel, *Civilization and Capitalism*, vol. II, *The Wheels of Commerce*, trans. Siân Reynolds (NY: Harper and Row, 1982), 349.

[95] Joanna Guldi, *Roads to Power: Britain Invents the Infrastructure State* (Cambridge, MA: Harvard University Press, 2012); Roy Porter, *English Society in the Eighteenth Century*, rev. ed. (London: Penguin, 1990), 191–192 (second quote); see also Philip L. Cottrell, "London as a Centre of Communications," in *Kommunikationsrevolutionen*, ed. North, 168–174; T. C. W. Blanning, *The Culture of Power and the Power of Culture: Old Regime Europe, 1660–1789* (Oxford: Oxford University Press, 2002), 127–129; Douglas W. Allen, *The Institutional Revolution: Measurement and the Economic Emergence of the*

The same can be said of Holland in the previous century or even earlier. Canals crisscrossed the watery nation to link the smallest of villages and the largest of towns. People and goods moved around and intermingled as nowhere else.[96] Private firms provided regular commercial transport: as a seventeenth-century Dutchman was proud to announce, "we have here [in Amsterdam] some very rich and prosperous people called *Expediteurs* [dispatchers] whom the merchants have only to ask whenever they have some merchandise to send overland. These dispatchers have carters and carriers in their service who work only for them."[97]

By the early seventeenth century, Holland also had a mail service to every one of its towns. Here, as in England, the rationale for this was to aid business in its quest for information. As a later head of the British Post Office stated, "the principle of the Post-office at its establishment . . . was to afford advantage to trade and commerce." By the 1760s, all the big cities of England had daily letter delivery to and from London and each other. Mail boats traveled twice a week between London and Amsterdam, propelled by demand for financial news: for merchants this drastically cut transaction costs involved with information seeking.[98]

Postal services extended globally and gave the Dutch and English unrivalled access to worlds beyond the oceans. The Dutch East India Company functioned as an international post office for its own and general Dutch business interests overseas.

By maritime or caravan routes, by ship, horse, or camel, the VOC sought out and received information on European consumer demand so that it could make price adjustments at its Indian and Indonesian spice factories. The company that was turning the continent-wide Indonesian archipelago into a Dutch-ruled territory relied on a preexisting intelligence network that involved Armenians, Jews, and other indigenous agents and contacts stretching from the Middle East to the Moluccas. Given the uncertainties of this system, the VOC sent messages in multiple routes and multiple copies, often on special VOC courier ships. The information, however it got to Amsterdam, was then processed

Modern World (Chicago: University of Chicago Press, 2012), 178–184; Grafe, *Distant Tyranny*, 211–212.

[96] Bernard Hendrik Slicher van Bath, "The Economic Situation in the Dutch Republic during the Seventeenth Century," in *Dutch Capitalism and World Capitalism*, ed. Maurice Aymard (Cambridge: Cambridge University Press, 1982), 29–30.

[97] Braudel, *Civilization and Capitalism*, vol. II, 357.

[98] Lesger, *Rise of the Amsterdam Market*, 238–239; McCusker, "Information and Transaction Costs in Early Modern Europe," 81 (post office quote); Blanning, *Culture of Power*, 131; Woodruff D. Smith, "The Function of Commercial Centers in the Modernization of European Capitalism: Amsterdam as an Information Exchange in the Seventeenth Century," *Journal of Economic History* (Dec. 1984), 991ff; Pettegree, *Invention of News*, 243.

by a growing number of clerks and retained in systematically organized files for short-term and long-term prediction of market activities.[99]

But it was slow, with one-way communication between Holland and the Spice Islands taking half a year at the fastest speed, and the VOC was constrained by its control-freak insistence that all goods and information sent to and from Asia had to go through Batavia, its capital on Java. This rigidity was absent among the British, who were able to monopolize information-gathering from India and shove the Dutch aside in South Asia.[100] Even more successfully than the VOC, the English East India Company used the data it so assiduously collected to forecast supply and demand, with subcommittees of its Court of Directors engaging in constant analysis of overseas dispatches and accounting records.[101]

If but a few large state-sponsored charter companies engaged in this kind of information sifting, it might not be noteworthy, but it was deemed essential for all levels of Dutch and British business. In Amsterdam, information was collected, compiled, analyzed, and disseminated with the seemingly ceaseless motion of an anthill. Thousands of seamen and shipmasters reported overseas news to merchants, which was supplemented by contact with spies and other Dutchmen living abroad. This was not just commercial information: as a seventeenth-century German resident of Amsterdam put it, "yes, [at the Amsterdam Bourse] one finds out the state of all the kingdoms and countries of the whole world, as well as whatever remarkable occurs in the same." The intelligence-gathering efforts of most European states centered on the Dutch capital, which hosted the largest number of foreign agents on the continent. The English East India Company itself posted a correspondent there specifically to collect information about its own Asian interests.[102]

Obtaining information about the world at large became a national passion, and in this period the Dutch and the British expanded their horizons internationally. Hundreds of people were involved in amassing

---

[99] René J. Barendse, "The Long Road to Livorno: The Overland Messenger Services of the Dutch East India Company in the Seventeenth Century," *Itinerario*, no. 2 (1988), 24–43; Om Prakash, "Commercial Communication and Monetary Integration in Early Modern India," in *From Commercial Communication to Commercial Integration*, ed. Markus A. Denzel (Stuttgart: Franz Steiner Verlag, 2004), 159–165; Smith, "Function of Commercial Centers," 1000–1003.

[100] Prakash, "Commercial Communication and Monetary Integration in Early Modern India," 162–163.

[101] K. N. Chaudhuri, *The Trading World of Asia and the East India Company, 1660–1760* (Cambridge: Cambridge University Press, 1978), 30–31, 74–78, 80, 135, 229, 303–304, 413–414, 436ff, 463–467.

[102] Lesger, *Rise of the Amsterdam Market*, 224 (quote), and chap. 6 passim; Smith, "Function of Commercial Centers," 987, 996.

and analyzing material objects acquired in commercial ventures. The Dutch, for instance, embarked on a project of cataloguing medicines from around the globe – the East and West Indies, Brazil, or wherever their ships landed. In science as in business, information collection, sorting, and categorizing were colossal enterprises undertaken by Europeans. Compare Asia once again: Japanese scholars (and one assumes scholars from elsewhere, too) were indeed very interested in European medicines, but they could not travel overseas; it was the Dutch who brought this knowledge to them, for it was the Dutch who had the global capability and the global perspective. In Japan and the rest of Asia, merchants had a lower social status than their peers in Western Europe; in Holland and England (as also in Spain, Portugal, and France), merchants were actively supported by mercantilist governments and created a globalized economy. Scientists followed in their wake. All of them brought news and knowledge of the wider world back home. Most Asians of that era could not even dream of doing anything similar.[103]

Due in part to the actions of the English monarchy, by the 1730s London was supplanting Amsterdam as the center of the information nexus. To oversee rapidly expanding British mercantile activity at home and abroad, in 1696 William III set up a permanent Board of Trade and an Inspector General of Imports and Exports. He also required all British consuls to assemble commercial data for submission to London. This was an early example of the quantitative approach to national economic analysis, or what was then called "political arithmetic." The purpose was to help the treasury to improve understanding of its tax base and administer the national economy, and it was the first time that a government made such an effort to gather regular trade statistics. But its repercussions were all the greater because of the way it used the information.[104] In the eighteenth century, German bureaucrats

[103] Harold J. Cook, *Matters of Exchange: Commerce, Medicine, and Science in the Dutch Golden Age* (New Haven: Yale University Press, 2007), chaps. 1, 5, 8–9. In this the other Europeans were following in the footsteps of the Spanish and Portuguese: see Hugh Glenn Cagle, "The Botany of Colonial Medicine: Gender, Authority, and Natural History in the Empires of Spain and Portugal," in *Women of the Iberian Atlantic*, ed. Sarah E. Owens and Jane E. Mangan (Baton Rouge: Louisiana State University, 2012), 174–195. See also Jeremy Black, *The Power of Knowledge: How Information and Technology Made the Modern World* (New Haven: Yale University Press, 2014), chaps. 2–3, 6.

[104] David Ormrod, "Northern Europe and the Expanding World Economy: The Transformation of Commercial Organisation, 1500–1800," in *Prodotti e tecniche d'Oltremare nelle economie europee secc. XIII–XVIII*, ed. Simonetta Cavaciocchi (Florence: Le Monnier, 1998), 689–691; John Brewer, *The Sinews of Power: War, Money, and the English State, 1688–1783* (NY: Knopf, 1989), chap. 8; Daniel T. Headrick, *When Information Came of Age: Technologies of Knowledge in the Age of Reason and Revolution, 1700–1850* (Oxford: Oxford University Press, 2000), chap. 3.

coined the word "statistic," which meant "knowledge of the state," with the implication that this was confidential information about the resources of the land that the ruler could exploit for his own purposes.[105] The English government, unlike any other central state, shared the statistics it collected with the general public.[106] It did so through the publication of parliamentary records and by allowing lobbyists for mercantile or industrial groups to make requests of government departments for copies of their statistical records.[107]

While England might have been the first to attempt such massive information collection, better record keeping was on the agenda for most government bureaucracies in Europe as they sought to become more effective servitors of their respective regimes. What was unique about England, though, was the pressure Parliament, special-interest groups, and the society at large were able to bring to bear on the monarchy to make information open access. As early as the sixteenth century, all customs documents were considered public records in England. With the power sharing between parliament and monarchy that was a condition of William III's accession to the throne, the principle was destined to be extended further.[108] In a similar spirit, censorship policies were lightweight in Holland and England by the late seventeenth century, not so much out of dedication to the principle of free speech as in capitulation to the impossibility of policing such a rapidly expanding newspaper and publishing industry; moreover, both governments relied on information generated in the press. In both places, censorship had largely disappeared except for restrictions provided by sedition, libel, and blasphemy laws.[109]

---

[105] Keith Tribe, *Governing Economy: The Reformation of German Economic Discourse* (Cambridge: Cambridge University Press, 1988), 8, 33. For the French experience, see Henry C. Clark, *Compass of Society: Commerce and Absolutism in Old-Regime France* (Lanham: Lexington Books, 2007), 196–201.

[106] The only previous instance that I am aware of was the practice of early modern Dutch municipal governments, which also shared with the public the business information they had commissioned or collected: see Ogilvie, *Institutions and European Trade*, 382–383.

[107] Brewer, *Sinews of Power*, 244ff.

[108] Brewer, *Sinews of Power*, chap. 8; John J. McCusker, *European Bills of Entry and Marine Lists: Early Commercial Publications and the Origins of the Business Press* (Cambridge, MA: Harvard University Library, 1985), 15ff; Ogilvie, *Institutions and European Trade*, 422–423.

[109] Otto Lankhorst, "Newspapers in the Netherlands in the Seventeenth Century," in *The Politics of Information in Early Modern Europe*, ed. Brendan Dooley and Sabrina A. Baron (London: Routledge, 2001), 153–156; Larry Neal, "The Business Press," and Arend H. Huussen, Jr., "Censorship in the Netherlands," both in *The Age of William III and Mary II*, ed. Robert P. Maccubbin and Martha Hamilton-Phillips (Williamsburg: College of William and Mary, 1989), 145–149 and 347–351, respectively; C. G. Gibbs, "Government and the English Press, 1695 to the Middle of the Eighteenth Century," in *Too Mighty to Be Free: Censorship and the Press in Britain and the Netherlands*, ed. A. C. Duke and C. A. Tamse (Zutphen: De Walburg Pers, 1987), 87–106.

These policies had a marked impact because so many people were active in the pursuit of knowledge. Literacy rates were climbing. A large reading public existed in Holland during the seventeenth century, with every level of society down to artisans and peasants showing an interest in books about national and international affairs.[110] By the eighteenth century, almost all English males in the middle and upper classes were literate and about half in the lower classes; across the board it was 40 percent of women. In London the rate was higher, reaching 90 percent for men and 70 percent for women.[111] Dutch universities allowed non-students to audit courses, and at least in mathematics, the general public did so in large numbers.[112] In England, too, there was a large demand for public lecturers and mathematicians, all to help advise and analyze the financial markets.[113]

Aside from universities and royal academies, institutions whose mission was to encourage research and invention proliferated. In Britain, most famously, the Royal Society for the Improvement of Natural Knowledge (1662), the Society of Arts (1754), the Royal Institution (1799), and the Mechanics Institute (1804) all offered public lectures and prizes. New ideas with the potential to generate a profit received financial backing from venture-capital banks, of which there were 370 in Britain by 1800. In both the Dutch Republic and the United Kingdom, merchants, artisans, farmers, and mechanics interacted in these nations that encouraged open science. Dutch scholar Jan Luiten van Zanden argues that the "birth of a European knowledge economy" took place as northwestern European societies lessened the gap between common skilled workmen and educated elites in the centuries between 1400 and 1800. These developments had no equivalent in any other part of the world.[114]

---

[110] A. T. van Deursen, *Plain Lives in a Golden Age: Popular Culture, Religion, and Society in Seventeenth-Century Holland*, trans. Maarten Ultee (Cambridge: Cambridge University Press, 1991), 140ff.

[111] Porter, *English Society in the Eighteenth Century*, 167, 221, 233; Blanning, *Culture of Power*, 113.

[112] Karel Davids, "Amsterdam as a Centre of Learning in the Dutch Golden Age," in *Urban Achievement in Early Modern Europe*, ed. Patrick O'Brien et al. (Cambridge: Cambridge University Press, 2001), 314ff.

[113] Murphy, *Origins of English Financial Markets*, 110.

[114] Jan Luiten van Zanden, *The Long Road to the Industrial Revolution: The European Economy in a Global Perspective, 1000–1800* (Leiden: Brill, 2009), pt. III. For further evidence in support of this argument, see Joel Mokyr, "The Institutional Origins of the Industrial Revolution," in *Institutions and Economic Performance*, ed. Elhanan Helpman (Cambridge, MA: Harvard University Press, 2008), 70–71, 81–82, and Jacob, *First Knowledge Economy*. Jonathan Lyons, *The Society for Useful Knowledge: How Benjamin Franklin and Friends Brought the Enlightenment to America* (NY: Bloomsbury, 2013),

Mounting literacy and popular demand for reading materials supported a large publishing industry that could grow without fear of government repression. Seventeenth-century Amsterdam has been called the "intellectual entrepôt of Europe." By the 1660s, over 780 publishing houses were in business in the Dutch Republic (a century earlier there were over a hundred), and forty presses in Amsterdam alone issued multilingual editions of every sort of book, with the number of Dutch-language titles in this period estimated at 100,000. Those who could not afford to buy them could go to the Amsterdam City Library, which first opened its doors to the public in the late sixteenth century. Books prohibited in other countries were published in Holland and smuggled abroad. And throughout the continent Dutch maps, atlases, and sea charts brought a high price. Their accuracy was renowned as cartographers, the best known of whom was Willem Jansz Blaeu, plied the wharves talking to ship pilots and reading their logbooks to add new detail and correct errors.[115]

Publishing also grew apace in eighteenth-century England. Printers and booksellers operated in every town, and hundreds of circulating libraries opened. As early as 1600, 6,000 titles had been published; by the 1790s the number was in the 50,000 range.[116] Among the largest categories were publications aimed at merchants: bookkeeping manuals, best business practices, compilations of commercial law, and books about the world. Dutch books in this field inspired similar kinds of works in England, including the oldest volume in the English language on the retail trade, William Scott's *Essay of Drapery* (1635), and a series of business self-help books that one can easily envision on the best-seller list today: *A Way to Get Wealth* (1625), *The Pleasant Art of Money Catching* (1684), and *Every Man His Own Broker* (1761).[117] This was also the age that saw the birth of the scholarly scientific journal,

---

chap. 4 and passim, shows it was in the same spirit that Benjamin Franklin and his contemporaries founded like institutions in the early United States.

[115] Paul Hoftijzer, "Metropolis of Print: The Amsterdam Book Trade in the Seventeenth Century," in *Urban Achievement in Early Modern Europe*, ed. O'Brien et al., 249–263 (with quote on 249); de Vries and van der Woude, *The First Modern Economy*, 315, 318; Violet Barbour, *Capitalism in Amsterdam in the Seventeenth Century* (Ann Arbor: University of Michigan Press, 1963), 65; Lesger, *Rise of the Amsterdam Market*, 216, 227–231.

[116] Porter, *English Society in the Eighteenth Century*, 234–236, 239–240; Blanning, *Culture of Power*, 137.

[117] Arthur H. Cole, *The Historical Development of Economic and Business Literature* (Boston: Baker Library, Harvard Graduate School of Business Administration, 1957), 3, 6–11; J. Roger Mace, "Finance," in *Age of William III and Mary II*, ed. Maccubbin and Hamilton-Phillips, 140.

which in England had a surprisingly broad popular readership.[118] It was a rich cross-fertilization: Roger Bacon and other progenitors of the Scientific Revolution borrowed from the methodology of merchants, whose printed handbooks amalgamated information collected from the natural world and applied inductive reasoning to assess it.[119]

The most transformative, influential, and democratizing information device was the newspaper, however. This, too, had no counterparts in the early modern world outside of Western Europe, and it was freest in Holland and England. Without the business press there could be no experiments in finance of the sort that were renovating the economies of those two nations. Why did a business press not appear in China or Japan, where print culture was so deeply rooted? Censorship was fairly light in both places before the eighteenth century, so the answer lies elsewhere.[120] The explanation has to do with the absence, anywhere in Asia, of the conditions prevalent in England and Holland, where high levels of speculative activity in the financial markets required ready access to public price information. Handwritten, then printed, price currents were unknown in Asia, but had already circulated widely in the late-medieval commercial centers of Europe. With the Dutch and British governments encouraging open access to trade data for the purposes of economic stimulation, newspaper publishers profited from the high demand for their services in tracking commercial news and prices. Elsewhere in the world, prices were still considered secret, proprietary information. It opened up a world of difference when the press made this kind of information readily available.

The first printed newspapers were in Strasbourg (1605), followed by Wolfenbüttel, Frankfurt am Main, Basel, Hamburg, and Berlin. The honor for having the first daily paper belongs to the German town of Leipzig (1650).[121] But in quantity and quality, Holland and England stood out. By 1626, Amsterdam had more than 140 different newspapers, each competing for market share. The Dutch were the first to make use of

---

[118] The earliest scientific journal was the *Journal des sçavans* (Paris, 1665), copied in London a few months later by *Philosophical Transactions*, which was loosely connected to the newly founded Royal Society. See Pettegree, *Invention of News*, 270–274; and Thomas Leng, "Epistemology: Expertise and Knowledge in the World of Commerce," in *Mercantilism Reimagined: Political Economy in Early Modern Britain and Its Empire*, ed. Philip J. Stern and Carl Wennerlind (Oxford: Oxford University Press, 2014), 100–102. See also Deborah E. Harkness, "Accounting for Science," in *The Self-Perception of Early Modern Capitalists*, ed. Margaret C. Jacob and Catherine Secretan (NY: Palgrave Macmillan, 2008), 205–228, for merchants' scientific literacy and frame of mind.

[119] Leng, "Epistemology," 105–113.

[120] Brook, "Censorship in Eighteenth-Century China."

[121] Johannes Weber, "Strassburg, 1605: The Origins of the Newspaper in Europe," *German History* (Aug. 2006), 387–411; Pettegree, *Invention of News*, 5–6, 184, chap. 9.

special correspondents to include coverage of international news from the rest of Europe, the Caribbean, South America, and Southeast Asia, which was of interest to business readers and politicians. Dutch papers and newssheets in French, German, Italian, and Spanish were distributed twice a week by boat to the main ports of Europe.[122] In the United States, they were still in high repute as late as 1790, when Thomas Jefferson wrote a compatriot in France, asking him to send copies: "The Leyden gazettes furnishing so good information of the interesting scenes now passing in Europe, I must ask your particular attention to the forwarding of them as frequently as it is possible to find conveyances."[123]

In 1620, Amsterdam was the birthplace of the first English-language newspapers, but by the next century journalism was well established in Britain. In the mid-eighteenth century, London had six weeklies, six thrice-weeklies, six dailies, and a few decades later fourteen morning papers. Provincial papers numbered thirty-five, with more being added every year. With his usual acuteness, Dr. Johnson observed that "knowledge is diffused among our people by the news-papers."[124]

Nowhere was that more true than among merchants, who were avid readers of the business papers that were the forerunners of the *Financial Times* and *The Economist*. The city brokers of Amsterdam began to publish price currents on a weekly basis from the 1580s onward. By the 1640s, ten were in print, listing hundreds of commodities, stock transactions, and information on bankruptcies and defaults that helped merchants assess the reputation of their colleagues. London followed suit, so that by the late eighteenth century business newspapers published in the two financial capitals of Europe included price currents reporting on commodities, exchange rates, and stock prices; bill-of-entry and marine lists reporting on overseas trade and shipping; and multiple combinations thereof.

---

[122] For this paragraph and those that follow on the newspaper, see McCusker, "Information and Transaction Costs in Early Modern Europe," 70–78, 80–83; McCusker, "Demise of Distance," 296n6, 298–307; McCusker and Gravesteijn, *Beginnings of Commercial and Financial Journalism*, 21–31; Barbour, *Capitalism in Amsterdam*, 20–21, 66–67; Michel Morineau, "Die holländischen Zeitungen des 17. und 18. Jahrhunderts," in *Kommunikationsrevolutionen*, ed. North, 34–37; Lesger, *Rise of the Amsterdam Market*, 232–235; Joad Raymond, *The Invention of the Newspaper: English Newsbooks, 1641–1649* (Oxford: Clarendon Press, 1996), 7; Smith, *The Newspaper*, 25, 58, chap. 3; Larry Neal and Stephen Quinn, "Networks of Information, Markets, and Institutions in the Rise of London as a Financial Centre, 1660–1720," *Financial History Review* (April 2001), 7–26 passim; Glaisyer, *Culture of Commerce in England*, 5, 19–23, and chap. 4; Cottrell, "London as a Centre of Communications," 166.

[123] Thomas Jefferson to William Short, April 6, 1790, in *Memoir, Correspondence, and Miscellanies, from the Papers of Thomas Jefferson*, ed. Thomas Jefferson Randolph, vol. III (Charlottesville: F. Carr, 1829), 51.

[124] Porter, *English Society in the Eighteenth Century*, 234.

The newspapers were of such importance to the economic vitality of the nation that governments gave them postal subsidies to minimize the cost of delivery. Business became dependent on newspapers as they allowed firms to shift the labors of their staff from investigating prices to more productive activities. They were expensive, but overall they lowered transaction costs and reduced risks, which could only stimulate commerce.[125] And the papers went to great lengths to provide accurate information lest they lose their customer base. As John Drummond, a director of the English East India Company, wrote in a report of 1724, "Amsterdam price currents ... [are] extremely punctuall [sic] and much to be depended on."[126] One of the Liverpool papers, by contrast, went out of business for its inaccuracies. The papers also raised the status of the stock broker, who, to quote Dr. Johnson again, had once been written off as "a low wretch who makes money by buying and selling shares in the funds."[127]

Business relied on up-to-date information, or, in the language of early modern England, "the freshest advices."[128] How much better it was to be able to find the freshest advices in the newspaper rather than every day having to search down and chat up one's contacts in the taverns, at the bourse, and on the wharves. Given the difficulties involved in extracting this kind of information, it had at one time been closely guarded, which capped the number of potential investors: only a relatively small clique of insiders was able to follow prices and judge deals and contracts.[129] But now, explained John Houghton, whose London newspaper *A Collection for the Improvement of Husbandry and Trade* was after 1692 among the first to list stock prices, by reading his paper "the whole Kingdom may reap Advantage," not just the few who previously had privileged contacts. "Without doubt," he continues, if newspapers like his made "those Trades ... better known, 'twould be a great Advantage to the Kingdom; only I must caution Beginners to be very wary, for there are many cunning Artists among them."[130] It was true that information could be manipulated: on the Amsterdam market, bear raiders would spread rumors that lowered the price of stocks which they would then snap up at bargain

---

[125] Douglass C. North considers the rise of the financial press to be itself evidence of a decline in the price of information, thereby reducing a key transaction cost. See his "Institutions, Transaction Costs, and the Rise of Merchant Empires," 40.

[126] McCusker and Gravesteijn, *Beginnings of Commercial and Financial Journalism*, 30.

[127] Morgan and Thomas, *Stock Exchange*, 21.

[128] McCusker and Gravesteijn, *Beginnings of Commercial and Financial Journalism*, 21.

[129] Gelderblom and Jonker, "Amsterdam as the Cradle of Modern Futures and Options Trading," 192.

[130] Neal, *Rise of Financial Capitalism*, 22; and see chap. 2 passim.

rates.[131] But thanks to the business press, information was made widely available on the Dutch and English exchanges. And even if one questions their accuracy and reliability, there is no doubt that the advertisements and background articles on investment opportunities and financial services made a difference in stimulating the speculative activity that brought financing to businesses and liquidity that benefited the broader economy.[132]

Newspapers were too expensive for most individuals to buy subscriptions, so people read them in coffee houses, those "Theatres of News and Politicks" as a Londoner of the 1720s described them.[133] This caffeinated beverage had been introduced from the Levant into Europe in the seventeenth century, and hundreds of café owners were making a living from it in all the major cities. Because of its stimulant effect, the coffee house replaced the tavern as a center of sociability and wheeling-dealing: alcohol-fueled stupors and fights were less conducive to business and intellectual discourse.[134] The Dutch-Portuguese Jew Joseph de la Vega wrote about the phenomenon in 1688:

Our speculators frequent certain places which are called *coffy-huysen* or coffee-houses because a certain beverage is served there called *coffy* by the Dutch and *caffé* by the Levantines ... You will meet there with visitors with whom you can discuss affairs. One person takes chocolate, the others coffee, milk, and tea; and nearly everybody smokes while conversing. None of this occasions very great expense; and while one learns the news, he negotiates and closes transactions.[135]

In London, too, buying and selling of stocks took place in coffee houses in the century before the Stock Exchange was built. The owner of one of them was Edward Lloyd, who called himself the "coffee man" and also collected shipping information from contacts located throughout England and Europe. He began issuing *Lloyd's List* weekly in the 1690s and daily in the 1730s, making it the second-oldest continuously published newspaper in the world today (the official *London Gazette* is in first place) and the oldest daily newspaper.[136]

---

[131] Edward Chancellor, *Devil Take the Hindmost: A History of Financial Speculation* (NY: Plume, 1999), 12–13. For an excellent fictional account of how unscrupulous stock speculators might manipulate price information, see the historical novel by David Liss, *The Coffee Trader* (NY: Random House, 2003).
[132] Murphy, *Origins of English Financial Markets*, chap. 4.
[133] McCusker, "Demise of Distance," 305n28.
[134] "The Internet in a Cup," *Economist* (Dec. 20, 2003), 88–90.
[135] Joseph de la Vega, "Confusión de Confusiones (1688)," in *Extraordinary Popular Delusions and the Madness of Crowds and Confusión de Confusiones*, ed. Martin S. Fridson (NY: Wiley, 1996), 199.
[136] See lloydslist.com; McCusker, "Information and Transaction Costs," 74; McCusker, *European Bills of Entry*, 52–59. The original title of *Lloyd's List* was: *Ships Arrived at, and*

Each coffee shop attracted its own specialized clientele. Literati frequented Will's or Button's; commodity traders favored Garroway's; stock traders huddled at Jonathan's (which evolved into the London Stock Exchange); and ship owners converged on Lloyd's. Given the maritime interests of Mr. Lloyd, he began to offer shipping insurance and provided a venue for other insurers and customers to come together. Thus did the venerable Lloyd's of London come into being, which functions to this day not as an insurance company, but as an insurance market – in basic conception, not that different from its coffeehouse days.

This was not the only London café selling insurance. Some of the more important developments in this industry took place in Slaughter's Coffee House. Here Abraham de Moivre, a Huguenot refugee, mathematician, and friend of Newton, parked himself and in return for a fee determined odds for gamblers and insurance brokers. He was able to do so by applying the actuarial studies and probability theories worked out by the Dutch mathematician (and prime minister) Jan de Witt and the English astronomer Edmund Halley. This interplay between science and business was nearly impossible in other parts of the world, where the separation between social categories was rigidly adhered to. De Moivre also represented the advance in information analysis taking place in Holland and England. Insurance itself was not new: in ancient Greece, maritime insurance was common for the thousands of commercial vessels plying the Mediterranean; in much of Western Europe from the Renaissance on, publicly sponsored life annuities raised funds for governments and provided financial security for individuals; in Mughal India, merchants could buy it to protect their investments. But what was new with English or Dutch insurance, beginning with de Witt, Halley, and de Moivre, was that mathematical tools were now available to fine tune the premium sold to each policy holder. The more sophisticated this assessment, the larger could this business grow, vital as it is to the reduction of risk in any commercial economy.[137]

Besides providing a congenial setting for this new information economy, coffee houses epitomize the retail trade that was flourishing in Western Europe, above all Holland and England, in the seventeenth and

---

Departed from Several Ports of England, as I Have Account of Them in London ... [and] An Account of What English Shipping and Foreign Ships for England I Hear of in Foreign Ports.

[137] Poitras, *Early History of Financial Economics*, 296; James M. Poterba, "Annuities in Early Modern Europe," in *Origins of Value*, ed. Goetzmann and Rouwenhorst, 208–213; Barbour, *Capitalism in Amsterdam*, 33ff. On insurance in Greece and India, see respectively Edward E. Cohen, *Athenian Economy and Society: A Banking Perspective* (Princeton: Princeton University Press, 1992), 140–141, and Irfan Habib, "Potentialities of Capitalistic Development in the Economy of Mughal India," *Journal of Economic History* (March 1969), 73.

eighteenth centuries. The so-called "consumer revolution" rode on a tide of rising incomes and improving living standards, but was made possible by the information nexus of early modern capitalism.[138] As people down the social scale had more money to spend on clothes, household goods, jewelry, and makeup, businesses responded by adopting production and sales strategies based on market research – which for the purposes of this book can be described as conveying information (true or not) about products and assessing information about customers' wants.

This is when product cycles became the routine among manufacturers. Styles were altered every year to meet the demand for novelty and to market the novelty to consumers. It is striking that the following communication dates to 1681: in that year the Court of Directors of the East India Company wrote from London to their factors in Bengal, India, a major center of textile production before the Industrial Revolution:

Now this for a constant and generall Rule, that in all flowered silks you change ye fashion and flower as much as you can every yeare, for English ladies and they say ye French and other Europeans will give twice as much for a new thing not seen in Europe before, though worse, than they will give for a better silk [of] the same fashion worn ye former yeare.[139]

The fashion cycle was born in France, where in the late seventeenth century the silk industry of Lyons designed annual fashions consciously intending to capture international market share and undermine the competition. Daniel Defoe, who published a survey of English trades in 1726, complained that "as soon as those silks came over, our weaver got the fashion, and made silks to the French patterns; but before they could dispose them, the French artfully invented other fashion'd silks which prevented the sale of those made here, and discouraged the English manufactures by changing fashions so often upon them that they could make very little of the silk manufactures."[140]

[138] Jan de Vries, "Between Purchasing Power and the World of Goods: Understanding the Household Economy in Early Modern Europe," in *Consumption and the World of Goods*, ed. John Brewer and Roy Porter (London: Routledge, 1994), 85–132. Maryanne Kowaleski, "A Consumer Economy," in *A Social History of England, 1200–1500*, ed. Rosemary Horrox and W. Mark Ormrod (Cambridge: Cambridge University Press, 2006), 238–259, dates the consumer revolution even earlier, to the Middle Ages.

[139] Prakash, "Commercial Communication and Monetary Integration in Early Modern India," 163.

[140] For this and the following two paragraphs, see Maxine Berg, "French Fancy and Cool Britannia: The Fashion Markets of Early Modern Europe," in *Fiere e mercati nella integrazione delle economie europee secc. XIII–XVIII*, ed. Simonetta Cavaciocchi (Florence: Le Monnier, 2001), 534–546 (with Defoe quote on 536); and Carlo Poni, "Fashion as Flexible Production: The Strategies of the Lyons Silk Merchants in the Eighteenth Century," in *World of Possibilities: Flexibility and Mass Production in Western*

This technique of the Lyons silk merchants was quickly copied by the British textile industry – the weavers of Norwich, the linen producers of Ireland and Scotland, the makers of Yorkshire woolens, the cotton exporters of India – to cash in on the desire for a yearly change of fashion that was becoming more common: a German traveler to England was astonished to find that even people in the "middling stations" had to have "at least three suits a year."[141] That could also be said of fashion accessories – jewelry, stockings, fans, umbrellas, buttons, medallions, and cameo pins – and also housewares, which saw new product designs introduced annually for Wedgwood ceramics, Chippendale furniture, and a wide selection of drinking glasses, porcelain, and children's toys. For Paris we can add fancy wigs and perfumes to the list.

Even then it was necessary for manufacturers to utilize all available marketing tools. One of them was brand new: shops outfitted with display windows, which Daniel Defoe called "perfect gilded theaters." Store windows with constantly changing contents were an informational device that attracted attention and gave potential customers quick knowledge of goods and prices. In the eighteenth century, window shopping became a new form of leisure activity, and the opportunities were great: according to Defoe, "I have endeavored to make some calculation of the number of shop-keepers in this kingdom, but I find it is not to be done – we may as well count the stars." Nor was this confined to London or Amsterdam, but took place all across England and Holland, where a dense forest of shops grew up, all announcing their wares to the public with now ubiquitous storefront signs and shingles.[142]

Shop windows and shop signs were forms of advertising; the newspaper provided another. Spreading the word about one's products in this forum could attract potential customers who did not normally pass by the shop or learn about it through word of mouth. Newspapers, magazines, and journals were themselves profit-making businesses, and to raise revenues and attract readers they sold advertisements. In Dutch papers of the Golden Age, you could find every service or commodity, from windmill construction and cotton textile

Industrialization, ed. Charles F. Sabel and Jonathan Zeitlin (Cambridge: Cambridge University Press, 1997), 37–74.

[141] Berg, "French Fancy and Cool Britannia," 539.

[142] Berg, "French Fancy and Cool Britannia," 546–552 (with first Defoe quote on 548); Porter, *English Society in the Eighteenth Century,* 190 (second Defoe quote); Simon Schama, *The Embarrassment of Riches: An Interpretation of Dutch Culture in the Golden Age* (NY: Knopf, 1987), 301–302; Gerard M. Koot, "Shops and Shopping in Britain: From market Stalls to Chain Stores," online at www1.umassd.edu/ir/resources/consumption/shopping.pdf.

"printing" to tobacco and chocolate.[143] Houghton's above-mentioned paper ran ads for items that appealed to late-seventeenth-century "yuppies" in London's financial district: "spaw water," "sago," "a super-fine Tea," coffee, and a variety of herbs and spices.[144]

Again, Dr. Johnson: "Promise, large promise, is the soul of advertisement." By the 1730s, 50 percent of print in English newspapers consisted of advertising. The provincial press spread London and Parisian tastes far and wide, as did the newly born fashion magazines: in Britain the *Gentleman's Magazine* (1730s) and the *Lady's Magazine* (1770s); in France the *Gallerie des modes et costumes français* and the *Cabinet des modes* (1770s–1780s); in Italy and Germany local equivalents. Other periodicals featured household design, clothing patterns, and sale catalogues. Of course the intellectuals were contemptuous of them all: the German philosopher Herder wrote that the "ruinous fashion journal[s] … induce variety, … [and] damage health [and] morality." He denounced the heavily advertised Wedgwood pottery designs for "destroy[ing] authentic Greek taste." For Goethe, all of it amounted to "illusionary gratifications."[145] But who in a bustling commercial and consumer society cared what they thought?

Retail business on this scale could only have arisen in a society with advertising, a means by which shop owners and manufacturers could provide information to customers, and by which customers could find information about products.[146] Not all of the information conveyed through advertising was honest, and it was always highly selective. But bombarding the consumer with advertisements was also a result of the communications advances occurring in the Netherlands and England, and it was an essential feature of what scholars have identified as a commercial revolution.[147] The information nexus grew even denser in these two nations because of the open political climate, the alliance between government and the free market, and a thriving press. Here were the true beginnings of capitalism.

---

[143] Leonie van Nierop, "Gegevens over de Nijverheid van Amsterdam: Bijeengelezen uit de Advertenties in de Amsterdamsche Courant, 1667–1794," pt. I, *Jaarboek van het Genootschap Amstelodamum*, 27 (1930), 261–311.

[144] I borrow use of the term "yuppie" from Neal, "Business Press," 148.

[145] Berg, "French Fancy and Cool Britannia," 552–555; Porter, *English Society in the Eighteenth Century*, 190 (Johnson quote); Daniel L. Purdy, *The Tyranny of Elegance: Consumer Cosmopolitanism in the Era of Goethe* (Baltimore: Johns Hopkins University Press, 1998), 8–10, 28 (Herder and Goethe quotes), and passim.

[146] For an economist's view of the original function of advertising in an information economy, see Stigler, *Organization of Industry*, 182.

[147] For contextualization of advertising in the expanding eighteenth-century economy, see Margaret Schabas, "Market Contracts in the Age of Hume," in *Higgling: Transactors and Their Markets in the History of Economics*, ed. Neil De Marchi and Mary S. Morgan (Durham, NC: Duke University Press, 1994), 117–134.

To put these world-shaping developments in sharper relief, we have already made some comparisons to Asia, and must now turn to the problem of France – because France, despite trend-setting retail fashions in Paris,[148] was on the whole resistant to following the path blazed by Amsterdam and London.

France: Absolutism and the absence of capitalism

Through London and Amsterdam we entered the modern world of information intensity and with it capitalism. The rest of Europe had not yet crossed the threshold. France looked like it might follow the Dutch and the English financial model in the 1710s after defaulting on high-interest loans taken during the War of Spanish Succession. This was when it agreed to adopt the solution proposed by the Scottish economist (and speculator, gambler, and murderer) John Law. A state bank issued paper money and floated stock in a government charter company, the Compagnie des Indes, to raise revenues for the state. Law tried but failed to contain the uncontrolled speculative fervor that engulfed the cafés of Paris. When the bubble burst, he fled the country in disgrace, and France fled from the notion of paper money and state banking for the next hundred years. It did create the Paris Bourse in 1724 to supervise trading in commercial paper, but it was not a stock exchange in the true sense as brokers were prohibited from investing on their own account and had to buy and sell only as agents for clients. The secondary market in securities remained minimal because of the tight restrictions dictated by the French state.[149]

At the same time, the British government had its own bubble crisis with the collapse of the South Sea Company, but stemmed the hemorrhaging of the markets by repackaging the debt and making the Bank of England the lender of last resort. The "Bubble Act" of 1720 restricted the role of joint-stock companies, but the stock exchange was allowed to continue to regulate itself. This was a balanced, less paranoid intervention than in

---

[148] Cissie Fairchilds, "The Production and Marketing of Populuxe Goods in Eighteenth-Century Paris," in *Consumption and the World of Goods*, ed. Brewer and Porter, 228–248.

[149] On French failure to adopt the Anglo-Dutch financial model, see Paul-Jacques Lehmann, *Histoire de la Bourse de Paris* (Paris: Presses universitaires de France, 1997), 7, and chap. I; Eric S. Schubert, "Innovations, Debts, and Bubbles: International Integration of Financial Markets in Western Europe, 1688–1720," *Journal of Economic History* (June 1988), 299–306; Neal, "On the Historical Development of Stock Markets," 66, 71; François R. Velde and David R. Weir, "The Financial Market and Government Debt Policy in France, 1746–1793," *Journal of Economic History* (March 1992), 1–39; Eugene N. White, "The Paris Bourse, 1724–1814," in *Finance, Intermediaries, and Economic Development*, ed. Engerman et al., 34–74.

France and ensured that the British crown would continue to attract investment in its bonds.[150] The autonomous free market remained alive in London, but in Paris was crippled by the absolutist state's fears of instability and losing its domination of the economy.

This attitude was even more evident in the weakness of the French press and publishing industry. If in the early sixteenth century per capita book consumption in France was double that of England and Holland, in the seventeenth and eighteenth centuries France fell far behind, with the positions reversed.[151] Severe government regulations, including censorship and a ceiling imposed on the number of publishers, forced most in the business to forego the mass market and produce small luxury editions for the wealthy buyer.[152] Corrupt French postal employees understood the hunger for information among merchants: they opened letters and sold the enclosed information to "commercial news hawkers."[153]

Even stricter rules applied to newspapers: the only one designated for discussion of political matters was the official *Gazette de France* (dating from 1631), while the *Journal des savants* (founded 1665) published book reviews and extracts hinting at news from abroad. The *Mercure galant* (1672–1724) provided poems, puzzles, and other forms of entertainment as well as lists of nominees for government office. In England, there were 7,000 copies of newspapers per week serving a national population of 6 million; in France, the *Gazette* came out in a print run of 9,000 copies for a population of 20 million.[154] As late as the mid-eighteenth century, the French government required pre-publication censorship involving submission of each sheet of print for approval. Independent French papers were printed in Holland and smuggled into France, but underground editions like these could not reach a broad national audience. Louis XIV had sought to repress their circulation, but read them

---

[150] Most trading on the London Stock Exchange for the next hundred years was in the repackaged, consolidated government debt (hence "Consols"), rather than private joint-stock companies, whose owners sought and found alternative means of organization and funding.

[151] Buringh and van Zanden, "Charting the 'Rise of the West,'" 421.

[152] Blanning, *Culture of Power*, 137–139, 141; John C. Rule and Ben S. Trotter, *A World of Paper: Louis XIV, Colbert de Torcy, and the Rise of the Information State* (Montreal: McGill-Queen's University Press, 2014), 11, 338ff.

[153] Rule and Trotter, *World of Paper*, 652n113.

[154] Stephen Botein, Jack R. Censer, and Harriet Ritvo, "The Periodical Press in Eighteenth-Century English and French Society," *Comparative Studies in Society and History* (July 1981), 464–490; Blanning, *Culture of Power*, 157; Emmet Kennedy, *A Cultural History of the French Revolution* (New Haven: Yale University Press, 1989), 14–15; Pettegree, *Invention of News*, 200–205, 231–236, 245; Jean-Pierre Vittu, "Instruments of Political Information in France," in *The Politics of Information in Early Modern Europe*, ed. Dooley and Baron, 160–178.

himself to find out news of his own realm.[155] As for the business press, the
few price currents available were intended for foreign merchants: in
Bordeaux it was in Dutch and in Lyons Italian; the only one in French
was issued in Marseilles.[156] Additionally, unlike the English, the
French government, in the most telling indication of its dread of the
free market, regulated bill-posting and shop signs. Advertising did
appear in newspapers, but only relatively late in the day: notices of
goods and services were sporadic before the 1750s and more standardized in rates and appearance only from the 1780s.[157]

The climate began to brighten for the periodical press after mid-
century. The first French daily newspaper was founded in 1777.
By the end of that decade, around forty government-sponsored weekly
advertisers were published in the regions of France. Called *affiches de
province*, they printed prices of commodities, mortgages, and equities,
and featured advertisements for real estate, employment, services, and
products. But these papers had a small circulation, largely among their
target audience of elites – unlike Holland and England, where people in
the lower social strata formed part of the readership.[158]

One of the major obstacles to the spread of information via the print
media in France was the existence of dozens of regional *patois*.
As enumerated by the abbé Henri Grégoire in 1794, millions of peasants
in France did not speak or understand French, but rather "Bas-Breton,
Bourguignon, Bressan, Lyonnais, Dauphinois, Auvergnat, Poitevin,
Limousin, Picard, Provençal, Languedocien, Velayen, Catalan,
Béarnais, Basque, Rouergat, and Gascon" – and he could have
added Flemish and German. The situation did not change until well
into the nineteenth century, after years of strenuous effort by Paris to
promote the French language and eradicate use of the others.[159]
The impact of this lack of a single national language on information
exchange and economic growth is incalculable.

All the above rebuts the claim that the underground manuscripts,
novels, and songs that spread political gossip made France an example

[155] Barbour, *Capitalism in Amsterdam*, 66–67.
[156] McCusker and Gravesteijn, *Beginnings of Commercial and Financial Journalism*, chaps. 10
(Bourdeaux), 26 (Lyons), and 27 (Marseilles).
[157] Christopher Todd, "French Advertising in the Eighteenth Century," *Studies on Voltaire
and the Eighteenth Century*, vol. CCLXVI (1989), 513–547.
[158] Jack R. Censer, *The French Press in the Age of Enlightenment* (London: Routledge, 1994),
7–12, and chap. 2; Louis Trenard, "La presse française des origines à 1788," in *Histoire
générale de la presse française*, vol. I, ed. Claude Bellanger et al. (Paris: Presses universitaires
de France, 1969), 323–402; Colin Jones, "The Great Chain of Buying: Medical
Advertisement, the Bourgeois Public Sphere, and the Origins of the French Revolution,"
American Historical Review (Feb. 1996), 17–21; Botein et al., "Periodical Press."
[159] Kennedy, *Cultural History of the French Revolution*, 325–326.

of an early "information society."[160] Government censorship of the news, the anemic business press, and the retreat from Anglo-Dutch financial methods squeezed the nation's capital market. Notaries used their knowledge of their clients' finances to conduct credit operations, but they were about the only ones who did, and their reach did not extend outside of the main cities.[161] Greater information about the nation's economic resources and potential could simply not be had without a free securities market and free press. Or, even more fundamental, without adequate roads and waterways. The central government's Corps des Ingénieurs des Ponts et Chaussées launched a program of improvement in the mid-1700s, but according to numerous contemporary accounts they remained in bad shape compared to those of England well into the next century, except perhaps for a few routes leading from Paris.[162]

Paris was on the sidelines of the integrated international capital network that branched out after the 1720s from Amsterdam and London to Hamburg, Frankfurt am Main, and Geneva – all cities where merchants rather than absolutist regimes dominated.[163] In the years immediately preceding the French Revolution, the state's control of the press and the financial markets began to break down, with a corresponding uptick in stock investment.[164] But that did not last long either as the revolutionaries forced the closure of the Paris Bourse and plunged first the country and then the continent into violence over the next quarter century. That is not to say that eighteenth-century France had been a laggard in every aspect of economic life – until the revolution it was an innovator in industrial technology. On the other hand, French pirating of more advanced English technology occurred

[160] Robert Darnton, "The News in Paris: An Early Information Society," in his *George Washington's Teeth: An Unconventional Guide to the Eighteenth Century* (NY: Norton, 2003), chap. 2.

[161] Philip T. Hoffman, Gilles Postel-Vinay, and Jean-Laurent Rosenthal, *Priceless Markets: The Political Economy of Credit in Paris, 1660–1870* (Chicago: University of Chicago Press, 2000), passim; Neal, "How It All Began," 132–136.

[162] Guy Arbellot, "La grande mutation des routes de France au milieu du XVIIIe siècle," *Annales* (May–June, 1973), 765–791; Roger Price, *The Modernization of Rural France: Communications Networks and Agricultural Market Structures in Nineteenth-Century France* (NY: St. Martin's, 1983), pt. I; Rick Szostak, *The Role of Transportation in the Industrial Revolution: A Comparison of England and France* (Montreal: McGill-Queen's University Press, 1991), chaps. 1–2; Stéphane J. L. Blond, "The Trudaine Atlas: Government Road Mapping in Eighteenth-Century France," *Imago Mundi*, LXV, no. 1 (2013), 64–79. A picture of the only faint interaction French provinces had with the wider world emerges from Emma Rothschild, "Isolation and Economic Life in Eighteenth-Century France," *American Historical Review* (Oct. 2014), 1055–1082.

[163] J. C. Riley, "Dutch Investment in France, 1781–1787," *Journal of Economic History* (Dec. 1973), 732–760; Schubert, "Innovations, Debts, and Bubbles," 299–306; Neal and Quinn, "Markets and Institutions in the Rise of London," 13–14.

[164] George V. Taylor, "The Paris Bourse on the Eve of the Revolution, 1781–1789," *American Historical Review* (July 1962), 951–977.

at a high frequency, providing evidence that France was behind.[165] The chasm separating educated elites and craftsmen was also much wider in France than in England, where the fusion of science, technology, and mechanical know-how were essential to industrialization.[166] And France missed out on economic stimuli because of its uneven level of consumerism and its conservative approach to state finance.[167] Capitalism, based as it is on the information nexus, took root in early modern Holland and England, but not yet France.

The sea change of capitalism began as commercial and financial undertakings surged with unimpeded flows of information.[168] In this the Dutch Republic and the United Kingdom had the competitive advantage over France, and Western Europe had the competitive advantage over Asia.

Geography figured in too: both Holland and England were compact nations where it was relatively easy to communicate and share information.[169] The technological advances of the nineteenth and twentieth centuries would eliminate this advantage and make it possible for an information nexus of an even greater density and intensity to take hold in the continent-sized United States. When it did, the modern corporation emerged as a new type of business organization devoted to managing the complex types of information generated in a mass market. That is the subject of Chapter 5.

[165] J. R. Harris, "Industrial Espionage in the Eighteenth Century," *Industrial Archaeology Review* (Spring 1985), 127–138.

[166] Jacob, *First Knowledge Economy*, chaps. 5–6.

[167] Its uneven consumerism was related to the relative poverty of the French population, which although changing over the course of the eighteenth century and less severe in the cities than in the countryside, was across the board not drastically improved by 1800: see Daniel Roche, *A History of Everyday Things: The Birth of Consumption in France, 1600–1800*, trans. B. Pearce (Cambridge: Cambridge University Press, 2000), 62ff, and chap. 8. Patrick O'Brien and Caglar Keyder, *Economic Growth in Britain and France, 1780–1914: Two Paths to the Twentieth Century* (London: George Allen and Unwin, 1978), argues that the economic gap between Britain and France was not as great as assumed in the nineteenth century, but its analysis does not apply to the early modern period as treated here. In *Reconceptualizing the Industrial Revolution*, ed. Horn, Rosenband, and Smith, chap. 2, O'Brien acknowledges British economic dominance of Europe in the mid-nineteenth century. Both Jacob, *First Knowledge Economy*, chaps. 5–6, and Joel Mokyr, *The Enlightened Economy: An Economic History of Britain, 1700–1850* (New Haven: Yale University Press, 2009), 11, and chap. 6, stress the French recognition of British industrial leadership, and GDP figures from "The New Maddison Project Database," online at ggdc.net/maddison/maddison-project/data.htm suggest that the French might have lagged into the late nineteenth century.

[168] For unimpeded diffusion of knowledge as the precondition of the "Industrial Enlightenment," see Joel Mokyr, "The Riddle of 'The Great Divergence': Intellectual and Economic Factors in the Growth of the West," *Historically Speaking* (Sept. 2003), online at bu.edu/historic/hs/september03.htmlbu.edu/historic/hs/september03.html# mokyr, pp. 4–5.

[169] Lesger, *Rise of the Amsterdam Market*, 246–247, makes this point for Holland alone.

5 The age of electricity and engines
America's mass market

In early modern Europe, the rapid circulation of commercial and financial information signified the rise of capitalism. It took place in a swath of territory that straddled the Alps from northern Italy to Lyons, Geneva, and Basel. It forked out to Paris on the one side and Frankfurt am Main on the other. But capitalism cut the deepest channels down the Rhine River basin to the Low Countries, from there arcing out across England and southern Scotland, and flowing east along the Baltic Sea coast to Stockholm.

In this territory, relatively small and politically open societies with strong but not oppressive central governments and good access to maritime, riverine, or overland communications routes held the advantage that they had accrued from abundant trade and a sense of widening economic horizons. Great Britain and the Dutch Republic were the most advanced of these information societies, as news and commerce traveled most voluminously in, around, and between Amsterdam and London.

The capitalist firmament expanded suddenly in the nineteenth century, when the railroad and the telegraph turned the United States into an immense, steam-powered, and electrified version of Holland or England. A compact coastal territory was no longer the requirement for rapid communications and intensive exchange of goods and information. Capitalism could now exist on a continental scale – wherever political conditions tolerated the freest and fullest transmission of information.

The size of the American economy – whose productive capacity was supercharged by industrialization after the Civil War – brought the first full-fledged mass market into existence. The mass market entailed new ways of doing business as new transportation and communications systems accelerated both supply and demand. Information technologies thus shaped the salient contours of capitalism in our time: internationally linked commodity markets; factory-based mass production; mass distribution in new types of retail stores; mass marketing; large corporations; and the meteoric rise of the stock market.

These are all the subjects of the current chapter, the first to interpret American capitalism from the perspective of the information nexus. But the story begins with the technological advances that generated the modern information nexus and undergirded capitalism in the nineteenth and twentieth centuries.

Steam and stamps, locomotion and lightning

Inventions in transportation and communications changed the ways passengers, goods, and information moved around – and exponentially increased the speed at which they traveled. With canal construction and the invention of the steamboat, mobility expanded and the cost of transport declined even before the coming of the railroad. In the early-nineteenth-century United States, canals cut shortcuts across regions and steamships plied the waters upstream as well as down. To give one example, these improvements reduced the time it took to travel or ship freight from New York to Cincinnati from fifty-two days to just six.[1]

By means of the railroad, steam conquered overland space. The average speed of stagecoaches was around 4 mph; sustaining 10 mph for a long period of time was extremely unusual. By horse-drawn coach or wagon it normally took sixteen days to travel between New York City and New Orleans, and more than a month to go from St. Louis to San Francisco.[2] The very first railroad locomotives propelled themselves forward at a teeth-rattling 15–20 mph, but by the 1840s they reached an average of 40 mph, with outer limits of 60 or 70. According to a British author writing in 1839, "distances were thus annihilated."[3]

The railroads carried people and goods fast and far, but in the United States the main information transmitter was the Post Office. As advocated by James Madison and enshrined in the 1792 Post Office Act, the US mail system was to circulate business and political news for the benefit of the public. The same year, an American legislator stated that the agency existed for "no other purpose" than the "conveyance of

[1] Jeffrey G. Williamson, *Globalization and the Poor Periphery before 1950* (Cambridge, MA: MIT Press, 2006), 8.

[2] Richard R. John, *Spreading the News: The American Postal System from Franklin to Morse* (Cambridge, MA: Harvard University Press, 1995), 74, 91; Maury Klein, *The Flowering of the Third America: The Making of an Organizational Society, 1850–1920* (Chicago: Ivan R. Dee, 1993), 5.

[3] Wolfgang Schivelbusch, *The Railway Journey: The Industrialization of Time and Space in the Nineteenth Century* (Berkeley: University of California Press, 1986), 34.

information" into "every part of the Union." To that end, the government subsidized the distribution of newspapers and government documents with low postal rates.[4]

The system as it developed was largely the brainchild of John McLean, Postmaster General of the United States 1823–1829 (previously a senator from Ohio and later a justice of the US Supreme Court). He expanded his predecessor Joseph Habersham's wheel-and-spoke pattern of post offices and distribution centers as part of a broader vision involving the efficient streaming of goods and information between regions of the country. Seeking greater transparency in the affairs of the nation, McLean wanted the postal system to broadcast market conditions far and wide so as to put an end to the practices of shady merchants who profited from their insider knowledge of prices in remote parts of the country. He commissioned private stagecoach companies to carry the mails; decades later, in the 1860s, the government inaugurated the Railway Mail Service. From the start, the USPO's "special agents" battled theft and corruption by postal employees. Those forerunners of the private eye ensured that sensitive documents as well as cash could be reliably sent via the US Mail. In and of itself this accounted for a large reduction in business transaction costs.

Already by the late 1820s, the United States had 13,500 post offices, or seventy-four for every 100,000 inhabitants. Considering how large the country was, it is an impressive number: in the United Kingdom, which also had a relatively advanced mail service, the number of post offices at the same time was only seventeen per 100,000; in France it was four, and as late as 1896 it was only three in the Russian empire. Russia, of course, was an autocratic nation whose leaders were suspicious of freely circulating information; but elsewhere in Europe, postal services expanded over the course of the nineteenth century and stimulated economic activity by spreading all manner of news, opinion, technical knowledge, and advertising.[5] Information access through the mails had grown more extensive in the United Kingdom after 1840, when a democratizing reform initiated flat rates and adhesive penny postage stamps: previously, recipients paid for delivery of letters, at the cost of around a day's wages.

---

[4] Richard R. John, *Network Nation: Inventing American Telecommunications* (Cambridge, MA: Belknap Press, 2010), 19.

[5] On the USPO, see John, *Spreading the News*, 5, 67, 73, 77, 83–84, 86; John, "Recasting the Information Infrastructure for the Industrial Age," in *A Nation Transformed by Information*, ed. Alfred D. Chandler, Jr. and James W. Cortada (Oxford: Oxford University Press, 2000), 55–74; Robert E. Wright, *The Wealth of Nations Rediscovered: Integration and Expansion in American Financial Markets, 1780–1850* (Cambridge: Cambridge University Press, 2002), 21; Daniel R. Headrick, "Information and Communication Technology," in *Oxford Encyclopaedia of Economic History*, ed. Joel Mokyr, vol. III (Oxford: Oxford University Press, 2003), 71.

The United States followed the British five years later with the 3-cent stamp – a rate, incidentally, that stayed the same for more than a century.[6]

The telegraph had as great an impact as the railroad and the post office. What contemporaries called "lightning wires" and the "lightning way" offered the first electrical means of transmitting writing, allowing contact between distant places at a previously unimaginable speed. On those grounds I would argue that electronic telegraphy was the key innovation in the rise of nineteenth- and twentieth-century capitalism: only with the telegraph was it possible for large enterprises and a mass market to come into being, dependent as they are on the fast circulation and coordination of vast amounts of information.[7] Compared to railroads, the telegraph network was cheap and easy to erect, involving stringing wires between poles dug into the ground. Samuel Morse and Alfred Vail built the first line in the United States from Baltimore to Washington, DC, in 1843 (the first line anywhere was in London, 1839). Eight years later, the telegraph extended across the entire continent, well before the completion of the transcontinental railroad.

The telegraph quickly went international. After the discovery of gutta-percha, the gum of a Southeast Asian tree that effectively insulated against saltwater, the first sea cables were laid across the English Channel between Dover and Calais in 1851. Over the next twenty years they were extended across the Baltic and Mediterranean seas, then the Atlantic and Indian oceans, and finally in 1871 over the Pacific. By 1900, some 350,000 kilometers of submarine cables stretched across the globe. Whereas it took surface mail on steamships two months to go between London and Sydney, Australia, or two weeks between London and New York, now messages could be transmitted in a couple of minutes. The January 3, 1880, issue of *The Electrician* reported what was then an astoundingly rapid use of the telegraph when a Wall Street broker could trade a number of stocks in only sixteen minutes![8] This is laughable when compared to the

---

[6] Catherine J. Golden, *Posting It: The Victorian Revolution in Letter Writing* (Gainesville: University Press of Florida, 2009), chap. 1 and 197.

[7] The paragraphs on the telegraph draw on the following sources: Richard B. Du Boff, "Business Demand and the Development of the Telegraph in the United States, 1844–1860," *Business History Review* (Winter 1980), 461 and 459–479 passim; Jorma Ahvenainen, "The Role of Telegraphs in the Nineteenth Century Revolution of Communications," and Robert Boyce, "Submarine Cables as a Factor in Britain's Ascendacy as a World Power, 1850–1914," both in *Kommunikationsrevolutionen: Die neuen Medien des 16. und 19. Jahrhunderts*, ed. Michael North, 2nd ed. (Cologne: Böhlau Verlag, 2001), 73–80 and 81–83, 90 respectively; Headrick, "Information and Communication Technology," 72; John J. McCusker, "Demise of Distance: The Business Press and the Origins of the Information Revolution in the Early Modern World," *American Historical Review* (April 2005), 295–298; Ranald C. Michie, *The Global Securities Market: A History* (Oxford: Oxford University Press, 2006), 112.

[8] Ahvenainen, "The Role of Telegraphs," 78–79.

speed of today's computer-based algorithmic trading, where transactions take place by the nanosecond, but for its day it was remarkable.

Businessmen were quick to grasp the lightning: they understood immediately the advantage the telegraph could give them by providing rapid transmission of commodities prices, exchange rates, and other kinds of news and commercial information. Markets worked better for all that, as telegraphy slashed transaction costs and gave a powerful jolt to economic activity.

The telegraph transformed the United States. Southern business journalist J. D. B. De Bow, writing in *De Bow's Review* in February 1854 explained: "In a country ... in which business is spread over a vast area, and thousands of miles interpose between one commercial emporium and another – the telegraph answers to a use the complexion of which is unique."[9] Before the railroads welded the disparate parts of the nation together, the telegraph lines spun a web of interregional ties between American merchants, bankers, brokers, and shippers. By the 1880s, almost 90 percent of messages circulating through Western Union – the main telegraph company – were commerce-related, but businessmen in the United States were already dependent on the telegraph as early as the 1840s and 1850s, as this statement from De Bow, this time in 1847, makes clear: "every day affords instances of the advantages which our business men derive from the use of the telegraph. Operations are made in *one day* with its aid, by repeated communications, which could not be done from two to four weeks by mail."[10] Information technology trumped the geographical immensity of the North American continent, and turned the political unity of the United States to advantage by allowing the coordination of the continent's vast and dispersed resources.

The effect of the telegraph on domestic life might give those of us who are addicted to the internet or our cellphones a sense of déja vu. In a speech he gave in 1868, New York businessman W. E. Dodge assessed the matter:

Now, reports of the principal markets of the world are published every day, and our customers are continually posted by telegram. Instead of making a few large shipments in a year [as previously], the merchant must keep up constant action, multiplying his business over and over again. He has to keep up constant intercourse with distant correspondents, [and] knows in a few weeks the results of shipments which a few years ago would not have been known for months.

[9] Du Boff, "Business Demand and the Development of the Telegraph," 462 (quote); and see 459–479 passim.
[10] Du Boff, "Business Demand and the Development of the Telegraph," 472 (quote); John, "Recasting the Information Infrastructure," 81–82.

So far so good, but Dodge goes on to illustrate the all-too-familiar down side: the merchant

is thus kept in continual excitement, without time for quiet and rest. [He] goes home after a day of hard work and excitement to a late dinner, trying amid the family circle to forget business, when he is interrupted by a telegram from London, directing, perhaps, the purchase of 20,000 barrels of flour, and the poor man must dispatch his dinner as hurriedly as possible in order to send his message to California. The businessman of the present day must be continually on the jump, the slow express train will not answer his purpose, and the poor merchant has no other way in which to work to secure a living for his family. He *must* use the telegraph.[11]

On the basis of such complaints, Dr. George M. Beard asserted in his socio-medical study *American Nervousness* (1881) that "before the days of Morse and his rivals, merchants were far less worried than now, and less business was transacted in a given time ... [The] continual fluctuation of [prices], and the constant knowledge of those fluctuations in every part of the world, are the scourges of businessmen."[12] What the complaints of Dodge and Beard indicate is that the telegraph, like telecommunications devices of our own day, anxiety-inducing though they could be, also sped up communications and commerce.

The telephone and radio soon supplemented the telegraph. Patented in 1876, the telephone developed first and fastest in the information-hungry and economically dynamic United States. The Bell Company began by marketing the telephone for businesses, but it took hold in homes, too: as Alexander Graham Bell predicted of his invention, "the day is coming when telegraph wire will be laid on to houses just like water or gas – and friends converse with each other without leaving home."[13] By the 1920s, to quote from *Middletown*, the classic study of American life, "around the telephone have grown up such time-savers for the housewife as the general delivery system for everything from groceries to a spool of thread" – plus a new mode of social interaction.[14] In 1913, one telephone switchboard operated per 527 residents in Russia; in France, there was one switchboard for every 146 residents; in Germany one per fifty; in Britain one per forty-seven; and in the United States one per fourteen. Giving a sense of the American advantage is the fact that there were more

---

[11] Dodge quote in Tom Standage, *The Victorian Internet: The Remarkable Story of the Telegraph and the Nineteenth Century's On-line Pioneers* (NY: Walker, 1998), 165–166.
[12] George M. Beard, *American Nervousness: Its Causes and Consequences* (NY: G. P. Putnam's Sons, 1881), 105.
[13] John, *Network Nation*, 200.
[14] Robert S. Lynd and Helen Merrell Lynd, *Middletown: A Study in Modern American Culture* (NY: Harcourt Brace Jovanovich, 1957 [1929]), 173–174.

telephones in New York City hotels at the time than there were in all of Spain.[15] In the inelegant language of the *Saturday Evening Post*, the United States was "the most betelephoned nation in the world."[16]

The first commercial telephone service between New York and London was introduced in 1927 and relied on wireless radio technology. Wireless transmission signaled the rise of private radio broadcasting as a new communications medium in the interwar decades. Radio was a powerful new player in the information nexus: business could saturate the airwaves with commercials, which reached potential customers both local and remote. The quality of radios steadily improved, the price steadily declined, and in the 1920s the number of radio owners grew into the many millions. Consumers became aware of new products. Farmers listened for information about climate or market conditions affecting their crops. Country people heard the news and advertisements as fast as city folk, so felt less isolated and more integrated into the national community. From the 1950s onward, the experience was replicated and deepened through the powerful mass medium of television.[17]

Commodity markets and international integration

Commerce in commodities expanded regionally, nationally, and internationally in tandem with the information network whose tendrils reached out through steamships, railroads, the telegraph, and, later, the telephone and radio. Commodities trading exploded with the introduction of refrigeration on ships and trains beginning in the 1870s.[18] The most sizeable trade was in grain, but a huge increase also occurred in the buying and selling of livestock and meats; fish; butter and cheese; vegetable oils and other greases; fruits, vegetables, and seeds; coffee and sugar; straw and feed grasses; cotton; metals; oil and natural gas.

With the new forms of transport and electronic means of communication, growth in commodities production and trading seemed

[15] Horst A. Wessel, "Die Rolle des Telefons in der Kommunikationsrevolution des 19. Jahrhunderts," in *Kommunikationsrevolutionen*, ed. North, 120, 123; John, "Recasting the Information Infrastructure," 100.

[16] Jack Alexander, "The World's Biggest Business Gets a New Boss," *Saturday Evening Post* (March 19, 1949), 19.

[17] Headrick, "Information and Communication Technology," 72–75; Margaret Graham, "The Threshold of the Information Age: Radio, Television, and Motion Pictures Mobilize the Nation," in *A Nation Transformed by Information*, ed. Chandler and Cortada, 137–176.

[18] For an overview of the history of refrigeration and its impact on one commodity, see Susanne E. Friedberg, "The Triumph of the Egg," *Comparative Studies in Society and History* (April 2008), 400–423.

unstoppable. Mechanization enabled mass production on the land. The first agro-businesses were the post–Civil War "bonanza farms" of the American Great Plains and California, where crops were grown on tens and hundreds of thousands of acres, veritable "factories in the fields."[19] In 1914, the United States shipped 600 million bushels of wheat to Europe, fifteen times the amount for 1850.[20] And products could be sent farther at a lower price: such was the volume that overseas freight rates on steamships dropped by 50–70 percent over those on clipper ships.[21] By 1900, the cost of transporting a ton of wheat across the Atlantic from the United States to Germany cost the same as it did to move it internally across Germany.[22] For the same reason, the prices of goods carried on railroads also declined: for example, with the introduction of the railroad in British India the cost of food grains fell 80 percent.[23]

The telegraph gave traders in any given commodity the opportunity to make instantaneous global price checks.[24] The owners of grain stored in elevators in, say, Duluth or Minneapolis could keep track of prices on a daily basis in the main markets affecting their particular specialty – Winnipeg, Montreal, Buenos Aires, Liverpool, Paris, Antwerp, Berlin, St. Petersburg, Odessa, and Calcutta – and decide whether to sell or hold back. Meatpacking firms had a more precise way of determining how many animals to slaughter and how much meat to ship – with far less spoilage than would have occurred before the telegraph. Nor was this restricted to the advanced regions of the world: by the early 1900s, villagers on the steppes of western Siberia had daily access to prices on the Berlin wheat

---

[19] Thomas J. Schlereth, *Victorian America* (NY: HarperCollins, 1991), 42–45 (with quote on 43). For more accurate numbers than Schlereth provides, see Harold E. Briggs, "Early Bonanza Farming in the Red River Valley of the North," *Agricultural History* (Jan. 1932), 26–37.

[20] John Micklethwait and Adrian Wooldridge, *The Company: A Short History of a Revolutionary Idea* (NY: Modern Library, 2003), 63.

[21] Williamson, *Globalization and the Poor Periphery*, 8–11ff.

[22] Sebastian Conrad, *Globalisation and the Nation in Imperial Germany*, trans. Sorcha O'Hagan (Cambridge: Cambridge University Press, 2010), 35.

[23] Ronald Findlay and Kevin H. O'Rourke, "Commodity Market Integration, 1500–2000," in *Globalization in Historical Perspective*, ed. Michael D. Bordo et al. (Chicago: University of Chicago Press, 2003), 36; Karl Gunnar Persson, *Grain Markets in Europe, 1500–1900* (Cambridge: Cambridge University Press, 1999), chap. 5.

[24] The paragraphs rely on Jonathan Ira Levy, "Contemplating Delivery: Futures Trading and the Problem of Commodity Exchange in the United States, 1875–1905," *American Historical Review* (April 2006), 312ff; William Cronon, *Nature's Metropolis: Chicago and the Great West* (NY: Norton, 1992), 120–132 and chap. 3 passim; John, "Recasting the Information Infrastructure," 82–83, 86; Steven Topik, "Integration of the World Coffee Market," in *Global Coffee Economy*, ed. W. G. Clarence-Smith and Steven Topik (Cambridge: Cambridge University Press, 2003), 21–49.

exchange.[25] Furthering all this trade from the 1850s onward was the introduction of standardized methods of sorting, grading, weighing, and inspecting.[26]

In the American Midwest, as transactions in every conceivable commodity multiplied to unheard-of levels, a coordinating body came into being in 1848, the year the telegraph reached Chicago. Merchants in the city founded the Chicago Board of Trade, still today the world's largest commodities and futures exchange. Their intention was to stabilize the grain trade by regularizing procedures and establishing a futures market that could offer protection for farmers and dealers against the vagaries of the economy and the weather. Similar markets also appeared thereafter in other cities around the United States and the world (although Britain's first commodities futures market was not opened until 1882).

Using the telegraph, farmers, dealers, and investors had no need to set foot in Chicago or wherever it was their products were bought and sold. They could now acquire nearly instantaneous knowledge of surpluses or shortages anywhere on earth. This capability firmed up the market: because more people had quick access to prices, volatility declined. Meanwhile, speculators provided liquidity by betting on future prices – giving growers, miners, or cattle farmers guaranteed profits, which helped reduce the risks involved in planting, digging, or increasing the herd. To be sure, this could also bring trouble. In a globalized economy speculative bubbles would have a wider impact when they burst, plunging the world's economy into recession. It is not necessarily commodities speculation that was to blame, as opposed to investment in the more volatile financial sector. But speculators were an inseparable part of this wider system of securitization.

Yet on the whole, the trends brought about by this type of trading in commodities had a stabilizing effect. The new transportation and information technologies encouraged prices to converge internationally in what looked like a synchronized dance of supply and demand by connecting the major urban marketplaces to the grain-, meat-, dairy-, and metal-producing frontiers of the United States, Canada, Argentina, Australia, South Russia, and Siberia. In 1870, the price of rice in London

[25] Armand Mattelart, *Networking the World, 1794–2000*, trans. L. Carey-Libbrecht et al. (Minneapolis: University of Minnesota Press, 2000), 8.
[26] James R. Beniger, *The Control Revolution: Technological and Economic Origins of the Information Society* (Cambridge, MA: Harvard University Press, 1986), 18, 164–165, 248–254. Striving for standardization of weights, measures, and packaging units of commodities was already apparent in medieval Europe according to Jessica Dijkman, *Shaping Medieval Markets: The Organisation of Commodity Markets in Holland, c. 1200 – c. 1450* (Leiden: Brill, 2011), chap. 6.

was double that in Burma; by 1913, the difference was only 20 percent.[27] Transoceanic shipping rates also became more uniform, another sign that globalization was intensifying by the late nineteenth century.[28] Commodities-driven world trade grew in the nineteenth and twentieth centuries at its fastest pace in history: whereas it had increased by 1 percent annually from 1500 to 1800, from 1820 on it increased by close to 3.5 percent per year.[29]

These results were not always beneficial for all regions of the globe. Commodity price declines benefited consumers in the more urbanized nations of the West, and where they occurred they put an end to a long history of food shortages and food riots.[30] But the drop in prices had a negative effect on underdeveloped parts of Europe like Italy. In the 1880s, steam navigation and railroads opened the door to imports into this predominantly rural society. Cheap American and Russian agricultural goods poured in, causing mass unemployment, poverty, and emigration.[31] The situation was similar in Africa and Asia, where the majority of the population were peasant farmers who suffered from the loss of income as prices dropped. Further weakening these economies was the decline of handicrafts production in the face of competition from European industrial machinery. In 1820, the average Englishman earned only twice that of the average Indian; by 1913, the income of the former was ten times higher than the latter's. The price shifts brought about by nineteenth- and twentieth-century capitalism seem to have hurt the economic development of the world outside of Europe, European settler societies, and a few places like Japan that successfully westernized. And that is even before taking imperialism into account. The Western nations (plus Japan) had all the advantages

---

[27] Daniel Cohen, *Globalization and Its Enemies*, trans. Jessica B. Baker (Cambridge, MA: MIT Press, 2006), 24.

[28] Süleyman Özmucur and Şevket Pamuk, "Did European Commodity Prices Converge during 1500–1800?," Giovanni Federico and Karl Gunnar Pederson, "Market Integration and Convergence in the World Wheat Market, 1800–2000," and Alan L. Olmstead and Paul W. Rhode, "Biological Globalization: The Other Grain Invasion," all in *The New Comparative Economic History*, ed. Timothy J. Hatton et al. (Cambridge, MA: MIT Press, 2007), 59–140.

[29] Findlay and O'Rourke, "Commodity Market Integration," 40. By reducing "information lags," the telegraph also improved the efficiency and integration of foreign-exchange and regional stock markets: see Kenneth D. Garbade and William L. Silber, "Technology, Communication, and the Performance of Financial Markets, 1840–1975," *Journal of Finance* (June 1978), 819–832.

[30] John Bohstedt, *The Politics of Provisions: Food Riots, Moral Economy, and Market Transition in England, c. 1500–1850* (Farnham: Ashgate, 2010).

[31] Franco Amatori, "Reflections on Global Business and Modern Italian Enterprise," *Business History Review* (Summer 1997), 315–316.

in a globalized information economy, and it would not be until the mid- to late 1900s that the imbalances began, in some places, to be corrected.[32]

Mass production for a consumer society

Commodities markets as we know them were embryonic in the early modern era and came of age with the information advances of the nineteenth and twentieth centuries. Information innovations also helped give birth to something that was completely new in history: large-scale production for a consumer-oriented society, otherwise known as the mass market.

It happened most extensively in the United States. By 1900, this was already the largest industrial nation of the world, producing one-third of global output. While the American population doubled between 1880 and 1910, industrial production quadrupled. Commodity output climbed 50 percent higher every decade. The number of businesses grew from 427,000 in 1870 to 1.2 million in 1900 and more than 1.8 million in 1920. The biggest companies employed high-salaried white-collar managers, whose ranks swelled in the early years of corporate capitalism from 120,000 in 1870 to 900,000 in 1910. GDP more than doubled in the same time frame, increasing from $530 to $1,260. Across the board, wages rose and the consumer price index declined. Giving an indication of the type of economy already in place by 1900, a full quarter of the workforce was employed in the service sector, a category that included the growing number of urban professionals.[33]

These trends toward a mass market and consumer society continued to strengthen over the next century. They also offered a sharp contrast with Western Europe, where for a host of reasons consumer demand was weaker than in America by the early twentieth century, among them

---

[32] Williamson, *Globalization and the Poor Periphery*, chaps. 5–6; Cohen, *Globalization*, 29.

[33] This paragraph and the next draw on Walter Licht, *Industrializing America: The Nineteenth Century* (Baltimore: Johns Hopkins University Press, 1995), xiv–xv; Maury Klein, *The Genesis of Industrial America, 1870–1920* (Cambridge: Cambridge University Press, 2007), 177–178; Klein, *Flowering of the Third America*, 111; Alfred D. Chandler, Jr., "The United States: Seedbed of Managerial Capitalism," in *Managerial Hierarchies: Comparative Perspectives on the Rise of the Modern Industrial Enterprise*, ed. Alfred D. Chandler, Jr., and Herman Daems (Cambridge, MA: Harvard University Press, 1980), 35–39; Susan Strasser, *Satisfaction Guaranteed: The Making of the American Mass Market* (NY: Pantheon, 1989), 6; Victoria de Grazia, "Changing Consumption Regimes in Europe, 1930–1970," in *Getting and Spending: European and American Consumer Societies in the Twentieth Century*, ed. Susan Strasser et al. (Cambridge: Cambridge University Press, 1998), 67–69ff; David W. Jones, *Mass Motorization and Mass Transit: An American History and Policy Analysis* (Bloomington: Indiana University Press, 2008), 1.

lower wages due to higher population density, a larger labor supply, and greater pre-existing income inequalities. Perhaps most important, but often overlooked in comparisons with the United States, the two World Wars devastated Europe's economy, infrastructure, and household incomes. In this environment the mass production of consumer goods in Europe got off to a rocky start.

Yet it was not lacking altogether, as Western Europe invented the consumer society in the early modern era. Despite everything, this was still one of the richest parts of the world, and in Britain, France, Germany, the Low Countries, and Scandinavia, a mass market had begun to appear by the late nineteenth century (much of Southern Europe had to wait until after World War II). With more people living in cities, where there was a higher concentration of economic power and a large middle class, demand was on the upswing even if it was not on par with the United States. In Britain, the value of goods and services rose 250 percent in the nineteenth century, and 300 percent in 1880–1980.[34] Nonetheless, Europe could not generate a mass market on the American scale until its wars stopped and its societies became less stratified – and that was not until after 1945.[35]

What was the mass market like as it developed in the United States? Prior to the Civil War, Americans were starting to buy manufactured textiles, and by 1880, most households had store-bought cast-iron stoves. But many products were still homemade, including clothing, and if families did not grow their own vegetables, then they bought them directly from the farmer. Just thirty years after the war, consumer products had moved from home production to mass production. Nearly all Americans were dependent on factory-made products: soap, toothpaste, and safety razors; cornflakes, canned goods, cheese, and chewing gum;

---

[34] Theodore S. Hamerow, *The Birth of a New Europe* (Chapel Hill: University of North Carolina Press, 1983), chaps. 3–4; John Benson, *The Rise of Consumer Society in Britain, 1880–1980* (London: Longman, 1994), 14–27, 36; Robert C. Allen, "The Great Divergence in European Wages and Prices from the Middle Ages to the First World War," *Explorations in Economic History*, XXXVIII (2001), 411–447; Ivan T. Behrend, "A Transforming European Society, 1870–1945," in *Entrepreneurship and the Transformation of the Economy (10th–20th Centuries)*, ed. Paul Klep and Eddy van Cauwenberghe (Leuven University Press, 1994), 364ff.

[35] Mancur Olson, *The Rise and Decline of Nations: Stagflation and Social Rigidities* (New Haven: Yale University Press, 1982), chap. 4, argues the opposite, that World War II cleared away special-interest organizations and social groups opposed to change in Germany, Japan, and France. This then led to an explosion of growth in the unexpected postwar era economic "miracle," whereas stability and the absence of invasion accounts for the slower growth rates of Britain in the same period. But he ignores long-term continuities evidenced by the rise of consumerist mass production in these nations dating to the nineteenth century and even earlier. These continuities suggest that the world wars did indeed stop economic development in its tracks.

shoe polish and thread; cigarettes, matches, and liquor; cameras and flashlights. Their houses were loaded with the latest in conveniences: central heating, running water, bathrooms with porcelain sinks, tubs, and toilets, electric lights, and soon electric appliances.

Besides consumer durables, in this era entertainment, travel, and sports were commercialized and packaged for mass consumption too. And in the half century after the 1870s, the expansion of consumer credit made all of these goods and services available as credit agencies developed a standardized nationwide credit-reporting network with over 1,400 bureaus that kept and shared financial records on 60 million Americans. These institutions and their information-gathering practices were not necessary earlier because store-owners knew their customers and their reputations and could make credit decisions accordingly. In a mass society that was no longer feasible.

The mass market is both the culmination of the early modern consumer revolution and something very different: that is because mass production displaced the handicrafts that were at the heart of the consumer society "phase one." Mass-produced items were not as finely made as individually worked artisanal articles, but they were good enough for most people, they were affordable, and they brought in a greater profit for manufacturers. Consider stockings and automobiles. Silk stockings were exquisite, but too expensive for the majority of women, which is why only 155,000 pairs were made in the United States in 1900. By 1949, sales of nylon stockings – not as good, perhaps, but good enough – amounted to 453 million pairs.

The same trajectory applied to automobiles. In 1906, Woodrow Wilson, then president of Princeton University, denounced automobiles as toys for rich people that presented a "picture of the arrogance of wealth." In less than two decades, they were on the way to becoming a former luxury good that was now an affordable necessity. As an Indiana housewife with nine children put it in the 1920s, "I'll go without food before I'll see us give up the car." With mass production, the gap in lifestyles between rich and poor, urban and rural, began to close – one of the most characteristic phenomena of recent history.[36]

---

[36] For the preceding four paragraphs, see Frederick Lewis Allen, *The Big Change: American Transforms Itself, 1900–1950* (NY: Harper, 1952), chap. 8 and 192–195, with car quotes on 107–108; Josh Lauer, "The Good Consumer: Credit Reporting and the Invention of Financial Identity in the United States, 1840–1940," *Enterprise and Society* (Dec. 2010), 686–694; Strasser, *Satisfaction Guaranteed*, 5ff; Klein, *Genesis of Industrial America*, 31, 178–179; Benson, *Rise of Consumer Society in Britain*, 36–45; Rosa-Maria Gelpi and François Julien-Labruyère, *The History of Consumer Credit*, trans. Mn Liam Gavin (NY: St. Martin's, 2000), chaps. 8–9.

The vehicle most likely owned by the Indiana housewife was the Ford Model T. In 1908 it retailed for $850, and the company sold 5,986 cars. By 1916, the price had dropped to $360, and 577,036 customers bought one. The trick was mass production, applied to cars in 1913 when Henry Ford adopted a conveyor-based, continuous-flow system to his automobile plant. This was actually nothing new. For decades before Henry Ford came along, assembly lines and mechanical conveyors had been used for packing meats, milling flour, filling beer bottles, canning vegetables, and making soap, cigarettes, matches, cans, and breakfast cereals. Ford and his production team borrowed from all these models as well as industries using precision-made interchangeable parts. As Ford announced upon touring Swift's Chicago slaughterhouse, "if they can kill pigs and cows that way, we can build cars that way."[37]

The assembly line was the culmination of a long series of developments related to information gathering in manufacturing.[38] Before the introduction of the factory, entrepreneurs complained that they had no precise idea what was happening with the materials they supplied to families who worked them in their homes or small shops. In 1809, the merchant in charge of yarn production at Slater's Mill in Providence, Rhode Island, observed that "we have several hundred pieces now out weaving, but a hundred looms in families will not weave so much cloth as ten at least constantly employed under the immediate inspection of a workman."[39] As soon as it was feasible, therefore, the old putting-out system was happily abandoned and production moved into factories, whose function was in part informational: in the new setting manufacturers were able to see – and correct – what their laborers were doing on the job. With factory supervision they could achieve better control over the quality of work and stop the hemorrhaging of profits. As demand for mass-produced goods rose, standardization and quality control were vital to sales, and those were best achieved in the factory setting. Additionally, as employers became intimately familiar with the skill levels and technical knowledge

---

[37] David A. Hounshell, *From the American System to Mass Production, 1800–1932: The Development of Manufacturing Technology in the United States* (Baltimore: Johns Hopkins University Press, 1984), 10–11, and chap. 6, with Ford quote on 241. See also Alfred D. Chandler, Jr., *The Visible Hand: The Managerial Revolution in American Business* (Cambridge, MA: Harvard University Press, 1977), 376.

[38] Not all factories used Fordist mass-production techniques. Custom and batch production were applied for a large array of products from machine tools to jewelry that were less amenable to standardization. But the basic points of the next few paragraphs about systematization and information in the factory or workshop remain the same. See Philip Scranton, "Diversity in Diversity: Flexible Production and American Industrialization, 1880–1930," *Business History Review* (Spring 1991), 27–90.

[39] Chandler, *Visible Hand*, 63.

of their workers they could make improved assignments in the division of labor.[40]

As industry grew in size and complexity, though, management found that they still lacked enough direct knowledge of the activities carried out on the shop floor, as foremen could deliver inaccurate reports about worker behavior and workers could continue to perform inefficiently or sloppily. Two solutions to these information deficits emerged: first, the assembly line, where supervisors easily spotted employees who could not keep up – as famously spoofed by comedians Charlie Chaplin in his film "Modern Times" (1936) and Lucille Ball in the "candy factory" episode of her television sitcom "I Love Lucy" (1952); and second, the application of performance indicators under the influence of Frederick Winslow Taylor, the impresario of the scientific-management movement.

Taylor published his *Principles of Scientific Management* in 1911, based on his experience as a foreman at Midvale Steel Company in Philadelphia. There he had experimented with ways of improving the pacing and productivity of the workers under his authority. Wielding clipboards, chrono photography, and stopwatches he and his disciples developed a series of time-motion studies and laid down work standards and incentives in order to increase efficiency through the "elimination of humanity's greatest unnecessary waste" of time and energy.[41] Taylor strove for enhanced information about performance, but for the personnel affected by scientific management it seemed exploitative if not maniacally inhuman. Ironically, the greatest enthusiasm for Taylorism was in the early Soviet Union, where it seemed to offer fulfillment of the communist-utopian dream of remaking human beings into "cogs" in the machine of the planned economy.[42] In the United States, factory owners, including Ford, were well aware of Taylor's prescriptions but realized that they could never be fully achieved: the range of worker activities was too great for them to catalogue and control, and when they

[40] Naomi R. Lamoreaux, Daniel M. G. Raff, and Peter Temin, "Beyond Markets and Hierarchies: Toward a New Synthesis of American Business History," *American Historical Review* (April 2003), 412–413; Joel Mokyr, *The Gifts of Athena: Historical Origins of the Knowledge Economy* (Princeton: Princeton University Press, 2002), 131–148.

[41] Frederick Taylor, *The Principles of Scientific Management* (NY: Harper Bros., 1911); Frank and Lilien Gilbreth, *Fatigue Study: The Elimination of Humanity's Greatest Unnecessary Waste: A First Step In Motion Study* (NY: Macmillan, 1916).

[42] Kendall E. Bailes, "Alexei Gastev and the Soviet Controversy over Taylorism, 1918–24," *Soviet Studies* (July 1977), 373–394; Michael Voslensky, *Nomenklatura: The Soviet Ruling Class* (Garden City: Doubleday, 1984), 147ff. The early-Soviet quote about cogs can be found in Orlando Figes, *A People's Tragedy: A History of the Russian Revolution* (NY: Viking, 1997), 742–743.

tried, it provoked conflicts with labor. It turned out that management could get more out of the workforce if they paid higher wages, a notion they resisted for many years, but ended up doing to ease acceptance of assembly-line discipline.[43]

The phenomenon of Taylorism points to some of the ideals – even if not fully realized – that lay behind the assembly line in factories geared up for mass production. And if Taylorist discipline was too drastic for manufacturers, they did introduce other measurement methodologies, less severe but more effective, as the size, scale, and scope of manufacturing continued to expand. In 1910, a Detroit newspaper captured the spirit when it referred to the constant testing of processes on the factory floor: time-keeping for speed and accuracy, rearrangement of machinery for efficiency's sake, and close adherence to production schedules, all components in a new drive for "system, system, system."[44] And if that was not evident to the man and woman on the street, the imposition of standard time zones across the United States in the 1880s, at the behest of the railroad companies, and the erection of clock towers atop railroad stations and factories that now governed daily routines were publicly visible symbols and symptoms of that same drive toward control of information in an industrial society.[45]

Retail stores and mass distribution

Massive factory output represented the supply side of mass production. On the other half of the equation, industrialists could expect growing demand from a larger and wealthier population of consumers. But mass production entailed more than a simple response to demand, because to *sustain* their heavy production levels, industrial enterprises came to rely on mass marketing and mass distribution. This also stemmed from new methods of collecting and generating information, and it brought forth a new stage in the epoch of consumerism.

Mass merchandising was embodied in the department store, chain store, mail-order house, and supermarket. All sprang up after the mid-nineteenth century alongside earlier types of retail outlets: specialty stores

---

[43] Lamoreaux, Raff, and Temin, "Beyond Markets and Hierarchies," 413, 418–419; Licht, *Industrializing America*, 130–131; Douglass C. North, *Structure and Change in Economic History* (NY: Norton, 1981), 178; JoAnne Yates, "Business Use of Information and Technology during the Industrial Age," in *A Nation Transformed by Information*, ed. Chandler and Cortada, 109–111; Hounshell, *From the American System to Mass Production*, 249–253.

[44] Hounshell, *From the American System to Mass Production*, 229ff.

[45] Alan Trachtenberg, *The Incorporation of America: Culture and Society in the Gilded Age* (NY: Hill and Wang, 2007), 59–60.

in the city, and in the countryside general stores and peddlers. These traditional distributors had been dependent on the wholesalers and middlemen "jobbers" who were able to tightly control access to goods and keep prices high because they had knowledge of market conditions that no one else did, due to the limited circulation of information in a society without electricity. Modern retailing was an altogether different beast.

The department store served well-heeled urban customers. The best known from the founding generation were Macy's (1858), Marshall Field (1860s), and John Wanamaker's (also 1860s). These were partly modeled after French prototypes like Paris' Le Bon Marché (c. 1850), whose features the novelist Émile Zola later immortalized in his novel *Au Bonheur des Dames* (The Ladies' Paradise; 1883). With an outsized role in city life, by 1911 the Wanamaker building in Philadelphia was the largest retail store in the world. This marble-clad colossus occupied an entire city block, with hundreds of elegantly appointed galleries radiating from a domed central atrium that made the purchase of mass-produced goods seem the height of luxury.

Targeting a different clientele were chain stores like F. W. Woolworth's (1879) and J. C. Penney (1902). Known as "five and dimes" or "variety" stores, they carried less expensive goods and essentials for lower-class consumers in towns across America. But if the chain store lacked the grandiosity of the department store, the guiding principle was the same. Before penning *The Wonderful Wizard of Oz*, L. Frank Baum was the founder of the National Association of Window Trimmers (1897) and editor of the professional decorators' journal; as he put it, retail stores of all types resorted to vivid displays to "arouse in the observer the cupidity and longing to possess the goods."[46]

Mail-order houses such as Montgomery Ward (1872) and Sears, Roebuck, and Co. (1880s) aroused these same longings through catalogues. Initially they targeted the rural market by offering consumer goods to people who lived far away from stores. Their method of distributing goods caused the extinction of the once-ubiquitous itinerant peddler. Initially, these companies did all their business by mail: they sent out catalogues by the tens of millions, took orders by mail, and shipped goods over the rail network or via the parcel post services offered by Adams Express, American Express, or Wells Fargo, and after 1913 the US Post Office.[47]

[46] Baum cited in Klein, *Genesis of Industrial America*, 186–187.
[47] For comparison's sake, nowadays in the US advertisers send around 100 billion pieces of junk mail each year, half the total number of items delivered by the US Postal Service – see Ciara O'Rourke, "Reducing the Junk-Mail Footprint," *New York Times* (March 16,

By 1906, the Sears building in Chicago had become the largest structure devoted to business in the world. According to its catalogue,

miles of railroad tracks run lengthwise through and around this building for the receiving, moving, and forwarding of merchandise. Elevators, mechanical conveyors, endless chains, moving sidewalks, gravity chutes, apparatus and conveyors, pneumatic tubes and every known mechanical appliance for reducing labor, for the working out of economy and dispatch is to be utilized here in our great Works.[48]

Resembling a factory assembly line, machines opened 27,000 letters contained in 900 sacks of mail per day. Two thousand employees sorted them, keeping a card index for every customer, indicating what they had bought, and which catalogue to send them – no different in intent than today's efforts to assess consumer preferences.

Somewhat later, the self-service grocery stores – called supermarkets by the 1930s – made their entrance in cities and suburbs. The first to introduce open aisles with customers pushing shopping carts were Clarence Saunders' Piggly Wiggly, founded in Memphis, Tennessee, in 1916, and Cincinnati-based Kroger in the 1920s. They were followed by A&P, which became the largest chain of any kind in the world, with 15,700 stores.

All four types of mass-retail store emphasized a large variety of products, high sales volume, and fast turnover. These traits kept prices lower than in traditional merchant establishments, where profits came from the markup on cost. All of them were designed to attract a large number of customers and move goods off the shelves. In a mirror of trends in the factory, a hierarchy of managers existed behind the scenes to control for the quality of service and the inflow and outflow of stock. Logistical information guided a complex sequence of warehouses, distribution centers, and dispatch facilities to regulate shipments to stores and orders from suppliers. In the realm of merchandising (the word is an Americanism dating from the 1920s), constantly changing floor arrangements made displays appealing and accessible to shoppers who strolled through the building.[49]

2009), online at green.blogs.nytimes.com/2009/03/16/reducing-the-junk-mail-foot print/.

[48] Quote in Micklethwait and Wooldridge, *The Company*, 58.

[49] The paragraphs on retail stores are based on Klein, *Genesis of Industrial America*, 114–121, 189; Klein, *Flowering of the Third America*, 119–120; Michael B. Miller, *The Bon Marché: Bourgeois Culture and the Department Store, 1869–1920* (Princeton: Princeton University Press, 1981), chaps. 1–2, 5–6; Rachel Bowlby, *Carried Away: The Invention of Modern Shopping* (NY: Columbia University Press, 2001); Susan Porter Benson, *Counter Cultures: Saleswomen, Managers, and Customers in American Department Stores, 1890–1940* (Urbana: University of Illinois Press, 1988), chaps. 1–2; Strasser, *Satisfaction Guaranteed*, 81; Beniger, *Control Revolution*, 155–161; H. Thomas Johnson, "Managing by Remote Control: Recent Management Accounting

As today with Walmart, small retailers were up in arms about the evils of the "monopolistic" department stores, mail-order houses, and chain stores whenever they appeared on the scene. Afraid for their survival, merchants in the 1920s organized the burning of sales catalogues, agitated against rural-free delivery and parcel post, and encouraged zoning laws to keep mass retailers out. Social critics decried the low wages and the "machinelike atmosphere" designed to vacuum up the wealth of local communities, profit Wall Street tycoons, and enact a "dictatorship of big money."[50] But to no avail. Consumers accepted Frank Woolworth's defense of his labor practices: "We must have cheap help or we cannot sell cheap goods."[51] As Gene Talmadge, later governor of Georgia, announced to an audience during one of his election campaigns: "The poor dirt farmer ain't got but three friends on this earth: God Almighty, Sears Roebuck, and Gene Talmadge." The voters must have agreed because they elected him and kept coming to the chain stores.[52]

Revenues in the mass-retail business depended on selling to large numbers of people. In this they were assisted by the artifice of displays, but also by the arrival of mass transit. As late as the 1880s, most commuters within cities traveled by foot. Horse-drawn carriages or omnibuses were too expensive for average people, who in any case lived close to where they worked and shopped. The introduction of the cable car, electric tramway, and overhead electric streetcar changed that. Invented by American and European engineers, these means of conveyance spread faster in the United States because of the greater number of private companies involved. On both continents, though, cities laid thousands of miles of track and strung webs of wire atop the streets, giving a new mobility to hundreds of millions of passengers up and down the social scale. By 1900, the first subways, in Boston, New York, London, and Paris, were shuttling traffic through giant underground

Practice in Historical Perspective," in *Inside the Business Enterprise: Historical Perspectives on the Use of Information*, ed. Peter Temin (Chicago: University of Chicago Press, 1991), 48; Lamoreaux, Raff, and Temin, "Beyond Markets and Hierarchies," 415–417; Susan Strasser, "Woolworth to Wal-Mart: Mass Merchandising and the Changing Culture of Consumption," in *Wal-Mart: The Face of Twenty-First Century Capitalism*, ed. Nelson Lichtenstein (NY: New Press, 2006), 35–36, 41.

50 Beniger, *Control Revolution*, 338 (monopolistic quote); Ben Price, "A Movement Diverted: How Corporations Neutralized Anti–Chain Store Campaigns of the 1920s and 1930s" (2005), online at http://celdf.org/wp-content/uploads/2015/08/A-Movement-Diverted.pdf (machine-like quote); and Paul Ingram and Hayagreeva Rao, "Store Wars: The Enactment and Repeal of Anti-Chain-Store Legislation in America," *American Journal of Sociology* (Sept. 2004), 451 (dictatorship quote). See also Lewis Atherton, *Main Street on the Middle Border* (Bloomington: Indiana University Press, 1954), 232–233, 240–241.

51 Strasser, "Woolworth to Wal-Mart," 31.

52 William E. Leuchtenberg, *The White House Looks South* (Baton Rouge: Louisiana State University Press, 2005), 124 (quote); Beniger, *Control Revolution*, 338–341.

tubes.[53] And where the tracks did not extend, workers all over Europe and the United States, especially in more rural areas, hopped on newly mass-produced bicycles.[54]

Then the automobile age arrived. Because of the comparatively higher disposable income of Americans and – at first – the presence of sufficient domestic sources of oil, the United States over several decades disinvested in mass transit. By 1925, it had a daunting lead over Europe in individual automobile ownership. Beginning in the 1930s, highways sliced through the American countryside, with service stations, diners, and roadside motor inns forming the landscape of our parents', grand-parents', and great-grandparents' generations. After World War II, the construction of the interstate expressway system, the steady rise of airmail and passenger air travel, and the rapid growth of the trucking industry at the expense (at least temporarily) of rail freight accelerated these trans-port and communications trends, which caused transaction costs for businesses and consumers to plummet. Altogether they created the sub-urbs, further eroded rural isolation, broadened labor markets, and encouraged the endless shopping that became the American way of life.[55]

Mass marketing: "Ceaseless propaganda"

Endless shopping was also a product of endless advertising. Mass produc-tion depended not only on mass transit, but also on mass marketing. The large output of factories was a response to consumer demand, but that could be fickle. In order to earn a profit while covering the high costs of the physical plant and a workforce, companies had to sell their products at a reliably steady if not rising rate. To do so they ratcheted up their advertising.

Businesses were more than ever aware of the need to generate demand that was not necessarily preexisting. A speaker at the Nashville Ad Club admitted to this in 1916: "It is all very well to get the sales of things that people want to buy, but that is too small in volume. We must make people

---

[53] George W. Hilton and John F. Due, *The Electric Interurban Railways in America* (Stanford: Stanford University Press, 1960); John P. McKay, *Tramways and Trolleys: The Rise of Urban Mass Transport in Europe* (Princeton: Princeton University Press, 1976); William D. Middleton and William D. Middleton III, *Frank Julian Sprague: Electrical Inventor and Engineer* (Bloomington: Indiana University Press, 2009), chaps. 3–4.

[54] David V. Herlihy, *Bicycle: The History* (New Haven: Yale University Press, 2004), chap. 13.

[55] Allen, *The Big Change*, chap. 8; Jones, *Mass Motorization and Mass Transit*, 1, 3ff, 7–10, 14–15, chaps. 2–5; Mark H. Rose, Bruce E. Seely, and Paul F. Barrett, *The Best Transportation System in the World: Railroads, Trucks, Airlines, and American Public Policy in the Twentieth Century* (Columbus: Ohio State University Press, 2006), chaps. 2–4.

want many other things, in order to get a big increase in business." Companies tried to make consumers think they could not live without their products – an idea brazenly expressed by Nabisco's "Uneeda Biscuit" (1898). Not long before the twentieth century's totalitarian regimes gave propaganda a bad name, the spokesman for the Campbell Soup Company referred to its advertising as "ceaseless propaganda for soup-eating" – just as General Motors called theirs "sales propaganda." Such relentless corporate campaigning and the persuasive powers of modern advertising altered the nature of the marketplace.[56]

To conjure up demand, the magicians of advertising depended above all on product branding. By giving the impression of familiarity and reliability, brand names sustained a regular customer base, which gave companies some protection from competition and the business cycle. But it also gave consumers an awareness of at least a modicum of quality, which is the same reason for the appeal of the chain store and chain restaurant: unadventurous travelers from South Carolina searching for food on the interstate in Nebraska know what they can expect from McDonald's or Burger King as opposed to unfamiliar local establishments. In this sense, branding does not just manipulate, although some of the advertising might, but also offers regularized information about a given product or establishment.[57]

Branding was not new to the industrial age, as English products from the eighteenth century like Wedgwood pottery attest.[58] For that matter, national flags have a similar function, none more recognizably so than the American stars and stripes.[59] But branding was uncommon until the invention of a number of packaging and informational devices: the paper-bag machine (1852); the square-bottomed bag and bags stamped with the name of the product inside (late 1860s); printing on cans (1870s); the folding cardboard carton, initially for breakfast cereals (1880s);

[56] For the preceding two paragraphs, see Strasser, *Satisfaction Guaranteed*, 27 (Nashville quote), 32, 35, 95 (Campbell's soup quote), and passim; Roland Marchand, "Customer Research as Public Relations: General Motors in the 1930s," in *Getting and Spending*, ed. Strasser et al., 102 (GM quote); Richard S. Tedlow, *New and Improved: The Story of Mass Marketing in America* (NY: Basic Books, 1990); Pamela Walker Laird, *Advertising Progress: American Business and the Rise of Consumer Marketing* (Baltimore: Johns Hopkins University Press, 1998).

[57] George A. Akerlof, *An Economic Theorist's Book of Tales* (Cambridge: Cambridge University Press, 1984), 21. For the role of branding in the French bread industry, see Steven Laurence Kaplan, *Good Bread Is Back: A Contemporary History of French Bread* (Durham, NC: Duke University Press, 2006), 224–227, 314.

[58] Hoh-Cheung Mui and Lorna H. Mui, *Shops and Shopkeeping in Eighteenth-Century England* (Montreal: McGill-Queen's University Press, 1989), 230–231.

[59] Bruce Cumings, "Still the American Century," in *The Interregnum: Controversies in World Politics, 1989–1999*, ed. Michael Cox et al. (Cambridge: Cambridge University Press, 1999), 294.

labeling boxes with brand names (1890s); mechanized bottle making (1903); aluminum foil (1910); and cellophane (1913). The captions to two photographs in a 1928 book called *Packages that Sell* capture the difference these devices made: the first describes the "interior of a typical old-fashioned grocery store before the era of modern packaging. Crackers and sugar in unsanitary barrels, tea and spices in bins – and only a few canned goods." The second features "a modern grocery store interior. Everything is packaged in sanitary containers which are designed not only to convey but also to sell the products they contain. A merchandising revolution has taken place."[60]

That revolution was protected by law in the United States, with the passage of trademark legislation in 1905 (which lagged behind English law by three decades). By then, many of the brands we are familiar with today were already in existence. The earliest was Singer Sewing Machine Company, founded in 1851, followed in the 1860s by Sherwin-Williams house paints; in the 1870s by Levi's jeans, Colgate toothpaste, Heinz ketchup, Budweiser beer, and Scott toilet paper; in the 1880s by Coca-Cola, Pillsbury flour, Kodak film, and Proctor and Gamble's Ivory soap; in the 1890s by Campbell's soups, Quaker oats, and Wrigley's chewing gums; and in the early 1900s by Gillette safety razors, Kellogg's corn-flakes, Hershey's kisses, and Jell-O gelatin – the latter a mix of sugar and powdered collagen wastes from slaughterhouses that aggressive marketing turned into a staple of American kitchen cupboards.[61]

Along with branding, the scale and scope of advertising began to change in other ways in the nineteenth century. In the 1880s, larger ads with artwork or photographs replaced the small classified notices of yore when magazines like *Scribner's*, *Harper's*, or *Ladies Home Journal* and the new mass-circulation newspapers of William Randolph Hearst and Joseph Pulitzer offered lower fixed rates for advertising. In the same decade the first billboards went up, utilizing the new techniques of poster lithography, and printed ads were tacked to the sides of horse-drawn streetcars. After the turn of the century, electric light bulbs lit up advertising displays on Times Square and heavily trafficked intersections in other major cities. In the 1920s, flashing signs and signs with glowing

[60] Bowlby, *Carried Away*, 80.
[61] For the section on the history of packaging and branding in America I have drawn on Strasser, S*atisfaction Guaranteed*, 29–32, 45ff, 53–55, 57; Klein, *Genesis of Industrial America*, 180–185; Beniger, *Control Revolution*, 264–271; and Gary S. Cross and Robert N. Proctor, *Packaged Pleasures: How Technology and Marketing Revolutionized Desire* (Chicago: University of Chicago Press, 2014), chap. 4. On the history of canning, see Sue Shephard, *Pickled, Potted, and Canned: How the Art and Science of Food Preserving Changed the World* (NY: Simon and Schuster, 2000), chap. 12.

neon tubes made their appearance.[62] Advertising began in movie houses in the 1890s, and with radio and later TV, it penetrated homes in the form of commercials, seamlessly insinuated into programs like the "soap operas" invented in the 1920s and 1930s by companies promoting their bath and cleaning products: Procter and Gamble and Palmolive in the United States, and Lever Bros. in the United Kingdom.[63] In one of his poems, Carl Sandburg captured the sudden ubiquity of advertisements in the United States:

> Another baby in Cleveland, Ohio,
> in Cuyahoga County, Ohio–
> why did she ask:
>> "Papa,
>> what is the moon
>> supposed to advertise?"[64]

The bombardment of product information through printed ads and commercials went hand in hand with the growth of the advertising profession. In the whole United States, only two advertising copywriters were at work in 1880s. By the late 1890s, the founding date of the Association of American Advertisers, their number was in the hundreds, with ten times again as many by 1915. In the same three decades, company spending on advertising rose from $200 million to well over a billion dollars.

As industry executive Bruce Barton explained in 1929, "the American conception of advertising is to arouse desires and stimulate wants." With that in mind, advertisers sought to understand the customer so as to better respond to his or her needs, anticipate shifts in taste, and assess the quality of products after purchase. This was a world away from the time when itinerant peddlers sold their wares and decamped. The randomness and uncertainties inherent in those days were to be eliminated by the new marketing profession, which made sophisticated attempts to gather information about consumers. One of the first American advertising firms, N. W. Ayer and Son, began conducting

---

[62] Strasser, *Satisfaction Guaranteed*, 90–91, 93; Klein, *Genesis of Industrial America*, 186–187; Beniger, *Control Revolution*, 19–20, 353–354. For parallel British developments, see W. Hamish Fraser, *The Coming of the Mass Market, 1850–1914* (Hamden: Archon Books, 1981), chap. 10.

[63] Alecia Swasy, *Soap Opera: The Inside Story of Procter and Gamble* (NY: Times Books, 1993), 109–111; Kate Bowles, "Soap Opera," in *The Australian TV Book*, ed. Graeme Turner and Stuart Cunningham (St. Leonards, NSW: Allen and Unwin, 2000), 118.

[64] Carl Sandburg, "The People, Yes," in *Complete Poems of Carl Sandburg* (Boston: Houghton Mifflin, 2003), 443.

market surveys for clients in 1879. By the late nineteenth century, it had become routine for individual stores and companies to collect statistics on customer satisfaction and wants, sometimes going house to house to do so.[65]

The procedures became more rigorous in the new century as academics got involved.[66] Walter Dill Scott, an applied psychology professor at Northwestern University, authored the first textbook on the subject, *The Theory of Advertising*, in 1903, and the next year began issuing regular studies of consumer behavior and the techniques of sales persuasion. Within the decade, universities were offering marketing courses and making their services available to industry: in 1913 Harvard's Bureau of Business Research published its first bulletin – on selling shoes.

Freudianism was a force in its time, too, especially after Jewish psychologists fled Nazi-occupied Europe for American shores. Eddie Bernays applied the intellectual breakthroughs of his uncle, Sigmund Freud, to the marketing profession. The Austrian-born advertiser introduced the notion of subliminal messaging to "control and regiment the masses according to our will without them knowing it." In his work for the American Tobacco Corporation, he developed ads featuring slender, attractive women holding cigarettes that he believed represented penises in the subconscious of viewers. But his main contribution was to theorize that people received emotional satisfaction from buying things, and to show advertisers how to exploit that insight to encourage sales.[67] Another refugee-psychologist from Vienna, Ernest Dichter, introduced "motivational research" and focus groups to ascertain the psychology behind shoppers' predilection for specific products.[68] His 1957 report for Frito-Lay on how to allay people's "fears and resistances" to eating potato chips established the game plan for the expansion of the entire junk-food industry.[69]

---

[65] For the preceding two paragraphs, see Strasser, *Satisfaction Guaranteed*, 95, 99, 148–161; Klein, *Genesis of Industrial America*, 185–189; Lamoreaux, Raff, and Temin, "Beyond Markets and Hierarchies," 416, 420; Jackson Lears, *Fables of Abundance: A Cultural History of Advertising in America* (NY: Basic Books, 1994), 226–233, with Barton quote on 227.

[66] For this paragraph and the two that follow, see Walter Friedman, *Birth of a Salesman: The Transformation of Selling in America* (Cambridge, MA: Harvard University Press, 2004), 5–10, 154–166, chap. 7, and passim.

[67] Mark Frauenfelder, *Made by Hand: Searching for Meaning in a Throwaway World* (NY: Portfolio, 2010), 25–28.

[68] *Economist* (Dec. 17, 2011), 119–123. See also Daniel Horowitz, "The Emigré as Celebrant of American Consumer Culture," in *Getting and Spending*, ed. Strasser et al., 157–166.

[69] Michael Moss, *Salt, Sugar, Fat: How the Food Giants Hooked Us* (NY: Random House, 2013), 325–327.

Taylorism also influenced marketing. Countless trade journals and books like Charles Wilson Hoyt's *Scientific Sales Management* (1913) urged the introduction of system to the sales force. Salesmen were supposed to become professionals rather than hucksters, and companies subjected them to as much rigid discipline and supervision as they did factory workers. Their bosses issued minute instructions for routes, sales targets, and how to relate to customers, including the number of jokes to tell before the sales pitch. And they carefully logged receipts for examination at headquarters – which shows us that collection of point-of-sale data in the Walmart era is also nothing new, albeit collated by computers.

The result of all this activity was that companies paid careful attention to consumer preferences, or what a Gimbel's department-store executive referred to in the 1930s as "X-raying the consumer."[70] Coca-Cola boss Robert Woodruff was one of the first to introduce scientific techniques in marketing his product. In 1923, he had the company's Statistical Department (formerly the Information Department), begin a survey of all the stores in the nation with soda fountains (115,000 in total) to ascertain whether store location and traffic related to sales. The surveys showed that it did, thereby laying down a core principle of retailing drinks from Coke to Starbucks. Company analysts also surveyed tens of thousands of customers to gauge why they came back for more, and its ad agencies kept tabs on demand by collecting bottle caps from trash cans near office-building coolers to find out what percentage was Coke.[71]

This set the standard for every other industry. Like bicycle and railroad-locomotive companies before it, General Motors began to introduce annual changes to its automobile models to both mold and keep up with demand.[72] And supermarkets embraced a scientific approach to marketing that governed shelf positioning, the alluring layout of the produce department, and the display of items designated to attract attention at the end of aisles. Today, grocery-store marketers continue to try to track and make sense of customer behavior with

[70] Lawrence R. Samuel, *Freud on Madison Avenue* (Philadelphia: University of Pennsylvania Press, 2010), 6 (quote); Marchand, "Customer Research as Public Relations," 85–109.

[71] Mark Pendergrast, *For God, Country, and Coca-Cola: The Definitive History of the Great American Soft Drink and the Company that Makes It*, 2nd ed. (NY: Basic Books, 2000), 161–163, 180. For the importance of store locations in the coffee business, see Tim Harford, *The Undercover Economist* (NY: Random House, 2005), 3–11.

[72] Sally H. Clark, *Trust and Power: Consumers, the Modern Corporation, and the Making of the United States Automobile Market* (Cambridge: Cambridge University Press, 2007), chap. 5; Herlihy, *Bicycle*, 262, 361; Philip Scranton, *Endless Novelty: Specialty Production and American Industrialization, 1865–1925* (Princeton: Princeton University Press, 1997), 18, 21.

security cameras and constant surveying, going so far as to solicit volunteer shoppers to undergo brain scans to better comprehend the deep mental processes of consumer behavior.[73] Digital technologies are also exploiting greater data-mining capabilities in stores and among customers, as Chapter 6 details.

Corporate giants

The mass market that I have been describing is what gave rise to the large corporation. American Progressives viewed corporate agglomerations as life-crushing octopi.[74] German scholar Max Weber warned that they were tantamount to constructing an iron cage that would imprison humanity in a life of capitalist-bureaucratic misery.[75] For decades, novelists and social critics have subjected the conformist "company men" who worked for these companies to scathing critiques.[76] And who can deny the validity of some of these views if we think of the generally amoral, but sometimes downright immoral and socially irresponsible, behavior of big corporations?[77] Yet, big business delivers what consumers want at a reasonable price, even if a portion of demand is artificially jacked up by advertising. The reality is that it takes giant, often inhuman-seeming and soulless corporate organizations to master the complexities of mass production and distribution.

Needless to say, maximization of profit is the end game: as I have argued earlier, that has always been the aim of business enterprise, large or small, Western or non-Western, modern or ancient. How the large corporation was able to come into existence and how it was able to make a profit in the mass market are the real questions at hand. The short answer to both is this: because it succeeded at acquiring and analyzing vast amounts of information.[78]

The large corporation was by no means the only kind of business organization in existence. Big firms came to prevail in heavy industry,

---

[73] Nicholas Carr, *The Big Switch: Rewiring the World, from Edison to Google* (NY: Norton, 2008), 207; *Economist* (Dec. 20, 2008), 105–107.

[74] National Humanities Center, Toolbox Library, Primary Resources in U.S. History and Literature, "Power: Taming the Octopus," online at http://nationalhumanitiescenter.org /pds/gilded/power/power.htm.

[75] Max Weber, *The Protestant Ethic and the Spirit of Capitalism*, ed. Richard Swedberg (NY: Norton, 2009), 96.

[76] Anthony Sampson, *Company Man: The Rise and Fall of Corporate Life* (NY: TimesBusiness, 1995).

[77] As chronicled by, among many others, Kurt Eichenwald in *The Informant* (NY: Broadway Books, 2001) and *Conspiracy of Fools* (NY: Broadway Books, 2005).

[78] Naomi R. Lamoreaux, "Management," in *Oxford Encyclopedia of Economic History*, ed. Mokyr, vol. III, 427–429.

and big retail chains then and now put the squeeze on smaller mom-and-pop outfits, but in specialty stores, the service sector, niche manufacturing, and construction, small or medium-size business has always been the norm. Barriers to entry are usually very high within industries dominated by big corporations, but if one thinks of IBM in the wake of Silicon Valley or the American car industry in the face of the Japanese challenge, it is evident that not even the largest, seemingly invincible company is immune to serious competition. And at no time did big business ever generate more than around half of GNP.[79] Nonetheless, the large corporation has been the most distinctive feature of American business life from the late nineteenth century to the present, and it is important to recognize that it took shape the way it did because of changes in both the marketplace and the information environment.[80]

Big business was born on the railroads, which required marshaling enormous quantities of materials and numbers of laborers during construction; the continuous upkeep of track, rolling stock, and stations; complex logistics scheduling passenger and freight transport; constant vigilance for the safety of workers and passengers; and clearance of colossal quantities of capital, revenues, and expenditures during every stage and for every aspect of the railroad company's existence.

The founding father of the American model of corporate management was Daniel C. McCallum, superintendent of the New York and Erie Railroad, who in 1854 began using telegraph records to determine costs and set efficient rates on his rail line.[81] He pinpointed the problem faced not only by railroad managers but by executives of all large companies yet to come: "A Superintendent of a road fifty miles in length can give its business his personal attention . . . [but] in the government of a road five hundred miles in length a very different state exists." The latter requires a new kind of managerial structure: "To be efficient and successful, [it]

---

[79] Mansel G. Blackford, "Small Business in America: A Historiographic Survey," *Business History Review* (Spring 1991), 1–26; Leslie Hannah, "Marshall's 'Trees' and the Global 'Forest': Were Giant Redwoods Different?" in *Learning by Doing in Markets, Firms, and Countries*, ed. Naomi R. Lamoreaux, Daniel M. G. Raff, and Peter Temin (Chicago: University of Chicago Press, 1999), 258–262, 287; Klein, *Flowering of the Third America*, 49; Klein, *Genesis of Industrial America*, 105–106; Micklelthwait and Wooldridge, *The Company*, 77–78.

[80] This chapter focuses on the United States, but for a summary of the parallel rise of the European vertically integrated industrial enterprise, which first occurred in the Rhine valley of Germany and Switzerland, see Alfred D. Chandler, Jr., "How High Technology Industries Transformed Work and Life Worldwide from the 1880s to the 1990s," *Capitalism and Society*, vol. I, no. 2 (2006), 2, 4–18.

[81] Alfred D. Chandler, Jr., "The Information Age in Historical Perspective," in *A Nation Transformed by Information*, ed. Chandler and Cortada, 11–12; Chandler, *Visible Hand*, chap. 3.

should be such as to give to the principal and responsible head of the running department a complete daily history of details in all their minutiae."[82]

Several developments followed from McCallum's observation: one, the invention of financial, capital, and cost accounting, the first significant innovations in bookkeeping since the Italian Renaissance. For centuries, it had sufficed to keep simple accounts using centuries-old methods, if any method at all. But the railroads required a more sophisticated approach. Financial accounting involved the collection and auditing of daily financial transactions on the railroad to establish performance indicators based on the ratios between revenues and expenditures. Capital accounting assessed depreciation of physical plant and equipment. Cost accounting laid bare comparative cost data for each branch of the company. As McCallum wrote in 1855: the "comparison [of division accounts] will show the officers who conduct their business with the greatest economy."[83]

It was Albert Fink, an executive of the Louisville and Nashville Railroad from the mid-1850s to the mid-1870s, who first applied McCallum's ideas. Other rail companies followed suit, as did most big firms between the 1880s and 1920s, when reams of data had to be made accessible to managers, billing offices, investors, federal and state tax and regulatory agencies, and human-relations departments. A list of white-collar positions new to companies in this period suggests the growing complexity of financial analysis: cost accountant; sales controller; production controller; financial controller; auditor; system manager.[84]

The second development to follow from McCallum's line of reasoning was the reorganization of the company. McCallum devised one of the earliest business-organization charts, which broke railroad companies into decentralized divisions, each reporting up the chain of command to central management. Production-expense reports gave upper executives the bird's-eye view of each division's performance. Division managers, in turn, applied cost-accounting tools to achieve a better view of their subordinates' performance.[85] In the words of business historian Alfred D. Chandler, Jr., railroad companies of the 1850s and 1860s were "the first American business enterprise to build a large internal organizational structure with carefully defined lines of responsibility, authority, and communication between the central office, departmental headquarters,

[82] Chandler, *Visible Hand*, respective quotes on 98 and 103.
[83] Chandler, *Visible Hand*, 109–120, with quote on 115.
[84] Yates, "Business Use of Information," 111 and passim.
[85] Chandler, *Visible Hand*, 39, 109ff; Lamoreaux, "Management," 427–428; Lamoreaux, Raff, and Peter Temin, "Beyond Markets and Hierarchies," 413.

and field units; and they were the first to develop financial and statistical flows to control and evaluate the work of the many managers."[86]

It bears repeating that the rationale for this type of corporate organization was informational. As Alexander Hamilton Church, one of the key members of the scientific-management movement, wrote in *Engineering Magazine* in 1900: "The object of the commercial, or, as it might also be termed, the administrative organization scheme, should be to collect knowledge of what is going forward, not merely qualitatively, but quantitatively: it should also provide the means of regulating as well as the means of recording."[87]

Sharing that sentiment, the chairman of General Motors, Alfred P. Sloan, Jr., reorganized his company in the 1920s to improve upon the model introduced decades earlier on the railroads. Sloan did so after recognizing that "we did not have adequate knowledge or control of the individual operating divisions. It was a management by crony, with the divisions operating on a horse-trading basis." He formed each brand of automobile into an autonomous division headed by its own general manager. The chief of each division answered to the GM board, which undertook strategic decision making within the company as a whole. Sloan called this arrangement the "concept of co-ordinated decentralization." To make that work, he later explained, "each division manager was required to submit monthly reports of his total operating results ... The divisional return-on-investment reports were constantly studied by the top executives ... The figures did not give automatic answers to problems. They simply exposed the facts with which to judge whether divisions were operating in line with expectations." Referring to his own plan, but unconsciously stating the essence of managerial capitalism, Sloan wrote that "it was a matter of making things visible."[88]

Visibility through multidivisional organization became the holy grail for all of American big business. From the 1920s onward, corporations like General Electric, Standard Oil, and US Steel followed GM and DuPont, the earliest companies to restructure themselves as multidivisional firms. Because of the coordination-and-control ability emanating from these arrangements, in the post–World War II era IBM, Xerox, and most

---

[86] Chandler, *Visible Hand*, 120.

[87] JoAnne Yates, *Control through Communication: The Rise of System in American Management* (Baltimore: Johns Hopkins University Press, 1989), 13.

[88] Alfred P. Sloan, Jr., *My Years with General Motors* (Garden City: Doubleday, 1964), 27–28, 142–143, 429. In the words of Frank H. Knight, "all management is largely a matter of prediction," its goal being a "reduction of the uncertainty in individual judgments and decisions." Respective quotes from Frank H. Knight, "Socialism: The Nature of the Problem," *Ethics* (April, 1940), 271–272; and his *Risk, Uncertainty, and Profit* (Boston: Houghton Mifflin, 1921), 291–292.

other Fortune 500 companies adopted them. After the 1970s, some of these gargantuan companies came under threat from competitors because of their size-induced bureaucratic rigidities – which obscured what Sloan wanted to make visible. But those that wanted to survive and thrive adapted, figuring out how to revive their original information-generating capabilities.[89] Ironically, GM was one of the ones that did not, going into bankruptcy in 2009 and government receivership before being reformed and resurrected in part by encouraging the internal circulation of information which had previously been smothered under layers of hierarchy.[90] Microsoft and other iconic firms of the IT revolution have run into some of the same problems, but have seen no better way to organize themselves.[91] Google, by contrast, maintains a "flat" administrative structure in order to optimize the flow of information and kindle innovation – a "wafer-thin" bureaucracy, radically decentralized and without middle managers, to encourage the movement of ideas not from top down but from bottom up as well as laterally between different work units.[92] However, since all major decisions are made at the top by its founders and chief executives, Google's structure is not as radically original as it seems, but reminds one of the family firms of pre-big-business days.

The organizational features of big business were supposed to maximize the flow of information, but the corporate behemoths were able to get off the ground and fly in the first place only because all kinds of new devices came along to meet their needs in gathering, storing, conveying, and analyzing information. Just as pilots of the new flying machines depended on their cockpit instruments, so business managers in the main office maneuvered through the heady atmosphere of the Gilded Age with theirs. It is for good reason that we consider the 1880s–1920s to be the golden age of office equipment.

Once upon a time, businesses were small and relatively simple affairs that could get by just fine with a few staff – an owner-manager and a couple of clerks working with primitive supplies: a quill pen, paper,

---

[89] Micklelthwait and Wooldridge, *The Company*, 58–59, 104ff, 117ff, and chaps. 6–7 passim; Lamoreaux, "Management," 428; Lamoreaux, Raff, and Temin, "Beyond Markets and Hierarchies," 421–422 and passim.

[90] On its bankruptcy and revival, see Ed Whitacre, *American Turnaround: Reinventing AT&T and GM and the Way We Do Business in America* (NY: Business Plus, 2013), 9–12, 38–40, 44, 175–176, 179.

[91] "Todd Bishop, "Microsoft Announces Major Reorganization," *Seattle Post Intelligencer* (Sept. 19, 2005), online at seattlepi.com/default/article/Microsoft-announces-major-re organization-trying-1183301.php.

[92] Gary Hamel, *The Future of Management* (Boston: Harvard Business Review Press, 2007), chap. 6.

and built-in pigeon holes for storing documents. Oral transmission of instructions and decisions was routine within the company, and most written records were of transactions with outsiders. But that was no longer conceivable in large corporations producing for the mass market. More formalized and systematic approaches were mandatory, and they set off an avalanche of paperwork. To help office staff cope, all kinds of new supplies and equipment became available.

Beginning in the 1880s, complex business machines manufactured by the National Cash Register Company and the Burroughs Adding Machine Company generated sales, salary, and production data; these were the first calculating machines to come into use since the invention of the abacus several thousand years earlier! Carbon paper and A. B. Dick's stencil mimeograph eased the inter-office distribution of multiple copies of memoranda and reports. Employees took notes with new writing implements: steel pens, or pencils with attached erasers. Such devilishly clever devices as the pin, paper clip, stapler, or binder clip held together the profusion of paper and put an end to the time-wasting practice of punching holes and sewing pages together for insertion onto wooden or metal pegs in heavy ledger books. The mass of material thus generated was stored for easy retrieval in new filing cabinets, whose contents were organized and made accessible using card indexes (an idea borrowed from those information warehouses, the libraries). If office staff needed to mail something, they placed it in mass-produced envelopes. Sales reps, accountants, and division managers could present data during meetings in the eminently comprehensible format of the graph, also a recent innovation. The boss might record memos for his staff on a Dictaphone, available for purchase as of 1907. And employees at all levels became more precise about keeping time with the coming of standard time, the presence of business clocks, and ever more common wristwatches.[93] All told, these devices increased the speed of information transmission. Adding machines, for instance, enabled calculations that were 600 times faster than doing them by hand with pencil and paper. That does not seem like much compared with computers, but relative to what had come before it was a large increase.[94]

Nothing epitomized the era more than the typewriter. According to an 1887 issue of *Penman's Art Journal*, "five years ago the typewriter was simply a mechanical curiosity. Today its monotonous click can be heard

[93] Yates, "Business Use of Information and Technology"; Yates, *Control through Communication*, chapter 2 and passim; Beniger, *Control Revolution*, 16, 282–283, 327; interview with railroad historian H. Roger Grant (July 22, 2009).

[94] Karl Gunnar Persson, *An Economic History of Europe* (Cambridge: Cambridge University Press, 2010), 109.

in almost every well-regulated business establishment in the country. A great revolution is taking place, and the typewriter is at the bottom of it." Invented in the mid-1870s by the Remington Typewriter Company, it allowed for the standardized transcription of information, an elemental feature of managerial capitalism. Eventually, most typists and stenographers were women, whose wages were low and hours long, but for many of them it was a desirable job that promised a route to a more independent life in the city. Female secretaries also signified, along with the growing legions of (comparatively better-paid) male office employees, the changing nature of American society: from 1900 onward, the number of clerical, professional, and other knowledge-based workers steadily increased; by the mid-1920s, they were more numerous than farmhands, and in the 1930s they surpassed industrial laborers.[95]

The existence of legions of office workers required the construction of separate managerial facilities. Because communications were now possible using the pneumatic tube, the telegraph, and the telephone, management did not have to occupy the same building as the production plant. As company headquarters moved out of the factory, downtown office districts swelled.[96] With Elisha Otis' invention of the safety elevator in the 1850s, businesses were soon able to move upward in that cathedral of corporate capitalism, the skyscraper – which the authors of a recent book on the history of the company aptly describe as a very tall "vertical filing cabinet."[97]

Press, patents, and pedagogy

So the big corporation was a product of the electrically charged information revolution of the nineteenth and early twentieth centuries. I would challenge the assumption of some American scholars that this was the *first* information revolution, on the grounds that they overlook the medieval and early modern precedents.[98] As in Europe in earlier times, it was also not restricted to a small number of business and political elites, but

[95] Margery W. Davies, *Woman's Place Is at the Typewriter: Office Work and Office Workers, 1870–1930* (Philadelphia: Temple University Press, 1982), 37 (quote) and passim; Klein, *Flowering of the Third America*, 111; James W. Cortada, "Introducing the Knowledge Worker," *in Rise of the Knowledge Worker*, ed. James W. Cortada (Boston: Butterworth-Heinemann, 1998), xv–xviii.
[96] John, "Recasting the Information Infrastructure for the Industrial Age," 100–101.
[97] Mickelthwait and Wooldridge, *The Company*, 104–105.
[98] See, e.g., Yates, "Business Use of Information and Technology," 107, and Gerald W. Brock, *The Second Information Revolution* (Cambridge, MA: Harvard University Press), 2.

society-wide, and drew on institutions that dug deep to dredge up information the world over.

First and foremost among these institutions was the press. Before the revolution, political journalism thrived in the American colonies, but merchants had to rely on English (or Dutch) papers to keep abreast of the latest commercial developments. Only in 1783 was the native business press born, with the publication of the *Philadelphia Price Current*.[99] After the mid-nineteenth century, the cost of printing fell steadily with the introduction of paper made from wood pulp, linotype machines, mechanical typesetting, and rotary presses that could print hundreds of thousands of pages every hour. By 1900, 2,226 daily newspapers were being published in the United States, with an average circulation of 15,000, but in some cases reaching 500,000.[100] Non-newspaper serial publications multiplied from around 2,500 in the Civil War era to 6,000 in 1905.[101]

Among them were scores of publications devoted to business, manufacturing, finance, and technology, whose coverage spread the news of the latest advances and opportunities.[102] Particularly important were the seminal contributions of Henry Varnum Poor, whose *American Railroad Journal* (founded 1832) became a model for press coverage of other industries. He also issued *Poor's Manual of Railroad Securities*, which evolved into the credit-rating and financial-reporting firm Standard and Poor's (1941). Imitations of his manual soon appeared in all other branches of economic activity. The Americans also borrowed from the English: *The Economist* originated as a general financial magazine in 1844 and inspired the first national business weekly in the United States, the *Commercial and Financial Chronicle* (1865). A broader interest in equities prompted two financial journalists in New York, Charles Dow and Edward Jones, to issue the Dow Jones Index in 1884, whose listings of

[99] McCusker, "Demise of Distance," 312ff.
[100] Paul Starr, *The Creation of the Media* (NY: Basic Books, 2004), 252; Beniger, *Control Revolution*, 18.
[101] Frank Luther Mott, *A History of American Magazines* (Cambridge, MA: Harvard University Press, 1938, 1957), vol. II, 4–5, 91ff; vol. IV, 11.
[102] The next three paragraphs rely on Arthur H. Cole, *The Historical Development of Economic and Business Literature* (Boston: Baker Library, Harvard Graduate School of Business Administration, 1957), 22ff and passim; Mott, *History of American Magazines*, vol. III, chaps. 5–6 (with *Sunnyside* at 132); vol. IV, chaps. 17–20; Paul J. Miranti, "Stock Markets," in *Oxford Encyclopedia of Economic History*, ed. Mokyr, vol. V, 23–24; Jonathan Barron Baskin and Paul J. Miranti, Jr., *History of Corporate Finance* (Cambridge: Cambridge University Press, 1997), 143–144; Chandler, *Visible Hand*, 109; Howard M. Wachtel, *Street of Dreams – Boulevard of Broken Hearts: Wall Street's First Century* (London: Pluto Press, 2003), 157–159; Alex Preda, "The Rise of the Popular Investor: Financial Knowledge and Investing in England and France," *Sociological Quarterly* (Spring 2001), 205–232.

securities prices investors could now peruse. In 1889, Dow and Jones converted their *Customers' Afternoon News Letter* into the *Wall Street Journal* a year after the equivalent *Financial Times* first came out in the United Kingdom. This is not to say that all the information in the press was accurate or that readers assessed it properly. Often it accelerated herd behaviors that plunged investors into speculative bubbles or the nation into recession.[103]

Nevertheless, more information was available than ever before. By the late nineteenth century, an endless cascade of materials poured out from firms, chambers of commerce, government agencies, and universities, all spreading the latest news of business activities. Even more astonishing was the mushrooming of technical, trade, and professional journals, which were devoted to every imaginable sphere of activity: engineering and mining; chemistry and mechanics; electricity and oil; railroads, later automobiles and aeronautics; medicine and law; finance and farming. They addressed a variety of local, regional, and national audiences, and serve as proof that the age of specialization had arrived. A sampling would include a stalwart such as *Scientific American*, or randomly selected titles from the Gilded Age like *American Gas Journal*, *Blast Furnace*, *Sewing Machine News*, *Textile Colorist*, *Lumberman's Gazette*, *Oil City Derrick*, *Druggists' Circular*, *American Hatter*, *Western Brewer*, *Insurance World*, *Prairie Farmer*, *Construction News*, *Motor*, *U.S. Egg and Poultry*, *Telephony*, and *Sunnyside* – the curious name for the in-house journal of a New York casket manufacturer. Likewise, in every country of Europe, analogous publications were appearing at the time with the similar effect of magnifying the latest developments in their respective fields.

These periodicals demonstrate the vast wealth of information that was oxygenating modern society. From 1817 to 2010, there were over 39 million papers published in scientific journals; in our day, they are appearing at the rate of well over a million a year.[104] The numbers themselves are expressions of an unprecedented quest for knowledge, but the way in which they spurred business, investment, and professional activity is evident from the experience of Henry Ford: the pioneer of the mass-produced automobile gave the press full access to his factory floor, and technical magazines like *The American Machinist*, *Engineering*

---

[103] Gary B. Magee and Andrew S. Thompson, *Empire and Globalisation: Network of People, Goods, and Capital in the British World, c. 1850–1914* (Cambridge: Cambridge University Press, 2010), 185–198.

[104] M'hamed [sic] el Aisati et al., "Genealogy of Science according to Scopus," online at http://aminotes.tumblr.com/post/4027872129/genealogy-of-science-according-to-scopus.

Magazine, and *Iron Age* ensured that his ideas and innovations would be emulated throughout American and world industry.[105]

Nor was the phenomenon of information access and acquisition through the periodical press restricted to elites. Just as in early modern Holland and England, a widespread interest in science and technology existed at all levels of American and European society in the nineteenth and twentieth centuries. Serious newspapers added columns devoted to science, and publishing houses on both sides of the Atlantic produced cheap books and magazines for mass consumption, including the venerable *Popular Science Monthly* (New York), in print continuously since 1872.[106]

One example illustrates the monumental importance of that trend as well as the theme of this book: in 1975, a cover article in *Popular Electronics* magazine reported on the Altair, a small personal computer designed by H. Edward Roberts, owner of the MITS Hobby Shop in Albuquerque, New Mexico. Adolescents Bill Gates, Paul Allen, and Monte Davidoff read the article, moved to Albuquerque, and wrote Basic programming for the Altair. Microsoft and the PC era had begun.[107]

The science reading of the American public thus fed into a frenetic tinkering and inventiveness.[108] Passage of the Patents Acts of 1790, 1793, and 1836 had opened the floodgates. The intent of the laws was to protect inventors, but also "to promote the progress of useful arts" by making the technical information filed with patents available to the public.[109]

---

[105] Hounshell, *From the American System to Mass Production*, 260–261. In the nineteenth century, access to these materials would have differed by region, with northern states far more likely to have public libraries than southern states. See Stephen Mihm, "Where Slavery Thrived, Inequality Rules Today," *Boston Globe* (Aug. 24, 2014), online at bostonglobe.com/ideas/2014/08/23/where-slavery-thrived-inequality-rules-today/iF5zgFsXncPoYmYCMMs67J/story.html.

[106] Jonathan R. Topham, "Publishing 'Popular Science' in Early Nineteenth-Century Britain," and Graeme Gooday, "Illuminating the Expert-Consumer Relationship in Domestic Electricity," both in *Science in the Marketplace: Nineteenth-Century Sites and Experiences*, ed. Aileen Fyfe and Bernard Lightman (Chicago: University of Chicago Press, 2007), chaps. 5 and 8; Mott, *History of American Magazines*, vol. III, 104–109, 495–499; vol. IV, 306–310.

[107] Brock, *Second Information Revolution*, 164–166. According to Peter Hall, *Cities in Civilization* (London: Weidenfeld and Nicholson, 1998), 440, "the beginnings of the personal computer really lay in a competition between two magazines, *Popular Electronics* and *Radio Electronics*, whose readers wanted a home computer and could not get one."

[108] For the equivalent story in the Nordic countries, see Kristine Bruland, "Reconceptualizing Industrialization in Scandinavia," in *Reconceptualizing the Industrial Revolution*, ed. Jeff Horn, Leonard N. Rosenband, and Merritt Roe Smith (Cambridge, MA: MIT Press, 2010), 127–128, 136–144.

[109] Patent Act of 1790, Ch. 7, 1 Stat. 109–112 (April 10, 1790); Patent Act of 1793, Ch. 11, 1 Stat. 318–323 (February 21, 1793), secs. 2, 3. The first government to grant patents was Venice, which issued 1,904 between 1474 and 1788: see Luciano Pezzolo, "The Via

A British telegraph engineer, William Preece, explained his admiration for the US Patent Office: "every new thing is freely published, and the patent laws are sound and within the reach of all" (1877).[110] People from across the socio-economic spectrum took advantage of the formalized procedures and protection of intellectual property rights.[111] Companies were also involved, first by buying up patents, then institutionalizing invention in corporate research and development facilities. The most famous were General Electric and Bell Labs, but by 1927 a good thousand were in existence. Their purpose was not just to create new technologies but to provide informed guidance to the managers and owners of firms. The point is that the application of scientific and technological knowledge, whether by rags-to-riches inventors like Thomas Edison or salaried researchers in the employ of corporate giants, was supported by firms, entrepreneurs, investors, publishers, and legislation, all feeding off of the information nexus.[112]

The advances in science and technology that companies brought to market were in part the fruits of investment in education. The Land Grant Acts of 1862 and 1890 mandated the founding of universities with an emphasis on "agriculture and the mechanic arts" – whence "A and M" schools. Similar efforts were underway in Germany with the establishment of its renowned polytechnic schools. By 1900, both the United States and Germany produced far greater numbers of scientists than Britain, which did not invest as much in similar initiatives until the twentieth century.[113]

Italiana to Capitalism," in *The Cambridge History of Capitalism*, ed. Larry Neal and Jeffrey G. Williamson, vol. I (Cambridge: Cambridge University Press, 2014), 294.

[110] John, *Network Nation*, 44.

[111] Naomi R. Lamoreaux and Kenneth L. Sokoloff, "Introduction: The Organization and Finance of Innovation in American History," in *Financing Innovation in the United States, 1870 to the Present*, ed. Naomi R. Lamoreaux and Kenneth L. Sokoloff (Cambridge, MA: MIT Press, 2007), 4–12.

[112] Naomi R. Lamoreaux and Kenneth L. Sokoloff, "Inventors, Firms, and the Market for Technology in the Late Nineteenth and Early Twentieth Centuries," in *Learning by Doing*, ed. Lamoreaux et al., 19–57; Ruth Schwartz Cowan, *A Social History of American Technology* (Oxford: Oxford University Press, 1997), chaps. 6–7; Michael Aaron Dennis, "Accounting for Research: New Histories of Corporate Laboratories," *Social Studies of Science* (Aug. 1987), 479–518; Kristine Bruland and David C. Mowery, "Technology and the Spread of Capitalism," in *Cambridge History of Capitalism*, ed. Neal and Williamson, vol. II, 93–98.

[113] Johann Peter Murmann, *Knowledge and Competitive Advantage: The Coevolution of Firms, Technology, and National Institutions* (Cambridge: Cambridge University Press, 2003), 51–62; Jürgen Kocka, "Rise of the Modern Industrial Enterprise in Germany," in *Managerial Hierarchies*, ed. Chandler and Daems, 95–96. Today, according to Mark Muro et al., *America's Advanced Industries: What They Are, Where They Are, and Why They Matter* (Washington, DC: Brookings Institute, 2015), 8, 38, while the United States still has strong research universities, in a ranking of highly cited scientific

Managerial education was another arena in which America held sway with the formation of business schools within universities. The earliest was the Wharton School of Commerce and Finance, founded at the University of Pennsylvania in 1881; a relative latecomer more than two decades later was Harvard's Graduate School of Business Education (1908). Programs such as these went a long way to creating a professionalized cadre of executives, financiers, accountants, and marketers that managed a good part of the American and world economies.

The management-consulting industry was also a by-product of the expansion of the business school in higher education. The pioneer was Frederick Winslow Taylor, who hired experts to propagate the virtues of scientific management. This was not just an American phenomenon: in the 1920s, German companies of this sort existed, too, offering services like research into the solvency of other firms, corporate strategizing, and, sometimes, industrial espionage. But the phenomenon was more prominent in the United States because of a raft of antitrust legislation from the Progressive era through the 1950s that, among other things, prohibited firms from offering customers both consultant services for, and sales of, the same product. This led companies to hire outside "knowledge brokers" like McKinsey and Company and many others which from the 1920s onward sold expert advice to firms and preached the American corporate gospel to Europe and beyond.[114]

The stock market: "Monte Carlo without music"?

For legal, historical, and economic reasons, in continental Europe and Japan what Harold James calls "relationship capitalism" was standard in big business, as opposed to the bureaucratic, multidivisional firm in the United States. This was not only because, as James emphasizes, so many families retained direct control over the big companies they or their ancestors founded, but also because these companies were all, in the words of Japanese scholar Etsuo Abe, "multi-layered production and distribution networks," meaning these firms cultivated close personal relationships between suppliers, clients, shareholders, and members of

publications per capita, Switzerland is in first place and the US tenth. The number of STEM (science, technology, engineering, and mathematics) graduates per capita has also been declining in the US.
[114] For the previous two paragraphs, see Chandler, *Visible Hand*, 464–468; Matthias Kipling, "American Management Consulting Companies in Western Europe, 1920–1990," *Business History Review* (Summer 1999), 190–220; Mattelart, *Networking the World*, 26; Christopher D. McKenna, *The World's Newest Profession: Management Consulting in the Twentieth Century* (Cambridge: Cambridge University Press, 2006), 16ff and passim – I take the term "knowledge broker" from him.

industry associations. The intimately held information that these contacts yielded concerning reputation and consistency of performance were vital to all of them, and often were of greater importance than even cost considerations.[115] Big British companies, however, tended to follow American models in adopting the multidivisional structure by the 1920s. So there was a distinct Anglo-American pattern, which also pertained to the different way companies in these societies raised capital.[116]

Throughout Europe, stock markets grew robustly before 1914 and after 1970, both eras of financial globalization separated by a period of stagnation brought about by the two World Wars and the Great Depression.[117] In reaction to that expansion, hostility toward the shares market spread widely across the continent. In the years before the financial crisis of 2008, mainstream politicians in Germany attacked private-equity funds as "locusts," which echoed late-nineteenth-century right-wing denunciations of the stock market as a Jewish-controlled "Monte Carlo without music."[118] In many countries, the opponents of securities traders succeeded in imposing restrictions on them, and businesses raised capital through family ties, financial pools funded by industrial cartels, or banks.[119]

---

[115] Harold James, *Family Capitalism: Wendels, Haniels, Falcks, and the Continental European Model* (Cambridge, MA: Belknap Press, 2006), 3 (first quote); Etsuo Abe, "Development of Modern Business in Japan," *Business History Review* (Summer 1997), 305 (second quote); Peter A. Hall and David Soskice, "Introduction," in *Varieties of Capitalism: The Institutional Foundations of Comparative Advantage*, ed. Peter A. Hall and David Soskice (Oxford: Oxford University Press, 2001), 23; Theodore C. Bestor, *Tsukiji: The Fish Market at the Center of the World* (Berkeley: University of California Press, 2004), chap. 6.

[116] Leslie Hannah, "Visible and Invisible Hands in Great Britain," in *Managerial Hierarchies*, ed. Chandler and Daems, 41–76; Hannah, "Marshall's Trees," 274, n36.

[117] Ranald C. Michie, "Reversal or Change? The Global Securities Market in the Twentieth Century," *New Global Studies*, vol. II, no. 1 (2008), 1–40. In 1910 there were eighty-nine major stock exchanges in the world, 56 percent of them in Western Europe. Twenty million investors traded $160 billion in securities at nominal value, of which British investors held 24 percent, Americans 21 percent, French 18 percent, and Germans 16 percent (Lance Davis, Larry Neal, and Eugene N. White, "How It All Began: The Rise of Listing Requirements on the London, Berlin, Paris and New York Stock Exchanges," *International Journal of Accounting* [Summer 2003], 118).

[118] *Economist* (July 25, 2009), 53 (locust quote); Joost Jonker, "Competing in Tandem: Securities Markets and Commercial Banking Patterns in Europe during the Nineteenth Century," in *The Origins of National Financial Systems*, ed. Douglas J. Forsyth and Daniel Verdier (London: Routledge, 2003), 83 (Monte Carlo quote). There is a continuing correlation in Germany between historically anti-Semitic regions of the country and distrust in financial investment. See *Economist* (Oct. 18, 2014), online at economist.com/news/finance-and-economics/21625878-new-research-finds-link-betw een-persecution-jews-and-distrust.

[119] Ranald C. Michie, "Anglo-American Financial Systems, 1800–1939," in *Finance and the Making of the Modern Capitalist World, 1750–1931*, ed. Philip Cottrell and Jaime Reis (Seville Secretariado de Publicaciones de la Universidad de Sevilla, 1998), 43–63;

These were, in any case, familiar and traditional ways of financing enterprise. In Europe and Japan, banks bought large blocks of shares or lent large amounts of money, greasing the wheels of finance with insider knowledge and personal relationships forged over many years. Information was still of the essence, but confined to the boardroom. The stock market was a riskier alternative. It took a great leap of faith to raise capital by relying on anonymous investors making decisions based on publicly available information. Not that banks have been unimportant in the United States – in 2009, they still provided financing for 30 percent of big businesses and 90 percent of small ones.[120] And from the 1980s onward stock-market capitalization on the European continent – and for that matter everywhere else in the world – increased substantially. But in general, the impersonal securities markets have played an outsized role in the Anglo-American variety of capitalism.

Their origins in the early modern era and steady rise in economic importance after the mid-nineteenth century are inseparable from the state of the information nexus; so was their disarray in 2008.

Over the past few centuries, equities markets came to exist in many cities of England, Europe, and America, but the premier stock exchanges were located in the City of London and on Wall Street in New York City. Chapter 4 examined the rise of London as a financial capital. In the United States, there was an information corridor stretching up and down the east coast, but New York was the main American port of call for European ships and the commercial capital of the young country. International commerce lured financial institutions to the city, and by the late eighteenth century other states were depositing their reserves in New York banks. In 1817, Wall Street brokers, who had previously conducted their business in coffee houses or on the street, gathered to found the New York Stock Exchange. Information access explains how the NYSE overtook its competitors in other states to become the major national institution of its kind; characteristically, it was the first stock market to rely on the telegraph for trading in stocks, almost immediately after its invention.[121]

Michie, *Global Securities Market*; Kocka, "Rise of the Modern Industrial Enterprise in Germany," 89–92; Richard Tilly, "Capital Markets after 1750," in *Oxford Encyclopedia of Economic History*, ed. Mokyr, vol. I, 326–334.

[120] *Economist* (Dec. 12, 2009), 14.

[121] Youssef Cassis, *Big Business: The European Experience in the Twentieth Century* (Oxford: Oxford University Press, 1997), 15–24, 73, 83–101, 114–124; Wright, *Wealth of Nations Rediscovered*, 18, 85–90, and chaps. 5–7 passim; Philip. L. Cottrell, "London as a Centre of Communications," in *Kommunikationsrevolutionen*, ed. North, 157–178; Stuart Banner, *Anglo-American Securities Regulation: Cultural and Political Roots, 1690–1860* (Cambridge: Cambridge University Press, 1998), 256–257; David E. Nye,

Keep in mind, though, that local stock exchanges continued to exist all the while throughout the United States – along with a decentralized banking system and in recent decades a substantial community of venture capitalists. They contributed the seed funding for unusual and uncertain undertakings like telephony and, ultimately, the dotcoms, which would not as readily have found credit institutions willing to give start-ups a shot in countries with more centralized financial sectors like Germany, France, and even England.[122]

In the grand scheme of the capitalist economy, the shares market was fairly insignificant before the later nineteenth century. Investors had a wild ride in the English financial revolution, until the South Sea bubble burst in 1720. After that, British laws restricted joint-stock companies on the assumption that only insiders understood their real worth: without independent reporting, neither the government nor outside investors could get a good picture of their financial condition, which made the risks too high. As yet, sophisticated mathematical analysis of stocks and companies' books was nonexistent. In any case, with small-scale production being the norm before the era of mass production, there was little need for men who had built companies to consider selling shares to outside investors. For the time being, it was sufficient to raise capital by borrowing from family members, friends, and co-religionists. Reducing labor costs was another option.[123]

To put the history of nineteenth-century American securities in perspective, we should note that the country's 4 million slaves served as one of the largest stores of capital in the US economy before the Civil War: they were worth $3 billion in 1860, more than all the real estate in the South, three times the value of all American factories and railroads, and seven times the amount of capital invested in American banks. In the southern states there was an active market for collateralized loans based on mortgages on slaves. These were funded and traded by local banks plump with investment from the financial institutions of England and the northern United States that was pouring into all aspects of the cotton

"Shaping Communication Networks: Telegraph, Telephone, Computer," *Social Research* (Fall 1997), 1072.

[122] Larry Neal and Lance E. Davis, "Why Did Finance Capitalism and the Second Industrial Revolution Arise in the 1890s?," in *Financing Innovation in the United States*, ed. Lamoreaux and Sokoloff, 129–161; Bruce Kogut, ed., *The Global Internet Economy* (Cambridge, MA: MIT Press, 2003).

[123] Baskin and Miranti, *History of Corporate Finance*, 63ff, 117–118, 123, 134–139; Miranti, "Stock Markets," 23; Philip Mirowski, "The Rise (and Retreat) of a Market: English Joint Stock Shares in the Eighteenth Century," *Journal of Economic History* (Sept. 1981), 571, 576–577; Geoffrey Poitras, *The Early History of Financial Economics, 1478-1776* (Cheltenham: Edward Elgar, 2000), chaps. 4–12 passim; Ranald C. Michie, *The London Stock Exchange: A History* (Oxford: Oxford University Press, 1999), online version, 17.

business at this early stage of industrialized textile manufacturing. Slave mortgages would have become more securitized and entered more financial portfolios had investing in the slave trade not been illegal in the United Kingdom (investing in slave-grown cotton was legal, though) and had slavery not come to an abrupt end in the United States.[124]

But the shares market as we know it began to roll with the railroads, which had large financing requirements and turned to capital markets to satisfy them. British, Dutch, and other European investors saw opportunity in the US railroad boom and poured money into American stocks.[125] It did not take much to convince Americans to follow their lead – as the French consul in San Francisco commented in 1849, the "Yankee is a stockjobber by nature." Another French traveler observed that in the United States, "public opinion and pulpit forbid sensual gratifications, wine, women, and the display of princely luxury; cards and dice are equally prohibited; the American, therefore, has recourse to business for the strong emotions which he requires to make him feel life. He launches with delight into the ever-moving sea of speculation."[126] Railroad tycoon Jay Gould's attempt to drive down the price of Erie Railroad stock in 1868 almost came undone because he did not realize how many working- and middle-class speculators would buy up stock when it hit a low point, nearly undermining his manipulations.[127] Experience with railroad securities prepared the ground for investment in other kinds of companies. But we are still not speaking of exceptionally large volumes – it was not until 1886 that the stock market had its first million-trade day.[128]

Two developments drove stock-market volumes ever upward: new legislation permitting the formation of limited-liability companies; and the large corporations' extraordinary thirst for capital.

[124] Bonnie Martin, "Slavery's Invisible Engine: Mortgaging Human Property," *Journal of Southern History* (Nov. 2010), 817–866; Steven Deyle, *Carry Me Back: The Domestic Slave Trade in American Life* (Oxford: Oxford University Press, 2005), 59–60; Walter Johnson, *River of Dark Dreams: Slavery and Empire in the Cotton Kingdom* (Cambridge, MA: Harvard University Press, 2013), 2, 11–12, 279, and passim; Marika Sherwood, *After Abolition: Britain and the Slave Trade since 1807* (London: I. B. Tauris, 2007), 27–57, 78–81.
[125] Jonathan Barron Baskin, "The Development of Corporate Financial Markets in Britain and the United States, 1600–1914: Overcoming Asymetric Information," *Business History Review* (Summer 1988), 208–212, 219–224, 230–235; Yousseff Cassis, *Capitals of Capital: The Rise and Fall of International Financial Centres, 1780–2005* (Cambridge: Cambridge University Press, 2006), 57, 68.
[126] Quotes from Banner, *Anglo-American Securities Regulation*, 194–195.
[127] Edward J. Renehan, Jr., *Dark Genius of Wall Street: The Misunderstood Life of Jay Gould, King of the Robber Barons* (NY: Basic Books, 2005), 145–146.
[128] Micklethwait and Wooldridge, *The Company*, 61.

Before limited liability, the owners of a firm were responsible for all of its debts. This made it difficult to attract small investors since not just their investment but their entire personal worth was at stake if the company sank into bankruptcy. With the introduction of limited-liability law in Britain in 1855 and in most of the United States by 1860, an investor was legally liable only up to the value of the shares he held in a company. Instead, the company itself, which acted as an individual in the eyes of the law (the term "corporation" derives from the Latin for a body), was answerable for its debts and obligations. This law came under attack for giving unfair protections to business interests. According to American writer Ambrose Bierce, the limited-liability corporation was "an ingenious device for obtaining individual profit without individual responsibility." But the reasoning behind limited liability was to protect workers and other small investors by making the purchase of shares less of an all-or-nothing proposition. Like the concept of insurance, limited liability was a risk-sharing innovation that encouraged economic growth by making investment safer than it was before. With this legislation, the joint-stock corporation gained momentum. Now, with a multiplicity of owners big and small, companies would outlive their founders. And people could own a piece of a business without having to be involved in its management.[129]

Through the burgeoning securities markets, firms could tap much larger pools of capital, which watered the growing mass market. For big companies, limited liability and incorporation promised access to large volumes of cash. In the 1890s, big American firms were won over to Wall Street. The new companies born in the turn-of-the-century industrial boom fattened themselves off the stocks and bonds they issued; existing companies recapitalized for expansion; and founding families sold blocks of shares to receive a return on what would have previously been irretrievable sunk capital. Because of Progressive-era trust-busting legislation, raising money by erecting monopolistic alliances was also no longer legal, which left incorporation as one of the only options. In those days, investment banks, especially J. P. Morgan and Co.; J. and W. Seligman and Co.; Chase National; and Kuhn, Loeb,

---

[129] Bishop Carleton Hunt, *The Development of the Business Corporation in England, 1800–1867* (Cambridge, MA: Harvard University Press, 1936), 116, 138ff, and chap. 6 passim; Herbert Hovenkamp, *Enterprise and American Law, 1836–1937* (Cambridge, MA: Harvard University Press, 1991), 53–55; Baskin and Miranti, *History of Corporate Finance*, 60-61; Kenneth Lipartito, "The Utopian Corporation," in *Constructing Corporate America*, ed. Kenneth Lipartito and David B. Sicilia (Oxford: Oxford University Press, 2004), 94–119. Bierce quote in Klein, *Flowering of the Third America*, 77.

and Co. grew rich and powerful by orchestrating the sale of corporate securities – which also gave them effective control over Wall Street.[130]

New information technologies saved time and lowered transaction costs. In the early decades, messengers called "pad shovers" gathered prices by running back and forth between brokerage houses and the stock exchange. They lost out to the stock ticker, a labor-saving device invented in 1867 by a telegraph operator named Edward A. Calahan. His machine printed the fluctuating prices as they streamed continuously over the telegraph lines. At first users had to fill the machine's batteries twice a week with buckets sloshing over with sulfuric acid, and on top of that the printing was blurry. But Thomas Edison and others made improvements, and by 1880 there were a thousand installed on Wall Street.[131]

The securities markets were responsive to the capital demands of industry, but they could not have reached the heights they did unless, on the other side, potential investors had greater access to information about companies whose shares they considered buying. If people (or, perhaps, more accurately, bankers) were going to invest their money, they needed to see company balance sheets. In the terminology of economics, informational asymmetries between firms and potential investors had to be corrected for the securities market to continue to grow.[132]

Gradual advances in the information nexus helped to make the correction. Financial analysis, beginning with railroad economics, provided the first rudimentary tools with which to hazard predictions of future growth in equities. The business press made a contribution by vigorously reporting on corporate activity. For the benefit of companies, investors, and the general public, the US Interstate Commerce Commission (ICC) and the US Commerce Department (founded in 1887 and 1903 respectively) – issued statistical compendia. The government as yet was not in the business of monitoring all corporations, but private firms filled the gap. Credit-rating agencies such as Poor's Publishing Company (established 1868; later Standard and Poor's) tracked companies' performance and standardized ticker symbols. Moody's Investor's Services (1909) conceived the letter-rating system and published its assessments comparing the risk of investment among individual firms. In 1869, in accord with its self-regulating nature, the New York Stock Exchange began

[130] Ron Chernow, *Titan: The Life of John D. Rockefeller, Sr.* (NY: Random House, 1998), 370–371, 374, 389; Thomas R. Navin and Marian V. Sears, "The Rise of a Market for Industrial Securities, 1887–1902," *Business History Review* (June 1955), 105–138.

[131] Wachtel, *Street of Dreams*, 157–158; Eric Owles, "Wall Street's Race to the 48-Millisecond Trade," *New York Times* (Aug. 15, 2012), online at http://dealbook.nytimes.com/2012/08/15/wall-streets-race-to-the-48-millisecond-trade/.

[132] On the concept of asymmetric information in securities markets, see the works of Jonathan Barron Baskin and Paul J. Miranti, Jr. cited in this chapter.

encouraging its member companies to file annual reports. At first they ignored the suggestion, but over the succeeding decades it became standard practice, certainly by the 1920s.[133]

In the mid-nineteenth century these arrangements were perhaps not unreasonable: the New York Stock Exchange tracked the creditworthiness of companies doing business with it, listing defaulters in the ruinous "Black Book." But by 1900, Wall Street was no longer a small community, and the old arrangements were no longer feasible. As businesses became larger, more numerous, and more complex, and as the divide opened up between professional managers and shareholding owners, laws imposing new standards of financial assessment and reporting were in order.

Yet the status quo resisted change. Into the early years of the twentieth century, many big firms still held no annual meetings and gave little information to potential investors or minority shareholders. Without uniform accounting rules (up to then legally mandated only for railroad companies), firms could cherry pick the most flattering financial data to show the public. A 1910 book on stocks advised readers that "all [corporate] prospectuses should be scanned in a spirit of jaundiced criticism, and with the most pessimistic readiness to believe that they are speciously alluring traps laid by some designing financier to relieve the reader of some of his money."[134] For company bosses, even those who did not want to scam investors, it was counterintuitive that they should open their books to public scrutiny. Standard Oil executive John D. Archbold argued that "private corporations should not be required to make public items of receipts and expenditures, profits and losses. A statement of assets and liabilities is all that can benefit the public. Items of receipts and expenditures, profits and losses, can only benefit the competitors."[135]

With a greater degree of voluntary disclosure by companies in the years before World War I, corporate financial conditions were more visible than they had once been, but still not what they could be. Shareholders

---

[133] This and the three paragraphs that follow rely on Miranti, "Stock Markets," 23–24; Baskin and Miranti, *History of Corporate Finance*, 186–190; Baskin, "Development of Corporate Financial Markets," 230; Nicolas Véron, Matthieu Autret, and Alfred Galichon, *Smoke and Mirrors, Inc.: Accounting for Capitalism*, trans. George Holoch (Ithaca, NY: Cornell University Press, 2006), 11–13; Rawi Abdelal, *Capital Rules: The Construction of Global Finance* (Cambridge, MA: Harvard University Press, 2007), chap. 7; Banner, *Anglo-American Securities Regulation*, chaps. 2–4, 8; Paul Johnson, *Making the Market: Victorian Origins of Corporate Capitalism* (Cambridge: Cambridge University Press, 2010), 202–204.
[134] Baskin and Miranti, *History of Corporate Finance*, 190.
[135] Quote from Allen, *The Big Change*, 63.

therefore tended to judge a company by its dividends, which were a clear and reliable measure of performance – although some buyers had enough knowledge now to start investing in stocks based on expectations of growth rather than income. The number of shareholders rose from half a million in 1900 to 2 million in 1920 and 10 million in 1930 – this growth was not just because of the loose credit and stock mania of the Roaring Twenties, but also the improved understanding that came from new founts of information.

As a result of the stock market crash and Great Depression, cloudiness in the investment atmosphere was further dissipated by the New Deal. Its legislative agenda was a belated tribute to the precept of the reform-minded, Progressive jurist Louis Brandeis that for financial markets "sunlight is said to be the best of disinfectants" (1913).[136] Aside from railroad companies, whose abuses the Hepburn Act of 1906 fixed by forcing open their financial records, other kinds of firms had been subject only to "blue sky" laws passed by the states, which were routinely evaded. After the catastrophic crash of the stock market and the onset of the Great Depression, the federal government under President Franklin D. Roosevelt took matters in hand. With the passage of the Securities Acts of 1933 and 1934, the Securities and Exchange Commission (SEC) came into being. Stringent rules now forced all companies issuing stocks and bonds to disclose what had once been secret information about their finances. In 1938, the rules were extended to the many traders operating outside the official exchanges; these brokers then formed the National Association of Securities Dealers (NASD; later NASDAQ, National Association of Securities Dealers Automated Quotations).[137] Wall Street was no longer self-regulating.

The skies were clearer now and there was a better view of business doings. Despite companies' anxieties about government intrusiveness, the new rules encouraged the circulation of information, the reliability of which bolstered investor confidence and helped capital markets to survive the Great Depression. The disclosure requirements also banished the secrecy upon which the investment banks depended. Deprived of their monopoly of information and intelligence, they lost their chokehold on Wall Street deal making.[138]

New Deal legislation cleared many of the previously clogged channels of information concerning investment in securities. But the next big

[136] *Economist* (Feb. 21, 2009), 78.
[137] Baskin and Miranti, *History of Corporate Finance*, 142–145, 183–189, 200–202; Thomas K. McCraw, "Regulate, Baby, Regulate," *New Republic* (March 18, 2009), 16–17.
[138] Ron Chernow, *The Death of the Banker* (NY: Vintage, 1997), 43, 80–81; Baskin and Miranti, *History of Corporate Finance*, 207, 228ff, 307–308.

expansion of stock market activity only took place in the three decades after the 1970s, when financial deregulation and new information technologies sparked a big bang that engendered "the new order" of globalized securities trading.[139]

We still live in that bewilderingly large universe. In 1913, global securities were valued at $2.4 trillion, representing 88 percent of world GDP. By 2003, they stood at 221 percent of GDP with a value of $82 trillion (listings on American exchanges accounted for a bit less than a quarter of the total).[140] Under 6 percent of households owned mutual funds in 1980; twenty years later it was up to half, and by 2009 they held $11 trillion in such investments.[141] Added to that were hundreds of trillions of dollars' worth of junk bonds and derivatives, all techniques of financing that barely existed before the 1980s and were now available to entrepreneurs who in an earlier era would have been snubbed by the clubby stock markets and banks.[142] The notional value of outstanding derivatives in 2011 was $800 trillion.[143] Reflecting all this activity were around 800 (sic) academic journals devoted to economic data analysis.[144]

While free-market ideology in the age of Reagan and Thatcher played its part, it was mainly necessity that drove deregulation of the markets. Rivalries between New York, London, and the other major stock exchanges of the world; competition from unregulated over-the-counter traders; movement toward European economic union; and privatization of nationalized firms in Western as well as Eastern Europe all pressured governments to loosen the tight national boundaries and controls imposed on the markets after the Great Depression. Deregulation of the financial markets, which encouraged leveraged buy-outs, was also a response to the weakness of owners (i.e., investors) vis-à-vis corporate managers, who could run a company without paying adequate heed to the interests of stockholders.[145]

Communications innovations produced a more global securities market. Among them were fiber-optic cables, satellite transmitters, and cellular technology, which allowed millions of people to make calls simultaneously without overloading the system. The cost of a three-

---

[139] Quote from Michie, "Reversal or Change?," 15.
[140] Michie, "Reversal or Change?" 18, 24; Michie, *Global Securities Market*, 7.
[141] "Meltdown Jolts Consumers from Financial Fairyland," AP (Sept. 20, 2009), online at dailyfinance.com/2009/09/20/meltdown-jolts-consumers-from-financial-fairyland/.
[142] *Economist* (Oct. 23, 2010), 83–85; (Nov. 14, 2009), 93–96; and (Feb. 16, 2008), 77–79.
[143] Andrew Palmer, "Playing with Fire: A Special Report on Financial Innovation," *Economist* (Feb. 25, 2012), 13.
[144] *Economist* (Nov. 20, 2010), 90.
[145] Michie, *Global Securities Market*, 13–14, chap. 8; Tilly, "Capital Markets after 1750," 332–333.

minute telephone conversation between New York and London fell precipitously, from (in 1966 prices) £63 in 1945 and £12 in 1970 to 50 pence in the 1990s. And the price of talking long distance dropped to a fraction of that with the advent of mobile phones and computer-based telecommunications services such as Skype.[146]

Of course, the computer was the technology most responsible for the quantum growth of the capital markets – for better or worse. Down to the mid-twentieth century, clerks on the stock exchange gathered price information the same way they had for two or three centuries: by walking the trading floors and asking the brokers who were doing the buying and selling. The clerks then conferred, compiled the numbers, and sent them off to the newspaper printers.[147] Fast forward to the 2000s, when computers began to supplant the brain of the investing individual. Scanning the markets at warp speed, financial software issues tens of thousands of flash orders 24/7, making and cancelling trades nearly simultaneously to win advantage for their brokerages. Every 500 microseconds (that is, every 500 millionths of a second), electronic exchanges register purchases and sales, bidding and withdrawal from bidding. High-frequency algorithmic trading now accounts for 50–60 percent of volume on the New York, London, and other major stock markets of the world. Ever more efficient computer programs are also in the offing that would configure transactions in response to national and international news.[148]

One would think that the availability of all this data was for the good, but the information tsunami has had some negative side-effects on the capital markets. Digital technologies make it possible for outsiders to compete for business with the elite club of the stock exchange by enabling electronic trading via laptops situated wherever there is internet access. Not that the doors have been flung wide open: rich firms can best afford the expense of high-frequency-trading software and computer hardware. And many of those involved are not interested in investing in companies in the long term, which would have a beneficial effect on the economy, but mainly engage in arbitrage so as to reap tiny but profitable fees from each of the thousands of trades they issue per microsecond.[149] Computer-modeled

---

[146] Michie, *Global Securities Market*, 306-307; Michie, "Reversal or Change?" 37.

[147] McCusker, "Demise of Distance," 301–302.

[148] *Economist* (Aug. 1, 2009), 64; Charles Duhigg, "Stock Traders Find Speed Pays, in Milliseconds," *New York Times* (July 24, 2009), online at nytimes.com/2009/07/24/business/24trading.html; *Economist* (June 23, 2007), 85; Frank Pasquale, *The Black Box Society: The Secret Algorithms that Control Money and Information* (Cambridge, MA: Harvard University Press, 2015), chap. 4; Christopher Steiner, *Automate This: How Algorithms Came to Rule Our World* (NY: Portfolio/Penguin, 2012), 49; and see chap. 1 on the spread and hazards of algorithmic trading on Wall Street.

[149] *Economist* (Nov. 14, 2009), 85.

investing is also, thus far, incapable of factoring in the effects of human psychology and fraud on market conditions: most of the quantitative (quant) funds that had run up the markets prior to 2008 performed abysmally once the financial crisis took hold.[150] With data storage online rather than on paper, it is also much more difficult for companies to keep proprietary information secret and prevent it from being leaked to corporate rivals; on the other hand, it does not seem to have made it any easier for the investing public or government regulators to breach the walls of secrecy corporations build for their executives to hide behind.[151]

Many of the problems in the securities markets that helped cause the financial crisis were rooted not just in computers, but in other informational deficiencies. With deregulation, global banks and international brokerages expanded in every direction, diversifying far beyond their initial specializations to offer a surfeit of financial services. This was supposed to spread the risk, so that even if one division suffered a reversal, the whole would be buoyed by success elsewhere within the larger firm. But executives were overextended, supervising activities with which they had little or no expertise, and oftentimes CEOs were unaware of everything their own companies were up to. The business had become "too complex to manage."[152]

Amplifying the confusion was the jumble of newly concocted and arcane derivatives. The logic behind those, too, was to parcel out the risk among institutions willing to invest and trade in them. But due diligence on the part of individual or institutional investors was nearly impossible when debts were chopped up and repackaged into CDOs (collateralized debt obligations) that were many instances removed from the original lender and borrower. In many cases, to track one of these securities from one end of the chain to the other would have required reading 30,000 pages of documentation. Even large companies specializing in them could not – and so did not – do it. But they were issuing or investing in CDOs by the millions.[153] It got to the point where almost no one knew how much these securities were worth.

---

[150] Scott Patterson, "The Minds behind the Meltdown," *Wall Street Journal* (Jan. 22, 2010), online at http://online.wsj.com/article/SB100014240527487045097045750190 32416477138.html; and see *Economist* (Nov. 29, 2014), 70.

[151] "Companies and Information," *Economist* (Feb. 26, 2011), 75–77.

[152] Jerry Z. Muller, "Our Epistemological Depression," *The American – The Journal of the American Enterprise Institute* (Jan. 29, 2009), online at https://www.aei.org/publication /our-epistemological-depression ("too complex" quote); Michael Kinsley, "The Financial Food Chain," *Time* (Oct. 24, 1994), 88.

[153] Matthew Valencia, "The Gods Strike Back: A Special Report on Financial Risk," *Economist* (Feb. 14, 2010), 4; Michael Lewis, *The Big Short* (NY: Norton, 2010).

In part that was because investors around the world, including conservatively run European pension funds, relied on old-line ratings and accounting firms to grade the safety of the funds they were buying into. Everyone assumed these were independent agencies that offered objective information about financial paper, but they had become corrupted. They were paid not by buyers, but by sellers whose interest was in getting the highest ratings. Companies issuing debt badgered or bought off ratings analysts by lavishing them with attention, favors, and the promise of changes to corporate governance that no one intended to implement.[154] In 1933, the British chairman of Shell Oil Company, Horace Samuel, identified the problem: "Though an auditor may be a watch-dog, he is yet a watch-dog who, in order to discharge his duties, may be compelled to bite the hand that feeds him."[155] In recent years they licked that hand and wagged their tails even as their paymasters engaged in fraud: a shocking 93 percent of all AAA-rated subprime-mortgage-backed securities issued in 2006 were assessed as junk-quality after the financial crisis. A bond specialist at Pimco, one of the world's largest investment firms, stated that it was as if the invisible hand was "having a party, a non-regulated drinking party, with rating agencies handing out fake IDs."[156]

None of this is what the theorists of the efficient market predicted. But no matter how mathematically sophisticated, computer-generated economic models are imperfect when the numbers they crunch are false and intentionally misleading.[157] Even when the data are accurate, markets do not always do the expected, and thus far software has been unable to anticipate financial panics; predicting earthquakes is a more advanced science. If the experts' advanced tools failed to register the seismic upheavals about to bring down the biggest firms on Wall Street, what about the rest of us whose futures depend on our investments? We are not much different than the crusty old Captain Cuttle, in Dickens' novel *Dombey and Son*, who "felt bound to read the quotations of the funds every day, though he was unable to make out, on any principle of navigation, what the figures meant."[158] As Professor Michael Yaziji asks, "do you even know the names of all the companies you invest in?" The answer is no – because most of us invest in countless equities and bonds through

---

[154] *Economist* (Feb. 6, 2010), 72. And see John C. Bogle, "Democracy in Corporate America, *Daedalus* (Summer 2007), 24–35.

[155] Johnson, *Making the Market*, 205.

[156] Paul Krugman, "Berating the Raters," *New York Times* (April 26, 2010), online at nytimes.com/2010/04/26/opinion/26krugman.html (quote); Valencia, "The Gods Strike Back," 6.

[157] George Cooper, *The Origin of Financial Crises: Central Banks, Credit Bubbles, and the Efficient Market Fallacy* (NY: Vintage, 2008).

[158] Johnson, *Making the Market*, 11.

mutual funds run by layers of fund managers.[159] How could the answer be yes, when none of the big institutional investors or financial companies knew what risks they were themselves taking? They were no better than Captain Cuttle. In the words of historian Jerry Z. Muller, "the financial system created a fog so thick that even its captains could not navigate it." Muller called the recent crisis "our epistemological depression" – because of the "failure of the private and corporate actors *to understand what they were doing*."[160] In 1908, the financier Henry Clews wrote in his memoir of his life on Wall Street that "speculation is frequently confounded with gambling, although the two are radically different. Speculation is based upon knowledge and facts, whereas gambling deals solely with chance."[161] By his definition, in the run-up to 2008 it was gambling.

With the financial crash of 2008, we came full circle to the South Sea bubble. In 1720, the financial markets had gotten far ahead of the government's and public's ability to understand what was happening. So many people were burned by joint-stock-company shares – new financial devices that they did not fully comprehend and that the government had been unable to regulate – that the British Parliament imposed severe restrictions that almost eliminated them as a means of funneling capital to business (although it did not go as far as the French monarchy and ban paper currency or the independence of the stock exchange). It is ironic that in our own so-called Information Age, with its digital technologies and their ability to analyze unfathomable quantities of data, we are faced with a situation similar to 1720. As former Federal Reserve chairman Alan Greenspan stated in 2011, the financial markets "are unredeemably opaque."[162] To what extent they can be brought under control without hindering their vitality, dynamism, and obvious advantages remains to be seen. But in this latest twist in the saga of capitalism the problem and the solution are both at bottom informational in nature. I would argue that

---

[159] Michael Yaziji, "Time to Rethink Capitalism?" *Harvard Business Review* (Nov. 2008), 27. This was nothing new, judging by the experience of British investors in the pre–World War I era: see Magee and Thompson, *Empire and Globalisation*, 180–185. According to a recent study of 2,862 mutual funds, an investor would have done just as well or even beaten the experts' performance by flipping a coin on stock picks: see Jeff Sommer, "How Many Mutual Funds Routinely Rout the Market? Zero," *New York Times* (March 14, 2015), online at nytimes.com/2015/03/15/your-money/how-many -mutual-funds-routinely-rout-the-market-zero.html?_r=0.

[160] Muller, "Our Epistemological Depression." Emphasis in the original.

[161] Henry Clews, *Fifty Years in Wall Street* (NY: Irving Publishing Co., 1908), 959. For a comparison between journalists and modern hedge-fund traders as "aggressive infor- mation machines," see Michael Wolff, "How Hedge Funders Are Like Journalists – and Why We're Hated," *The Guardian* (Nov. 26, 2012), online at guardian.co.uk/commen tisfree/2012/nov/26/steven-cohen-hedge-funders-journalists.

[162] Pasquale, *Black Box Society*, 2 (quote), 7.

once information is not free-flowing, as was clearly the case in 2008, we are no longer dealing with capitalism. That point received expression from Michael Mayo, managing director and financial services analyst for Calyon Securities (USA) Inc., in his testimony before the US government's Financial Crisis Inquiry Commission: "Capitalism did not cause the problems" – rather, it constituted a "lack of capitalism" when investment banks did not have "good information to make decisions."[163] A more explicit statement of this book's argument does not exist.

The Great Recession occurred because new kinds of securities were too complex to understand and new information technologies outran the government's ability to referee the markets (along with a healthy dose of fraud, neglect, and blind faith in the ever-upward movement of housing prices). But if the latest phase of the information nexus proved somewhat dysfunctional on Wall Street, it did transform manufacturing, shopping, and business logistics. And if electricity powered the mass market in nations like the United States, the new information and communications technologies globalized it. Chapter 6 examines those subjects and explores the extent to which capitalism has spread and taken root in the digital age.

[163] http://fcic.law.stanford.edu/videos/view/18.

6   The digital age and the globalization of capitalism

In the nineteenth and twentieth centuries, engines and electricity cut pathways for the extension of the information nexus and capitalism across the United States, Western Europe, and Japan. After World War II, with the dawning of the digital age, capitalism spread and intensified as new technologies and new means of data processing reconfigured, sped up, and deepened the transmission of information globally. Although the birthplace of the new information technologies (IT) was the United States, seminal contributions came from the United Kingdom, and major Japanese innovations also molded the era and helped to globalize it.[1] The military and economic advantages these technologies bestowed on capitalist nations was one motivation for the Russian Communist Party's push for reform from above that unintentionally led to the dismantling of the Soviet Union.[2] With their economic model in ruins, former socialist states had no choice but to adopt market (or quasi-market) economies, first among them being China, whose meteoric rise our notion of the information nexus can contextualize. Digital technologies have provided elements of the capitalist information nexus to India and underdeveloped nations in Africa, where pioneering developments are taking place. But is the "IT revolution" truly revolutionary? And can we apply the term capitalism to digital-age states that interfere with the functioning of the information nexus? The current chapter addresses those issues after providing an overview of the technologies responsible for this third phase in the history of capitalism.

---

[1] Although the United States is the epicenter, in certain aspects leadership of IT development has shifted between the US, the UK, Western Europe, Japan, and South Korea. See James W. Cortada, *The Digital Flood: The Diffusion of Information Technology across the U.S., Europe, and Asia* (Oxford: Oxford University Press, 2012), passim; and Bruce Kogut, ed., *The Global Internet Economy* (Cambridge, MA: MIT Press, 2003).

[2] William E. Odom, *The Collapse of the Soviet Military* (New Haven: Yale University Press, 1998), 75, 87, and passim; Joseph H. Nye, "Gorbachev and the End of the Cold War" (April 5, 2006), online at http://belfercenter.ksg.harvard.edu/publication/1531/gorbachev_and_the_end_of_the_cold_war.html.

Computing and telecommunications: The "digitization of just about everything"

The computer as we know it has its direct origins in a mechanical tabulator designed by the American engineer and statistician Herman Hollerith for the US Census Bureau in 1890. Crunching data registered on punch cards, his machine shaved years off the time it had previously taken the government to complete the census. Hollerith's Tabulating Machine Company merged with other firms and in 1924 was renamed International Business Machines. Under the decades-long presidency of Thomas J. Watson, Sr., IBM led the global production of computing equipment. As the company fattened due to sales in the 1930s to the American Social Security Administration, it opened branch offices around the world.[3]

During World War II, American computer development benefited from the advances made by British and American scientists and the code-breakers who waged the first cyberwar. Spurred on by that conflict and the subsequent Cold War, IBM built electronic digital computers for the American military's program in atomic-weaponry development and air-defense systems.[4]

But true to its name, IBM saw the greatest profit potential in sales, leases, and services to the business community. A press release of

[3] This section on the history of computers relies on Gerald W. Brock, *The Second Information Revolution* (Cambridge, MA: Harvard University Press, 2003); Martin Campbell-Kelly and William Aspray, *Computer: A History of the Information Machine*, 2nd ed. (Boulder: Westview Press, 2004); James W. Cortada, "Progenitors of the Information Age: The Development of Chips and Computers," in *A Nation Transformed by Information*, ed. Alfred D. Chandler, Jr. and James W. Cortada (Oxford: Oxford University Press, 2000), 177–216; James W. Cortada, *The Digital Hand: How Computers Changed the Work of American Manufacturing, Transportation, and Retail Industries* (Oxford: Oxford University Press, 2004); Alfred D. Chandler, Jr., *Inventing the Electronic Century* (NY: Free Press, 2001); Paul Freiberger and Michael Swaine, *Fire in the Valley: The Making of the Personal Computer*, 2nd ed. (NY: McGraw-Hill, 2000); David Reynolds, "American Globalism," in *Globalization in World History*, ed. A. G. Hopkins (NY: W. W. Norton, 2002), 258–259; Armand Mattelart, *Networking the World: 1794–2000* (Minneapolis: University of Minnesota Press, 2000); Daniel R. Headrick, "Information and Communication Technology," in *Oxford Encyclopaedia of Economic History*, ed. Joel Mokyr, vol. III (Oxford: Oxford University Press, 2003), 76–77; and Joel Mokyr, *The Gifts of Athena: Historical Origins of the Knowledge Economy* (Princeton: Princeton University Press, 2002), 112.

[4] The first digital computer, however, was the ENIAC, or Electronic Numerical Integrator Analyser and Computer, created at University of Pennsylvania in 1946 also mainly to do Defense Department calculations. It covered 167 square meters of floor space and weighed thirty tons. It evolved into the UNIVAC, the first commercial general-purpose computer, installed at the US Census Bureau in 1951. See Peter Marsh, *The New Industrial Revolution: Consumers, Globalization, and the End of Mass Production* (New Haven: Yale University Press, 2012), 11; and Nicholas Carr, *The Big Switch: Rewiring the World, from Edison to Google* (NY: Norton, 2008), 48–50.

September 14, 1956, announced the mass production of the company's 305 and 650 RAMAC mainframe computers: "Two electronic data processing machines using IBM's random access memory, a stack of [fifty aluminum, iron–oxide–coated] disks that stores millions of facts and figures less than a second from management's reach. Because transactions are processed as they occur, the fresh facts held in a random access memory show business as it is right now, not as it was hours or weeks ago." With consoles the size of a refrigerator, they stored, respectively, 5 megabytes and 24 megabytes of memory. For the 305, the monthly charge was $3,200 ($27,000 in 2012 money).[5] The successor IBM system 360 family of computers, introduced in 1964, provided, for the first time in the computer industry, upgrades and equipment compatibility. According to James W. Cortada, the 360 line was "in the same class as the Ford Model T automobile or the birth control pill in its transformative effects."[6]

In 1946, only ten computers existed in the world. Despite the costs, by 1960, 5,400 electronic digital computers were in use in the United States. That was seven times the number in the United Kingdom, France, West Germany, and Japan combined.[7] Half a century later, there were 306 million computers (mainframes and PCs) in the United States and 1.5 billion worldwide. A basic personal computer could process 3 billion commands a second, or 600,000 times more than the computers of the 1940s, and at 1/17,000th the price.[8]

Those statistics reflect the cascading decline in the size and cost of computers and an exponential increase in speed and capacity. Technologically, the key to reducing the size and increasing the power of computing equipment was the control of electrical current. The first pieces of equipment to do the job contained hundreds or thousands of vacuum tubes per machine, but they burned out too often. In the mid-1950s, a small, more efficient, and longer-lived semiconductor, called a transistor, replaced the vacuum tube. In 1959, Jack Kilby of Texas Instruments and Robert Noyce, a founder of Fairchild Semiconductor, co-invented the integrated circuit, or memory chip. With Intel's introduction of the microprocessor in 1971, more than two

---

[5] IBM Archives, online at www-03.ibm.com/ibm/history/exhibits/650/650_pr2.html; www-0 3.ibm.com/ibm/history/exhibits/storage/storage_350.html; and www-03.ibm.com/ibm/his tory/exhibits/mainframe/mainframe_intro.htm.
[6] Cortada, *Digital Flood*, 66–67.
[7] Marsh, *New Industrial Revolution*, 12–13; Brock, *Second Information Revolution*, 105.
[8] "Executive Summary," *Computers in Use Forecast by Country*," (Feb. 2012), 6. For every thousand people in the world there were nineteen PCs in 1980 and 140 in 2005 (Cortada, *Digital Flood*, 41).

thousand miniaturized transistors could be implanted on one chip.[9] With recent advances in nanotechnology, the high-speed integrated circuits imbedded on a single chip can now number in the billions. And if the cost of the average transistor in 1968 was 1, by 2008 it had shrunk to 0.00000001.[10] These ever smaller and cheaper yet vastly more powerful chips made all of the subsequent hardware innovations associated with the digital revolution possible, from mainframe servers to the PC and smartphone.

The digital era required the standardization of programming languages. Bill Gates, Paul Allen, and Monte Davidoff founded Microsoft in 1975 (an evolution out of their first programming company, Traf-O-Data, founded in 1972) to produce computer-operating software Altair Basic, followed by MS-DOS, and ultimately Windows, which allowed people who were not computer engineers to make the most of the computer technology. What Microsoft offered in digital data control was the equivalent of all the technologies that came into existence to manage the great volume of business information generated in the Gilded Age.

A standardized protocol language that would enable communication between computers was also vital, so that the content of all those computerized file cabinets could potentially be shared among billions of computer users. This initiative began in the US Defense Department in the early 1960s. By the end of that decade it had established the Advanced Research Projects Agency Network (ARPANET) to link computers at universities across the country where scientists were working on government research contracts. One of the fruits of that effort was the invention of email. In the 1980s, the National Science Foundation expanded the network and led the way to the internet and the World Wide Web, which appeared in the mid-1990s.[11]

The actual architect of the web was British computer scientist Tim Berners-Lee of CERN, the European Organization for Nuclear Research. As he recounted its origins, when people started using "word processors, they stored their data. They typed into the word

---

[9] See T. R. Reid, *The Chip: How Two Americans Invented the Microchip and Launched a Revolution* (NY: Random House, 2001).

[10] Cortada, *Digital Flood*, 11. According to William D. Nordhaus, "Two Centuries of Productivity Growth in Computing," *Journal of Economic History* (March 2007), 128–159, the real cost of computing has fallen by at least 1.7 trillion times, mainly since 1980.

[11] On the history of the internet, see Shane Greenstein, *How the Internet Became Commercial: Innovation, Privatization, and the Birth of a New Network* (Princeton: Princeton University Press, 2015); Janet Abbate, *Inventing the Internet* (Cambridge, MA: MIT Press, 1999); and Katie Hafner and Matthew Lyon, *Where Wizards Stay Up Late: the Origins of the Internet* (NY: Simon and Schuster Paperbacks, 1996).

processor on a disk somewhere on a machine, which generally wasn't accessible . . . So there was . . . the frustration that we didn't have access to the data that existed, even though it was there." The web, he said, "was designed in order to make it possible to get at documentation and in order to be able to get people – students working with me, contributing to the project, for example – to be able to come in and link in their ideas, so that we wouldn't lose it all if we didn't debrief them before they left. Really, it was designed to be a collaborative workspace for people to design on a system together. That was the exciting thing about it."[12]

The internet democratized access to the massive amounts of information stored on computers worldwide. With a graphical user interface born of experiments undertaken in the 1960s at the Stanford Research Institute (where the computer mouse was invented), the University of Utah, and the Pentagon's Advanced Research Projects Agency (ARPA), the computer diffused rapidly.[13] In 1970, every office in the world had typewriters, but they could not download external material or do word processing. By 2000, every office had a PC that was capable of performing those actions plus nearly any kind of calculation. And computers spread faster within households than television had in the 1950s. By 2010, more than 78 percent of the North American population had one in their homes; globally it was 34 percent, with Europe and Australia not far behind the United States and Canada.[14] There are now more than 1.7 billion networked PCs in the world.[15]

In telecommunications, as with computers, what had formerly been military technology or affordable only to big business became accessible to everybody.[16] Satellites were put to civilian use, the United States government broke up AT&T's monopoly over telephoning in 1984, and improvements to fiber optics contributed to dramatic increases in phone usage. That multiplied further in the 1970s and 1980s after Motorola's invention of the handheld mobile cellphone. Computers and mobile devices for communications soon rivaled landline telephones and postal systems, bringing the costs close to zero and reducing the relevance of

---

[12] Academy of Achievement interview with Tim Berners-Lee, online at www.achievement .org/autodoc/page/ber1int-1.

[13] Campbell-Kelly and Aspray, *Computer*, 235–239, 259.

[14] Internet World Stats, "Usage and Population Statistics," online at internetworldst ats.com/stats.htm; Robert J. Gordon, "Does the 'New Economy' Measure up to the Great Inventions of the Past?" *Journal of Economic Perspectives* (Autumn, 2000), 66; Robert J. Gordon, "The Demise of US Economic Growth: Restatement, Rebuttal, and Reflections," *NBER Working Paper* no. 19895 (Feb. 2014), 29.

[15] Robert Scoble and Shel Israel, *Age of Context: Mobile, Sensors, Data, and the Future of Privacy* (n.p.: Patrick Brewster Press, 2014), xiv.

[16] In general see Jon Agar, *Constant Touch: A Global History of the Mobile Phone*, revised ed. (London: Icon Books, 2013).

geographical distance. They put the telegraph out of business, with the last transmission taking place in 1999. Cellphone growth was phenomenal, from 92,000 American subscribers in 1984 to 90 percent of the adult population in 2014.[17] By 2014, there were 6.9 billion cellphone subscriptions globally, and around 2.3 billion for mobile broadband.[18] Between 2009 and 2013, the mobile phone industry spent $1.8 trillion on infrastructure worldwide.[19] With the rollout of the iPhone in 2007, and the appearance of rivals running the Android operating system, mobile phones metamorphosed into smartphones: pocket-sized computers with "more number-crunching capacity than NASA had when it put men on the Moon in 1969."[20] Smartphones have facilitated the explosion of social media, on which 1.5 billion people around the world are now active; a billion tweets are posted on Twitter every 48–72 hours. And currently 100,000 plus mobile-phone application publishers are in business, offering more than 1.2 million apps; by late 2012, these had been downloaded more than 45 billion times.[21]

Among smartphone apps are those that give firms the ability to link up potential customers and suppliers or employers. Uber (founded in San Francisco in 2009, now active in 53 countries with yearly sales of over $1 billion and valued at $41 billion), Handy (New York City), and Eden McCallum (London) are all companies that attempt to marshal the millions of freelancers and independent contractors in the economy. Uber does so with drivers or unused capacity in cars, Handy with small jobs, Eden McCallum by offering consultant services. They have an easier time functioning in the United States or Britain than in the more regulated labor markets of continental Europe: in Germany they have sparked a critique of "Plattform-Kapitalismus" for turning all remaining private human assets into commodities.[22] But these firms are doing what businesses in capitalist societies have always done, which is exploiting information-sharing capabilities that did not previously exist.

The digital landscape also encompasses "the Internet of Things," a phrase coined by British IT entrepreneur Kevin Ashton to apply to all the inanimate objects that communicate with people or machine to machine.

[17] US Government, FCC, "Trends in Telephone Service" (Sept. 2010), online at fcc.gov/wcb/iatd/trends.html; Pew Research Center, "Mobile Technology Fact Sheet," online at pewinternet.org/fact-sheets/mobile-technology-fact-sheet/.
[18] International Telecommunications Union statistics (see aggregate data online at itu.int/en/ITU-D/Statistics/Pages/stat/default.aspx).
[19] *Economist* (Feb. 28, 2015), 19.
[20] *Economist* (Feb. 28, 2015), 9 (quote); Agar, *Constant Touch*, 177–178, 190, and chaps. 23–25 passim.
[21] Scoble and Israel, *Age of Context*, 3–4.
[22] *Economist* (Jan. 3, 2015), 9, 17–20, and (Feb. 28, 2015), 20.

There are now 3.5 billion networked consumer appliances, including automobiles, which car-company executives call "a cognitive device," "like an iPhone on wheels." All of these products are networked via sensors, which are tiny, radio-frequency identification (RFID) microchips attached to goods and connected to the internet. In 2007, only ten million sensors were in place; one prediction is that there will be 100 trillion by 2030.[23]

Besides sensors and improvements in computer-processing power, many of the latest advances come from more sophisticated algorithms whose creator-entrepreneurs utilize the voluntary sharing of data, which can present their companies with marketing opportunities. Google, the most popular internet search engine, with around 1.2 billion unique visitors each month, handles 35,000 internet searches a second and can process a petabyte of information every hour – which breaks down to 1,000,000,000,000,000 bytes, the equivalent of the contents of a 16-million-drawer filing cabinet, or about sixty-six times the number of books in the Library of Congress. What pays for their search-engine results are "sponsored links," or keyword-based, pay-per-click advertising, which is assumed to feed demand for advertised products.[24] Facebook, founded in 2004 and valued at $60 billion ten years later, benefits from the information freely provided by its billion-plus users to help its advertisers target customers. Match.com and other dating sites use algorithms to adjust responses to the online behaviors of users. Waze, founded by Israelis Uri Levine and Amir Shinar in 2008, turns each car whose driver is running the app on their smartphone into a "traffic-speed sensor" that automatically sends data to Waze's servers and gauges traffic conditions in conjunction with digital maps and GPS location information. The program gets stronger and more refined as more and more people download the app and provide updates about accidents, traffic jams, police speed traps, and the like.[25]

---

[23] Scoble and Israel, *Age of Context*, xiv, xv (iPhone quote), 3 (Ashton quote), 11; Sue Halpern, "Creepy New Wave of the Internet," *New York Review of Books* (Nov. 20, 2014), 22, 24 (cognitive quote).

[24] Kenneth Cukier, "Data, Data Everywhere: A Special Report on Managing Information," *Economist* (Feb. 27, 2010), 3, 5, 15; wordstream.com/keyword-advertising; Elizabeth Lambourn and Stephen Brown, "Global History of Data Storage," post on H-NET List for World History (March 9, 2010), online at http://h-net.msu.edu/cgi-bin/logbrowse.pl?trx=vx&list=h-world&month=1003&week=b&msg=agoEaSgDEFcwIRjJZEr10A&user=&pw=.

[25] Erik Brynjolfsson and Andrew McAfee, *The Second Machine Age* (NY: Norton, 2014), 60–66, 69–70, with sensor quote on 69; Ryan Avent, "The Third Great Wave: A Special Report on the World Economy," *Economist* (Oct. 4, 2014), 4; David Gelles, "Inside Match. com," *Financial Times* (July 29, 2011), online at ft.com/intl/cms/s/2/f31cae04-b8ca-11e 0-8206-00144feabdc0.html#axzz3VV41Tx00; Sam Frizell, "Here's What Facebook

Commentators have observed that we are witnessing the "digitization of just about everything."[26] This is true in the country as well as in the city. A farmer in Leesburg, Indiana, remarked on the comparison between himself and his great-grandfather, who ploughed with a mule: "We've got sensors on the combine, GPS data from satellites, cellular modems on self-driving tractors, apps for irrigation on iPhones," all making him "hooked on a drug of information and productivity." Farming, he said, is now all "about multiplying information." Farmers use computers to regulate the plowing of furrows and the dispersal of fertilizer, and to collect and analyze data about moisture and yields. Drones survey flood irrigation, and robots are in the works to identify and pluck weeds. It is expensive, but assists those family farmers who can afford the IT equipment to survive in competition with agribusiness.[27]

This bird's-eye survey of the topography of the digital age raises the question, why was this digital age overwhelmingly an American creation? It is for the same reason that the United States took the lead in the development of a consumer-oriented mass market: for one, because American office-appliance firms had the advantage of not having been destroyed in World War II. This ensured that IBM would remain the major vendor of computers in all of Europe and Japan; alongside it, Remington Rand (later Sperry Rand), National Cash Register, Burroughs, and General Electric would also fill the breach in the industry's formative period.[28] And nowhere else in the world were there so many synergizing clusters of engineers and scientists sharing information as there were in the Midwest in Ann Arbor, Champaign-Urbana, Madison, and Minneapolis; on the east coast in Boston, New York state, and Philadelphia; and, above all, in California.[29]

In the 1950s, the Santa Clara Valley was the prune capital of the United States. We know it now as Silicon Valley, named after the element which is the base ingredient in microchips and transformed a farming region into the nerve center of the digital age. "An information-exchange

Can Do with Your Personal Data in the Name of Science," *Time* (July 7, 2014), online at http://time.com/2949565/heres-what-facebook-can-do-with-your-personal-data-in-the-name-of-science/.

[26] Quote from Brynjolfsson and McAfee, *Second Machine Age*, 66.

[27] Quentin Hardy, "Working the Land and the Data," *New York Times* (Nov. 30, 2014), online at nytimes.com/2014/12/01/business/working-the-land-and-the-data.html.

[28] Cortada, *Digital Flood*, 52 and chaps. 3–5 and 7 passim.

[29] Cortada, *Digital Flood*, 46–47 and chap. 2 passim; James Flanigan, *Smile Southern California, You're the Center of the Universe: The Economy and People of a Global Region* (Stanford: Stanford University Press, 2009), chap. 6. Although on a smaller scale, the same was true of the UK, with its similar networks of scholars and civilian and defense officials, what Jon Agar calls "overlapping expert movements." See his book *The Government Machine: A Revolutionary History of the Computer* (Cambridge, MA: MIT Press, 2003), with quote on 9.

system for technical know-how," Silicon Valley extends intellectually if not geographically to encompass San Francisco, Palo Alto, and Berkeley. Its foundations were laid in the late 1930s, when two Stanford graduates founded the electronics firm Hewlett-Packard in a garage, and in 1957 when the newly formed Fairchild Semiconductor introduced the use of silicon in transistors. During the Cold War, military contracting for computing and computers primed the pump, attracting high-tech companies, university researchers, and financiers. Today, Silicon Valley has the highest concentration of venture-capital activity in the United States. Its clusters of IT firms and academic centers have formed, to quote a specialist in urban development, "a regional network-based industrial system that promotes collective learning and flexible adjustment among specialist producers of a complex of related technologies . . . . Companies compete intensely while at the same time learning from one another about changing markets and technologies through informal communication and collaborative practices."[30]

Historian Thomas Hughes attributes the genesis of the IT revolution in the United States to the "military-industrial-university complex."[31] That is true insofar as the digital computer, satellites, and the internet originated in corporate or university laboratories under government contract and closely connected with the US Defense Department during World War II and the Cold War. In desperate geopolitical competition with the Soviet Union, the US government sponsored all major computer-development projects from 1945 to 1955, and by the early 1960s funded fully two-thirds of all scientific research in the country.[32] From the labs they spilled over into the civilian scientific sector and from there to the broader consumer society.

Yet Hughes' statement insufficiently explains the digital age. The Defense Department did unleash energies that sped up the development of computers during World War II and the Cold War, but that is not a complete picture. Outside of military circles, the success of the computer in American society is due to the fact that from the 1880s to the present a profusion of office-appliance companies have gotten their customers used to relying on machines for data processing.[33] And the movement of digital technologies from the business community to the military establishment and back to the broader consumer sector is in the nature of capitalism, which abhors the locking up of ideas behind the secretive confines of government. The digital age could not have occurred without

---

[30] Respective quotes from Peter Hall, *Cities in Civilization* (London: Weidenfeld and Nicholson, 1998), 432 and 453.
[31] Thomas Hughes, *Rescuing Prometheus* (NY: Vintage, 2000), 3 and passim.
[32] Cortada, *Digital Flood*, 47–50.   [33] Cortada, *Digital Flood*, 51–52.

relatively easy exchange of information between large industrial and scientific enterprises, universities, solo hobbyist computer builders, and gadfly software writers. All of them contributed to and drew upon a rich specialist literature and kept abreast of the latest developments through the mass media. Because of the capitalist information nexus, individuals who were not highly ranked within the military-industrial-university complex, or even directly connected with it, were able to seize the moment and move from the fringes of activity to the very center of the digital universe. After all, Microsoft and Dell were founded by university drop-outs, Facebook by a college kid, and Google by a couple of graduate students.

The creators of the digital era also took advantage of the short-sightedness of the big companies that had become assured of their domination of the computer business, as exemplified by IBM's underestimation of potential PC sales in early negotiations with Bill Gates's Microsoft. Managers at IBM and other bureaucratized IT firms had always looked down on programmers, as an article from *Fortune* magazine in 1969 spelled out:

Most experts agree that another barrier to the most desirable use of the computer is the immense culture and communications gap that divides managers from computer people. The computer people tend to be young, mobile, and quantitatively oriented, and look to their peers both for company and for approval ... Managers, on the other hand, are typically older and tend to regard computer people either as mere technicians or as threats to their position and status – in either case they resist their presence in the halls of power.[34]

In this spirit, Hewlett-Packard rejected its employee Steve Wozniak's idea for a home computer. He built one called the Apple in Steve Jobs' garage. With the first true PC, the Apple II, designed to look "about as intimidating as a granola bar," sales went from zero in 1976 to $100 million in 1980. In 2014, the company was worth more than IBM, whose valuation also lags behind Microsoft.[35] This feat would

---

[34] www.cnet.com/news/gates-ibm-missed-pcs-early-potential/; Nathan L. Ensmenger, "Letting the 'Computer Boys' Take Over: Technology and the Politics of Organizational Transformation," in International Review of Social History, Supplement.

[35] Hall, *Cities in Civilization*, 445 (granola quote); Kurt Badenhausen, "Apple, Microsoft, and Google Are the World's Most Valuable Brands," *Forbes* (Nov. 5, 2014), online at forbes.com/sites/kurtbadenhausen/2014/11/05/apple-microsoft-and-google-are-worlds-most-valuable-brands/#38ef716b6f0e.

have been difficult to imagine happening in countries with even more rigid corporate cultures and more limited venture financing.

We associate the digital age with new information technologies, but metamorphoses in manufacturing and a "retail revolution" are also crucial features.[36] Production and distribution in this so-called new economy were both culminations of continuing evolutions in the information nexus of capitalism. We turn to those subjects now.

Flowing data: Digitization of production and distribution

Computerization of inventory control and the collection of point-of-sale (POS) data began in the 1980s. In the next decade, with the arrival of the internet and inexpensive telecommunications, manufacturers adopted holistic "process flow scheduling" for "just-in-time" or "lean" production. Suppliers customized the final product according to known consumer wants (ascertained, as we will see, by POS and other digital data), which rendered once large and expensive inventories unnecessary. With these developments a new intensification of the information nexus took place. As the cost of communications, computing, and transportation declined, it became cheaper for manufacturers to purchase components of a product from all over the world (first and foremost in Asia) instead of making them themselves. Networks of suppliers and distributors choreographed every aspect of production as never before. New supply chains were forged. Factory-floor flows shifted course. Work life changed. And all of that altered the relationship among industries, retail stores, and consumers.

In manufacturing, "lean production," also known as "flexible mass production" or "mass customization," involves seeking information to reduce the waste that comes from holding unnecessary spare parts or producing excess amounts of goods. The method arose in the Toyota Motor Corporation, but it stems from the unique situation of Tokyo and southern Japan, which were among the most dynamic high-tech industrial areas of the twentieth century.[37] In this region, the Japanese

---

[36] The quotation comes from Nelson Lichtenstein, *The Retail Revolution: How Wal-Mart Created a Brave New World of Business* (NY: Picador, 2010).

[37] The following section on Japan relies on Hall, *Cities in Civilization*, 455–460; Masahiko Aoki, "Toward an Economic Model of the Japanese Firm," *Journal of Economic Literature* (March 1990), 3–7; G. J. R. Linge, "Just-in-Time: More or Less Flexible?" *Economic Geography* (Oct. 1991), 316–332; Cortada, *Digital Hand*, 131–143, and chap. 7; James W. Cortada, "Where Did Knowledge Workers Come From?," in *Rise of the Knowledge*

showed their supreme skills at "downstream R&D" – the evolution of new engineering and production processes for products invented elsewhere, or what physicist Makoto Kikuchi has called "adaptive creativity."[38] There, information technologies diffused rapidly after the war with the introduction of electronics from American companies like AT&T, Bell Labs, and RCA. Japanese companies then sold their products to the rest of East and Southeast Asia. From the 1960s onward, Tokyo served in its own right as the world headquarters for giant companies like Sony, which produced electronics for home and office, but relied on subcontracts with research firms to generate ideas and with small and medium-sized factories to produce parts – many of the Japanese supplier networks having existed prior to World War II.

These manufacturing methods and information networking were applied to the highest degree in the automobile industry. In part it was the way things were done in Japan – as in Germany, intimate banking networks, close relations with the state planners, and communitarian labor relations were typical, a different variant of capitalism than Anglo-American forms of corporate organization and financing. But for this industry, the high cost of warehouse space and parking in a densely populated country forced companies like Toyota to find a more flexible approach to coordinating production and responding to shifts in consumer preferences through information sharing and outsourcing to local firms which it either owned or with which it had long-standing relationships.

Toyota also borrowed ideas from the United States, including implementing procedures taken from Taylorist scientific management. Before the war, the company's founder had recruited American engineers and espoused the most efficient American production methods. Afterwards, Toyota applied American managerial ideas under the influence of the quality-control expert and statistician W. Edwards Deming, who was an advisor to General Douglas MacArthur, supreme commander of the Allied Occupation of Japan. In the 1950s, Deming lectured in the country many times, urging Japanese firms to monitor every step of the industrial process for quality and to link consumer research and product manufacturing. Taiichi Ohno, Toyota's chief production engineer who was most

Worker, ed. James W. Cortada (Boston: Butterworth-Heinemann, 1998), 13–18; Etsuo Abe, "Development of Modern Business in Japan," *Business History Review* (Summer 1997), 304–305; Marsh, *New Industrial Revolution*, 50–56; Michael Cusumano, *The Japanese Automobile Industry: Technology and Management at Nissan and Toyota* (Cambridge, MA: Harvard University Asia Center, 1986); James P. Womack, Daniel T. Jones, and Daniel Roos, *The Machine that Changed the World: The Story of Lean Production* (NY: Free Press, 1990), chap. 3 and passim.

[38] Hall, *Cities in Civilization*, 480–481.

responsible for introducing these systems at Toyota, was one of Deming's disciples. On a visit to the United States, Ohno found that he admired American supermarkets as much as car companies, especially "the way customers chose exactly what they wanted, and in the quantities that they wanted," and how these stores "supplied merchandise in a simple, efficient, and timely manner." What he first called the "supermarket system" became the "Toyota Production System," which combined mass production with customized variations based on supply and demand.[39]

It works as follows: specific orders dictate the level and type of production, rather than throwing a big net hoping to catch buyers by pumping out a pre-set number of cars on the assembly line. Production targets change depending on shifts in consumer demand with monthly, weekly, and daily revisions in response to market demand forecasts or trends in actual consumer orders. Both automated quantitative data and human observation of qualitative factors are the determinants in the movement of information, parts, and materials between Toyota and its suppliers. Components are ordered according to the "just in time" or *kanban* system – named after a tag which, before the internet, suppliers and the manufacturer sent between themselves several times a day to adjust requisitions.

Japanese auto firms place a premium on information exchange. Engineers rotate through design labs and production labs, sharing information between the two. There is careful quality control, including the training of workers specifically to detect flaws on the assembly line. Managers organize time and motion supervision over workers and coordinate their activities with all aspects of production. The metaphor used to describe these methods in Japan is that of draining a pond, which is when problems become apparent as underwater hazards are revealed. Critics, though, regard lean production as milking a dry cow – since so much of the cost is squeezed out it is hard to achieve further efficiencies.

Japan influenced American and global manufacturing patterns in two ways. In the first place, as Japanese companies presented intense competition for American firms, automakers slowly adopted Japanese methods

---

[39] Supermarket quote from Taiichi Ohno, *Workplace Management*, trans. Jon Miller (NY: McGraw Hill, 2013), 68; others from Marsh, *New Industrial Revolution*, 54. On Deming, see William M. Tsutui, *Manufacturing Ideology: Scientific Management in Twentieth-Century Japan* (Princeton: Princeton University Press, 1998), 191–201, and Andrea Gabor, *The Capitalist Philosophers* (NY: Times Business, 2000), chap. 7. German industrial managers in the 1950 and 1960s also borrowed extensively from American ideas of quality control that firms in the US largely ignored. In the 1970s, German companies started to learn from the Japanese instead: see Mary Nolan, "Anti-Americanism and Americanization in Germany," *Politics and Society* (March 2005), 97.

in the 1980s and 1990s, after Japanese firms Toyota, Honda, and Nissan built factories in the United States. It became the norm here as it had been in Japan for decades to outsource to layers of suppliers big and small while the company producing the name-brand product was often just the final assembly point.[40]

Second, in the 1980s Japanese multinationals were associated with the "Flying Geese" model of moving production throughout Asia in quest of the lowest labor cost.[41] This was actually an American contrivance, too, in which the Japanese found it easy to participate: in some respects it was putting into action the strategies of prewar Japan's colonial bureaucracy in a new guise.[42] The back story is that in the early post–World War II United States, American retailers still purchased their stock from wholesalers, and manufacturers set a legally binding minimum retail price for their products. Chain stores like Sears, JCPenney, or Federated Department Stores (now Macy's) were best positioned to profit from that circumstance through the high turnover of merchandise. Many small retailers were being driven out of business. As highway construction picked up speed in the 1950s to 1980s, large discount department stores located outside city centers began to mushroom: within months of each other in 1962, Walmart, Kmart, Kohl's, and Target all opened their doors. In subsequent decades, with land available for bigger stores in areas undergoing suburbanization, niche clothing stores like Gap, The Limited, and Old Navy grew into large chains, as did a long list of pharmacies, office or auto supply stores, and bookstores.[43]

Until 1965, American manufacturers supplied these chains. In that year the United States ran its first trade deficit with Japan, which worsened in later years with imports from Hong Kong, South Korea, Taiwan, and, eventually, China. All of the big American chains contracted with sourcing firms in East Asia: Sears, Kmart, and JCPenney opened offices in Taiwan between 1967 and 1971, and almost all the

---

[40] Tetsuji Kawamura, ed., *Hybrid Factories in the United States: The Japanese-Style Management and Production System under the Global Economy* (Oxford: Oxford University Press, 2010); and John Y. Shook, "Bringing the Toyota Production System to the United States: A Personal Perspective," in *Becoming Lean: Inside Stories of US Manufacturers*, ed. Jeffrey K. Liker (Portland, OR: Productivity Press, 1998), 41–69.

[41] Henry Tricks, "The Pacific: A Special Report," *Economist* (Nov. 15, 2014), 6.

[42] Laura E. Hein, "Growth versus Success: Japan's Economic Policy in Historical Perspective," in *Postwar Japan as History*, ed. Andrew Gordon (Berkeley: University of California Press, 1993), 105.

[43] This paragraph and the one that follows relies on Gary G. Hamilton, *Commerce and Capitalism in Chinese Societies* (London: Routledge, 2006), chap. 6.

others did so in South Korea. They were attempting to undercut US Fair Trade Laws, which protected manufacturers and small retail shops by disallowing discount pricing. By opening their own private labels on clothing or other items, chains became manufacturers and could set their own low prices. At first, private-label production moved to the American South, where labor costs were low, but southern manufacturers were overwhelmed and themselves began to open offices in Asia. Japanese firms like Mitsui served as intermediaries. By 1975, the experimental phase in contract manufacturing was over as Asian suppliers' markets were by then well established. Meanwhile, competition between chain stores led them to contract for manufactured goods abroad without owning the factories. The Gap, The Limited, Nike, and later Dell Computers never made anything themselves. What they did was to assess consumer demand, design products to satisfy it, buy the goods from Asian factories, and then merchandise them. Outsourcing involved information as much if not more than it did the competitive race to the bottom in terms of labor costs.[44]

Mattel's Barbie doll illustrates the evolution of these international production networks. Fifty years ago, she was made in Japanese and Taiwanese factories, with clothing hand-sewn in Taiwanese homes. Now she is assembled in China using American molds and pigments, Japanese or European machinery, nylon hair from Japan, a plastic body from Taiwan, and Chinese cotton clothing.[45] Cellphones are another example: nearly all of them are manufactured by companies abroad, mainly in China. But the materials come from all over the world: tantalum in the capacitators from Australia or Congo; nickel in the battery from Chile; rare earths from China and the United States; the microprocessor chips and circuitry from North America; the plastic casing and liquid in the liquid-crystal display manufactured from petroleum pumped globally; the molds from Taiwan. In the case of Apple's iPhone, a thousand supply-chain managers oversee its international sourcing from headquarters in Cupertino, California.[46]

---

[44] It is worth noting that the decisions to outsource or move offshore were choices made by companies and that some chose not to play the game. See, e.g., Beth Macy, *Factory Man: How One Furniture Maker Battled Offshoring, Stayed Local – and Helped Save an American Town* (NY: Little, Brown, 2014), and the host of industries listed in Mark Muro et al., *America's Advanced Industries: What They Are, Where They Are, and Why They Matter* (Washington, DC: Brookings Institute, 2015), 21.

[45] Marc Levinson, *The Box: How the Shipping Container Made the World Smaller and the World Economy Bigger* (Princeton: Princeton University Press, 2006), 264–265.

[46] Agar, *Constant Touch*, 18–19; Marsh, *New Industrial Revolution*, 87; Jay Greene, "Digging for Rare Earths," *CNET Magazine* (Sept. 26, 2012), online at www.cnet.com/news/digging-for-rare-earths-the-mines-where-iphones-are-born/.

What Barbie and the iPhone represent is the "supply chain" or "value chain," a form of "interconnected manufacturing" in which firms produce niche services or pieces of a product, adding value by supporting companies further up the chain. This activity is now so substantial that it involves hundreds of widely dispersed companies and individuals, with around 2 million people worldwide employed in the management of value-chain operations. By 2010, because of post–Cold War globalization and new information and communications technologies, 41 percent of world manufacturing took place outside of developed nations, compared with 27 percent in 2000 and 24 percent in 1990, with China currently the world's heavyweight producer. Total global foreign direct investment – meaning investment outside of home countries – now exceeds a trillion dollars. In 1960, just 6 percent of world GDP was in foreign-investment assets, in 1980 it was 25 percent, and in 2000 it was 92 percent – a leap propelled by digital-age technologies. Many large companies have also established R&D operations abroad: in 2010, the German engineering conglomerate Siemens had 12 percent of its 30,000 R&D staff in Asia. As of 2009, over a quarter of all research departments in US multinational corporations were located overseas. A hundred American companies currently have R&D offices in China, and fifty in India.[47] Reflecting this internationalization, the United States today has a trade deficit in R&D services with Germany, the United Kingdom, the Netherlands, Switzerland, and Japan.[48]

Global supply chains, flexible production, and lean retailing (more on which below) all rely on informational improvements in logistics, including the precisely scheduled tracking of goods in transit. The placement of digital technologies in trains, trucks, and ships transformed the transportation industry. So did intermodal freight, with the standardized container boxes that migrate between ocean-going ships, river barges, railroads, and trucks. They were originally devised by Malcolm McLean, a North Carolina trucking entrepreneur, who shipped the first such containers, fabricated out of reinforced truck trailers, from Newark to Houston in 1956. The Dutch port of Rotterdam, the busiest port in Europe, was the first to grasp the potential of containers and adapt their facilities to accommodate them. Container ships are getting bigger and bigger because "transport adds nothing to the final value of a good so cost

---

[47] Marsh, *New Industrial Revolution*, 17–19, 66–72, 77–78, 87; Yousseff Cassis, *Capitals of Capital: The Rise and Fall of International Financial Centres, 1780–2005* (Cambridge: Cambridge University Press, 2006), 242–244; Eamonn Fingleton, "America the Innovative?," *New York Times* (March 30, 2013), online at nytimes.com/2013/03/31/sunday-review/america-the-innovative.html?pagewanted=all.

[48] Muro et al., *America's Advanced Industries*, 37.

minimization is all-important," and the larger the ship, the lower the cost per container. The first container ships in the 1950s carried 480 containers; now they carry more than 15,000–18,000. Only twenty crew members man these behemoths. Cranes unload them at automated ports and deposit them onto trucks and trains. Every year, more than 300 million containers are shipped by sea, and many times that number on land. Trucks and trains all have sophisticated onboard computer systems to communicate with dispatchers and clients; guiding container ships are radar, satellite, GPS, internet, and both satellite and mobile-telephone communications, while computerized cargo monitoring informed by sensors traces container locations and contents in real time. The amount of time freight spends in storage or being shipped is declining, and because of that, the cost of transporting goods from factories to markets around the world is now less than 1 percent of the retail price. Before the digital age it accounted for up to 25 percent of the cost.[49]

Cheaper shipping and lean production were both counterparts of lean retailing, which emerged with another informational innovation, the Universal Product Code (UPC) barcode and electronic scanners. IBM engineers developed the first barcodes on the initiative of the National Association of Food Chains. The first scanning of a barcode was on a pack of Wrigley's Juicy Fruit chewing gum at Marsh's Supermarket in Troy, Ohio, in June 1974, near NCR headquarters in Dayton, which had designed the checkout counter and installed the IBM 3660, a laser-scanning point-of-sale barcode reader. In tandem was the organization of the Uniform Code Council in 1984 for assignment of codes to vendors. UPC codes combined with computerized inventory programs ease the management of huge stocks of goods, supplies, and components; purchase orders and shipping invoices; as well as keeping balances of income and expenditures. As cash registers scan purchases, they instantly update inventory and accounting records and also track marketing trends. With POS data analytics, companies can replenish stocks quickly and decide what to sell and where to position it in the store.[50]

[49] Levinson, *The Box*; Arthur Donovan and Joseph Bonney, *The Box that Changed the World: Fifty Years of Container Shipping* (East Windsor, NJ: Commonwealth Business Media, 2006); Cortada, *Digital Hand*, 118, and chap. 8; Douglas Long, *International Logistics: Global Supply Chain Management* (Norwell, MA: Kluwer Academic Publishers, 2003); Helen Sampson and Bin Wu, "Compressing Time and Constraining Space," in *International Review of Social History*, supp. 11: *Uncovering Labour in Information Revolutions*, ed. Blok and Downey, 128–129; *Economist* (Nov. 3, 2012), 76 (quote).

[50] Stephen A. Brown, *Revolution at the Checkout Counter: The Explosion of the Bar Code* (Cambridge, MA: Harvard University Press, 1997); Frederick H. Abernathy et al., *A Stitch in Time: Lean Retailing and the Transformation of Manufacturing – Lessons from the Apparel and Textile Industries* (Oxford: Oxford University Press, 1999), 60ff; Cummings

Although Kmart was first to adopt the technology in 1983, it was Walmart that was in the vanguard of the "retail revolution." By virtue of competition, all others had to follow, with "much of the global economy ... now driven" by global supply chains of big-box store companies that "have their nerve centers in Bentonville, Arkansas (Walmart), Atlanta (Home Depot), Minneapolis (Target), Troy, Michigan (Kmart), Paris (Carrefour), Stockholm (IKEA), and Issaquah, Washington (Costco)."[51] It made Walmart one of the largest and most profitable companies in the world: if Walmart were a country, its GDP would be about the size of Switzerland's. Walmart is the largest private employer in the United States, with over 3,811 stores where 100 million Americans shop every week. It has an additional 1,200 stores abroad: it is the largest retailer in Mexico and Canada, and number two in the United Kingdom. Worldwide, more than 7.2 billion people shop at Walmart each year. It sells more groceries than any other company and is the world's largest private employer with 1.6 million "associates." From 2000 to 2006, more than 70 percent of all new retailing jobs in the United States came from Walmart.

By the early 1990s, Walmart had impelled all retail operations in the United States to follow its lead in adopting sophisticated information technologies for inventory and supply-chain management. From the start, Walmart's success has been based on its meticulous scrutinizing of information, attempts to know and control everything about every aspect of its business activity in order to bring its costs down. To quote Rollin Ford, a Chief Information Officer at Walmart, "every day I wake up and ask, 'how can I flow data better, manage data better, analyze data better?'" – a comment that captures the essence of modern capitalism.[52]

Design, "History: The Uniform Code Council, Inc.," online at cummingsdesign.com/bar_codes101_UCC_History.htm.

[51] Quotes from Nelson Lichtenstein, "Walmart's Long March to China," in *Walmart in China*, ed. Anita Chan (Ithaca, NY: ILR Press, 2011), 17. The rest of the section on Wal-Mart relies on Nelson Lichtenstein, "Wal-Mart: A Template," in *Wal-Mart: The Face of Twenty-First Century Capitalism*, ed. Nelson Lichtenstein (NY: New Press, 2006), 3, 11; James Hoopes, "Growth through Knowledge: Wal-Mart, High Technology, and the Ever Less Visible Hand of the Manager," in *Wal-Mart*, ed. Lichtenstein, 87–94; Cortada, *Digital Hand*, 259–260, 272, 274, and chaps. 10–11; Cukier, "Data, Data Everywhere," 3–9; Daniel M. G. Raff and Peter Temin, "Sears, Roebuck in the Twentieth Century," in *Learning by Doing in Markets, Firms, and Countries*, ed. Naomi R. Lamoreaux, Daniel M. G. Raff, and Peter Temin (Chicago: University of Chicago Press, 1999), 240–243; Simon Head, "They're Micromanaging Your Every Move," *New York Review of Books* (Aug. 16, 2007), 42; Charles Fishman, *The Wal-Mart Effect: How the World's Most Powerful Company Really Works – and How It's Transforming the American Economy* (NY: Penguin, 2006), 3, 6, 12–13, 107, and chap. 6; Brynjolfsson and McAfee, *Second Machine Age*, 100–103.

[52] Quote from Cukier, "Data, Data Everywhere," 4.

In its quest for data-driven profits, Walmart was one of the first companies to make use of POS data collection; it now processes more than 1 million customer transactions per hour. To ensure the profitability and productivity of its stores, it also measures sales per foot of shelf space for every item it stocks. By the late 1980s, Walmart also had the largest private satellite communications network in the world. Its suppliers all acquire and use the same technologies and standards, like RFID (radio frequency identification) technology that pinpoints goods at all stages of production and distribution. The company is connected to an inventory-management system that allows suppliers to see how many of their products are on Walmart shelves at any given moment. "When Walmart sells a tube of toothpaste in Memphis that information flashes straight through to Bentonville, then on to the P&G headquarters in Cincinnati, the Ohio home-product manufacturer, which then immediately sends the electronic impulse directly to an offshore toothpaste factory, which adjusts its production schedule accordingly."[53] Sharing data with suppliers is supposed to have led to an increase in sales from $1 billion a week in 1993 to the same amount every thirty-six hours in 2001. More importantly, by replacing a guessing game with these and other data-mining systems, it has prevented the waste of billions of dollars of unsold inventories in chain stores. In part it is because of these relentless efficiencies that when Walmart and other big-box chain stores come to town they create jobs, but other stores close or lose business. Walmart is able to demand the lowest prices from its suppliers because the latter are hooked on the profits they make by supplying to Walmart. Smaller retailers cannot compete. Nationwide, all other distribution firms and retail chains have imitated Walmart.

In advertising even more than production and distribution, digital-age retailing has made perhaps its boldest departure. The internet has become a vast "marketing laboratory," in the words of Nicholas Carr. The goal is to correct the problem identified by mass retailer John Wannamaker in the nineteenth century: "Half the money I spend on advertising is wasted. The trouble is I don't know which half."[54] Across the chain-retail industry and online "e-tail," or electronic retail business, a trend toward "personalization" leads firms to collect data about customer transactions and demographics to tailor prices, products, and online displays to specific individuals.[55] Walmart alone gathers 2.5 petabytes

[53] Lichtenstein, "Walmart's Long March to China," 17–18.
[54] Quotes from Carr, *Big Switch*, 205–206.
[55] This paragraph relies on Charles Duhigg, *The Power of Habit* (NY: Random House, 2012), chap. 7; Charles Duhigg, "How Companies Learn Your Secrets," *New York Times*

(or 2.5 quadrillion bytes) of data every hour from customer purchases.[56] That began with expanded credit-card use in the 1980s, but now sophisticated algorithms and statistically based pattern analysis exploit individual consumers' data. Companies still apply the lessons of mass psychology in the layout of stores: in supermarkets they place produce and other healthy foods first so that people will feel virtuous about their purchases and less reluctant to throw junk food into their cart later. But such techniques apply to all customers who enter the building, and as with lean production, greater profits and less wasteful stocking are to be had with individualized marketing. A decade ago, chain retailer Target, one of the industry leaders in this activity, started building a data warehouse on individuals through a "Guest ID number" that tracked how that person shopped or searched Target online, also exploiting the information generated with its customer loyalty cards and credit-card purchases. The company also buys demographic information from firms that collect it online from public records. Target then sends coupons as inducements based on what they think each customer will buy. Most major retailers now have "predictive analytics" departments, whose function is to discern precise consumer preferences. So do music companies, which attempt to decipher listeners' habits in order to know which albums and songs to push them to buy.

Online firms that crunch data to learn about consumers induce the latter to make small changes in behavior that lead to "repeated incremental gains": such tiny adjustments maximize sales and accumulate to increase corporate earnings. Data-intensive advertising is responsible for $150 billion a year in economic activity. Amazon.com has Amabot, an algorithm that recommends books based on customer online-search behaviors. Online e-tailers do not buy old-fashioned forms of advertising that broad categories of people reading the newspaper might happen to see. Using pattern recognition, algorithmic bidding systems target individual consumers instead, as online pop-ups of items a person has searched for on one website appear on another. Now 10 percent of advertising is sold in this format, with digital advertising networks like Ad.com or DoubleClick bidding for space and selling ads as directed

---

(Feb. 16, 2012), online at nytimes.com/2012/02/19/magazine/shopping-habits.html?pa gewanted=all; *Economist* (May 28, 2011), 74; Stephanie Clifford, "Shopper Alert: Price May Drop for You Alone," *New York Times* (Aug. 9, 2012), online at nytimes.com/2012/ 08/10/business/supermarkets-try-customizing-prices-for-shoppers.html?page wanted=all.

[56] Andrew McAfee and Eric Brynjolfsson, "Big Data: The Management Revolution," *Harvard Business Review* (Oct. 2012), 62.

by automated computer trading that is itself guided by "programmatic buying" technologies.[57]

***

The computer and the mobile phone are the information machines of the digital age. The Internet, as they used to say in the 1990s, is the "information superhighway."[58] Algorithms direct more and more of the traffic. Intermodal freight containers supply the goods made by lean production and sold by lean retailing; concomitantly, many working-class jobs have been shipped overseas, and data mining extracts consumer preferences. One statistic tallies with the perception that we are living in a "new economy": twelve of the fifteen richest Americans either own digital-technology companies, such as Microsoft, or are members of the Walton family, descendants of Walmart's founder.[59] No wonder it feels as though we are living through revolutionary times. But are we really?

Is it a revolution?

Contemporary discourse speaks of the IT Revolution; the Digital Revolution; the Retail Revolution; the newest Industrial Revolution. We need some perspective. The new information technologies of the digital age make it seem as though we are living in a "new economy," with greater individualism, entrepreneurialism, collaboration, and decentralization.[60] In 1997, *Wired*, a magazine of emergent technologies, predicted that the digital age would produce a "new civilization, a global civilization ... marked by a singular understanding: 'We're one global society, one human race.'"[61] But this current revolution, whatever the adjective describing it, has by no means ushered in a new dawn for

---

[57] *Economist* (July 19, 2014), 60; Steve Coll, "Citizen Bezos," *New York Review of Books* (July 10, 2014), 28; Tanzina Vega, "The New Algorithm of Web Marketing," *New York Times* (Nov. 15, 2012), online at nytimes.com/2012/11/16/business/media/automated-bid ding-systems-test-old-ways-of-selling-ads.html; Frank Pasquale, *The Black Box Society: The Secret Algorithms that Control Money and Information* (Cambridge, MA: Harvard University Press, 2015), chap. 2.

[58] For the history of this expression, see http://en.wikipedia.org/wiki/Information_super highway.

[59] Sue Halpern, "How Robots and Algorithms Are Taking Over," *New York Review of Books* (April 2, 2015), 26.

[60] According to a keyword search on the database "Readers' Guide Full Text Mega," the term "new economy" began to appear in the periodical press with regularity beginning in 1983.

[61] Fred Turner, *From Counterculture to Cyberculture: Stewart Brand, The Whole Earth Network, and the Rise of Digital Utopianism* (Chicago: University of Chicago Press, 2006), 7, 233 (quote); see also Carr, *Big Switch*, 109, 124; and Mark Dery, *Escape Velocity: Cyberculture at the End of the Century* (NY: Grove Press, 1996), passim.

humanity, in which the "digital generation" and the personalized technology of the internet brings about a society free from the control of governmental and corporate bureaucracies.

We can put paid to that utopian dream by remembering some of the overly enthusiastic things that have been said about IT innovations in the past. Here is the English art critic and social thinker John Ruskin commenting in 1870 on the impact of telegraphs, railroads, and steamships: "Within the last few years we have had the laws of natural science opened to us with a rapidity that has been blinding by its brightness; and means of transit and communication given to us, which have made but one kingdom of the habitable globe."[62] In the 1930s, David Sarnoff, head of RCA, rhapsodized about the invention of the television:

When television has fulfilled its ultimate destiny, man's sense of physical limitation will be swept away and his boundaries of sight and hearing will be the limits of the earth itself. With this may come a new horizon, a new philosophy, a new sense of freedom, and greatest of all, perhaps, a finer and broader understanding between all the peoples of the world.[63]

In 1997, Cyberpunk novelist Bruce Sterling expressed a more cynical view of such zealous expectations for new technologies: "The Radio Age, the Aviation Age, the Atomic Age, the Space Age ... all of these so-called 'ages' are history. Soon our much-trumpeted 'Information Age' will have that same archaic ring."[64]

What *Wired*, Ruskin, Sarnoff, and Sterling all misunderstood is that the "Information Age" was not new to their generation. Rather, it is part of a continuum of capitalism that stretches back to early modern Europe and continues to unfold in our computerized times. As previous chapters have made clear, it is incorrect to say today that "data are becoming the new raw material of business: an economic input almost on a par with capital and labor."[65] That was the case all along with business, wherever it was, but especially with the emergence of the information nexus beginning in seventeenth-century Holland and England. Digital technologies are just the latest manifestation of the capitalist quest for useful knowledge. Some things have changed as a result, but much is not at all

---

[62] John Ruskin, "Conclusion to Inaugural Lecture (1870)," in *Empire Writing: An Anthology of Colonial Literature 1870–1918*, ed. Elleke Boehmer (Oxford: Oxford University Press, 1998), 18.

[63] David E. Nye, "Shaping Communication Networks: Telegraph, Telephone, Computer," *Social Research* (Fall 1997), 1075–1076.

[64] Greg Downey, "Commentary: The Place of Labour in the History of Information-Technology Revolutions," in *International Review of Social History*, supp. 11: *Uncovering Labour in Information Revolutions*, ed. Blok and Downey, 230.

[65] Cukier, "Data, Data Everywhere," 4.

new. In assessing the revolutionary nature of the digital age it is useful to apply a model from the historiography of the French Revolution expounded by François Furet: the revolution did significantly and wrenchingly transmute French society, and contemporaries "experienced [it] subjectively as a radical break." But there were also deep continuities that remained in place, such as the growing ambit of the central state. Furet felt it was incumbent to identify both trends for an accurate under-standing of the complex legacies of the French Revolution. It behooves us to do the same as we seek to make sense of the digital age.[66]

We begin with the continuity column. Economist Robert J. Gordon downplays the achievements of the digital economy and in so doing implies that our current era has not been the dramatic departure from the recent past that we often think it is. Well before World War I, he writes, the telegraph had already made global communications nearly instantaneous. More than the internet, it was radio and TV broadcasts that opened households to the wider world.[67] And earlier inventions had a far greater impact on peoples' lives and standard of living, among them indoor plumbing, electrification of households, the lightbulb, the telephone, the automobile, air travel, and air conditioning.[68] Those statements might not apply to the underdeveloped parts of the world, but we will leave that issue aside temporarily.

Nor have the predictions of a "post-industrial society" been borne out. The term comes from a 1973 book by sociologist Daniel Bell, who identified a trend away from industrial labor and production of goods and toward a service economy ruled by a new technocratic elite. We can see the fallacy in his classification schema, whereby a pre-industrial society is a "game against nature"; an industrial society is a "game against fabricated nature" centered on "man-machine relationships"; and a post-industrial society is a "game between persons" in which "intellectual technology" "rises alongside of machine technology."[69] If the argument of my book holds, the way Bell characterizes post-industrial society as based on information should apply to all capitalist societies old and new. For him, the hallmark of being post-industrial is the shift away from "the quantity of goods as marking a standard of living" to one that "is defined by the quality of life as measured by the services and

---

[66] François Furet, *Interpreting the French Revolution*, trans. Elborg Forster (Cambridge: Cambridge University Press, 1981), 15 (quote), 28, 78.
[67] Gordon, "Does the 'New Economy' Measure Up?" 68.
[68] Gordon, "Does the 'New Economy' Measure Up?," 60, 68; Gordon, "Demise of US Economic Growth," 23–24.
[69] Daniel Bell, *The Coming of Post-Industrial Society: A Venture in Social Forecasting* (NY: Basic Books, 1973), with quote on 116.

amenities – heath, education, recreation, and the arts – which are now deemed desirable and possible for everyone."[70]

But the numbers do not back that up. It is true that the growth in demand for financial, legal, travel, and leisure services has meant a decline in the comparative proportion of economic output taken up by manufactures: between 1980 and 2010, global industrial production dropped by 30 percent, from 24.1 percent to 17.6 percent of total output. But manufacturing is still growing in the world, and significantly, with production now more than 1.5 times higher than in 1990, and fifty-seven times higher than in 1900. This clearly indicates that the global economy continues to be industrial rather than post-industrial. In 2010, moreover, the world's industrial companies spent the not insignificant sum of $1.2 trillion on the development of new manufactured goods. As for employment in manufacturing, in the United States it has indeed fallen from about 30 percent in the 1950s to less than 10 percent today; jobs in services rose from less than 50 percent to 70 percent in the same period, and finally in 2003 the number of Americans working in retailing (14.9 million) surpassed the number in factories (14.5 million). But in the world as a whole, there are now more manufacturing workers than ever before, equaling about 10 percent of the global workforce, which has been the average for the past two hundred years.[71]

On the retail-distribution side of this evolving but still-industrial economy, continuities also prevail. While e-commerce grew in the United States alone to $227 billion a year in 2012, much has also stayed the same. That figure accounts for only 5.2 percent of retail turnover, with in-store sales totaling $4.3 trillion.[72] Shopping online is just a few degrees away from the experience of placing telephone orders from the Sears, Roebuck or other catalogues, as was common from the 1920s onward. And while Amazon.com is an exception, most companies still mass-mail paper catalogues to the home. In "e-commerce" and the "virtual" economy, stuff is still produced the old way, hands-on by laborers, and still has to be shipped by fossil-fuel-burning trucks, ships, or airplanes with a paper receipt from brick-and-mortar warehouses (although Amazon is experimenting with delivery by drone).

For all its global power and greater pressure toward standardization, Walmart acts like early mass merchandiser Sears, Roebuck, or chain

[70] Bell, *Coming of Post-Industrial Society*, 126.
[71] Marsh, *New Industrial Revolution*, 15–16, 27, 233–234, 240; Fishman, *Wal-Mart Effect*, 108; *Economist* (Jan. 18, 2014), 26.
[72] US Census Bureau, "US Retail Trade Sales – Total and E-commerce: 2012 and 2011," online at census.gov/econ/estats/2012/all2012tables.html.

grocery store A&P, both of which were dominant players in the retail industry and whose modus operandi was to obsessively control costs and make a profit on volume rather than markups.[73] No different than Walmart, they put a "relentless squeeze on suppliers," with A&P "pioneer[ing] the practice of carefully dissecting manufacturers' costs to determine what prices they should receive for their products" – a practice that shocks us all over again when we learn that Walmart or Amazon.com engages in it today.[74] Older companies like Sears, Roebuck, also kept inventory low by ordering products in the smallest possible batches and forced down prices of manufacturers' brand-name goods by virtue of their clout in the economy. Those companies, too, systematized distribution and provoked local resistance, but in the end they appealed to consumers because they saved them money, and they appealed to producers and suppliers because they guaranteed them sales.

Even in the age of the algorithm, the collection of vast amounts of intimate consumer data does not guarantee that a company will make better sense of them than in the past. Resume-sorting algorithms are often imprecise as they search for specific words and miss others, so that HR firms end up overlooking good candidates. Algorithm-based personality tests conducted by employers have the same flaws.[75] Personally, I rarely want to watch any of the movies Netflix recommends for me based on my viewing profile or to buy any of the books Amazon suggests I might like. Chain store Target, one of the most advanced in data mining, has been losing money hand over fist because of bad business decisions leading to the introduction of unpopular lines of clothing and a misguided and doomed entrance into the Canadian market.[76] Target compares badly with Spanish clothing giant Zara, which uses humans instead of computers to decide which clothes to make and which to sell. The latter's specialty is "fast fashion" aimed at young people: good, cheap clothes with short-term popularity, which computer-aided forecasting cannot select. Zara asks its store managers to order clothing that will sell at their location very quickly. Rather than relying on algorithms, they make their purchasing decisions by walking around the store and observing their customers.[77]

[73] Susan Strasser, "Woolworth to Wal-Mart: Mass Merchandising and the Changing Culture of Consumption," in *Wal-Mart*, ed. Lichtenstein, 31–32, 37–38, 40–41, 47–48, 52–54; Hoopes, "Growth through Knowledge," in *Wal-Mart*, ed. Lichtenstein, 91–92; Gordon, "Does the 'New Economy' Measure Up?" 70; Linge, "Just-in-Time," 320; Nye, "Shaping Communication Networks," 1072–1073.

[74] Marc Levinson, *The Great A&P and the Struggle for Small Business in America* (NY: Hill and Wang, 2011), 268–269.

[75] Pasquale, *Black Box Society*, 36–38.   [76] *Economist* (Feb. 28, 2015), 57–58.

[77] Brynjolfsson and McAfee, *Second Machine Age*, 193–194.

On the production side, as with mass retailing, significant continuities also persist from an earlier era. The greater sensitivity to consumer demand that just-in-time manufacturing and POS data collection are supposed to have engendered has been exaggerated. To be sure, flexible, lean production and new efforts at "mass personalization" have yielded a greater variety in mass-produced goods. According to one estimate, there are currently around ten billion unique manufactured products available for purchase in the world today.[78] But they are nonetheless mass-produced goods, with most of them as impersonalized as before.[79] Many types of factories also customized goods in the past, as not all mass production was Fordist in nature, making and offering only one variety of a product at one price. General Motors is a good example of a company that from the start tried to produce different lines of automobiles to suit different tastes and different incomes. Custom or batch production was necessary for a wide array of products, from machine tools to jewelry, that could not be standardized.[80] And taking a longer view, personalized production is not necessarily a radically new way of producing, but a reversion to the craftsman–consumer relationship of earlier centuries.[81] Just-in-time production is also not as much a novelty as is often thought. In Japan, most subcontractors and lead firms are all clustered fairly close to one another, and in the United States the maximum distance between them is eight hours' driving time. The much-vaunted low inventory is in some sense an illusion: as executives in Japan and the United States have admitted, trucks delivering components are effectively "warehouses on wheels," so the costs have just been shifted around.[82]

As for corporate structures, they have bent and swayed with the hurricane-force winds of change coming from globalization and digitization, but have not collapsed. Outsourcing and modularization of production through transnational production networks may have checked the old model of vertical integration; one scholar has described

---

[78] Marsh, *New Industrial Revolution*, 56 (quote), 59.

[79] Daniel Cohen, *Our Modern Times: The New Nature of Capitalism in the Information Age* (Cambridge, MA: MIT Press, 2003), 5. But cf. predictions about personalized production by Jeremy Rifkin, *The Zero Marginal Cost Society: The Internet of Things, the Collaborative Commons, and the Eclipse of Capitalism* (NY: Palgrave Macmillan, 2014).

[80] Philip Scranton, "Diversity in Diversity: Flexible Production and American Industrialization, 1880–1930," *Business History Review* (Spring 1991), 27–90.

[81] Linge, "Just-in-Time," 320. I do not include in these categorizations the potential of 3D printers to change everything in a more individualized direction. It has not happened yet, but Rifkin, *Zero Marginal Cost Society*, predicts that it will.

[82] Linge, "Just-in-Time," 326, 329.

the period as one of "vertical disintegration."[83] But the giant corporation has not shown any sign of dissolving. General Motors, General Electric, Procter & Gamble, Microsoft, and Intel are all big firms of the old hierarchical type; obviously, large companies like these can thrive as long as they adapt. After some shake-ups, IBM, for instance, has shown unexpected flexibility in meeting challenges from competitors, by transforming itself from a hardware producer to a high-tech consultancy.[84] And according to some studies, the growing economic inequality noted in America and Britain in the past three decades is related to the steady growth of bigger firms, which are best able to afford investments in upgraded IT infrastructure. These put downward pressure on the wages of unskilled employees and open a larger gap between wages at the top and the bottom.[85]

If the preceding paragraphs emphasize continuities, when we examine other subjects, equal stress has to be placed on a mix of both continuity and change. Regarding labor conditions, the trend toward managerial supervision that was the reason for the historical introduction of the factory continues. The application of more effective, digital technologies of control in that arena is a logical progression of the informational principles of capitalism.[86] Just-in-time production was in part a demonstration of the Japanese desire to apply the principles of Taylorism more vigorously than American companies were willing to do.[87] Even if factory workers have more responsibility and autonomy, many must still engage

---

[83] John Zysman, "Creating Value in a Digital Era," in *How Revolutionary Was the Digital Revolution?* ed. John Zysman and Abraham Newman (Stanford: Stanford University Press, 2006), 28.

[84] Richard Sylla, "Chandler on High Technology Industries from the 1880s to the 1990s," *Capitalism and Society*, vol. I, issue 2 (2006), 5; "Big Is Back," *Economist* (Aug. 29, 2009), 9; Cortada, "Introducing the Knowledge Worker," in *Rise of the Knowledge Worker*, ed. Cortada, xv. Microsoft is attempting to break up some of the hierarchical walls between divisions to spur innovation and sales: see Nick Wingfield, "Microsoft (Yes, Microsoft) Has Far-Out Vision," *New York Times* (April 30, 2015), online at nytimes.com/2015/05/03/technology/microsoft-yes-microsoft-has-a-far-out-vision.html?hp&action=click&pgtype=Homepage&module=mini-moth&region=top-stories-below&WT.nav=top-stories-below.

[85] *Economist* (March 14, 2015), 76; Holger M. Mueller, Paige P. Ouimet, and Elena Simintzi, "Wage Inequality and Firm Growth," *NBER Working Paper* No. 20876 (January 2015), online at www.nber.org/papers/w20876.pdf.

[86] Besides the sources cited, this paragraph and the two that follow draw on Simon Head, *The New Ruthless Economy: Work and Power in the Digital Age* (Oxford: Oxford University Press, 2003), chaps. 3–5; Head, "They're Micromanaging Your Every Move," 42–43; Cohen, *Our Modern Times*, 4–7, 25–31, 35–39; Lee S. Sproull, "Computers in U.S. Households since 1977," in *Nation Transformed by Information*, ed. Chandler and Cortada, 271–272; Gordon, "Does the 'New Economy' Measure Up?" 63, 65.

[87] Tsutui, *Manufacturing Ideology*, chaps. 5–6.

in repetitive activity on the assembly line, and at a faster, more intense pace. There is very little decision making by workers and even more managerial interference than before. Whereas some observers see the computerized workplace and the team work that is central to the Japanese production method as fostering a more collaborative environment and breaking up shop-floor hierarchies, others argue the opposite, that they only consolidate the superior position of management.[88]

Reflecting yet another mix of continuity and change, factory principles have entered retail stores too, enhanced by "enterprise-wide information systems" or workflow software, which can evaluate all employees "daily on over a hundred different indicators." This software involves extensive standardization and monitoring of personnel, which it treats little differently than it does inventory. As one advocate of workflow management has written, the purpose is "to optimize the use of key assets in processes – be they physical goods inventory, human resources, or financial assets – companies must be constantly aware of the location, availability, and best use of those assets."[89] Workplace technologies like scheduling software encourage efficiency and bolster the profits of companies that use them, but they can also ignore the personal needs of staff. Starbucks software determines "which of its 130,000 baristas are needed in its thousands of locations and exactly when" – which often means the place and hours of work are constantly varying, and not according to the wishes of the employee.[90]

This has not just occurred on the factory floor, retail outlet, or call center, but it is increasingly applied in offices, too, through the embrace of the principles of industrial psychology, employee testing, human-resources management, and the computer, all of which have turned the office into a kind of factory in its level of supervision. Alan Liu points to the irony of the high-tech industry appropriating the "culture of cool" (the youthful bosses sporting jeans or hoodies, lavish company-provided rec rooms at work, etc.) while actually enhancing and extending the bureaucratic corporate authority of the old industrial society.[91]

[88] Laurie Graham, *On the Line at Subaru-Isuzu: The Japanese Model and the American Worker* (Ithaca, NY: ILR Press, 1995); Shoshana Zuboff, *In the Age of the Smart Machine: The Future of Work and Power* (NY: Basic Books, 1984), 6, chap. 8.

[89] First quote from Frederic Adam and David Sammon, eds., *The Enterprise Resource Planning Decade* (Hershey: Idea Group Publishing, 2004), 6–8; others from Head, *New Ruthless Economy*, 76.

[90] Jodi Kantor, "Working Anything but 9 to 5: Scheduling Technology Leaves Low-Income Parents with Hours of Chaos," *New York Times* (Aug. 31, 2014), online at nytimes.com/ interactive/2014/08/13/us/starbucks-workers-scheduling-hours.html.

[91] Alan Liu, *The Laws of Cool: Knowledge Work and the Culture of Information* (Chicago: University of Chicago Press, 2004), 91–99, 108–140.

Of course, that is what capitalism does: it seeks information about everything, including managers. But the increased supervision has produced more stress for white-collar as well as retail employees. Reporting is constant and the computer creates the expectation that company staff can multitask or continue to work after leaving the office. For white-collar workers, prior to the advent of the PC the most work they brought home was what they could fit in their briefcases;[92] when connected 24/7 to the computer, the amount is infinite. As the magazine *Business Week* noted as early as 1970, increasingly white collar "clerical jobs are measured just like factory jobs."[93]

All of that pertains to the American workforce. Still in the category of dual continuity and change, but internationally, a common practice in outsourced supply-chain production is to rely on a subcontracted labor force. This disconnects the main manufacturing company from the people making its products, sometimes at three or more levels of remove. Apple, for example, employs 63,000 workers itself, but another 750,000 by contract who are hired by factories that produce the parts in China and Taiwan. New information and communications technologies make it easier to outsource, which is in alignment with the basic striving of the capitalist information nexus to open up business opportunities. When informational flows are weak, though, deviations occur. Labor subcontracting is convenient since companies can turn a blind eye to work conditions in the factories that produce for them. But in 2013, when more than 1,100 garment workers died in the collapse of the Rana Plaza Building in Bangladesh, denials of responsibility by the Western brand names whose clothing those workers had been making did not convince the public and generated a social-media campaign that pressured companies to pay compensation to the victims.[94] The Rana catastrophe, like the large number of forced laborers in the Malaysian electronics industry (30 percent of total employees), or the sweatshop conditions in factories the world over, are symptomatic of an unregulated worldwide manufacturing system and globalized labor markets, all bound together by information technologies – what one author labels "digital capitalism."[95]

---

[92] Jill Andresky Fraser, *White-Collar Sweatshop: The Deterioration of Work and Its Rewards in Corporate America* (NY: W. W. Norton, 2001).

[93] Zuboff, *In the Age of the Smart Machine*, 121 (quote), chaps. 3–4 passim.

[94] Robert Kuttner: "Why Work Is More and More Debased," *New York Review of Books* (Oct. 23, 2014), 52–53; cleanclothes.org/ranaplaza.

[95] Dan Schiller, *Digital Capitalism: Networking the Global Market System* (Cambridge, MA: MIT Press, 1999). On Malaysia, see Verité, *Forced Labor in the Production of Electronic Goods in Malaysia: A Comprehensive Study of Scope and Characteristics* (Sept. 2014), online at verite.org/sites/default/files/images/VeriteForcedLaborMalaysianElectronics_2014_0 .pdf; on iPhone factories in China, see Agar, *Constant Touch*, chap. 26; on sweatshop

As these arrangements generate less rather than more information to companies about work conditions, I would argue they are contrary to the way capitalism ideally functions – as was also the case with American capital markets in the run-up to the 2008 financial crisis. Considering the question of continuity versus change, the Rana disaster and countless other instances of miserable and exploitative work conditions betoken a departure from the government-monitored factories of the modern Western world, and a reversion to William Blake's "dark Satanic mills" of the early industrial era. As the scholar Donna Haraway has observed of our supposedly post-industrial age, "our best machines are made of sunshine; they are all light and clean because they are nothing but signals, electromagnetic waves, a section of a spectrum, and these machines are eminently portable, mobile – a matter of immense human pain in Detroit and Singapore."[96] In Victorian Britain, like the developing world of the early twenty-first century, many people, including women and children, sought out work in those factories as they either had no alternative or wanted to move to the city to escape rural drudgery.[97] But it does not mean conditions were ideal then, nor are they ideal today.

In industrialized countries, the most pressing matter facing the workforce is whether machines, automation, and digitized technologies are making human labor obsolete. If that came to pass, it might point toward a sharp divergence from past trends, but it would also demonstrate the existence of continuities as it repeats a Schumpeterian pattern of creative destruction going back to the beginning of the industrial era, if not earlier. The steep collapse in the price of computing since the 1980s has made it worthwhile for companies to replace costly human labor whenever possible.[98] Some analysts believe that up to 47 percent of American occupations are potentially replaceable by robots and computers.[99] As economists Lawrence F. Katz and Robert A. Margo put it, "changes in the organization of work associated with computerization raise the

---

conditions in factories around the world, see publications of the International Labor Rights Forum, online at laborrights.org/publications.

[96] Donna Haraway, "A Cyborg Manifesto: Science, Technology, and Socialist-Feminism in the Late Twentieth Century," in her *Simians, Cyborgs and Women: The Reinvention of Nature* (NY: Routledge, 1991), 149–181, online at wayback.archive.org/web/20120214 194015/http://www.stanford.edu/dept/HPS/Haraway/CyborgManifesto.html.

[97] Joel Mokyr, *The Enlightened Economy: An Economic History of Britain, 1700–1850* (New Haven: Yale University Press, 2009), chap. 14; Pietra Rivoli, *The Travels of a T-Shirt in the Global Economy*, 2nd ed. (Hoboken: Wiley, 2009), 109–119; William C. Terry, "Working on the Water: On Legal Space and Seafarer Protection in the Cruise Industry," *Economic Geography* (Oct. 2009), 463–482.

[98] David Autor, "Polanyi's Paradox and the Shape of Employment Growth," *NBER Working Paper Series* no. 20485 (Sept. 2014), 7.

[99] Avent, "Third Great Wave," 4.

demand for the cognitive and interpersonal skills used by highly educated professionals and managers and reduced the demand for the routine analytical (nonmanual) and mechanical (manual) skills that characterize many middle-educated, ordinary white-collar positions and manufacturing production jobs."[100]

Incomes have thus remained stagnant for lower-skilled people even where there is low unemployment – in the United States as well as in Europe. In part that is because although "new economy" companies like Skype, YouTube, and Craigslist generate great amounts of wealth and are growing fast, they are mainly built on software code and do not spawn the number of jobs the industrial giants of yesteryear did. Ford and General Motors created millions of jobs; Facebook, with over a billion active users, has just over 9,000 employees. Google has around 50,000 employees, but a valuation of $14 billion. Even more extreme is Instagram, a photo-sharing site, which Facebook purchased for $1 billion in 2012, when it had 30 million customers and thirteen employees. Compare that to Kodak, the camera and film company, which recently entered bankruptcy with 145,000 employees. Another example of the way in which digital companies come up short is Etsy, the online crafts site: 74 percent of its sellers consider themselves engaged in a "business," but many of them earn less than $100 a year from it.[101]

Moreover, many online companies like the restaurant-review site Yelp, Amazon with its book reviews, Wikipedia, YouTube, or photo-downloading site Flickr get people to provide most of the content on their sites gratis. These firms "harness free labor and turn it into valuable products and services" from which they profit. Some view this as a liberational "high-tech gift economy" unmediated and untarnished by money. But in fact it is all monetized and commercialized, creating wealth for the small number of owners of firms who benefit from their thousands or millions or billions of contributors. Meanwhile, because of the popularity of online news sources, traditional information outlets like the newspapers are hemorrhaging readers and advertising revenues and are laying off more and more employees.[102]

[100] Lawrence F. Katz and Robert A. Margo, "Technical Change and the Relative Demand for Skilled Labor: The United States in Historical Perspective," in *Human Capital in History: The American Record*, ed. Leah Platt Boustan, Carola Frydman, and Robert A. Margo (Chicago: University of Chicago Press, 2014), 44.

[101] Halpern, "Creepy New Wave of the Internet," 24; *Economist* (Jan. 18, 2014), 9, and (Oct. 4, 2014), 14; Avent, "Third Great Wave," 5; Facebook Newsroom, "Company Info," online at http://newsroom.fb.com/company-info/; Google Investor Relations, "2014 Financial Tables," online at https://investor.google.com/financial/tables.html.

[102] Carr, *Big Switch*, 132–142, 151–157.

While these leading-edge online companies have failed to make a positive contribution to the employment statistics, scholarly and popular authors alike warn against the "smart machines" and "robot overlords" in more established industries that will steal human jobs and create "long-term misery."[103] We need to be skeptical of these claims about the "new economy," for we have heard similar complaints many times before. It has been a perpetual theme since the early industrial era when in the wake of wage stagnation and employment dislocation nineteenth-century intellectuals tried to plug the hole in the dike of the old crafts economy by denouncing the introduction of machinery in the workplace.[104] Not long after the Great Depression, Elizabeth Faulkner Baker foresaw the imminent "displacement of men by machines" in the printing industry.[105] In the 1950s, Norbert Weiner, author of the classic work *Cybernetics*, prophesied that machines would displace people and lead to unemployment on a level that would make 1929 "seem a pleasant joke."[106] In his novel *Player Piano* (1952), Kurt Vonnegut projected that computers and robots would lead to a world of "production with almost no manpower."[107] In 1965, the economist Robert Heilbroner brooded that "the new technology is threatening a whole new group of skills – the sorting, filing, checking, calculating, remembering, comparing, okaying skills – that are the special preserve of the office worker . . . In

---

[103] Autor, "Polanyi's Paradox," 30–31. To explain the decline of middle-wage jobs, Autor and others point the finger at their replacement by new technologies. But these kinds of jobs seem to have been declining since the 1950s: see Heidi Shierholz, Lawrence Mishel, and John Schmitt, "Don't Blame the Robots: Assessing the Job Polarization Explanation of Growing Wage Inequality," *EPI-CEPR Working Paper* (Nov. 19, 2013), online at epi.org/publication/technology-inequality-dont-blame-the-robots/. According to two papers by Scott Andes and Mark Muro, "Robots Are Infiltrating the Growth Statistics," *Brookings Advanced Industry Series* no. 63 (April 27, 2015), online at brookings.edu/blogs/the-avenue/posts/2015/04/27-robots-growth-statistics-andes-muro; and "Don't Blame the Robots for Lost Manufacturing Jobs," *Brookings Advanced Industry Series* no. 64 (April 29, 2015), online at brookings.edu/blogs/the-avenue/posts/2015/04/29-robots-manufacturing-jobs-andes-muro, recent research shows that there is no correlation between the introduction of robots and the loss of manufacturing jobs. Rather, robots raise productivity and stimulate job growth. See also Timothy B. Lee, "This Chart Shows Why Robots Aren't about to Steal All Our Jobs," *Vox* (July 30, 2015), online at vox.com/2015/7/30/9069003/chart-robot-job-steal, which points out that only 178,000 robots were shipped worldwide in 2013.

[104] Maxine Berg, *The Machinery Question and the Making of Political Economy, 1815–1848* (Cambridge: Cambridge University Press, 1980), 2, 322–326; Amy Sue Bix, *Inventing Ourselves Out of Jobs: America's Debate over Technological Unemployment, 1929–1981* (Baltimore: Johns Hopkins University Press, 2000).

[105] Elizabeth Faulkner Baker, *Displacement of Men by Machines: Effects of Technological Change in Commercial Printing* (NY: Columbia University Press, 1933).

[106] Theodore Roszak, *The Cult of Information: The Folklore of Computers and the True Art of Thinking* (NY: Pantheon, 1986), 10.

[107] Kurt Vonnegut, *Player Piano* (NY: Dial Press, 1980 [1952]), 1.

the end, as machines continue to invade society, duplicating greater and greater numbers of social tasks, it is human labor itself – at least, as we now think of 'labor' – that is gradually rendered redundant."[108] A decade later, the OPEC oil embargo and the end of the postwar economic boom raised fears of "deindustrialization." Social theorist Jeremy Rifkin forecast the impending "end of work" in 1995, just as he would write twenty years later of the impending "eclipse of capitalism."[109]

Knowing that so far none of those predictions has come to pass is small comfort for the unemployed, underemployed, and underpaid worker of today. But opposed to the doomsayers, MIT economist David Autor argues that it will be very difficult to automate tasks only humans can do, such as "those demanding flexibility, judgment, and common sense." These are activities associated with professional and managerial occupations that require "problem-solving capabilities, intuition, creativity, and persuasion," but it applies too to manual labor like food service, janitorial work, grounds maintenance, barbering, health assistance, and security/ protective services. As Autor points out, when machines increase productivity in one sphere, the economic value of the remaining jobs increases, and those jobs involve types of work that only humans can do. For instance, using heavy machinery, construction workers can accomplish much more than they could with a shovel. But "construction workers supply tasks such as control guidance and judgment that have no current machine substitutes and which therefore become more valuable as machinery augments their reach."[110]

If the past is a guide, digital technologies will produce entirely novel fields of work. The new information technologies introduced in the businesses of the nineteenth century (see Chapter 5) increased by a factor of nine the number of office workers – bookkeepers, cashiers, accountants, clerks, stenographers, typists – between 1870 and 1900.[111] New industrial technologies, including electricity, caused a shift in employment away from agriculture, which dropped from 41 percent of the total in the United States in 1900 to 2 percent today. Yet agricultural production is as high as ever. No one could have imagined in the early twentieth century how many jobs and types of jobs would be created to replace

---

[108] Autor, "Polanyi's Paradox," 4.

[109] Downey, "Commentary: The Place of Labour in the History of Information-Technology Revolutions," 237–238; Rifkin, *Zero Marginal Cost Society*.

[110] Autor, "Polanyi's Paradox," 8–9, 11, 32–33, and passim. A similar argument can be found in Frank Levy and Richard J. Murnane, *The New Division of Labor: How Computers Are Creating the Next Job Market* (Princeton: Princeton University Press, 2004).

[111] Downey, "Commentary: The Place of Labour in the History of Information-Technology Revolutions," 237–238.

farm work, all the while sustaining one of the highest living standards in the world.[112]

Today there is certainly no hint of the replacement of humans in America's "advanced industries," that combination of manufacturing, energy, and service businesses that have the highest level of R&D per worker, absorb a large percentage of workers in STEM (science, technology, engineering, and math) fields, and make extensive use of digital technologies. They employ 80 percent of US engineers, undertake 90 percent of private-sector R&D, generate 85 percent of US patents, and churn out 60 percent of American exports. These industries make up 9 percent of total US employment, but produce $2.7 trillion in goods and services annually, or 17 percent of American GDP. Through supply chains and other multiplier effects, their impact is spread indirectly with additional employment of workers in ancillary businesses, in total accounting for a quarter of the jobs in the United States. Wages in these knowledge-intensive firms are strong: even for high-school graduates, they are higher by 50–70 percent than in other industries.[113]

Part of the wage problem in the United States is not due to IT per se, but globalization, itself a manifestation of communications and transportation advances. International outsourcing has brought jobs and higher wages to the non-Western world, but the glut of cheap labor works to adjust pay downward in industrialized societies. This is a relatively recent phenomenon for Western workers, a sign of change rather than continuity. But, as some experts have suggested, automation and outsourcing are likely to affect laborers in China and other Asian economies even more than in the West because of less adequate social safety nets and weaker public outcry against adverse decisions made by companies in societies without a free press.[114]

Shifting patterns of employment, retail distribution, and industrial production all reflect the unsettling impact of digital technologies. The pace of those developments has increased in lockstep with internet data-extraction capabilities. With that, too, we are witnessing some

[112] Autor, "Polanyi's Paradox," 38.

[113] Muro et al., *America's Advanced Industries*, 3, 21–27.

[114] Brynjolfsson and McAfee, *Second Machine Age*, 182–184; Avent, "Third Great Wave," 6; Gordon, "Demise of US Economic Growth," 16. The impact of digital technologies on productivity is hotly debated by economists, but the jury is still out and it is too early to assess the issue from a historical perspective. For the pessimistic case, see Gordon, "Demise of US Economic Growth," 1–41; and Tyler Cowen, *The Great Stagnation* (NY: Dutton, 2010). For the optimists' viewpoint, see Erik Brynjolfsson and Adam Saunders, *Wired for Information: How Information Technology Is Reshaping the Economy* (Cambridge, MA: MIT Press, 2010); and Dale W. Jorgenson, "Accounting for Growth in the Information Age," in *Handbook of Economic Growth*, vol. 1A, ed. Philippe Aghion and Steven N. Durlauf (Amsterdam: Elsevier, 2005), 743–815.

continuities, but we have to place more weight on the discontinuities. Each day sees the creation of 2.5 exabytes of data, or seventy times the data contained in the Library of Congress. Annually, the world's servers process around 10 zetabytes (10^{22}) of data, or the equivalent of 10 trillion pages of text. If all the data stored online were to be printed in bound volumes, it would cover the entire area of the United States in thirteen layers of books. Internet traffic increased twelve times between 2006 and 2011, and now surpasses 23.9 exabytes per month. Globally, the quantity of information (in mostly electronic form) has been doubling every two years. In 2011, the amount of information stored on all digital devices – including home and office computers, cellphones, and factory control systems – stood at 1,800 exabytes, or a mind-boggling 1,800 quintillion bytes.[115]

How can we possibly keep track of everything? These numbers have produced fears of information overload and the concomitant loss of human control over knowledge. As historian Anne M. Blair argues, such apprehensions have not been confined to the digital age. Ancient, medieval, and early modern authors "articulated similar concerns, notably about the overabundance of books and the frailty of human resources for mastering them (such as memory and time)." According to Blair, in the past they managed by "storing, sorting, selecting, and summarizing." She is confident that we will too, by means of old approaches and new electronic data-management techniques.[116]

But with secret algorithms implemented by private companies, we may have indeed entered new terrain in human information history. The algorithms that internet search firms use are not neutral if we consider that their financial interests configure the search results – as the European Union has alleged in its 2015 antitrust suit against Google.[117] When one searches on Google for videos, YouTube, a Google subsidiary, comes up more often than other video sites (although to be fair, it is also the most popular repository for videos on the web). In the words of Frank Pasquale, "the power to include, exclude, and rank is the power to ensure that certain public impressions become permanent, while

---

[115] McAfee and Brynjolfsson, "Big Data," 62; Cortada, *Digital Flood*, 5; "Global Data Storage," *BBC News: Technology* (Feb. 11, 2011), online at bbc.com/news/technology -12419672; Scoble and Israel, *Age of Context*, 5; Brynjolfsson and McAfee, *Second Machine Age*, 66–67; Marsh, *New Industrial Revolution*, 28.

[116] Anne M. Blair, *Too Much to Know: Managing Scholarly Information before the Modern Age* (New Haven: Yale University Press, 2010), 3; and see chap. 1 passim. See also Chad Wellmon, *Organizing Enlightenment: Information Overload and the Invention of the Modern Research University* (Baltimore: Johns Hopkins University Press, 2015).

[117] *Economist* (April 18, 2015), 55.

others remain fleeting."[118] Besides affecting what we see and learn on the internet, algorithms have a nontrivial effect on people's lives: algorithms that analyze our data derive credit scores or risk calculations. Data brokers, credit bureaus, analytics firms, and marketers all engage in profiling according to the information they collect from online searches. Yet those profiles can show wide variations, with 30 percent of scores differing between credit bureaus by fifty points. And with access to commercial data profiling, predatory lenders can target minorities with "ghetto loans." The algorithms are unregulated by government and cannot be challenged by the individuals involved. In finance, algorithms eliminate some inefficiencies, but they cement in place "some dubious old patterns of credit castes and corporate unaccountability."[119]

Furthermore, we may have crossed the threshold into a society in which privacy is unprotected and our personal information is anybody's business: a transparent society may be an intrusive one. Google's goal, according to the company, is to store "100 percent of a user's data" to achieve "transparent personalization."[120] Commercial email services – Google's Gmail, Yahoo! Mail, and Microsoft's Outlook (formerly Hotmail) – retain copies of all messages even after the user deletes them.[121] App vendors have arcane privacy policies and sell data on users without their knowledge.[122] Dating back to the 1960s, but all the more today, governments have used computers to dredge up information about their citizens.[123] Cybercriminals, terrorist groups, and nation-states routinely hack into private and state computer systems. Almost no device is invulnerable.[124] And the fear of cyber bullying could lead

---

[118] Pasquale, *Black Box Society*, 61. For manipulation of the search rankings by rogue "click farms," see Doug Bock Clark, "The Bot Bubble: How Click Farms Have Inflated Social Media Currency," *New Republic* (May 2015), 32–41.

[119] "Room for Debate: Is Big Data Spreading Inequality?" *New York Times* (Aug. 6, 2014), online at nytimes.com/roomfordebate/2014/08/06/is-big-data-spreading-inequality (first quote); Pasquale, *Black Box Society*, introduction and chap. 2, with second quote on 15.

[120] Nicholas Carr, *The Glass Cage: Automation and Us* (NY: Norton, 2014), 161 (quote), and chap. 10.

[121] Hal Abelson, Ken Ledeen, and Harry Lewis, *Blown to Bits: Your Life, Liberty, and Happiness after the Digital Explosion* (Upper Saddle River: Addison-Wesley, 2008), 57 and passim.

[122] *Economist* (Feb. 28, 2015), 9.

[123] Agar, *Government Machine*, chap. 9. For more recent developments, see the muckraking work of journalist Glenn Greenwald in *The Guardian*, online at theguardian.com/profile/glenn-greenwald.

[124] Halpern, "Creepy New Wave of the Internet," 24; and Victor Mayer-Schönberger and Kenneth Cukier, *Big Data: A Revolution that Will Transform How We Live, Work, and Think* (Boston: Houghton Mifflin Harcourt, 2013). That includes commercial airliners, which are apparently vulnerable to hackers: see Evan Perez, "FBI: Hacker Claimed to

to self-censorship and the elimination of many individualist, risky, but culturally and economically creative behaviors.[125]

All of these instances bespeak the unstoppable progression of the information nexus of capitalism, contrary to Jeremy Rifkin's suggestion that the Internet of Things spells the "eclipse of capitalism."[126] Besides being unsettling, they also call into question the ability of the information nexus to function as freely as it has in the past: when the proprietary algorithms of a few companies dominate, or when faulty algorithms rather than people make business decisions, it could portend the declining dynamism of capitalism. One might conclude that capitalism could reach a dead end due to its very success.

There are, however, countervailing tendencies, with many advantages to living in this world dominated by IT and algorithms. Much of the information digital data mining and sensors generate is convenient and beneficial: sensors voluntarily installed in cars or exercise sensors both enable data-driven underwriting, which can help insurance companies to make more accurate risk assessments.[127] Millions and millions of times every day throughout the industrialized world, much more efficient and flexible connections now exist between buyers and suppliers due to the transmission of price information by cellphone or over the internet.[128] All of this corresponds to a reduction of transaction costs stemming from the augmentation of the information nexus.

For consumers, the value gained from Google, Yahoo!, or Bing searches has not been quantified. No measures of these "informational complements" exist, but it is clear that the value of what Erik Brynjolfsson and Adam Saunders call a "consumer surplus" is astronomical.[129] Between that and POS data analytics, although there are worrisome privacy issues, consumers now have greater power over the market as retailers can figure out more precisely what they want and in turn tell producers what and how much of it to make. It is true that choices can be restricted: when a Walmart or other big-box retailers come to town, smaller stores, unfortunately, shut down.[130] But the internet compensates by giving people access to information, especially prices, and makes

Have Taken over Flight's Engine Controls," *CNN* (May 18, 2015), online at cnn.com/2015/05/17/us/fbi-hacker-flight-computer-systems/index.html.

[125] *Economist* (March 14, 2015), 85.

[126] Rifkin, *Zero Marginal Cost Society*, title and 2–9.

[127] *Economist* (March 14, 2015), 18, 20, 71–73.

[128] For the difference between then and now see the example of the Tokyo fish business in Theodore C. Bestor, *Tsukiji: The Fish Market at the Center of the World* (Berkeley: University of California Press, 2004), 198.

[129] Brynjolfsson and Saunders, *Wired for Information*, x–xi, xiv–xv, 2–5, and passim.

[130] Fishman, *Wal-Mart Effect*, chap. 6.

available an even wider range of goods for sale. Comparison shopping has never been easier and is especially important in generating efficiencies in the economy and making consumers better informed.[131]

For everyone living in the digital age and pursuing the quest for useful knowledge, the hyper-expansion of the information nexus has been a tremendous boon. This book could not have been written without access to thousands of journal and newspaper articles found on internet databases and retrieved online, and without books purchased online or read in e-book format on my desktop PC, laptop Mac, iPad, and iPhone. Despite warning our students about the reliability of Wikipedia, we are ever more dependent on this website, which is in a league with Google, Facebook, Yahoo!, and Bing as one of the most trafficked sites on the internet, with 4.7 million articles in English and millions of articles in two hundred other languages.[132] Google and its competitors are making constant attempts to improve analysis of "data exhaust" generated by users, and data-visualization specialists are churning out new ways of displaying information in order to make sense of it all, while fulfilling the function of the chart and graph makers of old.[133] Because the cost of information and communications technologies are so low, access to information so high, and search engines and databases so effective and accessible, businessmen, entrepreneurs, professionals, scholars, scientists, and laymen all have more ready access to knowledge than at any time in history. One assumes the rapid rise in patent applications in the United States has to do with IT and the expanding data universe: the numbers grew slowly from 90,000 in 1963 to only 112,000 per year in 1980, then leaped to 615,000 in 2014.[134] In the world's democracies, governments are posting more documents online, making statistics and information about their doings more readily available. Add to that Facebook and other social media, with thousands of online discussion

[131] Robert E. Litan and Alice M. Rivlin, *Beyond the Dot.coms: The Economic Promise of the Internet* (Washington, DC: Brookings Institution Press, 2001), chap. 4; Sproull, "Computers in U.S. Households," 272–274.

[132] Noam Cohen, "Wikipedia vs. the Small Screen," *New York Times* (Feb. 29, 2014), online at nytimes.com/2014/02/10/technology/wikipedia-vs-the-small-screen.html; http://en.wikipedia.org/wiki/Wikipedia.

[133] Mokyr, *Gifts of Athena*, 112–115; Cukier, "Data, Data Everywhere," 10–11, 14.

[134] US Patent and Trademark Office, "US Patent Statistics Chart, Calendar Years 1963–2014," online at uspto.gov/web/offices/ac/ido/oeip/taf/us_stat.htm; Brynjolfsson and Saunders, *Wired for Information*, 9. Note that Cowen, *Great Stagnation*, 3, 8–10, and passim, is unimpressed. He considers the high point of innovation to have come in the late 1800s, when the highest rate of global invention relative to world population was achieved. By contrast, for an especially optimistic perspective on technological innovation and the impact of digital-age technologies, see Joel Mokyr, "Is Technological Progress a Thing of the Past?" *VOX: CEPR's Policy Portal* (Sept. 8, 2013), online at v oxeu.org/article/technological-progress-thing-past.

groups, blogs, and news outlets, which help us to become more aware of government conduct.[135] This is all on a continuum with earlier eras in the history of the West, but represents a quantitative and qualitative change as well. Capitalism is hardly moribund in the digital age.

Let us also look at the threat to privacy, abuse of algorithms, and informational obstructions from yet another angle. All of these are problems of the rich world. In developing nations, there is a yawning gap in data collection. Population statistics, road maps, disease data, and so forth, are all lacking. That hinders economic growth and limits economic opportunities.[136] People in those places can only dream of the day when they have such troubles as we do with data overload or flawed credit-reporting algorithms. Then again, the sharpest discontinuities of the digital age are to be found in the developing world, where the revolution of the information nexus has the potential to be far-reaching.

"I heard the mobile phone would bring work": The digital age in the developing world

The digital age has brought more benefit than harm to the emerging economies of the developing world despite sometimes bad work conditions for the Asians who build and take apart the computers and cell-phones that are the workhorses of the new economy.[137] Due to the end of the Cold War, the discrediting of Soviet-style socialism and the embrace of the Japanese/Asian Tiger model of economic development, global capital flows increased and IT and manufacturing innovations spread from Japan, South Korea, and Taiwan throughout Asia. The sudden opening of Communist-ruled China to the market energized the entire Pacific rim. All of that has "produced the most sustained economic boom in modern history, a great surge in income that has brought unprecedented gains in wealth and economic opportunity to three billion people." The numbers are hard to fathom: between 1965 and 2007, gross national income per capita rose 15,046 percent in South Korea, 7,291 percent in Taiwan, 5,913 percent in Singapore, 4,352 percent in Hong Kong, 4,133 percent in Japan, and 2,605 percent in China.[138]

In South Asia, India's more modest increase of 764 percent is the outcome of lower investment in human capital and the heavily statist

---

[135] Sproull, "Computers in U.S. Households," 274–279; Cukier, "Data, Data Everywhere," 4, 11; Mayer-Schönberger and Cukier, *Big Data*, 116–118.
[136] *Economist* (Nov. 15, 2014), 61–62.
[137] Turner, *From Counterculture to Cyberculture*, 260–261.
[138] Michael Schuman, *The Miracle: The Epic Story of Asia's Quest for Wealth* (NY: HarperCollins, 2009), xxiv.

economic policies dating to its first post-independence president, Jawaharlal Nehru. Within Asia, India has the lowest IT expenditures as a percentage of GNP. Compared to the rest of the world it lags in the consumption of new information and communications technologies: the figure for PCs per hundred people in India is 2.79, compared to 15.32 globally; fixed telephone and mobile-phone usage in India is 60 percent lower than the world average. Yet, how far it has come since 1967, when an Indian Communist leader, K. Anirudhan, speaking before his nation's parliament, proclaimed, "The automation equipment that are being imported into this country on a very wide scale include those frightening monstrous machines called electronic computers." Today, IBM employs approximately 100,000 people in India, where important global IT firms Infosys, Wipro, and Tata are also headquartered.[139]

In Africa, poverty has been declining, too, although the numbers are nowhere near Asian levels and are in dispute. According to the African Development Bank, the middle class on the continent grew from 126 million in 1980 to 350 million people in 2010. But ADB considers those who earn $2 a day to have entered the middle class. It is all relative, but the OECD reckons a more accurate figure is 32 million, equivalent to the size of the population of Canada.[140] One indicator of the underdevelopment of the continent is that only 12 percent of Africa's trade is intra-African, whereas 60 percent of Europe's trade is between European nations and 53 percent of Asia's trade takes places within Asia.[141]

Seemingly insuperable obstacles make it hard for underdeveloped nations to replicate the Asian economic miracle. Most critical for that purpose would be capabilities in information and communications technology and value chains that expedite the coordination of complex lean production. In 2012, the value of the global "knowledge-intensive trade," or trade based on R&D or skilled labor, was $12.6 trillion, or half of the total trade flow in goods and services worldwide. Those assets are absent in poor countries, which can only offer pools of cheap labor. The latter might benefit specific firms capable of mobilizing it, but it is not conducive to long-term, well-rounded growth.[142]

Deficits in infrastructure are also particularly severe, especially as they pertain to information transmission. Besides poverty, paranoid politics figure in this, too, as suggested by the two years of negotiations it has

---

[139] Cortada, *Digital Flood*, 491 (quote), 492–495; Schuman, *Miracle*, xxiv.

[140] Nicholas Kulish, "Africans Open Fuller Wallets to the Future," *New York Times* (July 20, 2014), online at nytimes.com/2014/07/21/world/africa/economy-improves-as-middle-class-africans-open-wallets-to-the-future.html?_r=0.

[141] *Economist* (Feb. 16, 2013), 50, and (July 5, 2014), 52.

[142] *Economist* (Oct. 4, 2014), 14; Avent, "Third Great Wave," 11–14.

taken to string a few fiber optics cables from Zambia to Zimbabwe and South Africa to Zimbabwe.[143] Only 12 percent of the African population has access to landline telephones, which are ubiquitous elsewhere. Internet penetration is also low: in Africa, a mere 1 percent of the population has a wired broadband subscription, and no more than 10 percent have web access. The figure for the latter is 21 percent elsewhere in the developing world, which itself is far lower than the 71 percent of the population that has access in the developed world.[144] At a more basic level, in less developed countries roads are unpaved, if they exist in the first place. In Cameroon, only a tenth of the roads are paved. It takes truckers four days to travel 300 miles – not much faster than in the days of the stagecoach in Western nations. That pushes up the price of goods and shrinks the profits people can make from their crops.[145] Bad road or rail conditions force up transport costs, which raises consumer prices in Malawi, Uganda, and Rwanda by 50–75 percent. "Shipping a car from China to Tanzania on the Indian Ocean coast costs $4,000, but getting it from there to nearby Uganda can cost another $5,000."[146] Perhaps nothing, though, indicates the deficiencies in the capitalist information nexus more than the mail systems of the developing world, which are plagued by inefficient service and theft by mailmen. The US Postal Service handles 50 percent of the world's mail: 600 million items are posted per day, for an average of 700 items per capita per annum. By contrast, the poorest of the world's countries generate less than one.[147]

Cellphones are giving poor nations the chance to leapfrog over many (though not all) of the infrastructural gaps. For economist Jeffrey Sachs, they are the "single most transformative tool for development." According to World Bank estimates, distributing cellphones to 10 percent of the population would increase GDP handsomely, by as much as 0.8 percent. Furthermore, the price of new phones is dropping, and used phones from the rich world are recycled for resale. Access to mobile networks is also now available to 90 percent of the world's population. There are over 4 billion cellphones in use worldwide, three-quarters of them in the developing world. Even in Africa, 40 percent of the

[143] *Economist* (July 5, 2014), 52.

[144] UN – MDG Africa Working Group, Infrastructure, "Preliminary Plan of Action: Final Report" (July, 2008), online at www-wds.worldbank.org/external/default/WDSConte ntServer/WDSP/IB/2009/04/27/000334955_20090427102736/Rendered/INDEX/482 160WP0P111818B01PUBLIC10UN0Final.txt; UN, International Telecommunication Union, *The World in 2010: ICT Facts and Figures* (Geneva: ITU, 2010), 4, 6 (online at itu.int/ITU-D/ict/material/FactsFigures2010.pdf).

[145] *Economist* (Dec. 21, 2002), 37–39.   [146] *Economist* (Feb. 16, 2013), 50–51.

[147] Pierre Guislain, *The Postal Sector in Developing and Transition Countries* (Washington, DC: World Bank, 2004), online at http://go.worldbank.org/DEYRPFAMU0.

population owns one. Increasingly, they are smartphones capable of internet access.[148] In Africa over the past decade, use of telephones has climbed from 0.7 percent of the population to 60–70 percent because of the introduction of cellphones.[149]

Mobile phones eliminate the expense of installing landlines and compensate for the absence of infrastructure. But they are not a perfect solution: despite the declining price of phones, they are expensive for those who, like many Kenyans, earn only a dollar a day. Studies have found people skipping meals and walking to work instead of taking the bus to make sure they can pay for their phones.[150] In Nigeria, they are so costly that people call them *oku na iri ego* – "the fire that consumes money."[151] And while the information nexus depends on a steady, uninterrupted transmission of electricity, power blackouts are chronic in the underdeveloped world, where in any case by 2008 only 55 percent of the population had access to electricity – and in sub-Saharan Africa only 24 percent.[152] The Niumi region of the Gambia is typical. Nearly everyone has a cellphone at this point, but recharging the phones is a challenge when so few homes have electricity. To do so, people have to go to stores and pay for the use of twelve-volt car batteries – which also power televisions. When the car batteries themselves need recharging they have to be taken in a taxi to someone who owns a diesel generator.[153]

But the benefits are apparent in the poorest parts of Africa and Asia – which is why more people per capita make cellphone calls in Nairobi, Kenya, than they do in New York City.[154] In India, only about half the population has access to toilets, but nearly everyone in the slums of

[148] Tom Standage, "Mobile Marvels: A Special Report on Telecoms in Emerging Markets," *Economist* (Sept. 26, 2009), with Sachs quote on 4; *Economist* (Sept. 26, 2009), 13; UN, ITU, *World in 2010*, 1; Paul Taylor, "Developing World: 'Have-Nots' no Closer to Catching the 'Haves,'" *Financial Times* (May 28, 2009), online at ft.com/intl/cms/s/0/40031bd2-4a54-11de-8e7e-00144feabdc0.html#axzz3W4 KCiKPD.

[149] *Economist* (Oct. 20, 2012), 43; Agar, *Constant Touch*, 122, 131.

[150] *Economist* (Nov. 10, 2012), 52.   [151] Agar, *Constant Touch*, 121.

[152] UN – MDG Africa Working Group, Infrastructure, "Preliminary Plan of Action: Final Report" (July, 2008), online at www-wds.worldbank.org/external/default/WDSConte ntServer/WDSP/IB/2009/04/27/000334955_20090427102736/Rendered/INDEX/482 160WP0P111818B01PUBLIC10UN0Final.txt; William J. Hausman, Peter Hertner, and Mira Wilkins, *Global Electrification: Multinational Enterprise and International Finance in the History of Light and Power, 1878–2007* (Cambridge: Cambridge University Press, 2008), 3–6; Norimitsu Onishi, "Weak Power Grids in Africa Stunt Economies," *New York Times* (July 2, 2015), online at http://mobile.nytimes.com/2015/07/03/world/africa/weak-power-grids-in-africa-stunt-economies-and-fire-up-tempers.html?_r=0.

[153] Donald R. Wright, *The World and a Very Small Place in Africa*, 2nd ed. (Armonk: M. E. Sharpe, 2004), 258; Wright, *The World and a Very Small Place in Africa*, 3rd ed. (Armonk: M. E. Sharpe, 2010), 216, 233, 257.

[154] *Economist* (June 7, 2007), online at economist.com/node/9304146.

Mumbai has a cellphone, with cheap prepaid call cards readily available for purchase.[155] Mobile phones make it easier for Muslim women in East Africa to engage in commerce and maintain access to clients in a society where female segregation is still common. In 2002, Fatima, a Khartoum henna painter, explained to an interviewer why she had invested her savings in a cellphone: "I heard the mobile phone would bring work and that was exactly what happened."[156]

Extension of this portion of the information nexus has had an immediate and positive economic impact. Reductions in transaction costs have occurred throughout the underdeveloped world as farmers can now make a phone call and determine market rates or check text-based weather reports several times a day, both of which reduce the risks that come from diversifying their crops. One of the reasons the price of rice increased in Asia in 2008 was that farmers even in remote regions relied on cellphones to ascertain international price data and determine whether grain dealers were paying them enough for their harvest. In the grain markets of Niger, the introduction of cellphones between 2001 and 2006 reduced price variations between markets, including distant ones, by 6.4 percent. In the Indian state of Madhya Pradesh soybean farmers given access to internet kiosks could compare the prices they were being offered by local wholesale agents, which improved farmers' profits and led them to increase production. Similarly, in the fishing industry of Kerala, India, fish prices declined by 4 percent for consumers, but because fishermen were able to eliminate wasted catches by knowing how much to bring to market each day, their profits rose by 8 percent.[157]

Mobile phones have been especially important in banking and banking services, including credit and insurance, in a world in which more than half the world's adult population lacks bank accounts (the lowest numbers are in Africa and the Middle East, but also a majority in South Asia and Latin America, and a large number of poor American blacks and Hispanics). Seventeen million Kenyans, or two-thirds of the adult

---

[155] Ravi Nessman, "India: Land of Many Cell Phones, Fewer Toilets," *Bloomberg Business* (Oct. 31, 2010), online at businessweek.com/ap/financialnews/D9J6EKRG2.htm.

[156] Agar, *Constant Touch*, 125–126.

[157] This paragraph is based on Keith Bradsher, "High Rice Cost Creating Fears of Asia Unrest," *New York Times* (March 29, 2008), online at nytimes.com/2008/03/29/business/worldbusiness/29rice.html?hp; Naazneen Barma, "Emerging Economies in the Digital Era," in *How Revolutionary Was the Digital Revolution?* ed. Zysman and Newman, 155–159; Standage, "Mobile Marvels," 10; *Economist* (Sept. 9, 2007), 54, and (Jan. 9, 2010), 77; Brynjolfsson and McAfee, *Second Machine Age*, 95; Aparajita Goyal, "Information, Direct Access to Farmers, and Rural Market Performance in Central India," *American Economic Journal: Applied Economics* (July 2010), 22–45.

population, send money by text message thanks to the service provided by that country's M-Pesa (M stands for "mobile," Pesa is Swahili for "money"), founded by Safaricom in 2007 as a microfinance loan repayment system but converted by customers into a "mobile wallet." It now sees over ten billion dollars in transactions per year. In Kenya, payment behavior over M-Pesa forms the basis of credit ratings, which banks then use to give out loans to people who were previously off the grid and had no opportunity to borrow. Phone companies compete by offering free micro-insurance policies, which most people would not buy otherwise. Kenya is the innovator in P2P, or person-to-person, payment services globally, but by June 2013 there were "242 mobile-enabled e-money providers operating in eighty-nine countries," with 61 million active accounts. In nine African countries – Cameroon, Democratic Republic of Congo, Gabon, Kenya, Madagascar, Tanzania, Uganda, Zambia, and Zimbabwe – mobile-money accounts outnumber bank accounts. Only 14 percent of Tanzanian adults use banks, but 44 percent use mobile money. Furthermore, the Tanzanian government permits the use of cellphones to pay licensing fees, which reduces corruption by eliminating direct contact with officials.[158]

Transaction costs are declining as capitalism, defined as the information nexus, enters regions previously untouched by it except as natural-resource providers to advanced industrial nations. But the future development of capitalism in these societies hinges on the actions of government. It should be apparent from previous chapters that states have always played a leading role in capitalism, but they cannot be too weak or too oppressive. Dictatorships are far too common in the developing world, and they rarely provide the stability essential to the flourishing of capitalism: state secrecy and endemic corruption obstruct the clear signaling of rules and prices. Going hand in hand with weak contract enforcement and inadequate accounting, corruption, in the form of bribery, extortion, nepotism, and cronyism, encourages economic conservatism and drains entrepreneurial initiative. Corruption imposes a high invisible tax on business and consumers as it adds between 10 and 25 percent to costs.[159] Democracies like India and Brazil are not immune either: rampant corruption hinders the full potential of their market economies by saddling economic exchange with uncertainty, secretiveness, and routine bending of the laws. Corruption contradicts the notion

---

[158] Leo Mirani, "Beyond Mobile Money," *Quartz* (June 19, 2014), online at http://qz.com/218988; Agar, *Constant Touch*, 127–128; *Economist* (Nov. 10, 2012), 52, (Nov 15, 2014), 27–29, and (Nov. 22, 2014), 71.

[159] Transparency International, *Global Corruption Report 2009: Corruption and the Private Sector* (Cambridge: Cambridge University Press, 2009), online at transparency.org.

of the information nexus of capitalism, which functions best in conditions of greatest clarity.[160] That brings us to China, which appears as the great success story of the digital age – until we begin to trace the vicissitudes of the information nexus there.

China and the limits of capitalism

Thirty-five years of market reforms have fueled China's evolution from an isolated Communist nation to one of the great economic powers of the world. In 1978, its leader, Deng Xiaoping, asserted, "the basic point is: we must acknowledge that we are backward, that many of our ways of doing things are inappropriate, and that we need to change." They did change, dismantling the inefficient Stalinist economic system, restoring private farming, and opening the country to foreign trade and investment.[161] Total industrial output jumped from $91 million in 1980 to $3,728 million in 2013, with exports (including agricultural goods) climbing from $38 billion in 1980 to $4,265 billion in 2012. Up to 2007 at least, China's growth rates ranged from 8 to 10 percent per year. It has seen a tenfold increase in per capita income and lifted 400 million people out of poverty. With foreign firms in search of low labor costs, the state's support for production, and the good fortune of having Hong Kong's rich capital markets on its doorstep, China has by some estimates become the world's largest economy, leading manufacturing nation, and biggest exporter of goods, including high-tech materials and merchandise. It now contributes around a quarter of world industrial output – compared to 3 percent in 1990 and 7 percent in 2000. It makes 80 percent of the world's air conditioners, 70 percent of its mobile phones, and 60 percent of its shoes. It produces more aluminum, cars, cement, computers, steel, and textiles than any other nation, and has become the biggest consumer of electricity on earth. With its supply chains extending to the rest of Asia,

---

[160] *Economist* (Aug. 4, 2007), 55, (March 12, 2011), 47–48, and (March 26, 2011), 76–77; David Segal, "Petrobras Oil Scandal Leaves Brazilians Lamenting a Lost Dream," *New York Times* (Aug. 7, 2015), online at nytimes.com/2015/08/09/business/international/eff ects-of-petrobras-scandal-leave-brazilians-lamenting-a-lost-dream.html?hp&action=clic k&pgtype=Homepage&module=second-column-region&region=top-news&WT.nav= top-news; Alena Ledeneva et al., "Corruption and the Rule of Law," *Russian Analytical Digest*, no. 92 (Feb. 22, 2011).

[161] Joe Studwell, *How Asia Works: Success and Failure in the World's Most Dynamic Region* (NY: Grove Press, 2013), 221 (quote), 224–227; Yasheng Huang, *Capitalism with Chinese Characteristics: Entrepreneurship and the State* (Cambridge: Cambridge University Press, 2008), chap. 2 and passim; Jan Svejnar, "China in Light of the Performance of the Transition Economies," in *China's Great Economic Transformation*, ed. Loren Brandt and Thomas G. Rawski (Cambridge: Cambridge University Press, 2008), 68–90.

including low-cost labor in Burma, Indonesia, Thailand, and Vietnam, China is the heart of "factory Asia," which accounts for nearly half of the world's industrial goods. Chinese companies have also bought some of the world's most iconic brands, among them IBM's PC division, purchased by Lenovo, a computer maker, in 2004, and Volvo automotive, which the Chinese car company Geely acquired in 2010.[162]

In the 1980s, Americans expressed fears of Japan buying up American companies and outdoing the US economy. Now it is China that is setting off alarm bells with its potential for "toppling America."[163] But we need to keep the rise of China in perspective. A large divide still separates Western nations and China: in Britain per capita GDP is six times as high as in China, which is a greater differential than at the outset of the Industrial Revolution. China's level of wealth per capita is where the United Kingdom's stood seventy years ago. The figure for the United States is nearly eight times that of China.[164] The rapid growth of the Chinese economy is an unquestionable triumph, but it is not what it might seem: in 1912, when the Qing dynasty collapsed, Imperial China's GDP was comparable to that of Germany and the United Kingdom. In 1932, after the Japanese army had invaded Manchuria, China's GDP was double Japan's. So the size of the economy does not always reflect its quality or the strength of the nation.[165]

Along with Russia under Vladimir Putin, China is the leading exemplar of "state capitalism," or "bureaucratically engineered capitalism."[166] But those are oxymorons. If we apply the concept of the information nexus to the Chinese economy, we see how much it deviates from any economy that we would label capitalist. Rather than "state capitalism" or "crony

---

[162] Marsh, *New Industrial Revolution*, 144, 155, 157; Xiaolan Fu, *China's Path to Innovation* (Cambridge: Cambridge University Press, 2015), 3; Barry Naughton, "Economic Growth: From High Speed to High Quality," in *China Today, China Tomorrow: Domestic Politics, Economy, and Society*, ed. Joseph Fewsmith (Lanham: Rowman and Littlefield, 2010), 71–72; and Joanna Lewis, "Environmental Challenges: From the Local to the Global," in *China Today, China Tomorrow*, ed. Fewsmith, 259; *Economist* (March 14, 2015), 16, 69–70 (factory Asia quote).

[163] Hugo Duncan, "China 'Overtakes US as the World's Largest Economy,'" *Daily Mail* (Oct. 8, 2014), online at dailymail.co.uk/news/article-2785766/China-overtakes-U-S -world-s-largest-economy-IMF-says-economy-worth-11-trillion-America-falls-second -place-time-1872.html.

[164] Peer Vries, *Escaping Poverty: The Origins of Modern Economic Growth* (Goettingen: V&R unipress, 2013), 46, 219; World Bank data online at data.worldbank.org/indica tor/NY.GDP.PCAP.CD/countries/1W?display=default.

[165] Carl E. Walter and Fraser J. T. Howie, *Red Capitalism: The Fragile Financial Foundation of China's Extraordinary Rise*, rev. ed. (Singapore: Wiley, 2012), xiv; GDP figures from "The New Maddison Project Database," online at ggdc.net/maddison/maddison-pro ject/data.htm and ggdc.net/maddison/historical_statistics/horizontal-file_03-2007.xls.

[166] Ian Bremmer, *End of the Free Market* (NY: Portfolio, 2010), 23, 133–145, and passim.

capitalism," political scientist Bruce J. Dickson rightly calls it "crony communism" and a "socialist market economy."[167] China is led by a Communist dictatorship, many of whose officials are suspicious of private enterprise and are in a position to interfere with it. The survival strategy of the Chinese Communist Party was to rely on and coopt the private sector through state-sponsored business associations and a network of Leninist-style Communist Party cells inside companies. Unlike its Russian counterpart, which did not manage to prevent the collapse of the Soviet Union, the Chinese Communist Party held onto its political monopoly by transitioning to a market economy without losing its grip on the state. The goal of the regime has been to maintain the status quo through direct and indirect control over the economy. As a party manifesto stated, "the party must grasp not only the gun, but the asset economy as well."[168] The political elite consists of revolutionary families whose interest in the management of economic policy is paramount. China is a "family-run business" whose purpose is to create conditions for a "Harmonious Society," namely social and political stability. The private sector is tolerated to the extent that it supports that goal.[169]

In the first phase of reform, in the 1980s, the state encouraged the entrepreneurial energies of small private business in the Chinese countryside, but in the 1990s, the country altered course and opted for urban-centered, state-led development. This "great reversal" was in line with the Chinese desire to emulate the supposed path to wealth followed by other great economic powers of the world and reflects the elite's calculations of the threats an enlivened rural society presented to its own dominance.[170] That has left the private sector smaller than it might be: around a third of Chinese GNP is produced by companies in which the state owns a majority share. Under Mao, the Chinese state was master of nearly 100 percent of the nation's economy, so the current 70 percent that is in private hands represents an extraordinary shift.[171] But the state (however decentralized it has become in today's China) remains preeminent, and that has a bearing on the status of capitalism and the information nexus in China.

---

[167] Bruce J. Dickson, *Wealth into Power: The Communist Party's Embrace of China's Private Sector* (Cambridge: Cambridge University Press, 2008), passim.

[168] Usha C. V. Haley and George T. Haley, *Subsidies to Chinese Industry: State Capitalism, Business Strategy, and Trade Policy* (Oxford: Oxford University Press, 2013), 22.

[169] Walter and Howie, *Red Capitalism*, xv, 8, 22 (quotes); and see Barry Naughton, "A Political Economy of China's Economic Transition," in *China's Great Economic Transformation*, ed. Brandt and Rawski, 91–135.

[170] Huang, *Capitalism with Chinese Characteristics*, chap. 3 and passim.

[171] Huang, *Capitalism with Chinese Characteristics*, 10–12.

There are now ninety-five Chinese companies on the Fortune 500 list.[172] But most of them, like the Foreign Invested Enterprises (FIEs), which are joint ventures with foreign companies, draw on international management and capital markets and are hardly representative of Chinese industry.[173] Behind the dazzling, internationally respectable capitalist façade, the state is in the driver's seat in China when it comes to business enterprise. There are more than 4,000 large state-owned enterprises (SOEs), among them the "national champions," giant bureaucratic oligopolies controlled by elite families. These companies fashion industrial policy in the nation. The SOEs own a substantial portion of ostensibly private firms through cross-shareholding and over-lapping personnel in the Communist Party, People's Liberation Army, government, and company boards. Foreign investors are not often aware that is the case, and many do not understand that both CEOs and Party secretaries jointly run these companies. Through the SOEs, the state owns and coordinates production within much of the nation. Even if partly privately owned, the state makes the most important project deci-sions, decides on mergers, and hires, pays, and fires top management. In 2008, the total assets of the SOEs approximated $6 trillion, equal to 133 percent of annual economic output that year. The state sector is "a patronage system centered on the Party's *nomenklatura*." According to a government official, they are giant "cash machines" whose function is less to make a profit than to help the central and local governments prevent civil unrest. For that reason, they pay local officials and distribute social services, redistributing revenues from strong firms to weak firms to ensure full employment. Because the government does not allow them to collapse, they restrict competition in the wider economy.[174]

Like China's impressive internationally successful corporate sector, so its capital markets seem world class. More than 120 million accounts trade the shares of approximately 1,800 companies on the Shanghai and Shenzhen stock markets, which have a total capitalization of $3.6 trillion, or about the same as Tokyo's. Add in the Hong Kong stock exchange and China has the second largest equities market in the world after New York City. China's stock markets have modern electro-nic trading platforms and provide abundant information about listed

---

[172] "Global 500 2014," *Fortune*, online at http://fortune.com/global500/.
[173] Walter and Howie, *Red Capitalism*, 11, 13; Huang, *Capitalism with Chinese Characteristics*, chap. 1.
[174] Walter and Howie, *Red Capitalism*, 23–24 (quotes), 193; Haley and Haley, *Subsidies to Chinese Industry*, 5, 19–21, 23–27; Justin Yifu Lin, *Demystifying the Chinese Economy* (Cambridge: Cambridge University Press, 2012), 195–201.

companies. They make the country look modern and up to date, but since political rather than economic motives such as extending the interests of the Communist Party are operative, they are a "triumph of form over substance."[175]

Although stock markets and private venture capital are indispensable for financing innovation in real capitalist societies, in China their purpose is for show to the international community, to attract foreign investment, and for speculation involving surplus capital generated by government subsidies and bank loans. Private firms have less adequate sources of funding compared to SOEs, which can always depend on infusions from state banks or direct subsidies from the state. Executives of the national champions have an oversized influence on the capital markets, indeed the economy as a whole, because of their command of large cash flows. State companies on the stock market are never for sale and their valuation is arbitrary, based on market liquidity and speculative demand. The high trading volume only signifies that a large amount of money is floating through the economy. Buying a stock is a bet that the share price will go up, not an assessment of the company's worth (which, as we will see below, few people can really know). Through its "politicized equity markets," it is not independent financial markets, but the Communist Party that allocates resources in this economy.[176]

The true sources of funding for industry are state banks, which in essence "are China's financial system." Four of them manage 45 percent of China's total financial assets: the Bank of China; China Construction Bank; Agricultural Bank of China; and the largest in the world by assets, Industrial and Commercial Bank of China. In total, Chinese central and provincial governments control four-fifths of all banking resources in the country. The Communist Party tells banks to loan money and give preference in credit decisions to state enterprises no matter what, even if they cannot repay or are losing money. The state thus treats the banks as basic utilities like the energy supply and water system. Commercial bank executives, too, are subject to government pressure. Given the desire for liquidity and the political function of this financial system, many local and provincial banks make free or low-cost loans to SOEs: off-balance-sheet lending exceeded RMB 3.8 trillion in 2010 alone, more than doubling over

---

[175] Walter and Howie, *Red Capitalism*, xii, 164, 166.
[176] Stephen Green, *The Development of China's Stock Market, 1984–2002* (London: Routledge, 2004), 3 (quote) and passim; Studwell, *How Asia Works*, 249–258; Walter and Howie, *Red Capitalism*, 166–167, 194, 210–211.

2009 and rising. Around 80 percent of these bank loans would be unattainable for private companies.[177]

The government at all levels funds more than 30 percent of China's industrial output: it is through bank lending and other forms of state-subsidized finance that the Communist Party promotes its own interests and regional and local governmental agencies promote theirs.[178] Along with cheap loans, state subsidies help to explain the strength of Chinese manufacturing in general, but especially in steel, glass, paper, auto parts, and solar panels. Capital from below-market-rate bank loans is the only way many Chinese companies have become globally competitive.[179] On the other hand, in China and elsewhere around the world, SOEs have performed poorly because of the sloppy misallocation of state funding and the absence of a need to consider the interests of investors.[180] Recent reform initiatives that would raise interest rates and reduce state protections for the banking system may correct some of these arrangements that create obvious inefficiencies and distortions throughout the Chinese economy as well as contributing to global imbalances.[181] But these circumstances help to clarify the malfunctions of the information nexus in contemporary China, which is our focus in this segment of the book.

Accurate information about companies, let alone the government, is very hard to find.[182] Statistics are incorrect and misleading: officially, state treasury debt stands at less than 20 percent of GDP, but this is widely considered to be grossly understated, with the real number at around 80 percent.[183] No reliable public information exists on the exact extent of the loans made to SOEs or other favored companies. Companies that are fully owned by the state have no disclosure requirements, but the accounting in all other types of firms is also opaque, making them nearly

---

[177] Walter and Howie, *Red Capitalism*, xii, 27–30 (financial system quote), 34, 47; Haley and Haley, *Subsidies to Chinese Industry*, xvii, xix, 1–7, 19–21, 27, 33–35, 46–47; Lin, *Demystifying the Chinese Economy*, chaps. 9–10.

[178] Haley and Haley, *Subsidies to Chinese Industry*, xvii.

[179] Haley and Haley, *Subsidies to Chinese Industry*, 1–2.

[180] Shimin Chen et al., "Government Intervention and Investment Efficiency: Evidence from China," *Journal of Corporate Finance* (April 2011), 259–271; *Economist* (Nov. 22, 2014), 57–58.

[181] Neil Gough, "China Rethinks Safety Net for Its Banking System," *New York Times* (April 30, 2015), online at nytimes.com/2015/05/01/business/dealbook/china-rethinks-safety-net-for-its-banking-system.html.

[182] In general see Haley and Haley, *Subsidies to Chinese Industry*, 5–6, 19–21, 34–35, 46–47, 62; Walter and Howie, *Red Capitalism*, 96–97, 112, 166; Lin, *Demystifying the Chinese Economy*, 195–198, 209–210, 216–218; Tong Lu, Jiyin Zhong, and Jie Kong, "How Good Is Corporate Governance in China?," *China and World Economy*, vol. XVII, no. 1 (2009), 92; Xiaolan Fu and Rongping Mu, "Enhancing China's Innovation Performance: The Policy Choices," *China and World Economy*, vol. XXII, no. 2 (2014), 43.

[183] Haley and Haley, *Subsidies to Chinese Industry*, 5–6.

impervious to independent appraisal.[184] Even the leading internationally traded companies have been found to be deficient in the information they disclose about themselves. According to Transparency International, the firms with the least open accounts in the world are China's. For instance, Huawei Technology Corporation, a rival to Cisco Systems, the American networking equipment firm, and one of China's most successful companies, with sales revenues exceeding $5.7 billion and offices in ninety countries, is also backed by the Chinese military. This might explain its "medieval record-keeping practices" and why "our knowledge of its actual ownership structure is almost non-existent."[185] Or, to give another example, the 2009 IPO prospectus of the large Shenzhen property developer Kaisa, which drew large international investments before collapsing, was 837 pages long, but murky on its founders and their sources of capital. As one bondholder put it, "no one knew what was going on."[186]

In part, this opacity may be intentional, as, following a traditional pattern of suspicion toward government, many smaller privately owned companies keep different sets of account books: for the government, for the banks, and for themselves.[187] So despite layer after layer of bureaucratic monitoring, the flow of information to the government itself is impeded, in many cases intentionally. The principal-agent problem that appears whenever owners and managers are different sets of people is exacerbated here by the lack of public information available about companies and banks. In capitalist societies, these informational asymmetries are lessened by the ability to gauge risk through an assessment of prices, interest rates, bond spreads, stock-market valuations, and money-management by banks. That does not happen in China.

Weak freedom of the press amplifies these deficiencies of the information nexus. If problems with companies do threaten to come to light, the government leans on the press to gain favorable publicity. When criticism of the diversification strategy of Haier, a large electronics appliance firm, surfaced, an official from the China Securities Regulatory

---

[184] Better regulations and enforcement thereof have reduced informational asymmetries relating to domestic shares, which suggests one cause of the broader problem: see Rong Gong and Alastair Marsden, "The Impact of the 2007 Reforms on the Level of Information Disclosure by the Chinese A-Share Market," *China Economic Review*, vol. XXX (Sept. 2014), 221–234; and Lei Gao and Gerhard Kling, "The Impact of Corporate Governance and External Audit on Compliance to Mandatory Disclosure Requirements in China," *Journal of International Accounting, Auditing, and Taxation*, vol. XXI, no. 1 (2012), 17–31.

[185] Huang, *Capitalism with Chinese Characteristics*, 10–12.

[186] David Barboza, "In China, a Building Frenzy's Fault Lines," *New York Times* (March 13, 2015), online at nytimes.com/2015/03/15/business/dealbook/in-china-a-building-frenzys-fault-lines.html.

[187] Huang, *Capitalism with Chinese Characteristics*, 291.

Commission (CSRC) threateningly insisted that "Haier is an intellec-tually prestigious brand of our country and our people. We should all cherish such a brand ... We at CSRC are very confident of Haier's honesty and trustworthiness."[188] This kind of pressure on the media in China goes hand in hand with the government's obsessive concern for secrecy. China acts like the old Soviet-bloc dictatorships, which strictly limited typewriter usage out of fear of dissent. Understandably, this distrust now extends to the internet.[189] Over 500 million Chinese are active online, a number that has made the government nervous and prone to impose restrictions on the web, blocking social media and networking sites like Facebook, Twitter, and LinkedIn, along with many others. For everything else it maintains purposefully slow loading times of five to thirty seconds per page. In 2010, China expelled Google and now blocks most of its apps, including calendars and email. It does countenance some of its services, among them Google Maps and Google Earth, although the law requires publicly accessible cartography to be inaccurate.[190]

The secrecy and governmental intrusion also boost corruption, which itself raises transaction costs and hampers the flow of information. Asset stripping, insider buyouts, nepotism, and bribery are all common in SOEs.[191] With official interest rates on loans to SOEs close to zero versus "market" rates from pawn shops and other private lenders exceeding 25 percent, unscrupulous employees of the SOEs have taken the cheap money and lent it out themselves at a profit.[192] That kind of behavior is systemic despite publicly visible attempts to assert the state's authority by cracking down on corruption. Perhaps it is persistent because of Chinese popular attitudes, which are pro-education and pro-market, but also place a high value on personal connections.[193] It may be how individuals successfully navigate through a harsh and rapidly changing world, but it builds illegality into economic interactions nationwide. And the ensuing fogginess precludes the functioning of the information nexus.

---

[188] Guoping Li, "China's Stock Market: Inefficiencies and Institutional Implications," *China and World Economy*, vol. XVI, no. 6 (2008), 89–90.

[189] Nye, "Shaping Communication Networks," 1070.

[190] Cortada, *Digital Flood*, 482, 490; James Fallows, *China Airborne* (NY: Pantheon Books, 2012), 24–25, 208–215; email correspondence with Bruce J. Dickson (June 23, 2015); Gady Epstein, "A Giant Cage: China and the Internet: A Special Report," *Economist* (April 6, 2013). Cf. the Soviet Union, where, in my experience, city street maps were either unavailable or so undetailed as to be almost useless except to find major tourist sites.

[191] Dickson, *Wealth into Power*, chap. 7.

[192] Email correspondence with Bruce J. Dickson (June 23, 2015); Lin, *Demystifying the Chinese Economy*, 194–195.

[193] Carolyn L. Hsu, *Creating Market Socialism: How Ordinary People Are Shaping Class and Status in China* (Durham, NC: Duke University Press, 2007).

This presents a contrast with Japan and the other Asian Tigers, although the Chinese authorities thought they were emulating their strategies for growth with big, state-backed corporations running the economy and relying on cheap domestic labor. Elsewhere in post–World War II Asia, most industry was in private hands, even if elite hands, and private-property rights were secure. In China, contract law is a work in progress, although it seems to be moving in the direction of Western business law.[194] However, land is still not owned by individuals, but leased long term, and government authorities (more likely local than central) have been prone to confiscate it at will and without inadequate compensation, as two-fifths of farming villages have experienced in the past decade.[195] In Japan, South Korea, and Taiwan, while the state was supportive with investment in education and other forms of human capital, it did not involve itself as actively in the micromanagement or financing of industry. In the Japanese electrical industry, there was little state guidance and intense competition between firms.[196] In China, the real private sector is in a subordinate and precarious position. The pattern prevailing in China is closer to that of the Philippines or Indonesia, where corruption and weak legal protections have curtailed economic growth. Even if we ignore corruption as a factor, in China it is in the self-interest of its 40 million state officials to preserve the status quo.[197] As we have seen in previous chapters, there is also a clear link between freedom of the press and the vitality of capital markets and the economy. That condition was generally present in the Asian Tigers, but is not in China.[198]

Its informational shortcomings explain why, "after more than thirty years of economic reforms and having transformed from a low to a middle income country, China now faces significant challenges in moving from imitation to innovation."[199] Innovation, including the creation of new

[194] Donald Clarke, Peter Murrell, and Susan Whiting, "The Role of Law in China's Economic Development," in *China's Great Economic Transformation*, ed. Brandt and Rawski, 399–415; Ron Harris, "Spread of Legal Innovation Defining Private and Public Domains," in *The Cambridge History of Capitalism*, ed. Larry Neal and Jeffrey G. Williamson, vol. II (Cambridge: Cambridge University Press, 2014), 145ff.

[195] Studwell, *How Asia Works*, 229–231. On the other hand, people can sue the government or seek mediation challenging land seizures, environmental degradation, and other injuries caused by the actions of officials. The success rate is around 30 percent according to Jamie Horsley, "The Rule of Law: Pushing the Limits of Party Rule," in *China Today, China Tomorrow*, ed. Fewsmith, 61–62.

[196] Simon Partner, *Assembled in Japan: Electrical Goods and the Making of the Japanese Consumer* (Berkeley: University of California Press, 1999), 231–233, 238–239.

[197] Haley and Haley, *Subsidies to Chinese Industry*, 4–5, 22–23; Studwell, *How Asia Works*, xxvii; Huang, *Capitalism with Chinese Characteristics*, 239, 278–280, 294.

[198] Li, "China's Stock Market," 92.

[199] Xiaolan Fu and Rongping Mu, "Enhancing China's Innovation Performance: The Policy Choices," *China and World Economy*, vol. XXII, no. 2 (2014), 42.

technologies, new ways of management, and new institutional structures, is the key to sustaining long-term growth and a clear marker of capitalism in the views of nearly every commentator from Schumpeter onward. It is also closely linked to a well-oiled, freely functioning information nexus.[200] As with capital markets and world-class companies, on the surface China looks strong in this regard, with the number of patent filings rivaling or exceeding the long-time leaders Japan and the United States. Chinese patent laws of 1985, 1992, and 2000 were designed to stimulate innovation, and the number of patents vaulted from 39,725 in 1996 to 352,406 in 2008. The "Chinese National Patent Development Strategy," embedded in the state's 12th Five-Year Plan (2011–2015), urged even more rapid growth, with bureaucrats setting a target of 2 million patent filings by the end date.[201]

The Chinese government has increased expenditures on R&D by a factor of eleven or more in the past twenty years. Funds for this purpose rose from RMB 34.9 billion in 1995 to RMB 10,298 billion in 2012. The country's research spending doubled from 0.9 percent of GDP in 2000 to 1.7 percent in 2009. The total number of Chinese researchers in R&D also more than doubled in the same period. China is now the third largest global investor in R&D, behind the United States and Japan.[202] In its promotion of R&D cross-fertilization between the state, business, and universities – the "Triple Helix" model of digital-age economic innovation – China has been much more successful than Russia, the other leading model of "state capitalism."[203] Chinese authorities have made especially heavy investment in nanotech R&D at national, provincial, and local levels, including the establishment of nanotech science parks in Suzhou: bioBay, with forty-two firms, and a new one, Nanopolis, currently in design. The state provides venture funding and ongoing financial support, supplemented by additional investment from

[200] Fu, *China's Path to Innovation*, 4–5; Gene M. Grossman and Elhanan Helpman, "Endogenous Innovation in the Theory of Growth," *Journal of Economic Perspectives* (Winter 1994), 23–44; Philippe Aghion and Peter Howitt, "Growth with Quality-Improving Innovations," in *Handbook of Economic Growth*, vol. 1A, ed. Aghion and Durlauf, 67–110.

[201] Chih-Hai Yang, Chun-Chien Kuo, and Eric D. Ramstetter, "Intellectual Property Rights and Patenting in China's High-Technology Industries: Does Ownership Matter?" *China and World Economy*, vol. XIX, no. 5 (2011), 103, 106; Haley and Haley, *Subsidies to Chinese Industry*, 1–2; *Economist* (Dec. 13, 2014), 73–74.

[202] Yang, Kuo, and Ramstetter, "Intellectual Property Rights and Patenting," 103; Fu, *China's Path to Innovation*, 16; Fu and Mu, "Enhancing China's Innovation Performance," 44; Fingleton, "America the Innovative?"

[203] Harley Balzer and Jon Askonas, "Innovations in Russia and China Compared," *Russian Analytical Digest* (Sept. 23, 2014), 2–6. The concept is theorized in Henry Etzkowitz, *The Triple Helix: University-Industry-Government Innovation in Action* (NY: Routledge, 2008).

Chinese returnees and America's Silicon Valley.[204] To quote Rob Atkinson, president of the Information Technology and Innovation Foundation in Washington, DC, "the Chinese have the ability to throw a lot of resources at [R&D], and some will stick to the wall."[205]

But is the hope that something sticks to the wall a tactic that will yield the best results? Does it correspond to the way the information nexus functions? Compare the United Kingdom, the Dutch Republic, and the United States in earlier eras, in which investors armed with information through the business and financial press made an infinite number of decisions that flowed together to shape capitalism and the Industrial Revolution. China's approach to R&D ignores the information nexus that was accountable for most of the innovations leading to steady economic growth since the early modern era. As the authors of a study on China's push for nanotechnology conclude, the government is too involved and will likely "miss a truly revolutionary breakthrough" that would have come from pure science backed by independent investors.[206]

There are already plenty of indications that the Chinese approach is wanting. China has gained knowledge transfers and technical upgrades, either as spillovers from foreign companies in coastal regions or because of the increase in the state's R&D expenditures. But on the European Union's Innovation Scoreboard, China ranks only one-third as high as the United States, South Korea, and Japan, and is lower than the EU27, Canada, and Australia – although it does score higher than Brazil, India, Russia, and South Africa. China fares poorly on triadic patents, which are those filed successfully and simultaneously in American, European, and Japanese patent offices. Comparing the number of triadic patents per million workers, China falls below Chile, Greece, and South Africa. The United States and Japan have ten times as many triadic patents as China. Whereas over a third of Japanese patents are also filed in the United States or Europe, only 5 percent of Chinese patents are.[207]

---

[204] Cong Cao, Richard P. Applebaum, and Rachel Parker, "'Research Is High and the Market Is Far Away': Commercialization of Nanotechnology in China," *Technology in Society* (Feb. 2013), 55–64.

[205] Fingleton, "America the Innovative?"

[206] Cao, Applebaum, and Parker, "Research Is High," 63.

[207] Xiaolan Fu, "Foreign Direct Investment, Absorptive Capacity, and Regional Innovation Capabilities: Evidence from China," *Oxford Development Studies* (March 2008), 89–110; Fu and Mu, "Enhancing China's Innovation Performance," 45; *Economist* (Dec. 13, 2014), 73–74; Muro et al., *America's Advanced Industries*, 38; Albert G. Z. Hu and Gary H. Jefferson, "Science and Technology in China," in *China's Great Economic Transformation*, ed. Brandt and Rawski, 287, 297–298, 304–308. Örjan Sölvell and Ivo Zander, "International Diffusion of Knowledge: Isolating Mechanisms and the Role of the MNE," in *The Dynamic Firm*, ed. Alfred D. Chandler, Jr. et al. (Oxford: Oxford University Press, 1998), 402–416, argue that

Most of the latter are adjustments to design appearances or new models rather than substantive innovations. Most Chinese patents are not, as in the United States, invention patents, and they are not subjected to rigorous review. The reason for this state of affairs has to do with bureaucratic involvement in the patents game, which ends up emphasizing quantity over quality.[208] Enforcement of existing patent protections and intellectual property rights is also weak, letting domestic firms get away with violating copyright on products made by foreign firms.[209] Because of political interventions and informational asymmetries, the SOEs tend not to be technologically innovative.[210]

The relative lack of innovation in China is manifested in industry after industry. According to the Asian Development Bank, Chinese workers piece the parts of the iPhone together, but the country only contributes about 3.6 percent of the total value of the phone. The other 96.4 percent is a result of high-tech transfers from Japan, Germany, the United States, and South Korea in that order. In other words, China still contributes more brawn than brain.[211] Or take the Chinese airline industry, where the state monopoly over airspace and the machinery and metals industries has inhibited the ability to build a quality civilian aircraft or expand civilian air flights. Although the number of aerospace engineers and assembly workers employed at the center of the aviation industry, the city of Xi'an, is eight times higher than in the comparable American city of Seattle, the latter produces the bulk of the world's airplanes. China is good at the fabrication of cheap consumer goods, but not airplanes, with all of the intellectual and infrastructural complexity inherent in everything from parts to air safety.[212]

There have been various successes as some of the government's efforts have "stuck to the wall." Chinese companies are good at creating efficiencies within manufacturing operations and they have advanced

---

multinational enterprises are not as effective at spreading innovation from one society to another as is often thought.

[208] Eve Y. Zhou and Bob Stembridge, "Patented in China: The Present and Future State of Innovation in China," *Thomson Reuters Scientific Report* (2008), brochure no. CO 08 8245 C RE, p. 19.

[209] Yang, Kuo, and Ramstetter, "Intellectual Property Rights and Patenting," 103ff, 106.

[210] Xiaolan Fu and Yundan Gong, "International and Intranational Technological Spillovers and Productivity Growth in China," *Asian Economic Papers* (Spring 2009), 1–23; Xiaolan Fu and Yundan Gong, "Indigenous and Foreign Innovation Efforts and Drivers of Technological Upgrading: Evidence from China," *World Development* (July 2011), 1213–1255.

[211] Yuqing Xing and Neal Detert, "How the iPhone Widens the United States Trade Deficit with the People's Republic of China," *ADBI Working Paper*, no. 257 (Dec. 2010), online at www.adb.org/sites/default/files/publication/156112/adbi-wp257.pdf.

[212] Fallows, *China Airborne*, 40 and passim.

innovations in forms of e-commerce, including online gambling. But "in the industries where innovation requires original inventions or engineering breakthroughs, such as branded pharmaceuticals and automobiles, China has small shares of global markets."[213] In the state sector, the government's China Development Bank, the National Development and Reform Commission, and the State Asset Supervision and Administration Commission all stress market incentives and the quality of exported goods in the companies they invest in or administer. Some national champions nursed by state-appointed managers, like China Shipbuilding, are efficient and internationally competitive. But these are mainly companies that sell to other industries or governments. And even where China is strongest, in heavy industry and infrastructure projects, it often looks better than it is: a case in point are its high-speed railways, which are heavily reliant on foreign technology.[214] The Communist Party's prerogatives have had unintended consequences. For example, in a country with one of the highest levels of income inequality in the world, investment has shifted away from education and allowed the number of illiterate Chinese adults to grow by 30 million between 2000 and 2005, a self-evident drag on any potential for economic innovation.[215]

Some experts consider the Chinese state's "techno-authoritarian" approach to planning and development to be successful and adaptive.[216] Its accomplishments are nothing to scoff at, and there will surely be more. China is not North Korea after all. Its entrepreneurs are sensitive to domestic consumer demand and have access to the information nexus of the capitalist world. And current reforms aimed at liberalizing the financial system and weakening the SOEs' dependence on government subsidies will have a positive effect.[217] But judging by this book's

---

[213] Jonathan Woetzel et al., "The China Effect on Global Innovation," *McKinsey Global Institute Research Bulletin* (July 2015), 5 and passim.

[214] Studwell, *How Asia Works*, 234–249.

[215] Haley and Haley, *Subsidies to Chinese Industry*, 19; Carl Riskin, "Inequality: Overcoming the Great Divide," in *China Today, China Tomorrow*, ed. Fewsmith, 91–107; Dwayne Benjamin et al., "Income Inequality during China's Economic Transition," in *China's Great Economic Transformation*, ed. Brandt and Rawski, 729–775.

[216] E.g., Sebastian Heilmann, "Economic Governance: Authoritarian Upgrading and Innovative Potential," in *China Today, China Tomorrow*, ed. Fewsmith, 117–118, 124. Hu and Jefferson, in "Science and Technology in China," 286–336, see more gains in Chinese innovation than I do, but also stress that under current conditions they cannot be sustained. Edward Tse extrapolates from a few cases of successful, innovative Chinese firms to envision a bright future, but even he admits that it will require the state to continue to liberalize, which is not a certainty: see his *China's Disruptors: How Alibaba, Xiaomi, Tencent, and Other Companies Are Changing the Rules of Business* (NY: Portfolio/Penguin, 2015).

[217] *Economist* (April 18, 2015), 11–12.

assessment of the information nexus and the nature of capitalism, the outlook is not as bright as it could be. The difference between China and the nations of Western Europe, the United States, and Japan, is much the same as the contrast that existed in early modern Europe between the United Kingdom and the Dutch Republic on the one hand and absolutist France on the other.

**

The concept of the information nexus thus sheds light on the nature of economic prospects in China and the developing world. It helps to sort out the realities of the digital age in our own society. Put another way, the information nexus tells us where capitalism really exists in the world today and where and why it does not.

Conclusion

The core of this book's argument is that polemicist critiques and celebrations reflect a failure to understand capitalism. Both opponents and supporters of capitalism have obscured historical and present-day reality by using the term incautiously and inaccurately. Critics and advocates alike have distorted and blurred its distinctive attributes. The defining feature of capitalism is an intensification of information gathering that goes above and beyond what is possible in non-capitalist societies. This amounted to a qualitative transformation in the consistency, public accessibility, efficiency, and global reach of information flows, initially in Northwestern Europe. The emergence of the information nexus in the early modern era explains the "great divergence" in modern world economic history, as well as accounting for the strong continuities in the history of capitalism from its birth in the seventeenth-century Dutch Republic to the "IT Revolution" of the current digital age.

Despite the misconceptions surrounding the word "capitalism," we are probably stuck with it. Replacing it with something in line with my interpretation like "informationism" would be implausible.[1] But in light of the findings in this book, our understanding of the concept has to shift in the direction of the information nexus and away from capital, commodification, and the other features mistakenly identified as *unique* characteristics of capitalism. Several conclusions logically follow.

As opposed to those who would argue for the existence of two forms of capitalism in the world, a good capitalism based on entrepreneurialism and big firms versus a bad oligarchic or crony capitalism, the notion of the information nexus leads me to propose a new taxonomy altogether, excluding from the ranks of capitalism any economies in which access

---

[1] Deirdre Nansen McCloskey, *Bourgeois Equality: How Ideas, Not Capital, Transformed the World* (Chicago: University of Chicago Press, forthcoming), 9, proposes a few alternatives, including the equally unwieldy "trade-tested progress," as a substitute for "capitalism." My thanks to the author for sharing the proofs of her book with me.

to information is substantially blocked.[2] The fact that contemporary China or other authoritarian societies like Putin's Russia have basically market economies with stock markets, consumer marketing, and other epiphenomena associated with capitalism misses the point.[3] Calling them "state capitalist" makes no sense. Because of restrictions on the press, the opacity that surrounds so much economic policy, and the corruption that channels so much economic activity in these countries, we cannot describe them as capitalist if "capitalism" is defined as the information nexus.

That is not to say authoritarian market economies make all the wrong decisions and capitalist ones with a flourishing information nexus all the right ones. In the case of China, imperfect markets are preferable to Soviet-style central planning. Governments in capitalist nations, for their part, implement many counterproductive policies – such as the flawed and incomplete currency union represented by the euro, or precipitous cuts in state income taxes in the United States.[4] The capitalist states of Western Europe, North America, and East Asia have different levels of regulation, taxation, and social welfare that can be helpful or harmful to their economies. The legacies of racial and ethnic discrimination have condemned large portions of the Indian and black populations to poverty throughout the western hemisphere, even in prosperous societies. But as long as conditions foster the free exchange of political and economic information we can say capitalism is operative in all of these variations on the mixed economy, however slowly or fast their economies are growing in any given decade.

[2] E.g., William J. Baumol, Robert E. Litan, Carl J. Schramm, *Good Capitalism, Bad Capitalism and the Economics of Growth and Prosperity* (New Haven: Yale University Press, 2007).

[3] On stock markets in China, see chap. 6 above; on the flourishing of consumer marketing in non-capitalist societies, see, e.g., Pamela E. Swett et al., eds, *Selling Modernity: Advertising in Twentieth-Century Germany* (Durham, NC: Duke University Press, 2007); Natalya Chernyshova, *Soviet Consumer Culture in the Brezhnev Era* (NY: Routledge, 2013); Pamela Karimi, *Domesticity and Consumer Culture in Iran: Interior Revolutions of the Modern Era* (NY: Routledge, 2013).

[4] Shahin Vallée, "How the Greek Deal Could Destroy the Euro," *New York Times* (July 27, 2015), online at nytimes.com/2015/07/28/opinion/how-the-greek-deal-could-destroy-the -euro.html?action=click&pgtype=Homepage&module=opinion-c-col-right-region&regi on=opinion-c-col-right-region&WT.nav=opinion-c-col-right-region; William G. Gale, "State Income Tax Cuts: Still a Bad Idea" (July 28, 2015), online at brookings.edu/rese arch/opinions/2015/07/28-state-income-tax-cuts-bad-idea-gale?utm_campaign=Brookin gs+Brief&utm_source=hs_email&utm_medium=email&utm_content=20905560&_hse nc=p2ANqtz-9yatAdmaLpDHhDna-Q_3mWXPEiGiXvLSAqUL9rIL4ml3EIi4Gg 5RE1BPZ3e1hAwhBdV5BCGR2gd1AgPA4cxg6vNqYmJQ&_hsmi=20905560.

It is false to assert that the more laissez-faire a country is, the more capitalist it is. Rather, capitalism is correlated with democracy regardless of the level of state economic intervention for the purposes of correcting market failures and promoting social welfare. Capitalism, in other words, is the result of political, not economic, liberalism.[5] Governments cannot be too overbearing, corrupt, or weak if capitalism is to thrive. When they are it impedes the development and functioning of the information nexus, which can exist only with laws and institutions that countenance and sustain it.[6] We cannot project into the future, but historically, the polities that maintained capitalism as an information nexus have been economically the strongest and nimblest, and technologically the most innovative. Innovation in these economies is not absolutely certain to occur, and specific conditions facilitate or hinder it.[7] Moreover, the information nexus is by no means a cure-all for countries with entrenched poverty. But innovation is more likely to occur over the long run under conditions of capitalism as I have defined it than not.

In capitalist societies, though, four developments related to the very success of the information nexus threaten to sap the vitality of capitalism. First, the potential threat to low- and middle-skilled workers from globalization and expanding digitization in manufacturing. Second, information overload and the monopolization of data searches by a limited number of companies. Third, the unwillingness of more than 90 percent of nations to make public the data that allow for assessment of corruption and waste.[8] If the latter two trends continue, they could weaken the democratized access to information that has been an essential feature of capitalism from the beginning. Social stability and the economic success of nations are potentially imperiled by all three developments.[9] As I explained in Chapter 6, I am on the side of the

[5] Ricardo Hausmann advances a related argument in his article "Why Are Rich Countries Democratic?" *Project Syndicate* (March 26, 2014), online at www.project-syndicate.org/commentary/ricardo-hausmann-on-the-market-like-mechanism-in-advanced-econo mies--political-systems?barrier=true.
[6] This point coincides with Daron Acemoglu and James A. Robinson, *Why Nations Fail: The Origins of Power, Prosperity, and Poverty* (NY: Crown Business, 2012), which argues for the relationship between sustained economic growth and inclusive economic and political institutions.
[7] Edmund Phelps, "What Is Wrong with the West's Economies?" *New York Review of Books* (Aug. 13, 2015), 55–56.
[8] That statistic from Tim Berners-Lee, "The Wider World Web," in *Economist: The World in 2016* (Nov. 2016), 160.
[9] One might expect to see income inequality on this list, but considering its presence throughout history I do not view it as being inherent to capitalism, especially as defined here. On the problem, see Thomas Piketty, *Capital in the Twenty-First Century*, trans. Arthur Goldhammer (Cambridge, MA: Belknap Press, 2014). In a recent article, the historian Jerry Z. Muller sees the American obsession with accountability metrics as

optimists, but the case of the pessimists should not be dismissed out of hand.

Perhaps most fateful of all, however, is the fourth development, the environmental degradation brought about by the information nexus. Consumption of the earth's resources has doubled since 1970. In 2010, manufactured goods were made of 15.3 billion tons of materials: wood and other plants, metals, minerals, and fossil fuels. That number is only a quarter of the amount of materials used in construction, mining, and food production. Extracting, growing, working, distributing, and disposing of these materials all expend energy, mostly in the form of fossil fuels, which emit carbon dioxide, the main culprit in global warming.[10]

This is not a result of capitalism alone, but is a by-product of human activity over millennia.[11] Industrialization and mass consumption in both capitalist and non-capitalist nations have caused much of the damage. To enable the operation of automobiles in every type of society, for instance, "humanity has adapted the naturally occurring environment by leveling, re-grading, and covering with asphalt a non-trivial percentage of the earth's land surface."[12] The Soviet Union, hardly a capitalist economy, had one of the worst environmental records in history.[13] The world's largest emitter of greenhouse gases today is Communist-led China, a country known for its polluted cities and waterways – although it is making efforts to reverse these problems through the adoption of renewable sources of energy.[14]

But the information nexus of capitalism bears unique responsibility here. Industrialization itself arose in capitalist societies, and thus even in non-capitalist form, industrial economies' impact on the environment can be considered an outgrowth of capitalism. And businesses everywhere, with their relentless drive for information, locate global natural resources and systematically exploit them. It is worth repeating that capitalist

a form of information-seeking gone haywire that also threatens capitalist dynamism: see his "The Costs of Accountability," *The American Interest* (Aug. 3, 2015), online at the -american-interest.com/2015/08/03/the-costs-of-accountability/.

[10] Peter Marsh, *The New Industrial Revolution: Consumers, Globalization, and the End of Mass Production* (New Haven: Yale University Press, 2012), 120–122.

[11] See, e.g., Richard C. Hoffman, *An Environmental History of Medieval Europe* (Cambridge: Cambridge University Press, 2014).

[12] David Autor, "Polanyi's Paradox and the Shape of Employment Growth" *NBER Working Paper Series* no. 20485 (Sept. 2014), 32.

[13] Murray Feshbach and Alfred Friendly, Jr., *Ecocide in the USSR* (NY: Basic Books, 1992).

[14] Joanna Lewis, "Environmental Challenges: From the Local to the Global," in *China Today, China Tomorrow: Domestic Politics, Economy, and Society*, ed. Joseph Fewsmith (Lanham, Maryland: Rowman and Littlefield, 2010), 260–263; James Roumasset, Kimberley Burnett, and Hua Wang, "Environmental Resources and Economic Growth," in *China's Great Economic Transformation*, ed. Loren Brandt and Thomas G. Rawski (Cambridge: Cambridge University Press, 2008), 250–285.

nations are not the only ones to blame, but it is fair to say they initiated the practices that resulted in the depletion of many resources and the mutilation of many an ecosystem: to give one example, the systematic destruction of the old-growth forests of the southern Appalachians by logging companies in the early twentieth century. The pattern of discovering, stripping, and selling resources on global commodity markets for the world's consumers has repeated itself many times the world over.[15]

We ignore the warnings of environmentalists at our peril. But condemning "the hegemonic capitalist system" as an unmitigated evil is misplaced.[16] For if capitalism takes away it also gives through the information nexus – which is not conceivable under any other economic system. Social media and the press expose ecological offenses and pressure countries and companies to clean up the environment.[17] NGOs like the World Resources Institute make use of new information services, including Google Maps, to investigate and monitor environmental abuses on land and sea.[18] And companies in capitalist societies have been conducting extensive research, which they share, on the environmental impact of their own manufacturing processes for the dual purpose of cutting costs and attracting environmentally conscious customers. As the CEO of a Dutch carpet manufacturer put it, "the more we make our products more sustainable, the better our customers like it."[19]

With all of the preceding hazards, it is incumbent upon governments to adopt policies that ensure the vitality of the information nexus. The state in capitalist nations must function as it always has as the active patron and protector of the information nexus. Regulatory action would have gone a long way to preventing the financial crisis of 2008, which a misguided

[15] Donald Edward Davis, *Where There Are Mountains: An Environmental History of the Southern Appalachians* (Athens, GA: University of Georgia Press, 2000), chaps. 6–7. See also Wilma A. Dunaway, *The First American Frontier: Transition to Capitalism in Southern Appalachia, 1700–1860* (Chapel Hill: University of North Carolina Press, 1996), chap. 8, and for other regions of the world, Tom Burgis, *The Looting Machine: Warlords, Oligarchs, Corporations, Smugglers, and the Theft of Africa's Wealth* (NY: Public Affairs, 2015); and Richard P. Tucker, *Insatiable Appetite: The United States and the Ecological Degradation of the Tropical World* (Lanham: Rowman and Littlefield, 2007).

[16] Quotation from Michael Bastasch, "130 Environmental Groups Call for an End to Capitalism," *The Daily Caller* (July 23, 2014), online at http://dailycaller.com/2014/07/23/130-environmental-groups-call-for-an-end-to-capitalism/; see also Naomi Klein, *This Changes Everything: Capitalism vs the Climate* (NY: Simon and Schuster, 2014).

[17] For their role in Asia, see Mark Clifford, *The Greening of Asia: The Business Case for Solving Asia's Environmental Emergency* (NY: Columbia University Press, 2015), 36, 99, 185, 210, and passim.

[18] wri.org; Marc Gunther, "Google-Powered Maps Help Fight Deforestation," *Guardian* (March 10, 2015), online at theguardian.com/sustainable-business/2015/mar/10/google-earth-engine-maps-forest-watch-deforestation-environment.

[19] Marsh, *New Industrial Revolution*, 125–142, with quotation on 128; Clifford, *Greening of Asia*, passim.

understanding of capitalism allowed to occur. Significant damage could have been avoided had the responsible parties in the US government perceived capitalism as an information nexus that was no longer functioning properly on Wall Street, rather than as a no-holds-barred market free-for-all. Government legislation can curtail abuses involving privacy, civil liberties, and predatory behaviors that stem from data mining. It can encourage competition in the search-engine business. It can guarantee freedom of the press and continued popular access to government information. It can work to reduce greenhouse-gas emissions and mandate fixes to other environmental ills caused by the many companies whose cost-benefit analyses focus solely on profit-taking. It can safeguard the social safety net and provide retraining for workers affected by digitization and globalization.[20] And surely government support for pure and applied scientific research and world-class public education from pre-K through university is a wise investment in human capital.[21]

Such measures will fortify capitalism so that it can continue to be the world's most productive, inventive, and dynamic economic system. Implicit in all of them is the insight that capitalism and the information nexus are one and the same.

---

[20] Jerry Z. Muller, "Capitalism and Inequality: What the Right and the Left Get Wrong," *Foreign Affairs* (March/April 2013), 48, makes a similar plea.

[21] The number of jobs in the US that require a college degree has tripled since the 1920s, and demand for highly skilled workers continues to climb. Yet high-school graduation rates are stagnant. Fixing this problem is an essential first step. See Nora Gordon, "Explaining Trends in High School Graduation," in *Human Capital in History: The American Record*, ed. Leah Platt Boustan, Carola Frydman, and Robert A. Margo (Chicago: University of Chicago Press, 2014), 59–95, and Lawrence F. Katz and Robert A. Margo, "Technical Change and the Relative Demand for Skilled Labor: The United States in Historical Perspective," in *Human Capital in History*, ed. Boustan et al., 47.

Index